TEN BRAVE MEN AND TRUE

TEN BRAVE MEN AND TRUE

The Victoria Cross holders from
the Borough of Tunbridge Wells

RICHARD SNOW

MENIN HOUSE

Menin House an imprint of
Tommies Guides Military Booksellers & Publishers

Gemini House
136-140 Old Shoreham Road
Brighton
BN3 7BD
www.tommiesguides.co.uk

First published in Great Britain by Menin House Publishers 2012

ISBN 978-1-908336-38-5

Cover design by Tommies Guides
Typeset by Graham Hales
Printed and bound by
CPI Group (UK) Ltd, Croydon, CR0 4YY

CONTENTS

PREFACE

I had never heard of John Brunt. It was on a visit to Paddock Wood, Kent that I spotted the John Brunt V.C. Pub. This prompted me to wonder who he was. This was early in 2005 and I decided to research his life story.

This culminated with me talking to 30 people who were at school with John Brunt and remembered him. In 2006, I then published a book, *All for Valour, the story of Captain John Brunt V.C., M.C.* This was launched at the pub that bears his name, by his sister, the late Dorothy Miller who came over from Belfast. An updated version is included in this book (Chapter Ten).

The publication coincided with the 150th Anniversary of the Victoria Cross and the 400th Anniversary of Royal Tunbridge Wells. On 13 October 2006, H.R.H. the Princess Royal visited the Victoria Cross Grove in Tunbridge Wells to dedicate a memorial to the ten brave men of the Borough who had won the highest award for gallantry: Rear Admiral Charles Davis Lucas, 1834 –1914; Major General Matthew Charles Dixon, 1821–1905; Lieutenant Colonel William Temple, 1833–1919; Lieutenant John Duncan Grant, 1877–1967; Captain Douglas Walter Belcher, 1889– 1953; The Reverend William Robert Fountaine Addison, 1883–1962; Acting Captain Eric Stuart Dougall, 1886–1918; Lieutenant Colonel William Hew Clark-Kennedy, 1879–1961; Captain Lionel Ernest Queripel, 1920–1944; Captain John Henry Cound Brunt, 1922–1944.

It was there that Brian Best, Secretary of the Victoria Cross Society and Keith Hetherington, local historian suggested I should write about the other nine V.C.s associated with the Borough. As I had enjoyed writing about John Brunt, I agreed to take up the challenge. I decided to contact the Victoria Cross Society, The Victoria Cross and George Cross Association and the Victoria Cross Database Users Group, who provided the basic skeleton of each story. Gradually over the next five years in my spare time I visited various reference libraries, museums, graves etc. and ordered many books from the local library. Working on one V.C. at a time, I tried to contact a relative of each and obtain as much information as I could from all sources, however fragmentary or incomplete. These included fragments of letters, cuttings from newspapers and documents from family members of the Victoria Cross holders, as well as snippets from relevant websites. I felt it was important and different to cover their complete lives, not just how and where they won their Victoria Crosses.

This then, is their story. We must never forget any of these men, and all the others who so bravely fought for their country.

Richard Snow

FOREWORD BY DAN SNOW

It is impossible not to be fascinated by the Victoria Cross. It is the highest award for gallantry, given out only in the most extraordinary of circumstances to men who automatically seem to become a breed apart. They are marked out for life by the highest honour that society can bestow for service on the battlefield.

My uncle Richard has produced this painstaking work of scholarship, inspired by the connection of his home town, Tunbridge Wells, with ten Victoria Cross winners from the Borough. What shines through so powerfully is the sheer range of conflicts this country has been embroiled in over the past 150 years. The ten men served from southern Africa to the Himalayas, from northern France to the Baltic and Burma. They also reflect the diverse make up of the British Empire, an Irishman who won his VC in New Zealand, a Canadian Scot who won a VC in one of the forgotten victories in France in the summer of 1918, an Indian born Briton who was decorated for valour in Tibet. It is an extraordinary sample of the remarkable group of men who have won the VC, and contains those who were decorated for saving lives as well as taking them.

Richard has also faithfully recorded the hardships these men underwent on returning from the battlefield. It is a powerful reminder that those who win VCs are human after all and are as vulnerable to the terrible psychological scars that can affect any who witness the terrors of conflict.

Like my uncle Richard, the majority of the men featured were not born in Tunbridge Wells, but chose it. Perhaps it has a certain quality that men who have survived the battlefield look for. Richard's only battle has been the cut and thrust of Snow family life but we are indebted that he has put such a huge amount of work into preserving the memory of this extraordinary group of men.

ACKNOWLEDGEMENTS

This book could not have been written without the practical help, advice, encouragement and enthusiasm of a large number of people. My thanks to Ryan Gearing and the team at Tommies Guides for their help and encouragement and to Jenny Laing for her editorial advice and input. To the best of my knowledge and belief, all the text and illustrations used are either in the public domain or, if not, have been included with the permission of the copyright holders. If I have inadvertently transgressed in any way, or left anyone out, I apologise!

Chapter One
I am particularly grateful to Michael Adams, great grandson of Charles Lucas; Keith Hetherington; Richard and Doug Arman, Vic Tambling and Paul Oldfield, Victoria Cross Database Users Group.

Also to Didy Grahame, The Victoria Cross and George Cross Association; The Military Historical Society and the Lummis Collection, The National Army Museum; The Imperial War Museum; Tunbridge Wells Reference Library; The Ulster History Circle; Poyntzpass and District Local History Society; Griffith Wylie; Barbara Tomlinson, The National Maritime Museum, Greenwich; William Harrison; Andrew Wells; Mike Hinton; Brian Best; Beryl Watson; Penny Mitchell; The National Memorial Arboretum, Alrewas, Staffordshire.

Chapter Two
I am particularly grateful to Jeannette Grant (née Clarke), great granddaughter of Frances Maria Dixon; Simon Griffith, great great grandson of Frances Maria Dixon; Keith Hetherington; Richard and Doug Arman; Vic Tambling and Paul Oldfield, Victoria Cross Database Users Group.

Also to Didy Grahame, The Victoria Cross and George Cross Association; The Military Historical Society and the Lummis Collection; The National Army Museum; The Imperial War Museum; Tunbridge Wells Reference Library; Dr. A. R. Morton. Archivist/ Deputy Curator, Sandhurst Collection, R.M.A. Sandhurst; Iain Stewart, www.victoriacross.org.uk; Lieutenant Colonel Maxwell Macfarlane RA (Retd.); Barry Smith; The Friends of Kensal Green Cemetery; His Honour John Gower, Q.C.

Chapter Three
I am particularly grateful to Diana Williams (née Temple), great granddaughter of William Temple V.C.; William Temple, great grandson of William Temple V.C.; Keith Hetherington; Richard and Doug Arman, Vic Tambling and Paul Oldfield, Victoria Cross Database Users Group; Robyn Williams, Genealogical Computer Group, New Zealand.

Also to Robert Mills, Librarian, Royal College of Physicians, Ireland; Didy Grahame, The Victoria Cross and George Cross Association; The Military Historical Society and the Lummis Collection, The National Army Museum; The Imperial War Museum; Alexander Turnbull Library, Wellington, New Zealand – Papers Past Website and the Urquhart Album photos; The Manuscripts Dept., Trinity College, Dublin; Tunbridge Wells Reference Library.

Chapter Four

I am particularly grateful to Michael Turkheim, John Duncan Grant's great nephew; Fleur Turkheim, John Duncan Grant's great niece; Keith Hetherington; Richard and Doug Arman; Vic Tambling and Paul Oldfield, Victoria Cross Database Users Group; and Chris Kempton.

Also to The Imperial War Museum Department of Documents; The National Army Museum, Department of Printed Books; Didy Grahame, The Victoria Cross and George Cross Association; Brian Best, Secretary of the Victoria Cross Society; Tunbridge Wells Library and Museum; Zoe Edwards, Information Librarian, East Sussex County Council; Jill Barlow, Cheltenham College Archives; Dr. A. R. Morton, Archivist/ Deputy Curator, Sandhurst Collection; Gavin Edgerley-Harris, The Gurkha Museum, Winchester.

Chapter Five

I am particularly grateful to Brian Belcher, son of Douglas Belcher; Virginia Roberts and Mary Luxford, Granddaughters of Douglas Belcher; Keith Hetherington; Richard and Doug Arman; Vic Tambling and Paul Oldfield, Victoria Cross Database Users Group; John King, Senior Deputy Head, Tiffin School, Kingston-on-Thames.

Also to Didy Grahame, The Victoria Cross and George Cross Association; The Military Historical Society and the Lummis Collection, The National Army Museum; The Imperial War Museum; Tunbridge Wells Reference Library; Christine Pullen, The Royal Green Jackets Museum; Chris Woods; Kingston-on-Thames Library; Janet Watkins, Church Administrator, Holy Trinity Church, Claygate.

Chapter Six

I am particularly grateful to Betty Milne, niece of Marjorie Addison; Barbara Cullen, niece of Marjorie Addison; Keith Hetherington; Richard and Doug Arman; Vic Tambling and Paul Oldfield, Victoria Cross Database Users Group.

Also to Didy Grahame, The Victoria Cross and George Cross Association; The Military Historical Society and the Lummis Collection; The National Army Museum; The Imperial War Museum; Tunbridge Wells Reference Library; John Robson; Betty Carman, Cranbrook Museum Archivist; Mrs Kircaldie, Cranbrook Parish Council Office; Fred Bruce; Mike Butterfield; John Cryer; Alan Mallett; Geoff Williams; John Harding, Coltishall Parish Council; Sherry Taylor, School Office, Robert May's School, Odiham; Sheila Millard, The Odiham Society; Peter Donnelly, Curator, King's Own Royal Regiment Museum; David Blake, Museum of Army Chaplaincy; Zoe Edwards, Info. Librarian, Library and Information Services, East Sussex County Council; Kathy Kromm.

Chapter Seven

I am particularly grateful to Alison Harker, cousin once removed of Eric Dougall; Lucian Warwick-Haller, cousin twice removed of Eric Dougall; Mr N. McBride, Fellow Librarian, Pembroke College, Cambridge; Mrs P. Aske, Librarian, Pembroke College, Cambridge; Keith

Hetherington; Richard and Doug Arman, Vic Tambling and Paul Oldfield, Victoria Cross Database Users Group.

Also to Didy Grahame, The Victoria Cross and George Cross Association, The Imperial War Museum; Mrs B. Matthews, Senior Librarian, Tonbridge School; Tunbridge Wells Library; Tonbridge Library; Lt. Col. M. Macfarlane (RA Retd.)

Chapter Eight

I am particularly grateful to Lt. Col. A. J. C. Kennedy, M.C., senior male cousin; Keith Hetherington; Richard and Doug Arman; Vic Tambling and Paul Oldfield, Victoria Cross Database Users Group. Also to Charlotte Buswell, Development Officer, Westminster School; Didy Grahame, The Victoria Cross and George Cross Association; The Military Historical Society and the Lummis Collection, The National Army Museum; The Imperial War Museum; Library and Archives, Canada; Dumfries and Galloway Reference and Local Studies Library; Tunbridge Wells and Southborough Libraries.

Chapter Nine

I am particularly grateful to Mrs Rose Robinson, Lionel's late sister and her late husband Dick; Keith Hetherington; Christian Thoma; Col. Robin McNish, Deputy President, The Royal Sussex Regimental Association; Richard and Doug Arman; Vic Tambling and Paul Oldfield, Victoria Cross Database Users Group.

Also to The Imperial War Museum and National Army Museum in London; Tunbridge Wells Library and Museum; Didy Grahame, The Victoria Cross and George Cross Association; Brian Best, Secretary of the Victoria Cross Society; John Baines, Royal Sussex Living History Group; R.H. Myles and Brian Hudson, Regimental Secretary, The Royal Sussex Regimental Association; Martin Evans and Penny Redman, The Marlburian Club; Dr. Terry Rogers, Hon. Archivist, Marlborough College; Dr. A.R. Morton, Archivist/ Deputy Curator, Sandhurst Collection; Jules McColl, Sandhurst Foundation; Alan Readman, West Sussex Record Office; Egremont British Legion Club; Dave Reynolds, Editor, Pegasus Magazine; The Airborne Forces Museum, Aldershot.

The following individuals also very kindly supplied information: Nigel Anderson, Hugh Baker Bill Balcombe, Michael Birley, Major Philip Brown, Sue Clark, David Clemmow, Harry Dicken, Gerry Dimmock, Kenneth Dunlop, Bill Freeman, Eileen Gall,Richard Gosling, Michael Gregson, Frederick Hicks, Tim Johnson, Richard Kingzett, Jock Knight, Martin Middlebrook, Hector Munro,Vanda Pitcher, Lt. Col. John Powell, Paula Powell, Lew Read, Guy Robinson, Ton Schemkes, Greville Selby-Lowndes, John Spare, John Swan, David Swann, Dr. Allan Thom,Guy Voice, Col. John Waddy, David Wakefield, Alan Welford.

Chapter Ten

I am particularly grateful to Mrs Dorothy Miller, John Brunt's late sister; Steve Rowan, Heritage Assistant, Museum of Lincolnshire Life, which contains the Museum of the Royal Lincolnshire Regiment; John Harvey, Honorary Secretary of The Old Ellesmerian Club.

I am very grateful to so many people for their help including: John Brunt Miller, John Brunt's nephew; the Libraries at Tonbridge, Tunbridge Wells and Paddock Wood; The Imperial War Museum and National Army Museum in London; Major Oliver Hackett, Mr I. G. Edwards, Archivist and Andrew McDougall at the Sherwood Foresters Museum; The Trustees of the Museum of The Royal Lincolnshire Regiment; Tunbridge Wells Planning Department; Rita Dixon and Nigel Everett of the John Brunt VC Pub, Paddock Wood; Nichola Reay, Town Clerk of Paddock Wood Town Council; Clive Blakeway of The Shropshire War Memorials Association, Didy Grahame of

The Victoria Cross and George Cross Association and Steve Finnis, Regimental Researcher for the Queen's Own Royal West Kent Regiment Museum.

The following individuals also very kindly supplied information: Bob Akehurst, Eric Aspland, Alan Baddeley, Denise Barr, Michael Barton, Lt.Col. Leonard Bell D.S.O., M.C., Brian Best, Peter Bevin, John Blake, Walter Bull, John Carter, Frank Chapman, Jack Chapman, Tom Chewter, Kenneth John Clarke, Charlie Emberton, Ethel Furnell, Kathleen Gibson, Bill Goddard, Ron Goldfinch, June Gray, Bill Hardcastle, Robert Harding, Oliver Hardy, Spencer Harrison, Sue Harvey, John Hedley, Keith Hetherington, Mary Hooper, Doreen Ives, Mabel Jenner, A. A. Jilani, Tom Johnson, Freddie King, Eric Knight, Roy Lambert, Malcolm Love, Terry Macdonald, Ethel Mockett, Peter Northcote, James Ogden, Norman Packer, Terence Priest, Dorothy Raleigh, Geoffrey Rice, Vic Rowles, Geoffrey Sale, Gordon Sceal, Peter Scott, Jim Shepherd, William Shepherd, Eric Silletto, Colin Smith, Percy Smith, Steve Snelling, John Taylor, Bill Thomas, Elizabeth Thomas, Malcolm Thomas, Terry Thornton, Reginald Tindall, Mr & Mrs Vicary, Edna Whenmouth, Gordon Whittaker, Peter Wright.

SPONSORS

I am very grateful to the following sponsors of this book, enabling me to donate any profits to "Help for Heroes":

Denise Barnes
Knight Frank, Estate Agents, Tunbridge Wells
Alex King, Deputy Leader, Kent County Council
Cripps Harries Hall, Solicitors, Tunbridge Wells

THE VICTORIA CROSS GROVE,
TUNBRIDGE WELLS

All ten Victoria Cross Holders remembered in this book are commemorated in the Victoria Cross Grove in Dunorlan Park, Tunbridge Wells.

Twenty-one young oak trees were planted over the winter of 1994–95. Until September 2011, when it was stolen, a plaque on the ground told us:

The Ten V.C.s

The Victoria Cross Grove was dedicated by the Worshipful the Mayor of the Borough of Tunbridge Wells, Councillor Hugh Wright, on 8th May 1995, the 50th Anniversary of Victory in Europe Day, to honour the Borough of Tunbridge Wells Holders of the Victoria Cross. A Commemorative Book on the Borough of Tunbridge Wells Victoria Cross recipients is displayed in Tunbridge Wells Museum and Art Gallery.

On 13 October 2006, a stone memorial created by artist Charles Gurrey was unveiled in the Grove by H.R.H. The Princess Royal. It includes extracts from a poem to the V.C. holders written especially by Poet Laureate Andrew Motion in November 2005. The poem, entitled "Remembrance" was commissioned as part of the 400th Anniversary of Tunbridge Wells Celebrations. It is reproduced here by kind permission of Andrew Motion:

The breaking leaf-buds, then the speckled sun;
The clattered branches, then the freezing gaps;
The life-lines, then the lists of names and dates;
The men who breathed, and then the history.
Lest we forget, this grove memorial
Keeps every season new but stays the same,
So hero-hearts survive as what they were
And we honour each one as we should.
The battle, then the haven with its hush;
The courage, then the bird-song and the nests;
The sacrifice, then shade the wind slides through;
Remembrance, then the march of time to come.

In addition, access to the Victoria Cross Grove was improved with the introduction of new park gates and a viewing area where visitors can read about the ten brave men of the Borough.

On 17 July 2009, Lance Corporal Johnson Beharry V.C. visited the Grove prior to attending a parade to welcome home soldiers from his regiment, 1st Battalion, The Princess of Wales's Royal Regiment, from tours of Afghanistan and Iraq.

The Memorial

Johnson Beharry V.C.

Johnson Beharry V.C. at the Grove

Portrait of William Temple V.C. This was painted from a photograph by a Temple cousin, Pauline Mitchell Innes. It hung in Reginald Temple's house (son of William) and now hangs in Diana Temple's house (great-granddaughter).

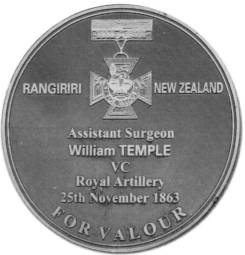

This plaque to William Temple V.C. commemorates his V.C. won at Rangiriri New Zealand. It is at the National Memorial Arboretum, Alrewas, Staffordshire, with others from the Royal Army Medical Corps.

Portrait of William Addison V.C. at Robert Mays School. This was commissioned by the Chairman of the Governors of Robert May's School, Odiham at his own expense in 1919. The artist is unknown. William Addison attended the school in 1892.

The grave of William Addison V.C. at Brookwood Cemetery before restoration. Addison died on 7th January 1962 in Hastings.

The grave of William Addison V.C. at Brookwood Cemetery near Woking, Surrey after restoration in 2007. The Brookwood Cemetery Society arranged the restoring of the grave with Pankhurst Graphic Masonry of West End, Woking.

Dougall's Medals. Eric Dougall's V.C. and M.C. were given to his sister Ellen Mary Dougall at Buckingham Palace on 10th July 1918. His medals were donated to Pembroke College, Cambridge, his old college in 1969. His two pocket diaries and New Testament were also given to the college.

Eric Dougall V.C. died on 14th April 1918, aged 32, just four days after his V.C. action. He was buried in the village of Westoutre, Heuvelland at the CWGC British Cemetery some seven miles south-west of Ypres. He has a special memorial which means that he is buried there, but the exact location is unknown.

Major-General Matthew Charles Dixon V.C.

John Brunt V.C. original pub sign. On September 3rd 1947 the Kent Arms in Paddock Wood was formally renamed "John Brunt V.C." The sign was unveiled by his father, Tom Brunt and was designed by Kathleen Claxton and built at Whitbread's Wateringbury Brewery. This sign disappeared in 1997 when the pub was renamed "The Hopping Hooden Horse". It changed back to "John Brunt V.C." in 2001.

The new John Brunt V.C. pub sign. A new pub sign was unveiled at the John Brunt V.C. pub, Paddock Wood on Remembrance Sunday 2008 by Eric Knight, schoolboy friend of John Brunt. The sign was designed by Alex Atkinson, former pupil at Mascalls School in the town. The author arranged sponsorship and making of the sign by Sign 2000 Ltd of Paddock Wood. Left to right, John Leigh (bugler), Eric Knight (friend of John Brunt), Richard Snow (author).

THE VICTOR

EVERY MONDAY

Price 5d

No. 230
JULY 17th
1965

BRUNT V.C.

On December 9th, 1944, during the Second World War, a platoon of the Sherwood Foresters, commanded by Captain J. H. C. Brunt, was attacked by a large formation of the German 90 Panzer Grenadier Division supported by Panther Mark IV tanks, north of Florence, in Italy.

UP AT THEM! THEY'VE NO HEAVY WEAPONS LEFT!

IT WOULD BE SUICIDE TO GO UP THERE JUST NOW.

THEY'RE NOT GETTING ANY NEARER! WE'VE GOT THEM!

WE'VE GOT TO RETIRE TO THE COMPANY POSITION, SIR!

RIGHT, SERGEANT! I'LL GIVE COVERING FIRE WHILE THE MEN GET BACK!

CONTINUED ON BACK PAGE

CONTINUED FROM FRONT PAGE

I'LL BE ABLE TO KEEP THE JERRIES AT BAY TILL THE LADS ARE CLEAR.

EVERYBODY HAS GONE! IT'S TIME I GOT OUT OF HERE.

HERE COMES MISTER BRUNT NOW! I HOPE HE MAKES IT!

EVERYBODY GOT BACK, SIR!

GOOD!

A little later.

JERRY HAS HAD ENOUGH FOR NOW—WE'LL GO BACK AND COLLECT THE WOUNDED.

NOT FAR TO GO NOW!

We'll soon have you out of here and back to the first aid post.

WE'LL SOON HAVE YOU OUT OF HERE AND BACK TO THE FIRST AID POST.

Despite the German fire around them, Brunt and his small party managed to collect all the wounded and bring them to safety.

Later.

KEEP FIRING! HERE THEY COME AGAIN.

I THOUGHT WE WERE GETTING TANK SUPPORT.

GOOD! THE TANKS HAVE ARRIVED. I'LL BE ABLE TO DIRECT THE FIRE BETTER FROM UP HERE.

TRAVERSE RIGHT! A BUNCH OF JERRIES ARE GATHERING OVER THERE.

Brunt continued to direct the fire and support his men for the rest of the day — but near dusk he was killed by a mortar bomb. For his bravery he was awarded the Victoria Cross.

NEXT WEEK—Another thrilling, true war story.

Printed and Published in Great Britain by D. C. THOMSON & Co., Ltd.,12 Fetter Lane, Fleet Street, London, E.C.4.
© D. C. THOMSON & CO., LTD., 1965.

V

THE STIRRING STORY OF HOW A CAPTAIN OF THE RED DEVILS WON THE BRONZE CROSS IN THE BITTER BATTLES OF ARNHEM!

THE VICTOR

EVERY MONDAY

Price 4½d

No. 83
SEPT. 22nd
1962

The COURAGE of CAPTAIN QUERIPEL

During nine hours of confused and bitter fighting at Arnhem on September 19, 1944, Captain L. E. Queripel, 1st Airborne Division, displayed the greatest gallantry. Although wounded in both arms, Captain Queripel stayed behind to cover the withdrawal of his men.

LOOK AFTER THE SERGEANT. I MUST GET BACK.

REGIMENTAL POST

BUT WHAT ABOUT YOUR OWN WOUND, SIR?

NO TIME FOR THAT! I MUST GET MY MEN ORGANISED.

WE'VE GOT TO SMASH THAT STRONG-POINT. IT'S HOLDING UP THE WHOLE ADVANCE. STAY HERE. I'LL TACKLE IT ALONE!

CONTINUED ON BACK PAGE

NEXT WEEK "Atlantic Rescue" — an amazing incident from the war at sea!

PRINTED AND PUBLISHED IN GREAT BRITAIN BY D. C. THOMSON & CO., LTD., AND JOHN LENG & CO., LTD., 12 FETTER LANE, FLEET STREET, LONDON, E.C.4. REGISTERED FOR TRANSMISSION BY CANADIAN MAGAZINE POST. © D. C. THOMSON & CO., LTD. 1962.

vii

John Duncan Grant V.C. portrait. This hangs in Cheltenham College, his old school. The original portrait lent by John Duncan Grant in 1957 was stolen. David Gibson, a local artist was commissioned to paint a copy.

The plaque in memory of John Duncan Grant V.C. at the Kent and Sussex Crematorium, Tunbridge Wells. It was unveiled beneath a cherry tree by Michael Turkheim, great nephew of Grant on 7th July 2009. Also pictured is Fleur Turkheim, great niece to John Duncan Grant. He was cremated in 1967 at a private funeral with no memorial.

Belcher cigaratte card. Produced by Gallaher Ltd. This is card number 44 in their Great War Series 2, 1915 Victoria Cross heroes. There were 25 cards in each series.

This paper wedding napkin is from the wedding of Douglas Belcher V.C. and Emily Francis Luxford on 31st January 1917 at St. Mark's Church, Surbiton where he had been a boy chorister.

Queripel Close. On 26th May 2007, the Mayor of Tunbridge Wells, Councillor Ron Weeden, hosted a road naming ceremony at Barratt Kent's new homes development in High Brooms. Five roads have been named after local V.C.'s. The Mayor is 2nd from the left, the author Richard Snow is on the right.

Rose Robinson, Lionel Queripel's late sister and her family at the Royal Sussex Regiment Museum, Eastbourne. Rose holds Lionel's sword and admires the new display of his deeds. September 2007.

CHAPTER ONE

The Very First V.C. – the Story of Rear Admiral Charles Davis Lucas 1834–1914

FOREWORD

In 1648, Sir Charles Lucas defended the town of Colchester for the Crown against the Roundheads during the English Civil War. Despite finally surrendering, he was executed for his pains. His sister Margaret married the "Great White Duke" of Newcastle, who was similarly defeated by the Roundheads at the Battle of Marston Moor during that same war.

His descendant, Rear Admiral Charles Davis Lucas also fought for the Crown, this time during the Crimean War and is immortalised as 2 the first to earn the Victoria Cross.

Thus is gallantry remembered, sometimes as an apparent failure, at other times as a glorious achievement.

When I had the honour of carrying my great grandfather's medals the length of the nave of Westminster Abbey in June 2006, it was as part of a glorious pageant in celebration of the 150th Anniversary of the institution of the Victoria Cross and the 50th Anniversary of the Victoria Cross and George Cross Association and the gallant recipients of both of those medals.

In September, my family attended a more personal and local ceremony at the church where he is buried, St. Lawrence's in Mereworth, Kent. Of all the memories of that day, the most abiding was of a local lady who tends his grave and who proudly told me how she loved looking after "my Admiral".

From what I have learned of my gallant ancestor, a brave but modest man like so many V.C.s, I have often wondered which of these occasions would have touched him most: the formal appreciation of his bravery or this gesture of Kentish affection.

Michael Adams
Great-grandson of Charles Lucas

A SAILOR IS BORN

The youngest of four sons, Charles Davis Lucas was born on Wednesday 19 February 1834 in Druminargal House, Poyntzpass, County Armagh, Northern Ireland.

Druminargal House

His father, Davis Lucas was a wealthy landowner. His mother was Elizabeth Hill of Drumargole, daughter of Captain Thomas Hill. Charles was born into one of the old county families of Ireland, being descended from the Lucas-Scudamores of Castle Shane, County Monaghan. They were an English family settled in Ireland.

So Charles Davis Lucas came from a distinguished family. However his mother Elizabeth died on 10 January 1837, when he was nearly three years old. It is thought he was reared by his mother's parents, Captain and Mrs Hill. He may have attended the local village school, but it is more likely that he was educated privately, as the standard of education in the village schools at the time was very poor, and as yet not organised. He had three sisters, Ellen, Elizabeth and Charlotte.

The Lucas family had a long tradition of service in the army and it is thought that Captain Hill was the influence behind Charles joining the Royal Navy. So he joined the Navy as a Cadet on 13 February 1847, just days before his 13th birthday.

THE SECOND BURMESE WAR

Charles joined H.M.S. *Amazon* on the Mediterranean Station. The *Amazon* was a 1,078-ton 46-gun frigate launched on 5 August 1821. In 1844, she was converted to carry 24 guns and was eventually sold in 1863. She was at the time commanded by Captain James John Stopford and was stationed in Lisbon and the Mediterranean.

Charles transferred as a cadet, in 1848, on to H.M.S. *Vanguard*, an 80-gun 2,609-ton second-rate ship of the line, launched on 25 August 1835 at Pembroke Yard. At the time she was the broadest ship ever built in England. She was a fully rigged sailing ship, with a complement of 700–750 officers and men. She was commanded by Captain George Frederick Rich in the Mediterranean from 6 November 1847 until *Vanguard* was paid off on 28 March 1849 in Plymouth.

H.M.S.*Vanguard*

Following this pay-off, Charles transferred to H.M.S. *Dragon* in 1849 off the coast of Ireland. The previous year, Ireland had been in open rebellion under the leadership of Smith O'Brien, in the suppression of which the *Dragon* took a very active part.

H.M.S. *Dragon* was commanded by Captain William Hutcheon Hall, Charles's future father-in-law who was noted for his prominent role during the First Opium War in 1841. Charles stayed with her until 8 June 1850 when she returned to Portsmouth. H.M.S. *Dragon* was a second-class frigate launched on 17 June 1845. She was 1,270 tons and had six guns.

On 23 July 1850, Charles transferred to H.M.S. *Fox* as a Midshipman and proceeded to India under Commodore G. Lambert. H.M.S. *Fox* was a 46-gun fifth-rate sailing frigate launched in 1829. A fifth-rate sailing frigate had 32–40 guns mounted on a single deck. These ships acted as fast scouts or independent cruisers and included a variety of guns from thirty-two 12-pounders to 36, 38 or even 40, 18-pound guns. Tonnage ranged from 700–1,450 tons and they carried 250–300 men.

Friction between the British and the Burmese increased after Pagan Min became King of Burma in 1846. The Burmese seemed to ignore the Treaty of Yandabo, signed on 24 February 1826 that had ended the first Burma War and guaranteed the protection of British merchants and commerce.

During 1851, Captain Sheppard, master and owner of a trading vessel, was charged with throwing a man overboard. He was fined 900 rupees and imprisoned by the Burmese Governor of Rangoon. Other acts of oppression followed and the merchants of Rangoon applied to the Governor General for protection. This resulted in Commodore Lambert being sent to Rangoon with H.M.S. *Fox* and two other ships, the *Prosperine* and the *Tenasserim*, to restore confidence. He demanded the removal of the Governor of Rangoon, and the payment of 9,000 rupees to Captain Sheppard for the indignity he had been subjected to. The Burmese court agreed to these terms and the Governor was relieved of his post and the money paid.

When the new Governor arrived, officers from the ship were treated with insolence by his servants. In retaliation, on 6 January 1852, Commodore Lambert seized the King's ships then in the Rangoon River, and declared the Rivers Rangoon, Bassein and Salween to be in a state of blockade.

On 10 January, having taken on board H.M.S. *Hermes*, the inhabitants of Rangoon who sought the protection of the British flag, Commodore Lambert set sail. The Burmese opened fire from their stockades and the ships replied. They proceeded to Calcutta where Lord Dalhousie, Governor General, approved the strong measures that had been taken. He hoped to avoid war by negotiation, but war was inevitable. On 12 February 1852 it was decided to send a second expedition to Burma.

That month Lord Dalhousie sent a letter to the King of Ava, really an ultimatum calling for various apologies, compensation payments, reception of a British Political agent and the removal of the Governor of Rangoon. Satisfaction on these points was to be given by 1 April 1852.

In March, Lord Dalhousie organised a force of 7,000 men under the command of Major General Sir Henry T. Godwin. The force arrived before Rangoon on 2 April. In addition a fleet of ships was brought in to assist.

Before commencing operations against Rangoon, General Godwin decided to strike a decisive blow against the town of Martaban. As soon as the British ships arrived opposite the stockades they were fired upon by the defenders. On 5 April H.M.S. *Fox* was part of the small squadron that attacked the heavily fortified town to great effect. A landing party attacked and captured the enemy stockades, spiking their guns and destroying their ammunition. This first engagement was a complete success.

At about 9 o'clock on the morning of 11 April, the British warships opened fire on Rangoon on the left bank and Dallah on the right. The enemy replied with some vigorous and accurate fire. However by 11 o'clock the fire from the defences of Rangoon was silenced, with the stockade and part of the town in flames. On the Dallah side, the Burmese stayed with their defences. Sailors were sent in boats as a storming party. After landing on low mud banks they quickly formed up and rushed the defenders. Their attack was so fierce that the enemy abandoned their works and fled.

Shortly after daybreak the next day, the ships once more opened fire from Rangoon and two brigades landed. When they were ready, the First Brigade went into action with the Second Brigade in support. Four companies of the 51st Light Infantry covered the British advance, accompanied by four guns of the Bengal Artillery. After about a mile, the British found themselves in contact with the enemy, under direct fire from the defences sighted on the line of advance. The enemy were ensconced in a white masonry building. The artillery opened fire on the building with four guns at a range of 800 yards, but had to cease as they had little ammunition.

This was followed by an assault party consisting of the 51st Light Infantry and Sappers and Miners. Despite heavy fire from the building they were able to raise scaling ladders. Having scaled the ramparts, the enemy evacuated the building and ran into the jungle. British losses were considerable.

After camping overnight on the open plain, on the 14th, they prepared for the main attack on the Great Pagoda. At daybreak the entire force advanced in two brigades. The British guns fired at the Pagoda with little apparent effect upon the morale of the Burmese defenders. Over a space of 800 yards an assault was made, heavily exposed to fire. The leading company, led on by its officers, rushed up the stone steps, followed closely by the whole attacking force. This caused the enemy to panic and they fled into the jungle. British losses in two days' fighting were 2 officers and 15 men killed, 14 officers and 118 men wounded.

In the next few months the rain set in, and with it, fever and dysentery. The temporary hospitals were packed with sick men, and medical officers were at a premium. Despite this it was decided to attack Bassein, an important settlement in South Arakan. Bassein was strongly fortified, with an estimated force of 7,000 men. The defences were about a mile in length, with a strongly built mud wall occupying the left of the line, while in the centre was a huge pagoda.

General Godwin led about 800 men in the assault. On the 18 May at around 4 p.m. they were opposite the town. They landed without interference, and attacked the mud fort. The storming party found it fully garrisoned and well-armed. The attack was very determined as was the defence obstinate. It was bravely stormed but several officers and men were severely wounded. The whole affair was over just after 6pm.

In the intervening time a rebellion at Pegu had broken out. Troops had mutinied and taken possession of the city, but were shortly driven out and order, to a certain extent, was restored. The British authorities at Rangoon resolved to take advantage of this in order to take control of the city. Major Cotton was sent to occupy it and demolished its defences on 4 June, after which he returned to Rangoon.

At the beginning of July an expedition advanced up the Irrawaddy to Prome, at the time a large and populous city. Captain Tarleton R.N. conducted this expedition, and finding little opposition, he landed on 9 July and took possession capturing 20 guns, many of them of large calibre, and many war boats, barges etc. This operation is said to have brought to a close the first phase of the Second Burmese War.

Additional British reinforcements arrived at Rangoon in September 1852. British ships sailed up the river, bombarded the stockade at Prome, and the British occupied the deserted town on 10 October 1852. The British retook the town of Pegu after a short sharp fight on 21 November 1852. The British annexed the province of Pegu shortly after. After this annexation a number of Burmese officials resisted. One of these was Myat Htoon, Commissioner of the Danchen district north of Danubyu. The British attempted to overthrow him by marching against his stockade in February 1853, but the Burmese ambushed the British force, killing or wounding more than 80 soldiers. Charles Lucas took part in this attack under Captain Lock R.N. Captain Lock himself was killed. The force had been obliged to retreat, command of the rearguard devolved on 19-year-old Midshipman Lucas. The retreat lasted nine hours, during which the rearguard was warmly engaged in keeping back the enemy. Brigadier General Cheape with a 1,100 man force, supported by guns and rockets, was then given the mission. After a 24-day-long fierce battle, Cheape's force defeated the Burmese. The British lost 130 killed or wounded, plus more than 100 dead from cholera.

As the British prepared to march on the capital of Ava, King Pagan Min was deposed by his brother Mindon, who wanted to end the war. The British, in addition to the province of Pegu, demanded hundreds of additional square miles that included valuable teak forests. The Burmese protested but had to accept, although King Mindon refused to sign the formal peace treaty. A ceasefire ended the war and was declared on 30 January 1853. The end of the war resulted in the annexation of most of Burma by Britain.

Charles was gazetted on 5 March 1853 for his part in the severe and gallant action in the vicinity of Danubyu. He was also awarded the Indian Service Medal for his efforts with the clasp for Pegu. The Indian Service Medal was awarded from 1854 until 1895. Major campaigns that previously merited medals of their own were now reduced to bars. The "Pegu" bar was awarded for action between 28 March 1852 and 30 June 1853. On 1 July 1853 he became a Mate. His bravery and presence of mind under fire were noted by his superior officers.

H.M.S. HECLA AND THE BALTIC EXPEDITION

Charles Lucas returned to England in May 1854, and at once proceeded to the Baltic, where he joined H.M.S. *Hecla*, under the command of Captain W. H. Hall (his former captain on the *Dragon*.) He joined the ship on 6 May, and remained with her in the Baltic until July 1854.

That year war had broken out between allies Britain and France on the one hand and Russia. Known as the Crimean War because most of the significant action took place in the Crimea Peninsula on the northern shores of the Black Sea, it was ostensibly fought to stop Russia expanding into Turkey. There were also actions in the Baltic.

H.M.S. *Hecla* was part of a fleet of warships dispatched to the Baltic when hostilities broke out, with the aim of blockading the Russian Baltic fleet, inflicting damage on their defences and diverting some of the Russian army away from the Crimea. The British fleet were under the command of Admiral Sir Charles Napier. The main body of the fleet had left Spithead on 9 March.

The *Hecla* was an 817-ton wooden steam paddle-ship launched on 14 January 1839 with six guns. This was the third ship to be named *Hecla* after a volcano in Iceland. She left Hull on 19

February 1854 with a team of surveyors, who drew charts and sought suitable anchorages for the large Anglo-French fleet. She had a crew of 135, and two 8-inch guns (on pivots) and forward and aft, two 32-pounders. She had superior speed enabling her to outrun the Russian frigates.

It was *Hecla* and H.M.S. *Arrogant* that first engaged the enemy on 20 May at Eckness among the Aland Islands, which lie at the mouth of the Gulf of Bothnia. Eckness was a town situated on the banks of a river 12 miles in the interior. The *Arrogant* had been detached from the fleet for a considerable time, employed in reconnoitring the enemy's posts and the shores around Hango Bay. While so employed, the *Hecla* joined her. Both ships planned a little expedition of their own. After capturing a fishing boat, they used the crew to guide them in looking for enemy merchant ships. They proceeded up a narrow river, and on anchoring on the evening of 19 May, were fired upon by the enemy from behind a high sand bank, in a thickly wooded place. While passing through this narrow waterway, the Russian battery opened fire, only to be silenced by the 46-gun *Arrogant*. The next morning at 2 a.m. both ships again weighed anchor and with the *Hecla* leading, proceeded up river with both ship's companies standing by their guns. After about three hours quietly feeling their way along the intricate navigation of the river both ships came suddenly within range of an enemy's battery. The *Hecla* found herself within range of the guns of a Russian fort. She returned fire but was unable to compete. Luckily *Arrogant*, under Captain Yelverton, arrived shortly after and fired a broadside which silenced the enemy guns. When the smoke cleared, a troop of horse artillery was observed scampering away. A prolonged and heavy fire of musketry now ensued from the wood, and Minie balls fell thick on board both ships. The *Arrogant* now went aground within 20 yards of the battery. However, before attempting to haul the ship off, the enemy's guns were dismounted by a broadside and the ship then hauled to safety. On passing the fort where the guns had been dismounted, a terrible sight was witnessed – gun carriages blown to fragments, guns dismounted, helmets and knapsacks scattered about without owners. The town of Ekness lay before them. They found three merchant ships, two of which had run aground. The *Arrogant* had to anchor here, as the water was shallow. The *Hecla* proceeded on, but another battery now opened fire on her. The *Arrogant* swung broadside on, while the *Hecla* passed, firing shells on the enemy as she did so. She ran up alongside a barque, took her in tow, and steamed away with her much to the horror of the inhabitants. *Arrogant* had two killed and four wounded. *Hecla* had five wounded and one man killed, and Captain Hall was wounded in the leg by a musket ball.

While they were returning they were joined by the *Dauntless* – she had been sent to ascertain the cause and source of firing, which was distinctly audible as the squadron steamed into Hango-roads. The *Hecla* had several shots through the funnel, steam-pipe and hull, one shot passing through the ship's side.

They rejoined the fleet on 21 May, off Hango Head. The Commander-in-Chief, Sir Charles Napier hoisted the signal "Well done, *Arrogant* and *Hecla*". Sir James Graham in Parliament mentioned the incident as "one worthy of the brightest annals of British naval warfare".

This skirmish was followed on 22 May by *Dragon*, *Magicienne* and *Basilisk*, later joined by *Hecla* shelling the Hango fortification for five hours. Both sides hailed the engagement as a great victory, the English losing four officers and some men. On 29 May, Captain Hall visited Stockholm with H.M.S. *Hecla*, which was a great sightseeing attraction.

For several days the weather was quite threatening, and nothing happened except the Paddle Steamer *Driver* and Surveying Vessel *Lightning* were despatched to the Aland Islands. They returned on 10 June and reported that the island of Bomarsund was strongly fortified, and garrisoned by about 2,500 men. The fortifications consisted of solid granite, with two tiers of guns, and were supported by three round towers. The fortress guarded the entrance to the Gulf of Bothnia.

By now the British fleet consisted of 27 ships, and the French, of 19 vessels. On the evening of 21 June 1854, the *Hecla* (Captain Hall) along with the *Odin* (Captain F. Scott) and *Valorous* (Captain C. M. Buckle) attacked the fortress. It was defended by more than 80 guns and a fierce encounter ensued which lasted most of the night.

Captain Hall had been sent by Sir Charles Napier, with instructions to Rear Admiral Plumridge to join the fleet at Baro Sound, in order to procure provisions for his squadron in the Gulf. So Admiral Plumridge left Captain Hall in command until his return. He also ordered the captains of the squadron to obey the orders of Captain Hall as their senior officer. Captain Hall was to observe the enemy in the Gulf of Bothnia.

Captain Hall was to proceed, in the first instance, off Lagskaren lighthouse, where he would rendezvous with the *Valorous, Vulture* and *Odin*, until the admiral returned. Here he was to leave one ship with the information as to the whereabouts of the other ships. These orders were given on 19 June. On 21st, Captain Hall wrote to Admiral Plumridge that he had been fortunate enough to obtain a pilot for the southern part of the Aland Islands. Taking advantage of this, he had proceeded up as far as Flaka in Rod Bay, where he had cut out a Russian brigantine. On his return to the rendezvous he found the *Valorous* and *Odin*, who had joined him to reconnoitre as far as Ango Sund.

On the 22nd, Captain Hall reported to the admiral that he had attacked Bomarsund. To everyone's surprise Captain Hall thought his three steamers sufficient for the purpose. What should have been a reconnaissance developed into a bombardment by three lightly armed ships against a heavily armed fortress. Captain Hall led his ship and the two 16-gun paddle steamers *Odin* and *Valorous* through the narrow channel to Bomarsund. The ships were fired on by riflemen and artillery from the shore and the main fort batteries also opened fire. All three ships anchored at about 9 o'clock that night (it being midsummer and light in those latitudes until nearly midnight) and began a spirited bombardment which lasted until 1 o'clock the next morning, but without doing much lasting damage. Captain Hall was later commended by the King of Sweden but criticised by the Admiralty for using so much ammunition.

Captain Hall described the situation in a letter:

> Adverting to my letter of yesterday, wherein I mentioned having cut out a merchant brig at Flaka and procuring pilots, I have the honour to inform you, that on my return to the rendezvous off Lagskar lighthouse, I found there H.M. ships Valorous and Odin, and proceeded with them to reconnoitre the Russian fortifications at Bomarsund.
>
> I thought it right to put on board both vessels a Finland pilot; and having arranged with Captains Buckle and Scott my plan of operations, and ordered them to be prepared against red-hot shot, rifle shot, and the likelihood of getting on shore &c., I proceeded through the archipelago of the Aland Islands – the channel being only from one to two cable lengths wide, but with not less than five fathoms water, HECLA leading the way in close order.
>
> At 4.30 p.m. entered the narrow channel of Ango Sund, firing on the woods as we passed to prevent a surprise from riflemen, and, on opening the strong fortifications of Bomarsund, I made the preconcerted signal (white ensign at the main) to engage forts, and opened fire from the HECLA's 10-inch guns with shot and shell, which was followed by the other ships.
>
> The enemy did not for some time return our fire, evidently wishing to draw us within range, which, however, I carefully avoided, finding that our shot and shell reached the fort. At 5.35 the largest battery, a casemated battery of two tiers, mounting between 70 and 80 guns, opened on the squadron, and a masked battery of 6 guns, from the southern part of the bay, much nearer to us, opened a smart flanking fire with shot, shell and rockets, and a body of riflemen from the same quarter kept up a continuous fire.
>
> I directed a heavy fire to be kept up from the ships to silence the 6-gun battery and the riflemen, which were accompanied by a body of Horse Artillery, all of which were finally driven from their position apparently with great loss.
>
> At 8.50, from the numerous shoals and the danger of getting on shore while manoeuvring and firing at the different batteries, signalised to the squadron to anchor with springs on their cables, to enable them to bring their broadsides to bear on the forts in a part of the bay least exposed to the enemy's fire, continuing the action without intermission.

At 10 observed that the shell of the squadron had set fire to the public storehouses and buildings in the rear of the fort, and part of the fortress. At this time, nearly every shot and shell fired by the squadron appeared to take effect. The action was continued with great spirit until after midnight, when I made the signal to discontinue the engagement, the squadron having expended nearly all their shot and shell for the large guns, and the fire from the enemy having slackened to only an occasional shot.

At 12.58 weighed and proceeded with squadron in company through the same channel by which we had entered to Rod Bay, where we anchored at 4 a.m. this day, having left the extensive military government storehouses in rear of the fort and part of the forts still in flames, and the fire increasing.

I cannot speak too highly of the assistance afforded me by Capts. Buckle and Scott, throughout the whole of the engagement, and of the admirable manner in which both ships were manoeuvred in such narrow waters. Capts. Buckle and Scott speak in the highest terms of their lieutenants W. Mould and Jos. Edye, as well as the whole of their officers, seamen and marines. I have also great pleasure in being able to speak in the highest terms of the conduct of Lieut. Battiscombe, Mr. E. Tucker, Master of the HECLA, as well as the rest of the officers, seamen and marines, and Mr. LUCAS, Mate; and with regard to Mr. LUCAS, I have the pleasure to report a remarkable instance of coolness and presence of mind in action – he having taken up and thrown overboard a live shell thrown on board the HECLA by the enemy, while the fuse was burning. I have also to mention that Capt. Thomas Lyons, who is on board as a volunteer, from his knowledge of the language rendered a most efficient service.

I beg to enclose a list of casualties during the action, which I am delighted to say is slight: only five men were wounded. The ships were hulled repeatedly by the enemy's fire, and the spars and rigging also suffered, and the boats of the HECLA were rendered, for the time, unserviceable. I beg also to enclose a rough tracing of the squadron's track from the sea to Bomarsund, also an outline of the position of the ships in the bay, and a rough sketch of the principal forts, etc.

For further details I beg to refer you to Capt. Scott of the Odin, who is the bearer of this despatch.

I have, &c

W. H. HALL, Captain

It is interesting to note that in an action of only eight hours duration, Captain Hall's ships expended nearly all their shot and shell. Sir James Graham praised the skill of Captain Hall in Parliament. Captain Hall exaggerated the damage inflicted upon the Russians and earned a stiff rebuke from the Admiralty for putting his ship in unnecessary danger and expending all his ammunition to little effect. The action proved a godsend to the government at the time, and the news was well received by a British public hungry for some offensive movement from their much-vaunted navy. Bomarsund became a topic of conversation and a new coal mining village near Newcastle was even named after the Baltic fortress. However the Commander-in-Chief was getting repeated injunctions from home to be sparing of shot and shell for practice, the Board of Ordnance having only a limited supply. This was lamentable proof of our unprepared condition for war. While the action was of no consequence, neither the fort nor the ships suffering any damage, Lucas's actions earned him immortality.

On 22 June, the combined fleet weighed anchor and proceeded towards Cronstadt. On the 26th the combined fleet moved forward. At 8 a.m. the *Imperieuse* spotted the Russian fleet at anchor, and telegraphed the information to the admiral. During the ensuing mist the Russian fleet made for the shelter of the fortified harbour, thus avoiding coming into contact with the Allied fleet. On the 28th the fleet was much surprised by the approach of the *Hecla*, with the signal flying, "Bomarsund has been successfully bombarded".

Admiral Napier, having considered the strength of Cronstadt, decided not to risk his ships in making an attack on the fortress. On 4 July the *Hecla* met the *Leopard* at Orengrund, the former having brought despatches from the Commander-in-Chief, and ammunition and stores for the *Odin* and *Valorous*. The ammunition and stores were sent on in the *Hecla* northwards.

On 18 July the French and English squadrons again weighed anchor and stood to sea, leaving the *Imperieuse* and *Dragon* at anchor in Baro Sound.

Meanwhile on 18 July Charles Lucas was promoted to Lieutenant on the *Dauntless*.

SHELL OVERBOARD!

So what did Charles Lucas do in all this?

When the British fleet began its attack on the well-defended Russian positions at Bomarsund, Lucas was an 18-year-old acting mate in command of a battery of six guns aboard H.M.S. *Hecla*. His self-possession and initiative had already been noted by his superiors, but his most glorious moment was about to come.

As soon as the British began attacking, furious fire was returned – the range was about 500 yards and each of the Russians' 24lb shells hit its target. The *Hecla* and her sister ships shook under the impact. Suddenly a screaming shell landed on the deck of the *Hecla*, not far from where young Lucas stood directing his men. It rolled to a stop and lay there, its fuse burning rapidly away. In an instant the panic-stricken seamen dropped down and covered their heads, waiting for the dreaded blast … all except Lucas.

The young midshipman sprang forward, seized the terrifying object and, its fuse hissing in his face, carried it to the railing and heaved it overboard. A moment later, with a terrible roar, it exploded in the sea, without causing any major damage. The ship received some minor damage, but thanks to Lucas's action no one was killed or seriously wounded.

Doncella Cigarette Card

Many years later Lucas recalled the situation in an American magazine, published in 1903:

We had been doing nothing for some time, and, feeling tired of inactivity, Captain Hall, of the Hecla, determined to wake the Russians up. So, happening, while detached from the fleet, to fall in with the small paddle frigates Valorous, Captain Buckle, and Odin, Captain Frank Scott, Captain Hall asked Captains Buckle and Scott if they would join him in an attack on Bomarsund. They replied that he (Captain Hall) was senior officer, and that if he would take them under his command and take also the responsibility, they would be delighted. Consequently we went for Bomarsund – the Hecla leading her little squadron.

We arrived off Bomarsund on June 21, and at once opened fire on the large fort, which as quickly returned fire. We had no charts of that coast, and so we were obliged to approach the fort very slowly for fear of the rocks, which we dreaded more than the forts. While proceeding in this leisurely manner a masked battery of six or eight guns opened fire upon us at about 600 yards – every shell striking the ship. I was an acting mate and had command of the after battery, consisting of six guns. I was standing on the small skylight of the captain's cabin, to be able to see above the men's heads, when a shell struck the skylight. I fortunately came down on my feet, and seeing the men – very properly – lying down, as the shell was amongst them with its fuse still burning, I picked it up and threw it overboard.

When he was asked how he felt at that moment he replied, "Oh, you're asking me to go back a hundred years. It's effect upon me was simply this: 'There you are and you must get out of that!' One didn't stop to think much. You can't funk or cast about for an elaborate plan of action when Fate suddenly puts a pistol at your head. All you do is let nature work, and nature's infallible plan is to get rid of the pistol. I just called to the men to lie down, and scrambling on my feet, I ran at the shell, picked it up with both hands, and heaved it overboard as soon as possible. It was good to hear it go fizz into the water!"

Asked if it exploded, he replied, "Oh, yes, it hadn't come all that way for nothing. When it went off it was about four feet down, and did no damage. It was a great mercy, for the *Hecla* had her fair weight of lead that day".

For his bravery in saving the lives of his fellow men, Lucas was awarded the Royal Humane Society Medal. This large 51mm diameter medal was not intended for wearing, but Lucas had a ring and blue ribbon fitted. He also had the original silver medal gilded. In 1869, official permission was granted for the wearing of the medal and a 38mm diameter medal was produced with a scroll suspension and navy blue ribbon. This was a replacement medal issued to Lucas in 1879. He also had this medal gilded. These medals are held at the National Maritime Museum in Greenwich.

Lucas's Humane Society Medals.

For his gallantry Lucas was promoted to Lieutenant on the recommendations of Hall and Napier. The former wrote to the admiral on 22 June:

> With regard to Mr. Lucas, I have the pleasure to report a remarkable instance of coolness and presence of mind in action, he having taken up, and thrown overboard, a live shell thrown on board the 'Hecla' by the enemy, while the fuse was burning.

In forwarding Hall's report to the Admiralty on 28 June, Napier added:

> Their Lordships will observe, in Captain Hall's letter, the great courage of Mr. C. D. Lucas, in taking up a live shell and throwing it overboard; and I trust their Lordships will mark their sense of it by promoting him.

Lucas's promotion was dated from 26 June, two days before Napier wrote his report. A promotion for gallantry in action was not unusual. There were no suitable gallantry awards, and sometimes a financial reward might be awarded. Having had Lucas promoted, he also recommended Lucas for the Victoria Cross when the decoration was instituted.

At the outbreak of the Crimean War only senior officers were eligible for orders of chivalry, but their juniors, and other ranks, received no formal recognition of acts of gallantry.

There is a strong case for thinking that Lucas's act of bravery led directly to the creation of the Victoria Cross. The incident was widely reported and discussed and it was certain that his action was greatly admired by Queen Victoria herself. In December of 1854, ex-Navy Captain Thomas Scobell MP proposed in the House of Commons, "that an Order of Merit to persons serving in the army or navy for distinguished and prominent personal gallantry to which every grade should be admissible" should be created.

The idea was taken up by The Secretary of State for War, the Duke of Newcastle, and received the enthusiastic support of the Queen and Prince Albert. The new award was announced on 29 January, 1856. It took some time to agree the form of the award, name, material etc. The shape of a cross was generally favoured and Prince Albert is credited with insisting that it should be called "The Victoria Cross". The metal was to be taken from two Russian cannon captured in the Crimea. The Queen herself was responsible for the inscription "For Valour". Originally the V.C. ribbon was blue for the navy, dark red for the army, but since 1918 it has been the same crimson shade for all the services. Recipients of the Cross were to receive an annual pension of £10.

It was not until 26 June 1857, that the Victoria Cross was presented for the first time. There was a lot of debate about whether it should be confined to only those who had served in the Crimea, but Queen Victoria insisted that the award should be retrospective and that the Navy be included. On 12 June, the Queen informed the new Secretary of State for War, Lord Panmure, that she had "come to the conclusion that it will be best to have a Review in Hyde Park", where she would attend on horseback. The list of those who were to receive the award was not published until three days before the presentation ceremony.

On 26 June 1857, in Hyde Park, Queen Victoria presented the new Victoria Cross to 62 members of the army and navy. It was a unique occasion, the first on which officers and men were decorated by the monarch together. The Queen was wearing a semi-military dress. The body of it was scarlet like a military tunic, and a gold sash was worn over the left shoulder. On parade were a large body of troops under Sir Colin Campbell, comprised of Life Guards, Dragoons, Hussars, Royal Engineers, Artillery and Line regiments, together with a detachment of Bluejackets from the Royal Navy. A few minutes before 10 o'clock the officers and men who were to receive the medal marched in single file across the park to the Queen's position. She was escorted by the Prince Consort, the Crown Prince of Russia, the Prince of Wales and the Queen's son Prince Alfred (Duke of Saxe-Coburg-Gotha). The Victoria Crosses lay upon a small table covered with a scarlet cloth. The V.C. recipients passed before the Queen who was mounted on a charger and leant from her saddle to pin the Cross on each of the soldier's and sailor's breasts. They came forward one at a time as Lord Panmure read their names. "So quietly and expeditiously was this done in every case", commented *The Times*, "that the whole ceremony scarcely occupied 10 minutes, and must have been over before the general but very distant public in the background were aware it had commenced".

The V.C.s then stood opposite the Queen while the troops marched past between – the infantry twice and the cavalry and horse artillery three times.

Charles Lucas was the first to earn the Victoria Cross, and he was the fourth to receive it. He accepted the award with pride and calm dignity. His V.C. Citation appeared in the *London Gazette* 21971, page 654, dated 24 February 1857. It stated that: "This Officer was promoted to his present rank on the 21st June 1854, for his gallantry in throwing overboard a live shell, at the first attack on the batteries of Bomarsund". The letters from Captain Hall and Sir Charles Napier were then quoted.

He was the first man ever to perform an action which was subsequently rewarded with the Victoria Cross. More properly his action was chronologically the first to be so rewarded. With "Senior Service" (Naval) awards being presented first, in order of rank, three naval commanders received their awards before Lucas. In order of presentation they were Commander H. J. Raby, Commander John Bythesea, and Commander H. T. Burgoyne.

It is interesting to note that the Navy and Royal Marines had their awards presented in order of rank, while the army had their crosses presented on order of regimental precedence.

1854–1873

Following his promotion to Lieutenant, Charles Lucas joined H.M.S. *Dauntless* in the Baltic, until November 1854. The *Dauntless* was a wooden-hulled steam screw-frigate, launched at Portsmouth in 1847.

In 1854, she sailed with the main fleet to the Baltic, until in December she transferred to the Black Sea taking with her artillery details and stores. Her commanding officer from December 1853 was Captain Alfred Phillipps Ryder R.N.

Lucas's next appointment was as Lieutenant on H.M.S. *Calcutta* at Sheerness from 26 February 1855. She was based in home waters. This 2,291-ton 84-gun second-rate ship-of-the-line was launched on 14 March 1831 in Bombay. She had a complement of 720 men (38 officers, 69 petty officers, 403 seamen, 60 boys and 150 marines). In 1855, she had been in reserve, but was recommissioned for the Baltic Wars. After two months she had been sent home again, as being useless for modern naval actions.

On 12 October 1855, Lucas became Lieutenant on H.M.S. *Powerful*, in North America and the West Indies until October 1856. The *Powerful* was commissioned by Captain Thomas Massie on 12 September 1854 for service in the North American West Indies Station, which generally meant being based in Jamaica.

On 12 December 1857, Lucas joined the steamship H.M.S. *Edinburgh* until February 1858. Then on 1 March 1858 he became Lieutenant on H.M.S. *Cressy* at Sheerness. *Cressy* was a third-rate wooden screw ship, launched at Chatham on 21 July 1853. She had 80 guns and 750 men. She had served in the Baltic War, then the Mediterranean. On 1 March 1858, command was taken up by Captain Edward Pellew Halstead. From 10 May 1858, provisions and stores were ordered to be taken on board the screw steam guardship of ordinary *Royal George*, and the screw steam guardship of steam reserve *Cressy*. If required for immediate service they were ordered to be manned from the different coastguard stations attached to their district.

From 12 June 1858, the three depot ships of the steam fleet in reserve, including the *Cressy* were ordered to form members of the Channel fleet.

On 19 May 1859, the *Cressy* steamed out of harbour at Sheerness for Spithead, to join the Channel fleet. She saluted the flag of the Commander-in-Chief, and at 12 o'clock fired a Royal salute, in commemoration of Her Majesty's birthday

From 26 September 1860 until 26 May 1861, Charles Lucas was with *Cressy* in The Mediterranean, captained by Thomas Harvey. He, Lucas was promoted to commander on 19 February 1862 and joined the frigate H.M.S. *Liffey* on 18 August 1862 in the Mediterranean. She was launched at Devonport on 6 May 1856 and was a wooden screw frigate with 51 guns and 560 men. She was captained from 17 July 1862 until 31 October 1865 by Captain George Parker, in the Mediterranean and from March 1865, in North America and the West Indies. Lucas served with her until October 1866 as second in command.

On 18 October 1866, Lucas joined H.M.S. *Indus* in Devonport until 3 November 1867. He was then attached to H.M.S. *Vixen* from 17 June until 23 August 1867, to be commander for comparative trials with *Viper* and *Waterwitch*. *Vixen* was an armoured composite gunboat and was the first Royal Navy vessel to have twin propellers.

Charles Lucas

From 17 June 1867 she was captained by Commander Lucas for trials with her sister ships. The trials attracted considerable attention in August 1867. The results were disappointing and led to the abandonment of hydraulic propulsion for naval ships until the last few decades. The *Vixen* and *Viper* were considered too slow as well as unseaworthy and were withdrawn from service in 1887 and towed to Bermuda in 1888 as coastal defence ships.

Commander Lucas then transferred back to H.M.S. *Indus* from 23 August 1867 until 3 November 1867. He was promoted to the rank of Captain on 25 October 1867. The 1871 census shows him as being with his brother-in-law Sir George de la Poer Beresford and Lady Beresford at their home at Gate Fulford in Yorkshire. Also listed at that address was Charles's brother Edward, a retired farmer aged 39.

On 1 October 1873, aged 39, Lucas retired to Scotland, and went to live with his sister and brother-in-law in the Western Highlands.

IN RETIREMENT

From 1873–1883, Charles Lucas commanded the 13th Argyll Rifle Volunteers (the Ballachulish Corps) in Scotland as Brigadier General. Prior to 1861 there were 13 corps raised in Argyll totalling 16 companies. Most of them wore the sombre grey tunics and trousers of the day. In 1861, the scattered companies were gathered together and reorganised into the 1st Administrative Battalion, Argyllshire Volunteers which in 1863 adopted Highland dress. In 1880, the Battalion was consolidated into the 1st Argyllshire Highland Rifle Volunteers. The following year it was incorporated into the Argyll and Sutherland Highlanders. When he resigned his commission he was granted permission to retain his rank and wear the uniform of the Argyllshire Highlanders.

Sometime between 1878 and 1879 Lucas is believed to have left his V.C. and other medals on a train, possibly on one of his trips to Scotland. However there are various stories about how he lost it. It is also believed he may have sold it to pay for an illegitimate son in South America. He was however issued with a duplicate medal.

On 22 April 1879, Charles Lucas married Frances Russell Hall, only child of his former captain on *Hecla*, Admiral Sir William Hall, K.C.B., F.R.S., and the Hon. Lady Hall (née Hilare Caroline Byng) a daughter of Admiral (the sixth) Lord Torrington. He was George Byng of Yotes Court, Mereworth, near Maidstone. There was a certain irony here in that Torrington's ancestor was Admiral Byng, famous for being executed on his own quarter-deck upon the orders of the Lords of the Admiralty for refusing to take his ships in to attack the French land batteries at the siege of Minorca. He recognised that

Lucas's V.C., India Service Medal and Baltic War Medal

his men would be destroyed to no purpose, but in his case his action resulted in condemnation.

It is understood that Lucas had been summoned to the deathbed of his old captain, William Hall, who made an extraordinary request. He died at his residence, 48 Phillimore Gardens, Kensington of apoplexy on 25 June 1878, and was buried at Mereworth, Kent on 29 June. He begged Lucas to take care of his wife Hilare and to marry his only daughter. Lucas, an incurable romantic, agreed.

Charles Lucas V.C.

However the marriage was not a great success. Frances was arrogant and violent-tempered and far too aware of her position as a member of the Byng family.

In the 1881 census, Charles (age 47) and Frances (age 31) were living at Kinlochlaich House, Lismore and Appin, Argyll, Scotland. Her mother Helen Hall (age 66) was residing with them. Also listed at the house were three servants and a cook. They included Sarah Roberts (age 33) who stayed with the family for 35 years. Their eldest daughter, Hilare Caroline Lucas was born here around 1880. Charles was a J.P. for Argyll.

By 1882, the family had moved to 48 Phillimore Gardens, Kensington, where their daughter was born – Frances Byng Lucas. On 1 June 1885, Charles Lucas was promoted rear admiral on the retired list. The youngest daughter, Caroline Louisa Byng was born around 1887 in Brighton.

The 1891 and 1901 census returns show the family at 48 Phillimore Gardens. The only difference is that in 1901 they had four servants (two in 1891). The faithful Sarah Roberts is listed as Domestic Maid.

TUNBRIDGE WELLS

Sometime in the late 1890s the Lucas family moved to Great Culverden, Mount Ephraim, Tunbridge Wells, Kent, in order to live with Caroline Louisa, the widow of James Master Owen Byng, son of George Byng, 6th Viscount Torrington. His wife, Frances, was George George Byng's grand-daughter, and James's grand-niece.

Great Culverden House was built in 1830 by Jacob Jeddere Fisher. He came from Ealing and moved to Tunbridge Wells in 1828 with his two sons and twin daughters. He came with enough money to buy Culverden House (built 1740–60), have it demolished and then instruct Decimus Burton to design a new house, which he called Great Culverden. Great Culverden Park was a small nine and a half acre wood. The house was an imposing, square, stone-built house rendered in cement. The first Culverden House was built on the highest point in the wood (which later became the Kent and Sussex Hospital car park).

Great Culverden House

Only seven years after the completion of the new house, Fisher died. His widow Elizabeth continued to live there. When she died the estate was acquired by the Hon. James Owen Byng. James had followed his father into the navy, but following an accident, was forced to retire. In 1856, he married Caroline Cook of Royden Hall.

Caroline Louisa Byng and her husband James had come to Great Culverden in November 1868. James died in May 1897. He left the Great Culverden estate to be enjoyed by his widow, Caroline, during her lifetime, and left legacies of £10,000 each to Frances' three daughters. Frances had married Charles Lucas at about the same time as James Byng died. It is likely that Caroline moved out of the house to make way for the Lucases and took up residence in Culverden Lodge, her personal property, which then became known as the Dower House, although they may have also looked after her as she suffered poor health in the last years of her life. When Caroline died in April 1906, Frances inherited the estate, except for Culverden Lodge. The family then lived there until Frances died in 1925.

She left nearly £190,000. A notice appeared in *The Times* on 30 June 1906:

> The Hon. Caroline Louisa Byng deceased. Notice is hereby given that all creditors and other persons having any claims or demands against the estate of the Hon. C. L. Byng late of Great Culverden Tunbridge Wells widow deceased who died on 2 April 1906 (will with 10

codicils was proved in the Principal Registry of the Probate dated of the High Court on 14 June 1906 by Admiral Charles Davis Lucas V.C., Sir Charles Pontifex K.C.I.E. and Reginald Duke Hill executors).

Admiral Lucas was a director of the Phoenix Fire Assurance Company, a trustee for the Army and Navy Club, and J.P. for Argyllshire and Kent. He was for many years a county magistrate, and was President of the North Ward Conservative Association, having been elected chairman in 1909.

Byng Hall

He was also a Vice-President of the Central Association. He regularly placed one of the best rooms at Great Culverden at the disposal of the North Ward Association. He took a keen interest in all things connected with the welfare of Tunbridge Wells. His appearances before the public were chiefly concerned with his work on behalf of Unionism, of which he became one of the staunchest supporters in the district, particularly in respect of the Home Rule question.

In 1900, Charles Lucas officially opened the Byng Hall in Tunbridge Wells. The original cost of the Hall was £3000 but a further £2,000 was needed. The vicar visited his friend, Caroline Louisa Byng at Great Culverden. She agreed to raise her original donation from £300 to £1500. When her husband James died in May 1897 she kindly donated £100 to the St. John's Church Tower fund in his memory. She later took on the financial responsibility to enable the tower to be completed.

Her greatest gift was the Byng Hall, a lofty building which could accommodate 500 people. It was to serve as a Parish Room and Institute. It had open roof-timbers, was well lit, and had a gallery at one end. There were club rooms and classrooms for men, youths and women, together with a gymnasium.

The crowded Hall was officially opened by Admiral Lucas on Wednesday 17 October 1900. In naming the Hall, he said that the name Byng was an ancient and honourable one, a Kentish name that had been known and respected in the county for many centuries. The members of St. John's Choir were in attendance. Frances opened the remainder of the Hall when it was completed the following year. It was eventually sold to Skinners School in 2003.

Charles Lucas died at the age of 80, at home at 4 p.m. on Friday 7 August 1914 – three days after the start of the First World War. He had been ill for about three weeks, finally having a relapse from which he never recovered. He was interred at Mereworth Churchyard on Wednesday 12 August, the burial place of Mrs Lucas' family, the Byngs of Yotes Court. The Rector (the Rev. W. Moore) officiated.

The funeral arrangements were carried out by Mr. James Booty of The Pantiles, Tunbridge Wells. Lucas's remains were encased in a panelled oak coffin, with solid brass furniture. The coffin was borne in a motor-hearse, and the mourners conveyed to the Churchyard in motor cars. He left unsettled property valued at £4,729 gross of which the net personality amounted to £2,900. Probate was granted to Frances on 26 September.

After Charles Lucas died and Frances lived there, some economies were made, for the nursery gardens and greenhouses were let off to Mr Holland at £190 per annum. The Park was used for many fêtes and bazaars in aid of local charities, including the fund for a new general hospital.

Frances died on Saturday 3 January 1925 at Great Culverden and was buried at Mereworth on 7 January. The service was conducted by the Rev. Moore, Vicar of Mereworth. The chief mourners were her daughters Miss C. Byng Lucas, Captain and Mrs Byng Stamper, Mrs Adams, and Mr Douglas Byng Stamper, son of Captain

Lucas's Grave, Mereworth

and Mrs Byng Stamper. Many beautiful floral tributes were sent by friends. Probate from her will was granted to her daughters Caroline Louisa Byng Lucas and Frances Byng Byng Stamper. She left £10,637 gross and £8,114 net. Charles Lucas's V.C. was given to the National Maritime Museum by his daughter, Hilare.

Trustees then tried to wind up the Estate putting it on the market as a whole, through Bracketts. They described the property as "occupying an exceedingly valuable position on high ground, less than half a mile from Tunbridge Wells station on the Southern Railway, comprising a stone built Mansion with Finely-Timbered Park-like Grounds, Farmstead, Bailiff's House, Cottages and about 74 acres". But money was tight in the aftermath of the war and there were few who could at that time afford to run an estate of that size. At the auction the bidding was disappointing and only reached £36,000 – 4,000 below its reserve, so it was withdrawn. It was then split up and in 1927 Great Culverden was demolished and the estate divided into lots and auctioned. At the second auction one of the principle bidders was the Tunbridge Wells Hospital Committee, who bought the 11 acres fronting on Mount Ephraim. The remaining 63 acres were purchased by Colonel John Egginton and Charles Hillman, who developed the land as the Royal Chase Estate.

The Foundation Stone for the new Kent and Sussex Hospital was not laid until 19 July 1932, and the Hospital opened in July 1934. It finally closed its doors in September 2011 when patients were transferred to a new hospital at Pembury.

THE LADIES OF MILLER'S

Two of Charles Lucas's daughters, Frances Byng Stamper and Caroline Lucas became well known in Lewes in Sussex. Frances was known as "Bay" to her friends and Caroline as "Mouie". They bought Millers, a sixteenth-century timber-framed house on St. Anne's Hill, in 1939. It was called Millers because the house of which it was once the stable, originally belonged to a miller.

The third daughter, Hilare committed an unforgiveable sin in the eyes of her mother and sister. She married Captain Alexander Adams at St. Giles, London in 1915. He was a Roman Catholic, and she adopted her husband's faith. She was cast out from the family and never spoken of again. She became Lady-in-Waiting to Princess Louise (the Duchess of Argyll) and died in 1951.

Frances Lucas had married Welshman Edwin Byng-Stamper in 1909 (son of a respectable Pembrokeshire doctor who was also a Lieutenant in the Royal Welsh Fusiliers). They had a son, Douglas in 1910, who was tragically killed when he fell from a moving train on 4 August 1927.

Caroline pleased her mother by developing her artistic talents and remained single. She became Frances' darling child to whom she bequeathed her entire estate. However she was not fond of her mother and lost no time at her death in 1925 in putting her inheritance at the disposal of her sister and brother-in-law. Caroline studied art in Paris, Rome and London. In the mid-1920s, using an inheritance from their mother, they bought the Northease estate at Rodmell (now Northease Manor Independent School). This consisted of a fine Queen Anne manor house, a sheep and dairy farm, 20 cottages and 1,000 acres. Edwin left the army and joined them running the estate, and being a gentleman farmer, they extensively and lavishly developed the farm. Frances ruled the household with a rod of iron, while Caroline spent her time painting in her bedroom and going hunting. However Douglas's death had a profound effect on the family. Frances and her husband, united only in their love for their son, grew apart. They lost interest in the estate, which was now in financial difficulties and decided to sell up. From then on the sisters determined to throw themselves into the arts.

In 1932, they sold the estate and lived between Pembrokeshire (where they rented Manorbier Castle) and London, where Caroline painted and learned sculpture. She also exhibited in Paris and Rome. Frances co-founded the Contemporary Arts Society, and was widowed in 1939. They decided to return to Lewes.

The two eccentric genteel sisters were enthusiastic patrons of the Arts and maintained a close association with the members of the Bloomsbury Group. The latter had a rural retreat at nearby Charleston Farmhouse. During the Second World War they converted the stables in the back garden at Millers into an exhibition area which opened in 1941 and staged over 40 art exhibitions, concerts and lectures. They also bought other properties in Lewes and used one as an art school. They often bought up period buildings that were in danger of falling down but then did little to preserve them.

After the war they set up the "Millers Press" to commission lithographs and monotypes from leading artists. This operated from 134 High Street, Lewes from 1945. Artists involved included Vanessa Bell, Duncan Grant and Hercules Enslin du Plessis.

The sisters established the Society of London Painter-Printers in conjunction with the Redfern Gallery. They inaugurated the Byng-Stamper Prize for Landscape Painting and began an appeal to restore the ruins of Lewes Priory.

The gallery and press closed in the mid-1950s, after the ladies found their lithographic activities too taxing and the

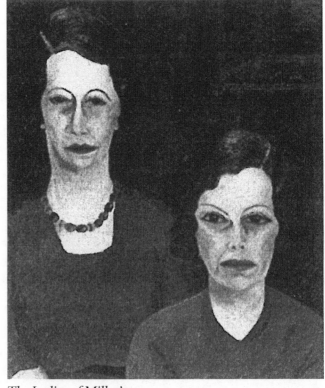

The Ladies of Miller's

press was disbanded. In the 1960s the sisters were very frail and became permanent residents of the nearby Shelley's Hotel, where they died. Caroline died on Boxing Day 1967 aged 81 and a distraught Frances died on 26 May 1968. They were both buried at Rodmell. Caroline's painting of Adelaide Crescent is in Brighton and Hove Art Gallery. The stables were demolished in 1972, their possessions split up and most of their correspondence destroyed. There is still a "Millers" at 134 High Street, which is currently a guest house. It is situated at the top end of the High Street, and Shelley's Hotel is still open for business.

The sisters, together with Edwin are buried at St. Peter's Church, Rodmell. Their little headstone is in the far corner of the lovely churchyard.

LEST WE FORGET

In June 1956, a celebration of the centenary of the instigation of the Victoria Cross was organised, which included an exhibition of V.C.s held in Marlborough House, London from 15 June until 7 July. Charles Lucas's duplicate V.C. was lent for the exhibition.

It appears that at the time it was not realised that Charles Lucas had lost his original medal. A report in the *Daily Express* for Thursday 26 April 1956 was headed "The first V.C. goes on show – as fake".

> When the exhibition was being arranged an expert looked at the medal and said: 'This is a fake'. Hancocks, the jewellers who have made all the V.C.s agreed with him. Said Commander Edward May, deputy director of the National Maritime Museum, last night: 'It is an absolute mystery. The medal was given to us in complete good faith. We have a photograph of the Admiral wearing the fake. It may be he lost his medal and had an imitation made. Or maybe he valued the original so highly he wore an imitation'.

In 1980, a set of 24 cigarette cards was issued by John Player and Sons, Imperial Tobacco Ltd. The Doncella set depicted the History of the V.C. and Number One featured an artist's impression of Lucas's action at Bomarsund (page 29).

In an article in the *Times* in July 1982, Paul Pickering wrote: "Lucas was the first V.C. Nowadays he would be lucky to get a mention in despatches for the same act". Michael Naxton, a Sotheby's medal expert said, "In the Baltic campaign and the Crimea they handed out V.C.'s extremely liberally; but as we get nearer and nearer the present time the authorities have been less willing to grant the award". Diana Condell from The Imperial War Museum said, "In the case of (Mate Charles) Lucas, at a time of unmechanized warfare he actually picked up a bomb. It would be like someone doing something against an Exocet today. It is not so much a question of the actual act's degree of gallantry, as to what we have come to expect".

On 12 September 1998 (European Heritage Day), at the instigation of the Local History Society, a plaque was unveiled in his honour at the British Legion Hall, Poyntzpass:

Charles Davis Lucas V.C. R.N.
1834–1914
Born Druminargle House, Poyntzpass
(Later Rear Admiral)
Awarded
The First Victoria Cross for Valour
At Bomarsund 21st June 1854

A two-foot sculpture of Charles Lucas receiving his V.C. from Queen Victoria was unveiled at the National Memorial Arboretum, Alrewas, Staffordshire on 26 June 2002. In 1995, Colonel Stuart Archer GC, OBE, ERD, Chairman of the V.C. and G.C. Association realised there was no National Memorial commemorating the recipients of the Victoria and George Cross. He approached the authorities to request a statue to be placed on a spare plinth in Trafalgar Square. This was part of a competition to find a permanent statue at that time. He thought of the idea of a statue to be of Queen Victoria investing the very first V.C. to Charles Lucas. The authorities refused permission for this. However in 2003, Colonel Archer's perseverance paid off when a commemorative stone to V.C. and G.C. holders was unveiled in Westminster Abbey.

David Childs, Founder of the National Memorial Arboretum wrote to the V.C. and G.C. Association, volunteering the Arboretum as a home for the finished work if it was not successful. Colonel Archer engaged the services of a sculptor, Simon Dyer, who sculpted a model in deep brown wax approximately two feet in height. It was placed in a glass cabinet provided by the Association, and is now sited permanently in the reception area at the National Arboretum memorial. Twelve holders of the V.C. and G.C., or their widows, attended the presentation. The statue has had to be recast in bronze as the wax warmed under the heat and started to melt the figure of Lucas.

Statue at National Memorial Arboretum

An inscription plaque attached to the case states: "H.M. Queen Victoria Decorating the First Recipient of the Victoria Cross, Mate Charles Lucas, Royal Navy, on the occasion of the First Victoria Cross Investiture held on 26 June 1857 in Hyde Park, London".

On Wednesday 14 May 2003, a Service was held at Westminster Abbey to dedicate the Victoria Cross and George Cross Memorial. It was attended by the Queen and the Duke of Edinburgh and 11 V.C.s. In addition, 1,400 descendents of past recipients of both awards attended the ceremony. These included Michael Adams and Suzy Davis, great-grand-children of Charles Lucas. Suzy Davis presented a bouquet to the Queen at a reception following the service.

A Service was held at St. Lawrence's Church, Mereworth, in June 2004 to mark the 150th Anniversary of Lucas's action.

On 21 June 2004, a Memorial stone made of granite from the Bomarsund Fortress and dedicated to the three V.C.s including Lucas, was unveiled in Bomarsund, Finland. The other V.C.s named on the memorial are Stoker William Johnstone and Lieutenant John Bythesea. This was to mark the 150th anniversary, and the ceremony was performed by the British Ambassador to Finland, Mr Matthew Kirk. The memorial stands on a grassy slope near the fortress overlooking the water. In passing it is interesting to note that there is a Bomarsund Welfare Cricket Club located in a village of the same name in Northumberland. The club was founded in 1958.

On 29 January 2006, Jersey issued a £2 Miniature Stamp Sheet, depicting the V.C. In the margin of the sheet is a picture of H.M.S. *Hecla* and Charles Lucas. The artist was Andrew Robinson. In the same year Alderney issued a sterling silver £5 coin as the first in a series "The VC Winners Silver Coin Collection". The limited edition of 30,000 coins features a portrait of Lucas.

A set of six stamps was issued on 21 September 2006 by The Royal Mail to mark the 150th Anniversary of the Victoria Cross. The 64p stamp featured a portrait of Charles Lucas and an account of his brave deed.

A Service of Commemoration to mark the 150th Anniversary of the Institution of the Victoria Cross and the 50th Anniversary of the Victoria Cross and George Cross Association was held on Monday 26 June 2006 at Westminster Abbey. It was attended by H.R.H. the Prince of Wales and H.R.H. the Duchess of Cornwall. Michael Adams carried his great-grandfather's duplicate V.C. and medals up the aisle at the Service.

On Sunday 17 September 2006, at 11.15 a.m. a service was held at St. Lawrence's Church, Mereworth, Kent to mark the same anniversary. Again Michael Adams and his family attended and he read a lesson. More than 100 people attended including families of other V.C.s together with Sea Cadets, Army Cadets and members of the Maidstone branch of the Royal Naval Association. The service was taken by the rector of Mereworth and West Peckham, Rev. Noel McConachie, and the sermon was given by the archdeacon of Tonbridge. After the service a wreath was laid at Charles Lucas's grave by Michael Adams's sister Susan Davis, and the Last Post sounded. This was followed by two minutes silence, "They shall not grow old ..." followed by Reveille.

Apart from the grave at St. Lawrence's Church there is a plaque in the church. This is situated in the northwest (Yotes Court) chapel, which is now a vestry.

Plaque in St. Lawrence's Church

On the walls are memorials relating to successive owners of Yotes Court and their relations.

Hilare Caroline, sister of the 7th Viscount Torrington, and her husband, Vice-Admiral Sir William Hutcheon Hall, KCB, FRS are also commemorated in a tablet above that of Charles Lucas.

The wording on Charles Lucas grave is as follows:

IN LOVING MEMORY OF
CHARLES DAVIS LUCAS
REAR ADMIRAL V.C.
BORN FEBRUARY 19 1834. DIED AUGUST 7 1914
AND OF FRANCES RUSSELL HIS WIFE
BORN APRIL 23 1856. DIED JANUARY 3 1925.

On the Reverse:

> ALSO
> IN EVER LOVING MEMORY OF
> DOUGLAS CHARLES BYNG
> BYNG STAMPER
> BORN SEPTEMBER 29 1910
> DIED AUGUST 4 1927
> AGED 16 YEARS.

Another celebration was held in Portsmouth at the Royal Naval Club on 23 February 2007 and at Portsmouth Cathedral, where all Royal Naval recipients who were members of the club were duly honoured and where the Duke of Edinburgh met families and descendents. He also unveiled an official plaque to the memories of the recipients. Sir Jonathan Bland, the First Sea Lord gave a brief talk.

The memorial is in a corridor leading from the Reception area of the Royal Naval Club and Royal Albert Yacht Club, Pembroke Road, Portsmouth. It records the 19 members upon whom the Victoria Cross was conferred.

Each V.C. includes a picture and a write-up. Charles Lucas's reads as follows:

> Rear Admiral
> Charles Davis Lucas VC
> Born – Drumargole, Armagh, Ireland, 19 February 1834
> Died – Great Culverden, Kent, 7 August 1914
>
> Place and date of VC
> HMS *Hecla*, The Baltic Sea, 21 June 1854
> Rank – Mate, Royal Navy
> Aged 20 years
> The first deed of valour to be awarded with the Victoria Cross
> Commanded the Ballachulish Corps in Scotland 1873/83
> With the rank of Brigadier General
> Club Member 1868

Also in Portsmouth is a large boulder in Broad Street, Old Portsmouth – on the water side of the road by the Round Tower. The inscription on this, tells us:

> During the Russian War (1854) a landing party from HMS Hecla was attacked by a large body of Cossacks and many would have fallen had it not been for the courage of two sailors who taking cover behind this stone kept the enemy at bay until the safety of the whole party was assured. Captain Hall had this boulder carried to his ship and transported to Portsmouth.

On 5 April 2006 Dix Noonan Webb auctioned a rare and historic commission appointing Charles Lucas, RN, as acting mate on the steam sloop *Hecla,* in which vessel, one month later he won the very first V.C. It sold for £1,300.

On Thursday 26 April 2007, the Mayor of Tunbridge Wells, Councillor Ron Weedon, hosted a road naming ceremony at Barratt Kent's new homes development at Connaught Park, Sandhurst Road, High Brooms, Tunbridge Wells. Five roads were named after local V.Cs including "Lucas Close".

The Ulster History Circle unveiled a Blue Plaque to Charles Lucas at his birthplace, Druminargal House, 29 Poyntzpass Road, Scarva at 11.30 a.m. on Tuesday 26 June 2007. The event was held in conjunction with Poyntzpass Local History Society and was sponsored by Armagh City and District Council. This was 150 years to the day after he had been awarded the V.C. The Mayor pointed out that this was the first Blue Plaque in the District and commented that it was fitting that it honoured another first, the first V.C., and to an Armagh man at that. After the unveiling, Doreen Corcoran, Chairman of the Ulster History Circle, presented the Megaw family, then owners of the house, with a framed copy of the Ulster History Circle's citation on Lucas.

The Blue Plaque at Druminargal House

On 20 December 2007 Charles Lucas's V.C., India General Service Medal and Baltic War Medal were loaned to the National Museum of Ireland in Dublin. They were included in their new exhibition entitled "Soldiers and Chiefs – The Irish at War at Home and Abroad from 1550". They are still on loan at the Museum. Only his Royal Humane Society Lifesaving Medal and duplicate remain in Greenwich, though not on public display.

His name is also on the V.C. Roll of Honour at the Union Jack Club, Sandell Street, Waterloo, London SE1 8UJ.

CHAPTER TWO

Commanding the Guns at Sevastopol – The Story of Major General Matthew Charles Dixon 1821–1905

FOREWORD

I am very lucky and privileged, as a distant relative, to have become the custodian of the medals and other artefacts of Major General Matthew Charles Dixon, V.C. I have only known about his military career and exploits in the Crimean War in more recent times as the items I have were in the possession of my grandmother for many years. My father inherited them from her and likewise they have been passed on to me. I am very pleased that Richard Snow has put all the history that I already had together with all the extra research he has done. He has written this up in a way that puts it all into perspective. Matthew Charles Dixon married a Bosanquet and, strangely enough, my aunt also married a Bosanquet so my first cousins are both Bosanquets. The Clarke connection is also there in that my great-grandmother was a Clarke before marriage and the historical items came my way via this relationship. Both my father and my aunt spoke of memories of visiting "Aunty Dixon", his widow, when they were young.

Simon Griffith.
Great-great-grandson of Frances Maria Dixon, Major General Dixon's youngest sister

A MILITARY PEDIGREE

In his *Reminiscences*, General M. C. Dixon V.C. gives the early origins of the family:

> The Dixon family originally from Durham has been represented in Military or Naval services of the country for many generations. My Great Grandfather, General Matthew Dixon R.E (1725–1793) served in the Battle of Minden 1758 and was selected by the Duke of Richmond to erect fortifications around Plymouth and Devonport.
>
> His eldest son was Manley Dixon who was born in 1757. He joined the Royal Navy and was married twice. Manley Dixon rose to be Rear Admiral in 1808, then Vice Admiral from 1813 and was appointed Commander-in-Chief at Plymouth from April 1830–April 1833. He was also made a Knight Commander of the Bath. He retired to Exmouth where he died of influenza on 8th February 1837. His career was summed up as 'he has been uniformly successful in every service to which it has fallen to his lot to be employed'.

Manley Dixon had three sons by his first wife, Christiana Hall: Manley Hall Dixon, John Taylor Dixon, and Matthew Charles Dixon, the father of our V.C. hero who also carried his name.

Manley Hall Dixon was born on 8 June 1786. He entered the navy in June 1794 as First Class Volunteer on board the *Porcupine*. He served under his father until August 1801 as Midshipman, Master's Mate and acting Lieutenant in the Channel, North Sea, Irish and Mediterranean stations, witnessing the surrender of Malta. On 4 June 1807, he joined the *Horatio* and on 10 Feb 1809, as First Lieutenant of that frigate, he was badly wounded by a ball entering the left groin, passing through the thigh. For his gallantry in this action, which resulted in the capture of the frigate *Le Juno* he was promoted to commander from the date of the action, and received a gratuity from the Patriotic Fund, as well as receiving a pension of 250 shillings. He married his cousin Harriet Foot on 18 April 1815 but they had no family. He became a Vice Admiral on 7 February 1855. He resided at Stoke Damerel, Devon until his death on 3 March 1864.

Admiral Manley Dixon

Manley Hall Dixon's brother was Matthew Charles Dixon (father of our V.C. hero). He was born in 1791. He joined the Royal Engineers as a Temporary Second Lieutenant on 2 April 1806. His only war service was in North America 1812–1815. He was wounded at Sundusky on 2 August 1813 and taken prisoner at Moraviantown on 5 October 1813. He was awarded a gold medal for the capture of Fort Detroit at which he was the only engineer present and granted the brevet rank of Major on 12 December 1814. After his wife's death in Montreal he returned to England with his children and was quartered at Gravesend. He died aged 69 years on 30 January 1860 in Southampton.

His first wife was Susan Phillips, daughter of Captain Phillips, ADC to General Wolfe. Their children included William Manley Hall Dixon, who was born in Canada on 7 January 1817. He joined the British Army as a Lieutenant in 1835. He rose to be a Major General in the Royal

Seal of Manley Hall Dixon

Artillery. On 20 May 1871, he was appointed Commander of the Bath, retiring on full pay on 23 December 1871. He married his stepmother's niece – Frances Ann Haden Bertram. He died on 19 March 1888 at Hornchurch, Essex.

Matthew Charles Dixon's second wife was Emma Dalton. They were married in 1820. Matthew Dixon was frequently stationed overseas and the Dixon family used Jersey as a home base. He had issue by this marriage of three daughters and four sons.

The eldest son by marriage to Emma was Matthew Charles Dixon. After five years at Gravesend, Matthew and Emma retired to Avranches in Normandy, when he was placed on half pay. Matthew Charles, their eldest son was born here on 5 February 1821.

Matthew recalls in his *Reminiscences*:

> About 1826 he (his father) was recalled to full pay and sent on foreign service, first to Barbados where his family accompanied him. Some 3 years later he had to proceed to Wexford, Ireland to 'Duncannon Fort' where I was sent to school at Waterford, and later I was sent to a prep school at Shooters Hill and passed into the Academy (Woolwich) with tolerable credit.

The date of the notification of his appointment to the Royal Military Academy was 29 January 1835, aged 14 years. He joined the RMA on 23 February, receiving his commission into the Royal Artillery on 19 March 1839, as Second Lieutenant in the 62nd Battalion at Woolwich. "In October I was attached to a company proceeding to Ceylon".

Up until 1854, the only entry into the Royal Artillery had been to the R.M.A. where the cadets went from fourteen to fifteen and a half years of age. There they were drilled and instructed until they joined the Practical Class in the Arsenal. A cadet worked his way from the 4th or Junior

Academy to the 1st or Senior Academy by passing satisfactorily severe exams at the end of each six-month term. From the 1st Academy he had to pass a strict exam to get into the Practical Class; after a year there he passed his final exam and received a commission in the Engineers or Artillery.

On 11 April 1841, he was promoted to Lieutenant and on leaving Ceylon in June 1848, he became a second captain on 30 June that year.

> In 1848 we were ordered back to England touching at the Cape and St. Helena in our freight ship. When near the Azores we passed a big vessel outward bound which signalled 'a revolution in France'. Louis Philippe resigned and Napoleon having escaped from his priory at Ham was made President.
>
> I was shortly after ordered to Jamaica, promoted to a second captaincy, and was shortly left in military command there.

In fact, he served in Jamaica from 27 December 1848 until 16 January 1854. When he returned he was promoted captain on 17 February 1854, before proceeding to the Channel Islands.

He is however listed in the 1851 Census as being with the family at Moyle Road, St Peter Port, Channel Islands with his father Colonel M. C. Dixon, mother Emma, and Susan E. Dixon, William M. H. Dixon, Frances M. Dixon, and Matthew M. C. Dixon, grandson. He is listed as being a "2nd Captain Rifle Battery Full Pay (British subject)".

His service in Jersey was brought to a halt with a Call to Arms by Lord Raglan to serve in the Crimea.

JOINING THE GUNS IN THE CRIMEA

In 1854, the regiment consisted of seven Troops of Royal Horse Artillery and twelve battalions of Royal Artillery, each battalion being made up of eight companies. Each troop of company was commanded by a captain, who had under him a second captain and two or three lieutenants. Woolwich was their headquarters.

The last months of 1853 found Russia and Turkey at war and France and Great Britain as allies. The fleets of the two Western Powers were already in the Bosphorus, and early in the New Year war seemed inevitable. The British Government summoned an expeditionary force to Turkey, and in the middle of March troops left England and disembarked at Scutari. The expedition was assembled without due consideration of the size of the task, and without any adequate prior reconnaissance. But London and Paris had decided that Russian power in the Black Sea must be broken by crippling the great naval base at Sevastopol.

On 28 March 1854 war was declared against Russia by France and Great Britain and a combined flotilla assembled in the Black Sea on 7 September. A week later allied forces landed unopposed at Eupatoria on the Russian coast.

By 20 March, the Royal Artillery had embarked for the East. Even before they sailed from the dockyard, it was apparent that the numerical strength of the regiment was insufficient, and during the next two years continual additions were made to the establishment. In January 1854, the Royal Artillery had 13,859 men of all ranks and 1,388 horses. By mid-July two troops and 17 companies were assembled in the neighbourhood of Varna.

The British Army consisted of five Divisions and a Light Cavalry Brigade. Each Division was formed of some 5,000 infantry and 12 field guns. The Cavalry Brigade numbered 1,000 troops with six guns. Lord Raglan was Commander-in-Chief. In addition to some 300 Royal Sappers and Miners and the Siege Train, the British contingent consisted of 26,000 infantry and 1,000 cavalry and 60 field guns. The total allied force (including the French and Turks) consisted of some 60,000 infantry, 1,000 cavalry and 128 guns. On 14 September, the landing of the combined armies began near Eupatoria in the Crimea.

The Russian forces consisted of 76,000 fighting men under Prince Menshikov, but they were not all in place. So he assembled his field army on hills south of the Alma River, and reconnoitred the ground in the area.

The Allies landed on an open beach between 13 and 18 September, some 30 miles north of Sevastopol. Bad weather and the weakened condition of the troops caused delays. They advanced on 19 September and soon after noon Lord Cardigan crossed the Boulganak with his two leading regiments, where they met skirmishers. There was some minor fighting.

The Battle of the Alma on 20 September is usually considered the first battle of the Crimean War. The Allied attack crossed the river without much difficulty, but the British then found themselves faced by a steep slope, which was won only after a hard fight. The Anglo-French force under General St. Arnaud and Lord Raglan defeated the Russian army, which lost around 6,000 troops. The Allies lost about 3,000 men. However the Allies failed to gain a decisive victory by pursuing the Russians, which enabled them to regroup, recover and prepare their defences.

The Allies were now in sight of Sevastopol, where the harbour had been blockaded by sunken ships, which made any naval assistance impossible from the north. However the Allies needed a base, and marched around the south side of the fortress to establish bases at Kamiesch and Balaclava. They thus regained contact with the fleet: the British based at Balaclava and the French at Kamiesch.

On 28 September, the disembarkation of the Siege Train began. The British Siege Train, consisting of 65 pieces, with 520 rounds apiece, was successfully landed at Balaclava in five days under Lieutenant Colonel Gambier in command. The Siege artillery was to bear the brunt of the campaign. The Command of the Right Attack was in the hands of Major Collingwood Dickson (later General Sir. C. Dickson, G.C.B., V.C., Colonel Commandant).

The southern defences of Sevastopol had not yet been completed, which meant an immediate assault might have been successful. But the Allies were still grouping and preparing for a prolonged siege, and so by 17 October, when the first bombardment opened, the Russians had completed their fortifications. The bombardment and counter-battery fire resulted in serious losses on both sides but no permanent damage to the works. The fleet was commanded by Admiral Sir Edmund Lyons.

The British were allocated to the defence of the right flank of the Allied siege operation, for which Raglan had insufficient men. Taking advantage of this the Russian General Liprandi with some 25,000 men, prepared to attack the defences around Balaclava, hoping to disrupt the supply line between the British base and their siege lines.

Hence on 25 October, the Battle of Balaclava commenced with a Russian artillery and infantry attack on the Ottoman Turkish redoubts that formed Balaclava's first line of defence. The Turks initially held firm but were eventually forced to retreat. The Russian cavalry then engaged the second defensive line held by the Turks and the Scottish 93rd Highland Regiment in what became known as "The Thin Red Line". This line held and repulsed the attack, as did General Scarlett's British Heavy Brigade who charged and defeated the greater proportion of the cavalry advance, forcing the Russians onto the defensive. However a final Allied cavalry charge, following a misinterpreted order from Lord Raglan, led to arguably the most famous and ill-fated event in British military history – the Charge of the Light Brigade. This resulted in 247 men and 497 horses being lost, out of 673 mounted officers and men. The Russians retained possession of the Vorontosov ridge, commanding the Balaclava-Sevastopol road. The Allies had retained Balaclava, but the Russians saw the battle as a victory.

Using intelligence gained by a reconnaissance by the Russians, they launched a main attack on the same position one week later on 5 November to start the Battle of Inkerman. They tried once again to forge a gap between the besieging troops and their field support. The brunt of the action fell on the British in an all-day struggle. The arrival of Bosquet's French Division finally tipped the balance, and Menshikov withdrew.

After Inkerman the Russians realised that Sevastopol would not be taken by a battle in the field, so moved their troops into the city to support the defenders. Around the edge of the city along its fortifications stood a number of redoubts that were to be fought over during the siege: the Malakoff, the Redan, Flagstaff Bastion, the Little Redan and others. A heavy storm on 14 November wrecked some 30 transports lying at Balaclava, and destroyed most of the existing rations, forage and clothing. The British troops were starving, without adequate clothing or shelter, and cholera raged. Many men died and this led to the establishment of proper medical and hospital facilities under the inspiration of Florence Nightingale.

During the winter of 1855 a new road and railroad over the mud plain was built to link the Balaclava base to the siege corps. This enabled delivery of more than 500 guns and plentiful ammunition.

On 17 February 1855, the Battle of Eupatoria was fought. The Russian field army planned to take the Turkish garrison by surprise. But this failed to happen as both the Turkish garrison and the Allied fleet anticipated the attack. The Russian artillery and infantry attacks were countered with heavy fire. Having lost 750 men, the Russians retreated. The garrison pursued them, and the retreat was turned into a rout. Menshikov was now replaced by Prince Michael Gorchakov.

The Russians now sought to strengthen their defences, with 6,000-10,000 men working continuously day and night.

Captain Matthew Dixon recalls:

> In Jan. 1854 I got my orders to proceed to the front in command of one of the two batteries of artillery ordered out. At Gibraltar I disobeyed the order of the Governor over a matter of quarantine, some of our men having developed smallpox. I had requested him to let me land them there. He refused and we were told to consider ourselves in quarantine for a fortnight. As I knew our presence in the camp at the front was much desired I took upon myself the responsibility of ordering the Captain of Transport to sail immediately to carry us to our destination with all possible speed. I had had to use my judgement as C.O. and felt I could do nothing other than to hasten to join my corps.
>
> At Constantinople I handed over my sick to the medical at Scutari then under the management of Miss Florence Nightingale.
>
> Our ship across the Sea of Marmara and the Black Sea struck violent gales and I was glad when we arrived in the little harbour of Balaclava which we found so blocked with Men of War transports etc., that it was with greatest difficulty that we were able to make our way in.
>
> After landing we had a four mile march through deep mud to our camp which was on the right of the Malekoff Tower. We found it strewn with skulls, human bones and other disagreeable things. Our work in the trenches was very arduous owing to constant bombardments. We had to turn out every six hours for duty.

Thus it was that reinforcements to the Siege Train arrived. One of these, in March 1855, led to the arrival of Captain Dixon, who was placed in command of four officers and 131 men posted to No 5. Company, 9th Battalion with the Right Attack. His fellow officers were Second Captain H. Heyman, Lieutenant C. E. Burt and Lieutenant B. G. Humfrey. The previous month Lieutenant Colonel E. Warde had taken over command of the Siege Train, and he made very strong representations regarding its weakness and the necessity for more companies.

From 11 March until 22 March, a daily average of 100 rounds was fired from the Right Attack against the Russian works on the Mamelon Hill. On the night of the 21st, two 9-pounder guns, placed in the advanced right approach drove out the Russian riflemen from the Mamelon Trench.

On the night of the 22nd, 5,500 Russians swept back the French. The Russians then advanced in four distinct bodies on the British. They succeeded in penetrating the Right Attack. The British lost about 80, including 3 officers and 16 men killed and the Russians about 1,300. On the 24th, a burial truce was agreed upon.

All was now ready for the 2nd Bombardment, which it was intended should be followed by an assault. The French now had some 70,000 men. The British, though men were rapidly coming off the sick list, did not number more than 20,500 – excluding those landed from the fleet.

By early April, the effective strength of the Siege Train was some 1,800 all ranks and the number present when the 2nd Bombardment began was 1,200. Since the afternoon of the 8th April, work had been carried out in two reliefs, and both officers and men were becoming exhausted. They were continually wet, their feet were so swollen by constant standing in, and walking to and from the batteries, that many of the men were afraid to take their boots off in case they should not be able to get them on again. Many were fitter for the hospital than for duty, yet comparatively few fell out and shorthanded as they were, they carried on with a patient heroism. The remaining pieces were now almost ready to join the action, but men could not be found to work them. The much-needed reinforcements for the Siege Train had not yet arrived, and Lord Raglan asked for help from the Royal Navy.

The plan was to open fire on 9th April, and to maintain this for 24 hours, after which the Council of War would reconvene to decide on the best method of attack. As a rule, the Right Attack continued to fire some 100 rounds a day against the Mamelon and rifle-pits, and the Left remained silent. But on 5 April, a combined fire of 18-inch mortars was opened from both Attacks against the Redan, the Malakoff and the Mamelon, which were actively holding up the French advance. Some 300 rounds were fired, silencing the Russians.

The garrison of Sevastopol in April consisted of 34,000 infantry and 9,000 artillery and seamen gunners. Although the Russian guns were more numerous, they were on the whole lighter than those of the Allies, who had more than double the number of mortars. The siege batteries were on the whole on commanding ground, and encircled the Russian works.

8 April fell on Easter Sunday and the inhabitants of Sevastopol observed the sacred festival without much disturbance. However, the morning of the 9th opened to the roar of 400 guns. Shortly after 5.30 a.m. when the outlines of the Redan and the Malakoff were in view, the British opened fire, speedily followed by a hundred others in the Left and Right Attacks. The French had joined in with 300 guns. Captain Dixon's 9th Battery consisted of eight 8-inch guns in the Right Attack.

The Russians, taken by complete surprise, did not respond until 6.00. By evening it was clear that a breach had been made in the wall north of the Central Bastion. This work and its adjacent defences were silenced. During the night the Russians worked hard to rebuild their defences.

On the morning of the 10th the Allies re-opened fire and the Russians duly responded. Much damage was done to the Russians, but the French did not press their advantage and seemed reluctant to carry out a full assault.

On the 14th, the Right Attack brought forward all its pieces, except three mortars, and for the first time during the bombardment No. 9 Battery was manned. It was within 450 yards from some Russian rifle-pits, and in order to screen the gunners, Colonel Collingwood Dickson devised a makeshift mantle of bullock-hides stuffed with hay. They were soon not needed, for by using short fuses, so that their 8-inch common shell burst over the Russian pits, the British gunners swiftly drove the enemy from their defences.

On 17 April, the magazine of No. 9 Battery blew up when a shell fell on it, killing and wounding 10 men, disabling five guns. A large crater appeared, the parapet was partially knocked down, and all the guns but one were buried in debris. The Russians manned the parapets and cheered, and opened a concentrated fire on No. 9 Battery. However, its remaining gun was at once turned on the enemy. The officers in the battery at the time were Captain M. C. Dixon and Lieutenant C. H. Owen. They continued firing until sunset (some seven hours), despite the heavy concentration of fire from the Russian batteries. The battery was so entirely commanded at first by the Russian riflemen, and such a hail of bullets was poured into it, that it was nicknamed the "lead mine". This was also the only English battery which blew up throughout the whole course of the siege.

Charles H. Owen sent his own account of what happened to the Editor of *Navy and Army* in March 1915, when he was a Major General. This was in response to their account of the explosion given in the magazine on 24 October 1914. There are a number of anomalies in the account including the date of the action, Captain Dixon's rank, and the number of casualties and guns. As it was written over 60 years later, it is prone to exaggeration.

> The Battery was in the Right Attack and was armed with 8in shell guns. It was constructed to fire on the batteries below the Malakoff Tower, about 1,000 yards distant. Lt-Col. Dixon and I took a relief in it for some two months or more. As we were short of men, the battery was made by the French, and one of the magazines was placed directly in rear of the battery, a very faulty position, as it was in the line of fire. Not on the day mentioned in the account given, but on April 16th, 1855, a large mortar shell fell on top of the magazine behind the battery. I shouted to the gunners to get under the travelling gun carriages, which afforded some protection from the falling masses of earth, the magazine being behind my four guns on the right of the battery. Lt.-Col Dixon wisely withdrew his men outside the left flank of the battery. When the shell burst it exploded the magazine, the terre plein of the battery was forced up, seven guns, not five, as in the account, were rendered unserviceable by masses of earth thrown up, and some of the gunners were jammed against the parapet, and others buried below. Eleven men were killed or wounded, and of the magazine man only his toes were found. Lt.-Colonel M. Dixon decided to go on firing with the gun on the left of the Battery, the only one in a serviceable state. The Russians poured a very heavy fire on us, but failed to silence this gun. Your account says that the gun was turned on the advancing masses, which were kept at a distance. No Russian troops advanced on the Battery, which was separated by 1,000 yards of open ground from their works.

Captain Dixon's own account again has discrepancies on the number of casualties:

> The first bombardment I was engaged in was a very exciting affair and we hoped to capture the Malakoff Redoubt and other works on the southern side which defended Sevastopol. I was first in a battery of eight guns of 8-in calibre. We fired so many shells that our guns became very heated. I feared they would burst.
>
> I was very fortunate on several occasions with my field magazines placed in the rear of the batteries and which exploded more than once causing great loss to our men. I had a very narrow escape myself once when a shell burst just behind me grazing my tunic and cutting my face. Seven of my guns were so bespattered with mud that I could not use them again but as soon as I was able to rally my gun detachments I reopened fire with the one remaining gun. Before the enemy had ceased cheering our men lost about 16 killed and wounded. The remainder were so dazed and bewildered I had to run after them, and drag them back by main force to their places. Once back they were as cool and efficient as before. Colonel Dickson was very kind and seemed satisfied I had done my duty.

The second bombardment of Sevastopol ended without any decisive result, after eight days incessant firing with some of the heaviest guns and mortars ever used at a siege. The British lost 265 men killed and wounded, the French 1,685 and the Russians 6,130. Allied field commanders and home governments then argued via telegraph about the conduct of the operations. The French General Canrobert, angered by the interference, resigned his command to be replaced by General Pelissier. It was then decided to bring extra guns to the trenches, before considering a general assault.

By now, the strength of the Russians was on the wane. During the past month, the garrison had lost over 10,000 men. The total Russian force could not have exceeded 100,000 men, while the Allies numbered 188,000. Pelissier now determined to press the siege.

On 24 May, a joint French and British expedition cleared the Sea of Azov at the port of Kerch thus disabling Russian communications with the interior. During the whole of May, except for some weak mortar fire, the allied batteries were virtually silent. All efforts were put into replacing damaged items, and bringing up new ordnance.

Under a bright sky the third bombardment of Sevastopol began at 2.30 p.m. on 6 June. For three hours opposing artilleries shared the spoils, until the Russian left flank began to show signs of exhaustion. The Russian defences were badly hit that day. The bombardment continued the next day. By 8 a.m. all Russian guns to the east of the Middle Ravine appeared to have been disabled; but the Redan repeated its obstinate resistance of the previous day. About 10 o'clock, one of the shells from the Redan resulted in the explosion of a second magazine in No. 9 Battery, Right Attack. Though on this occasion no damage was done, once again the Russians manned their parapets and cheered. The two officers present on this occasion were again Captain Dixon and Lieutenant Owen.

By midday, all was ready for an assault, with the French attacking the White Works and the Mamelon, following which the British would advance against the Quarries. The guns were to fire at the Malakoff and the Mamelon. Three 8-inch Guns in No. 9 Battery, which commanded the communications between the two works, were specifically ordered to prepare for shrapnel fire against the Russian infantry. The Mamelon was captured by the French, followed by three 8-inch guns in No. 9 Battery firing shrapnel on the retreating Russians. The victory proved costly with the Allies suffering 5,443 casualties.

Two columns now advanced against either flank of the main Russian contingent at the Quarries, which began the start of a ten-hour encounter. After valiant resistance, the Russians fell back on the Redan.

On 10 June, a Council of War proposed that a bombardment lasting 48 hours should precede a general attack on the fortress by a number of columns. The French were to assault the Town Front, which would operate against the Quarantine, Central and Flagstaff Bastions; the British were to assault the Redan, and the French the Malakoff.

On 16 June, the Russians had 1,129 pieces mounted on the south side of Sevastopol. The infantry garrison now amounted to 48,000 bayonets, and a further 21,000 men in the vicinity. In the fortress itself were 10,697 artillerymen and seamen gunners. At daylight on the 17th the batteries opened fire for the fourth time upon Sevastopol. The British efforts were mainly directed on the Redan, the heavy mortars of the Right Attack providing assistance to the French by directing their shells on the Malakoff.

Pelissier then decided to attack at daybreak the following day. This was a mistake as it meant attacking the strongest positions on Sevastopol before they had been weakened by artillery fire. It also left no time for the siege guns to prepare the ground for the assault.

On 18 June, the French penetrated the Gervais Battery, which was the signal for the British to attack the Redan. They were immediately assailed by a heavy fire of grape and musketry. After vainly trying to advance, the columns were directed to withdraw into the trenches. However, by then almost all of the senior officers had been killed or wounded. The attack had again failed. Lack of co-ordination resulted in complete failure. The British lost 1,505, the French 3,551 and the Russians 5,446.

On 26 June, Lord Raglan became unwell, and died on 28th. He had aged greatly, and seemed much affected by the venom of the English Press. He was succeeded by General Sir James Simpson.

The siege batteries continued to fire fitfully until the end of June. During July and August Russian losses were draining Sevastopol's strength – some 350 a day during July. They decided to make one final effort to break through the allied line between Balaklava and the fortress. On 17 July Captain Dixon was promoted to Brevet Major.

On 16 August, the Battle of the Traktir Ridge took place between the French and Russians. A five-hour combat ended in Russian defeat, which had been the last hope for relieving Sevastopol. The British played little or no part in this battle.

The fifth bombardment began with heavy firing for two days. The period 17–21 August is assigned as the period of the bombardment, but fire was kept up with more or less intensity until 5 September. At 5 a.m. on 17 August a salvo of three shells fired into the Redan from No. 13 Battery Right Attack, gave the preconceived signal for opening fire, and all the British guns came into action. On the right the allied guns contributed their share to the siege against the Malakoff, and from both Attacks mortar fire lasted through the night. The bombardment continued the next day.

By 3 September, it was decided that the time for a general assault was now imminent. They recommended a three-day bombardment prior to an assault to start on 5 September. At 5 a.m on that day the Allies opened fire against both Town and Faubourg Fronts, and very soon the Malakoff was rendered defenceless. During the next two days a similar bombardment continued, and again the night sky was lit up by burning shipping and bursting mortar shells. By noon on the 8th the fire of the French on the Malakoff front suddenly ceased: the time for the assault had arrived. Thirteen allied divisions and one allied brigade (total strength 60,000) began the last assault.

By midnight, the Malakoff was safely in French hands. A simultaneous British assault on the Redan was repulsed, but from the Malakoff the French now turned their fire on the Russians in the Redan and succeeded in driving them out with heavy loss. The Russians decided to cease further resistance, and after setting fire to the fortifications they evacuated Sevastopol, allowing the allies to enter and occupy the fortress the next day, 9 September, after a 322-day siege. In all the allies lost more than 10,000 casualties in this final assault, the Russians 13,000.

After the fall of Sevastopol, a combined force of the Allies remained in the city, the British contingent consisting of the 3rd Buffs and 500 men from the Siege Train. The Allies began the destruction of the seaward ports and the docks of Sevastopol.

Matthew Dixon's report continued:

> I had a capital view on Sept. 8th of the attack by the French against the Malakoff and the Redan which was mined. At 4 p.m. next day the French were in possession of the Malakoff which being higher ground than the Redan was important. We were to attack the Redan with Sir Colin Campbell's Highlanders next day but this was frustrated by the retreat of the Russians during the night. We were however able to afford the French material help in their attack on the Malakoff of which their officers were well aware. In the darkness, the Russians, having cast their field pieces into the sea and left their sick and wounded behind, were able to effect during the night following our assault they moved to the harbour and by daybreak all their forces were on the other side. They burned the rest of their Black Sea Fleet.
>
> The visit we paid to Sevastopol next morning was interesting and exciting. Public buildings and churches mostly destroyed totally, and all kinds of things strewn about – some fine bells were taken, but we drew lots with the French and lost them.
>
> In Jan 1856 the siege train returned home under my command and landed at Gravesend where Queen Victoria came down on purpose to review us, as we were without our proper uniforms, hair and beards untrimmed.

On 2 November 1855, Brevet Major Dixon was promoted to Brevet Lieutenant Colonel. At the end of the campaign the Siege Train consisted of 29 companies, 11 of which were sent to garrison the forts at Balaclava, while a large number of gunner-drivers were transferred to the field batteries to make good casualties or replace weak and sick men.

By the middle of February 1856, the demolitions in Sevastopol were completed by the engineers, and at the end of the month an armistice was signed, and on 30 March peace was declared, by the signing of the Treaty of Paris. This declared the Black Sea neutral territory, closing it to all warships and prohibiting fortifications and the presence of armaments on its shores. It marked a severe setback to Russian influence in the region.

When the first contingent of the Siege Train arrived in Woolwich in March 1856, they had a good reception. The veteran commandant, Sir E. C. Whinyates bared his head in their honour as they passed him, and the sovereign herself came to Woolwich to review them and inspect the various trophies they brought home. Queen Victoria was again present at Woolwich on 14 July to review the troops and field batteries drawn up on the Common for her inspection: on this occasion her Majesty was mounted on her favourite chestnut horse and wore a scarlet habit trimmed with gold lace, the sash and plumes of a General Officer, and the ribbon of the Garter.

DECORATED IN PORTSMOUTH, MARRIED IN ENFIELD

In June 1856, the Muster Roll tells us that "3rd Lt. Col. M. C. Dixon was in command of No. 5 Company" after he was ordered to the Channel Islands.

His Victoria Cross was announced in the *London Gazette* No. 21971, on 24 February 1857, p. 655:

> Royal Artillery Brevet Lieut.-Colonel Matthew Charles Dixon
> On the 17th April, 1855, about 2 p.m., when the battery he commanded was blown up by a shell from the enemy, which burst in the Magazine, destroyed the parapets, killed and wounded ten men, disabled five guns, and covered a sixth with earth; for most gallantly re-opening fire with the remaining gun before the enemy had ceased cheering from their parapets (on which they had mounted) and fighting it until sunset, despite the concentrated fire of the enemy's batteries, and the ruined state of his own.

He was not decorated at the very first investiture in Hyde Park on 26 June 1857. It is possible that, as he was serving in the Channel Islands, the place was thought to be so remote that he was not considered able to attend.

He was actually decorated with the V.C. by H.M. Queen Victoria on Southsea Common, Portsmouth on 2 August 1858. Also decorated with the V.C. were twelve men, ten of whom were awarded the Cross for bravery in the Crimean War. The other two won the award for bravery in India.

The Times of 3 August 1858, reported:

> Yesterday evening another of those impressive ceremonies which have done so much to foster a military pride and spirit among the people took place at Portsmouth, and Her Majesty for the third time since the institution of this great order of valour conferred the Victoria Cross upon her soldiers. The weather, of course, was fine, the arrangements were excellent, and the whole affair passed off with an enthusiasm and completeness that did the authorities at Portsmouth the highest credit, and from which those entrusted with the management of such fetes in London might well derive a lesson.
>
> A marquee was pitched just under the esplanade on the Common for the accommodation of Her Majesty, and before this was a raised dais covered with scarlet cloth, on which the Royal party stood during the distribution. In advance of this again was the place reserved for the gallant recipients of the cross, and in rear of these, so as to stretch in one line of contiguous columns and form an immense semicircle, were the troops of the garrison. Behind the Royal pavilion, on the extensive slope forming the esplanade, stood the general public, and on each side of the Royal dais was a small square enclosure, each capable of containing 600 people, and to whom admission was only to be gained by tickets.
>
> Our readers to fill in the picture for themselves must imagine a faultless day of Queen's weather – the long bank along the esplanade side of the common decorated with flags and banners of all nations – a bright, cool, crisp-looking sea, with a noble fleet dressed in colours in the middle distance, and the picturesque shore of the Isle of Wight for a background.

When our readers have imagined this, with crowds of yachts, pleasure boats, and thousands of holiday people, they will have a fair idea of what a scene Southsea Common presented yesterday evening.

The line of recipients was a very thin one, for there were only 12 men in all, nine commissioned, two non-commissioned officers, and one private soldier.

It was getting full on half-past 4; the people were anxious, and the Queen's reputation for punctuality seemed in danger, when the guns, commencing again for the last time from the saluting battery, showed that her Majesty was really near at hand. The Royal party had landed at the Queen's stairs, and thence proceeded through the town.

Her Majesty, with the Royal children, was seated in an open carriage. On her right rode Prince Albert; on her left the Duke of Cambridge, both in full uniform. Behind came her staff.

General Yorke Scarlett sat in front of the line of troops, and as the Royal cortege came upon the ground the whole force, with a simultaneous movement, gave the Royal salute, presenting arms and lowering colours, with most impressive effect.

The Royal party immediately proceeded down the line minutely inspecting the trim of the men, and then returned at once to the dais. As they did so the staff were joined by some of the Lords of the Admiralty.

Her Majesty stood upon the dais with the Prince Consort and the Duke of Cambridge on her right, and immediately proceeded to confer the Crosses. Each recipient advanced in order, (with Lt. Col. Dixon being second to receive his), saluted Her Majesty, and then stood while the Queen with her own hands affixed the Cross to their breasts.

The decoration over, the Victoria Cross heroes formed in a line on the left of Her Majesty, while all the troops on the common marched past. The troops then resumed their original stations, and advancing at slow time again gave a grand Royal salute, and this concluded the ceremony of the day.

The Royal party then left the ground, and, accompanied by the same manifestations of loyalty, returned through Portsmouth and embarked for Osborne, the fleet manning yards and saluting as before.

The Queen had arrived in Southsea from Osborne on the royal steam yacht *Fairy*. Her Majesty's being at Osborne no doubt explains why the ceremony was held at Southsea.

Further acts of bravery in the Crimea brought Lieutenant Colonel Dixon the Campaign Medal (1854–56) with clasp Sebastopol, and he was made a Knight of the Legion of Honour. The latter was announced in the *London Gazette* Issue 21996, on 1 May 1857. He also received the 5th Class of the Medjidie, and the Turkish Crimea Medal 1854–55. The translation of the Diploma attached to the Decoration of the Medjidie says:

> The glory and the splendour of my Imperial Throne requiring that those who afford proof of zeal, devotion and fidelity in the cause of my empire, and who give pledge of their constant attachment to its interests, should be the object of my Imperial munificence, and Lieutenant-Colonel M.C. Dixon having by the efforts that he has displayed for the welfare of my state, acquired a right to my consideration. I thereby confer upon him the decoration of my Imperial Order of the Medjidie of the 5th Class, and consequently, the present Imperial diploma is committed to him. Written on the sixth day of the Rebialevvel lunar month of the year of the Hegira. Twelve Hundred and Seventy Six.

The Order of the Medjidie was instituted in 1852 and was awarded in five Classes, with the First being the highest. It was issued in considerable numbers by Sultan Abdul Mejid as a reward for distinguished service to members of the British forces who came to the aid of the Turkish Empire and who fought in the Crimean War. In Britain, it was worn after any British gallantry and campaign medals awarded, but before the Turkish Crimean War Medal.

Interestingly a set of three full-size replica medals (The Victoria Cross, Crimea Medal with Clasp and Turkish Crimea Medal) held by him came up on Ebay in June 2009. They were offered for £24.95.

In January 1859, Lieutenant Colonel Dixon served with 5th Company, 9th Battalion until in April they were designated to become 2nd Battery, 3rd Brigade. They were stationed at Devonport, Plymouth. In April 1860, Captain Inglefield (No. 1 Battery) and Lieutenant Colonel Dixon (No. 2 Battery) of the 3rd Brigade, who were then stationed at Plymouth Citadel, were given orders to proceed to the Channel Islands to relieve two batteries ordered to Portsmouth, where they were to do duty for two batteries of the 3rd Brigade who were to join the headquarters in the Citadel.

On Monday 27 August 1860, H.M.S. *Emerald* sailed from Spithead for Alderney with two batteries of Royal Artillery on board, under the command of Colonel Dixon and arrived at Alderney the same evening, taking up moorings beside the breakwater at 7.00 p.m. The following morning two batteries of the 15th Brigade under Major Lennox left for Spithead.

It appears that Lieutenant Colonel Dixon was backwards and forwards from Alderney at this time. He went from Gosport to Alderney in September, and again in January 1861; it was reported that the 15th Brigade of Royal Artillery, under the command of Colonel Franklyn, C.B., were under orders to move from Gosport; six batteries under Colonel F. Mullin proceeding to Pembroke, two batteries under Lieutenant Colonel Dixon to Alderney and two to Kinsale.

In his *Reminiscences* he continues:

> In 1862 I was ordered again to Woolwich and became intimate with the family of Admiral
> Charles Bosanquet of Wildwood, a very pretty place on the borders of Middlesex and Herts.
> On the 13th May 1862 I was married at Enfield parish church to his eldest daughter.

She was Henrietta Letitia Eliza Bosanquet, who was born in London in 1834, and therefore 13 years younger than him. The wedding was performed by the Rev. Claude Bosanquet, who himself married Henrietta's younger sister Amelia.

> We went to Maidenhead and then to Lynton and other places in Devon for our tour.
> I was then ordered to Shoeburyness and we took a house in Southend.

On 28 June 1862, Lieutenant Colonel Dixon was appointed Brevet Colonel, and then "after two months we were ordered to Jamaica and had a house on a coral rock about 100 yards from shore at Port Royal". They were there from 31 October 1862 until 26 July 1866.

> After two and a half years there we went to New York and Canada on leave, at the
> time of Abraham Lincoln's assassination. We spent the summer at Wildwood. I was
> sent out to Jamaica again in the autumn and thence to Chester.

They were in Gibraltar for a year from 15 January 1867 until 19 January 1868.

> The Governor there being Sir Richard Airey who had been Lord Raglan's A.G. in the
> Crimea, the whole period he was in command. Previous to our departure from there we
> made an interesting excursion to Tangiers and Algeciras. We finally returned to England
> through Spain, Malaga, Cordova, Granada, Seville, Madrid and the Pyrenees and also Paris.
>   Returning to England we went to Portland Place where my father in law was then living
> and soon after I expected full pay retirement after 30 years' service. After travelling in

Switzerland and a time in Bonchurch and the Isle of Wight we purchased a little property near Tunbridge Wells at Pembury recommended to me by a brother officer Major Lempriere.

On 28 August 1868, he was appointed Regimental Colonel, and on 19 March 1869, he retired from the army aged 48 on full pay with the honorary rank of Major General R.A. This was announced in the *London Gazette* Issue 23484, dated 2 April 1869.

Major General Dixon *Matthew and Henrietta*

THIRTY-SIX YEARS IN PEMBURY

Woodsgate House, Pembury, near Tunbridge Wells, Kent was an Inn in 1785 on the road from London to Rye and Hastings. At one time it was the halfway posting and coaching inn from London to Hastings. General and Mrs Dixon lived there with their nephews and nieces the Bosanquets, and they all took a very active part in village life. In addition, General Dixon was a member of the Kent Archaeological Society.

Woodsgate House (on right)

His gardener at Woodsgate for many years was Charles Gower (1860–1935). He described the Dixons as ideal employers. They were sincere and devout Christians, caring for the welfare of those who worked for them. On Sundays, Mrs Dixon ran a bible class for the local lads – some of them of a very young age. She seems to have been a kindly lady.

Charles Gower's grandson, His Honour John Gower Q.C., remembers his father telling a tale of his brother, Charlie, then only about eight, insisting upon recounting to the class how "Father killed a girt old rat in the stable yard yes'd,y". Mrs Dixon listened patiently before gently reminding Charlie that it was Sunday, and that they should be thinking of "higher things". On another occasion she read to her class from the book of Ruth. When she read the account of Ruth at Naomi's suggestion going in to Boaz to spend the night with him on the threshing floor, an oafish youth interjected "Dirty old Boaz". Mrs Dixon unruffled as ever rebuked him gently: "Be reverent, dear boy; be reverent!"

Charles Gower worked hard and loyally for the Dixons, building up a relationship of mutual respect. He passed on to his son the maxim "Boy, make yourself indispensible to your governor". The General became frail and doddery. Each day Charles would walk with him around his small domain. The old man would ask: "Chickens laying well Gower?". "Cow milking well Gower?". "Pigs well Gower?" To each question Charles would answer resoundingly, "Yes, General" regardless of what the situation really was. It was important not to worry the General.

Charles and his family occupied accommodation over the stable at Woodsgate. After his first wife died, he remarried and the space became very cramped. He foresaw that the likely increase in the number of children following his new marriage could lead to impossible overcrowding. He also thought that his first wife had succumbed to an infection caused by noxious exhalations from the stable. He gave in his notice, explaining his reasons for leaving and expressing regret. Mrs Dixon would not hear of it. She promised him a new cottage, built to order within the grounds of Woodsgate.

"Cherry" Chantler was the Dixons' coachman, and he was deeply religious. On one occasion Mrs Dixon emerged from her milliner's in Tunbridge Wells to find her carriage with "Cherry" on the box surrounded by a group of jeering cabbies. She soon dispersed them. On her enquiring what it was all about, "Cherry" explained that he had been "doin' the Lord's work". One of the cabbies had drawn

him out on the subject of his Christian faith, ending by enquiring whether he would describe himself as a "Man o' God". After momentary reflection, "Cherry" assented to this description of himself. The cabbie then shouted to his mates, "Come on chaps. Now's yer chance to meet a man o' God". They accepted the invitation joyfully to the accompaniment of vociferous blasphemy. Mrs Dixon's reaction to the explanation was to say to "Cherry": "To do the Lord's work is always praiseworthy, but there is a time and place for everything, Chantler. Don't do it again when with my carriage in the public street".

After Mrs Dixon's horse died, Cherry then pushed her about the village and to church on Sundays in a bathchair, still wearing his coachman's coat and top hat, complete with cockade and big gloves.

The 1881 Census shows Matthew and Henrietta Dixon living with Ellen Jasper, 31, Parlour maid and Jane Judd, 22, Housemaid. John Parkes, 32, was the Gardener, and his wife Emma, 35, was the Cook. Their daughter Annie, 13, was listed as a Scholar.

Matthew and Henrietta in their Conservatory in 1904

By 1901, Amelia Bosanquet, sister-in-law, age 65, and Charles Bosanquet, 35, nephew, had joined the Dixons. At Number 2, Charles Gower was the Gardener, with his wife Emily, and sons Henry (houseboy), Albert, Charles, Cecil and James.

Major General Dixon died on Saturday 7 January 1905 (his grave says 8 January), aged 84, at his home. His death was certified by Dr. Cyril H. Crawford MRCS and the cause of death was listed as "senile decay, valvular heart disease and influenza". The informant was his nephew Charles R. Bosanquet of Woodsgate.

As a mark of respect to the many friends he had made in the village, the first part of the funeral service on Thursday 12 January was held in Pembury Church at 10.30 a.m. Afterwards the remains were conveyed to Kensal Green, London for burial in the family grave at 2.00 p.m. His grave is Square 103/2 Plot 22977 in Kensal Green cemetery.

The Dixon Family Grave

His obituary in the *Kent and Sussex Courier* stated:

Profound regret is felt in Pembury at the passing away of the gallant soldier, who had been an esteemed resident of the village for upwards of 30 years. The village will miss a valued and honoured resident, whose sympathies were ever practical, although of late years increasing infirmity had impaired his once splendid mental and physical powers.

The officiating clergy at the funeral were the Rev. A. C. D. Clarke (nephew), the Rev. H. S. Brooke (Vicar of Pembury), the Rev. Claude Bosanquet and the Rev. Reginald Bosanquet (nephews). Mourners included Mrs Dixon (widow), Captain Dixon (nephew) and Mrs Dixon, Miss Dixon (niece), Mrs Bosanquet (sister-in-law), Mr C. R. Bosanquet, Mr E. F. Bosanquet (nephews), Mr G. Jacob (nephew), Miss Jacob (great niece), Lieutenant Bosanquet R.N., and the servants at Woodsgate.

Mrs Dixon was still at Woodsgate in 1919 but in 1922 she was living at 8 Calverley Terrace in Tunbridge Wells with Charles Richard Bosanquet (born 21.4.1865), who was Chairman of Pembury Parish Council from 1917–1922. He died on 14 January 1944 and is buried in the burial ground behind Pembury School, along with his brother Rev. Reginald Albert Bosanquet M.A. (born 14 June 1867) who died on 11 November 1940. Woodsgate was occupied by John Cowper Knocker. Mrs Dixon remained in Calverley Terrace until her death aged 93 on 3 September 1926. She was buried with her husband and family at Kensal Green.

Henrietta in 1923 aged 90

WOODSGATE DEMOLISHED AND MEMORIALS

After being a private house and cottages, Woodsgate became a country club and restaurant in the 1940s and 1950s before being demolished in March 1960. This was to make way for Woodsgate Way housing estate, and 5,000 square feet of garage, an extension to the Woodsgate Garage.

An article in the *Kent and Sussex Courier* for 8 April 1960 recalls:

Mr O. L. Young, a 78-year old retired schoolmaster, who had just returned to Tunbridge Wells remembered 'one fine afternoon, 70 years ago', when he was one of a party of children, playing with the grandchildren of the then owner of Woodsgate, General Dixon.

'About 1890, when General Dixon lived there, I was at a children's party', said Mr Young. 'We were playing hide-and-seek and chasing a fat boy down one of the upstairs passages. He took a flying leap down a couple of stairs – and promptly went through the floor. We had discovered a highwayman's hiding hole, long boarded over and forgotten. It was very small, but we were assured that Dick Turpin had once taken refuge there. It seems more probable that it had been a smuggler's cache.'

Woodsgate Guest House

Woodsgate Lounge 1930–1940

Mr Young recalls a village legend that General Dixon was one of the first VC's. Village fetes were held at Woodsgate and an archery club practised in the grounds.

'Opposite the front door – the road there was only half as wide as it is now – there used to be a pond,' said Mr Young. 'In wet weather this pond overflowed, and water used to stream through the house.

'When I knew General Dixon, he was a little senile. He always stopped the old one-horse buses to see if his wife was on – even she had left for Tunbridge Wells only 10 minutes before. He was a loveable old man.'

Postscript: The village legend about General Dixon's V.C. was wrong – as wrong, probably, as the legend of the Woodsgate ghost. In fact he never won the award.

(The legend of the ghost was that there was a skeleton in the cellars, which belonged to a smuggler, who died trying to escape the Bow Street Runners. His ghost was said to have roamed the house, rattling doors and drinking a daily pint of beer.)

The following week a letter appeared in the Courier from Miss Ivy P. F. Bosanquet and Mrs Nancy V. F. Richardson of 5 Rusthall Road, Tunbridge Wells:

> In last week's issue under the heading 'Where Smugglers Hid at Old Hotel', it is stated that 'the village legend about General Dixon's V.C. was wrong ... in fact he never won the award.'
>
> We are great-nieces of General Dixon and spent most of our childhood at Woodsgate, and we should like to correct this statement.
>
> General Dixon won the V.C. in the Crimean War, his being one of those in the second list of awards. His medals, including the V.C., are in the possession of his great-great-nephew. A memorial to General Dixon is in St. Peter's Church, Pembury.
>
> We have been very interested in your accounts of Woodsgate and remember well some of what, we, as children, called secret rooms.
>
> EDITOR'S NOTE: We regret the error and are pleased to make it clear that in fact General Dixon DID win the Victoria Cross.

Another story concerning his Victoria Cross had appeared in the Kent and Sussex Courier in September 1956, which stated that the relatives of the late Major General were seeking information about the medal, claiming it had been lost and that, during the V.C. Centenary Year, the relations were hoping to regain it.

The following week Miss L. Bosanquet wrote from 14 Wilman Road, Tunbridge Wells that she was the General's great-niece and stated that the medal was in the possession of his great-great nephew, to whom it was left by Mrs Dixon. She stated that the V.C. and other medals had been on show at the Centenary Exhibition at Marlborough House, London (15 June – 7 July 1956). At the beginning they had not been labelled, but when her sister visited the exhibition they drew the attention of the authorities to this omission and the correct caption giving Major General Dixon's name etc. was put on the medal case.

His name does not appear in any official listing of those medals on display. It is a little peculiar that the exhibition authorities would display a V.C. without identifying it, especially as the recipient's name is engraved on the reverse.

The medals were left to Lady Griffith (née Jacob) whose mother was Clarke. She passed them on to her son John R. C. Griffith and then to his son, Simon who holds them now, together with Dixon's sword and his "Shako" and army commissioning papers. Simon is the great-great-grandson of Dixon's youngest sister, Frances Maria, who had 13 children, 12 of whom lived to grow up.

In 1980, the medals and sword and commissions were exhibited on indefinite loan in the Military Heritage Museum in Albion Street, Lewes, Sussex in their Artillery Cabinet. When the Museum closed in the late 1980's the items were returned to Simon.

Dixon's Sword Handle

Major General Dixon's Medals

Tributes to Major General Dixon include a Brass Memorial Tablet in St. Peter's Church, Pembury:

> In Loving Memory of
> Matthew Charles Dixon
> Major General Royal Artillery V.C.
> Of Woodsgate in this parish
> Who entered into rest Janry 7th 1905 Aged 84.
> "As many as received Him, to them gave He the right to become
> Children of GOD, to them that believe on His Name". John 1.12

* * * * *

His name was included on the former memorial at the Royal Artillery Chapel in Woolwich.

* * * * *

His name is also on the V.C. Roll of Honour at the Union Jack Club, Sandell Street, Waterloo, London SE1 8UJ.

* * * * *

Matthew Charles Dixon

Captain (later rising to Major General) in the Royal Regiment of Artillery

Born in 1821, the son of a Major General and grandson of an Admiral, Captain Dixon gained his Victoria Cross soon after he was ordered to the front at the outbreak of the Crimean War.

On April 17 1855, the battery Captain Dixon was commanding was blown up by an enemy shell which destroyed the parapets at Sevastopol.

Ten men were killed or wounded, five guns were disabled and a sixth was covered with earth. Dixon took control of the remaining gun and, despite heavy enemy fire, continued firing until sunset brought relief.

Major General Dixon lived in Pembury soon after retiring from the army in 1869 until his death in 1905. A memorial tablet to the Major General can be seen in St Peter's Church, Pembury.

Other honours
Companion of the Order of the Bath, Knight of the Legion of Honour

Image courtesy of the Victoria Cross Society

Dixon's Write-up at the Victoria Cross Grove, Tunbridge Wells

CHAPTER THREE

Heroism in New Zealand – The Story of Lieutenant Colonel William Temple 1833–1919

FOREWORD

Throughout my childhood Colonel William Temple's portrait hung in our family dining room, firstly at my grandfather Lieutenant General Reginald Temple's house, and then when he died, in our home. He was always referred to as "The V.C.". His portrait was fresh and bright. It had actually been painted from a photograph for my grandparents by a Temple cousin, Pauline Mitchell Innes. There were also the portraits of his parents, Doctor William Temple and his wife, traditional country paintings, probably done when they were newly married. The V.C. with its accompanying New Zealand Campaign medal were displayed in a special frame, together with my grandfather's medals and were always on show in the study. Nevertheless, no one ever talked about these people. We knew so very little about any of these men. The award of the V.C. had in effect overshadowed all this particular man's other achievements.

For example, involvement in medicine as a career meant that both father and son were highly respected for their skills in this field. William Temple V.C. had also been an early photographer. His pictures of his family remain with us. His remarkable photographs of the pioneering work of the army in New Zealand are now regarded as a key historical resource in Wellington's National Museum.

Thankfully, the research done in recent years by my husband, my son (who is also a regular soldier serving in the Irish Guards) and now Richard Snow have thrown a great deal more light on the remarkable lives of both William Temple "the V.C.". and his father, the respected doctor of Monaghan Town; we have been delighted by all that has been revealed. I feel we have now readdressed the balance and can give proper acknowledgement to all that was achieved by this remarkable man and his father through long careers in the military and in the life of County Monaghan respectively.

Dr William Temple senior, trained at the Medical School at Edinburgh University, where he wrote his qualifying thesis on typhus fever, in Latin. Colonel William Temple V.C. trained in medicine at Trinity College, Dublin, and became that great institution's first V.C. Both the Royal Artillery and the Royal Army Medical Corps claim him as "their man". In fact, Colonel Temple trained at the Military Academy at Woolwich (known as "the Shop") before joining the Royal Horse Artillery as an Assistant Surgeon. My father, Major William Vere Temple M.C., R.E. was in the last "batch" to enter "the Shop" at Woolwich in 1939, before it was closed forever at the onset of the Second World War. I am sure his grandfather would have approved his choice and that he entered "top of his class".

Diana Temple, great-granddaughter of William Temple V.C.

IRISH BEGINNINGS

William Temple's father, also William, was born around 1790. He married Anne, daughter of Hugh Hamill of Rooskey, Ireland, and they lived at The Terrace, Monaghan. He received his M.D. at Edinburgh in 1819.

His entry in the Medical Directory for Ireland for 1852 reads as follows:

> TEMPLE, William, Monaghan – M.D. Edin.1819; L.S.A. Ireland; Lic. in Midw. Dub. Lying. in Hosp.; Med.Off. Union Workhouse and Fever Hosp.; Phys. Monaghan Fever Hosp.; Med. Att. Scotstown Disp. and Constabulary; late Med. Att. Castleshane Disp.

The entry for 1854 reads the same but ends:

> Med. Att, Monaghan Dist, and Constabulary, and formerly Med. Att. Castleshane Disp., and late of the Ballanade Disp. and Constabulary.

William died in July 1872 and his death was announced in the *Medical Press and Circular* of 3 July, 1872:

> This week is marked by the death of one of the best and most revered of the old school of provincial practitioners in Ireland, who, in his green old age of eighty-two, has passed from the ranks of the Profession, to which during nearly sixty years of practice he did nothing but honour. The role of a Workhouse Medical Officer is not one in which honour and notoriety can be rapidly accumulated; yet there are few men in the locality in which Dr. Temple had carried on his practice who could be less easily spared, or whose death would be more universally regretted. *The Monaghan Standard* says:
>
> > Dr. Temple's private practice was extensive. His uniform geniality of disposition won the friendship of those with whom his professional avocations brought him in contact. In 1817 he first commenced practice in this town, having been appointed in that year Medical attendant to the Fever Hospital; and we believe we are correct in stating that since that period until within a few weeks of his death he diligently performed the duties of his several appointments almost without intermission. Naturally possessed of a vigorous constitution, conserved by regular habits, he was capable of, and did endure, without exhaustion, an amount of labour that to others would be oppressive. Thus it need not be a matter of surprise that at the age of eighty-two years he was still found in possession of those fine faculties by which all through life he had been distinguished. To this community it is superfluous to recapitulate his many fine qualities, or dwell on the deep sorrow with which the announcement of his death has been received. We all recognised in him a skilful physician, an honourable gentleman, a good citizen, a true friend, and a most charitable and benevolent Christian.

On 10 July 1872, the *Medical Press and Circular* carried a piece headed "Monaghan Union":

> The Board placed in their minutes the following resolution:- The Board of Guardians assembled this day have to record their regret at the death of William Temple, Esq., who has been Medical officer of the house since its first opening, now thirty years ago, and who discharged the duties of his office to the entire satisfaction of the Board.

The Chairman said that Dr. Temple, as Medical officer of the Workhouse, discharged his duties with great humanity and, at the same time, with perfect economy. He did not squander the rates at all. He acted with judgement and discretion. At the same time nothing could exceed the health of the inmates of the house. No number of children in any other rank of life assembled together had on an average the same good health, while there was a smaller average of deaths. The Poor-law Inspectors had always borne testimony to the fact.

The main Workhouse in Monaghan housed 900 paupers and was built on a seven and a half acre site. There were four Workhouses in Monaghan, in which the inmates were separated from their families and carried out hard labour, while hungry and fevered, for two meals a day. According to an 1845 Monaghan County History these institutions were "repulsive to the habits and feelings of a people". The "intolerable overcrowding" was relieved in only two ways: through forced emigration, or "when death helped to empty the workhouses through fever and disease".

In April 1844, a body of 21 commissioners was established to take over the running of Monaghan, and William was one of the first commissioners. He was still a commissioner in 1855.

His first child was Annie Temple, born on 12 May 1832 (died 12 November 1908). William Temple, the only son, was born on 7 November 1833 in Monaghan. His second sister Jane was born on 31 April 1835 (died 25 November 1913) and the youngest Elizabeth Alice was born on 1 September 1836 (died 23 May 1865). They were all christened in Monaghan. William was privately educated at Rev. John Bleckley's School in the 1840s. John Bleckley was a Presbyterian Minister, who in 1852 was elected Moderator of the Presbyterian Church of Ireland for the ensuing year. The boarders were sons of the gentry and professional men of two or three neighbouring counties, and the day boys were sons of the principle townspeople. There were around 50 pupils, all Protestants or Presbyterians. Mr Bleckley was a careful and assiduous teacher. In the Monaghan County Directory for 1862, William's father is listed as the School's Medical Officer.

William's sisters remained in Monaghan, apparently breeding carriage horses. There was a substantial stable yard behind the House and Surgery in Monaghan Town. William went on to Trinity College, Dublin in October 1851, aged 17 years, as a pensioner, meaning he paid a fixed annual fee for his education. Here he obtained a BA in the spring of 1856 and an MB in summer 1858. He became a Licentiate for the Royal College of Surgeons, Ireland in the same year. He was, in due course, to become the first Victoria Cross holder from Trinity College.

NEW ZEALAND AND THE MAORI WARS

Following a short period in civilian medical practice, William joined the army on 1 November 1858, as Assistant Surgeon, Army Medical Department until 10 January 1859. The following day he transferred to the Royal Regiment of Artillery as Assistant Surgeon. This was announced in the *London Gazette* 22217, dated 11 January 1859, page 1.

On 20 November 1860, he sailed for New Zealand with "C" Battery, 4th Brigade, Royal Regiment of Artillery (later 94 (New Zealand) Battery R.A.). He sailed from Woolwich on the *Norwood*, an 850-ton ship, under Captain H. Bristow. On board were Captain Mercer, Captain Watson, Captain Hunter, Lieutenant Magennis and Lieutenant Pickard, and Assistant Surgeon Temple, 219 rank and file, 31 women and 33 children. They arrived in Auckland, New Zealand on 5 March 1861.

The year 1860 saw the start of the first Taranaki War and British troops being despatched to New Zealand. This war was an armed conflict over land ownership and sovereignty and took place between March 1860 and March 1861. Taranaki is in North Island and the war was fought between the Maoris and the New Zealand Government. The 4th Brigade R.A. was under the command of Captain Henry Mercer, and they were equipped with six RBL 12-pounders. The guns arrived safely together with other stores and a quantity of ammunition and other equipment including two 10-inch and two 8-inch mortars. The total cargo amounted to 700 tons. The ship was not allowed to unload at the main wharf, presumably because she carried ammunition, so she had to anchor some distance out in the harbour and be discharged by a lighter. This task was completed by the gunners in less than a week.

On 12 March, Captain Mercer and Lieutenant Pickard, with three 12-pounder Armstrongs and four mortars, received orders to proceed to Taranaki, where Sir T. Pratt, KCB, together with about 2,000 men was still fighting the Maoris. They boarded the colonial war steamer "*SS Victoria*" in Auckland, and they arrived at the Waitara River on the morning of 13 March. The stores and equipment were landed in surf boats, and the guns were cleaned and assembled. The battery had moved by sea on H.M.S. *Cordelia*, *Niger* and *SS Victoria*. The troops mustered at Huirangi on 17 March 1861.

Major General Sir T. S. Pratt directed Captain Mercer to select a suitable area for the guns. At the same time Lieutenant Pickard put the men through their paces on gun drill after their long voyage from England. On 15 March the guns and mortars, drawn by six bullocks each, set out at 6 a.m. The 10-inch mortars travelled in carts. Three hours later the guns arrived at a redoubt occupied by the 14th Regiment called Te Arei. A position for the guns was taken up near the redoubt.

Captain Mercer and Lieutenant MacNaghten proceeded to the forward infantry positions to observe the enemy at close quarters during a three-day cease-fire. The Maoris were entrenched in lines of rifle pits along the crests of the hills forming a curve of some 2,000 yards. The scrub and bush provided good cover for them. The troops never saw more than the head and shoulders of the hostile natives, and never more than two or three were seen together. After the truce ended, during the three days that the Armstrongs were in action about 100 rounds were fired from them. While laying a small mortar Lieutenant MacNaghten, R.A. was killed on 17 March. On the following day Sergeant Christie, R.A. was wounded near the same spot. However, early on the morning of the 19th, the Maoris surrendered.

By 30 April 1861, the entire regiment was concentrated in the Albert Barracks, Auckland except for 84 men in Taranaki. The Taranaki detachment finally rejoined the regiment in June 1863. On 1 August 1861 at an inquest held at the Garrison Library, Albert Barracks, Assistant Surgeon William Temple, in medical charge of the battery, gave evidence in the enquiry into the death of Charles McCleary. The latter was a gunner, Royal Artillery, aged about 30, who had a reputation of being addicted to drink. Temple had called to see him and found him dead. The verdict of the hearing was that McCleary died from excessive drinking.

At the beginning of May 1861, the three Armstrong Guns were ordered back to Auckland. They were taken in pieces to H.M.S. *Fawn* which took them to the Manukau harbour. Here they were disembarked, re-assembled and taken to Auckland.

On 27 May 1861, William Temple attended a Levee arranged by His Excellency the Governor at Government House in Auckland in honour of the Queen's Birthday. The Levee started at 3 p.m. but "was not as large as on previous occasions due to the late hour at which the review terminated. The Otahuhu Cavalry attended in their blue serge shirts, but the Auckland Rifle Volunteers did not arrive at Government House until the Levee was over".

During 1861 and until December 1862, the regiment was engaged in paving the stables and stable yard and in building, along with the other regiments in the country, the Great South Road south from Auckland in preparation for the invasion of the Waikato. Governor Sir George Grey prepared for war. At the end of 1861 he had ordered Lieutenant General Duncan Cameron, in command of the Imperial and Colonial Forces in New Zealand, to extend the Great South Road from Drury to the Waikato River. The Survey of this road was seen by the Maoris as a threat to their sovereignty. Blocking the path of the surveyors was one tactic used by the Maoris; others included the removal of survey pegs and surveyors' tools. At the same time a series of redoubts and stockades were built in South Auckland and along the lower Waikato River.

The Governor Sir George Grey had requested that construction of the Great South Road be undertaken by the troops. The first units included one officer and 57 men of the Royal Artillery. The first detachment of troops left Auckland on 24 November 1861 via Otahuhu to Drury, a distance

Maoris Protesting at Pokeno. (Photo taken by William Temple. Photo archive, Alexander Turnbull Library, New Zealand).

of 14.5 miles. The detachment of the 2nd Battalion, 14th Regiment and some Royal Engineers marched from camp Otahuhu under Colonel Alexander. They pitched camp near the native settlement of Pokeno.

Drury was the principle headquarters of the troops during the formation of the road in 1862, and also the movement of troops to the front in 1863. The main camp was east of the village, sometimes known as Camp Hill. It was overlooked by a two-storey house, which General Cameron adopted as his H.Q., his staff camped in tents nearby.

Camp at Drury (Photo taken by William Temple. Photo archive, Alexander Turnbull Library, New Zealand.)

Work on the road commenced on 1 January 1862. The men were to work from 8 a.m. to 12 noon, and from 2 p.m. to 5 p.m. except on Saturdays when work ceased at noon. Actual metalling of the road commenced at the end of January. This had been put back to allow bullock traffic to use the road.

By May 1862, although labour had continued through the winter, the hard work and perseverance had nearly completed the road. Orders were therefore given for the return by stages of troops to the main camp at Otahuhu. The main artery to the south had now been opened up giving access to the Waikato River. In May 1862, General Cameron fixed on a site for a major forward base to be known as "Queen's Redoubt".

On 5 September 1862, William attended The Subscription Ball, an anxiously awaited event held at the Brunswick Music Hall, attended by members of most of the leading families of the city and neighbourhood. The Ball was organised by a Committee which included Colonel Mould. Three of his daughters were to attend the Ball. Music was provided by the Band of the 40th Regiment, and the Ball was attended by around 220 ladies and gentlemen. The local paper at the time reports that

> …by ten or eleven o'clock, the greater portion of the company had assembled, and dancing might then be considered as commenced in real earnest. The younger portion could not have entered with greater spirit in 'the mazes of the mystic dance" while the elders enjoyed themselves by 'quiet hands at whist and other favourite games' … the evening was spent in 'unalloyed enjoyment and recreative indulgence'.

On 21 October 1862, William Temple married Anne Theodosia Mould at St. Paul's Church, Auckland. She was the fourth daughter of Colonel (later Major General) Thomas Rawlings Mould CB, RE, who was commanding the Royal Engineers in New Zealand. His wife was Annie Stirling and Anne Theodosia was born in 1844, one of 13 children. Commissioned into the Royal Corps of Engineers from Woolwich as a Second Lieutenant on 22 September 1826, Mould and his six daughters arrived in Auckland late in December 1855. In June 1861, he had written an important memorandum outlining the need for a line of fortifications south of Auckland to protect the city and its surrounding districts. He also proposed that the roads south of Auckland be extended and improved to facilitate the occupation of Waikato. Both proposals were acted on, and Mould himself

Anne Theodosia Mould, Temple's wife.

General Mould

72

directed much of the work. As an active member of the Anglican Church, in 1863 he enlarged St. Paul's Church, Auckland. In July he joined Lieutenant General Cameron's staff for the invasion of Waikato, overseeing the construction of the roads, bridges and fortifications which were central to British operations. He was at Rangiriri with William. In 1866, Colonel Mould returned to Britain, where in 1867 he was promoted to Major General; he retired from the army on full pay in 1872. He died in Bayswater, London on 13 June 1886.

Work started again on a new line to Mangatawhiri in November 1862 under the direction of Colonel Mould. In December 1862, the battery went for practice to a range of about 1,760 yards on land a few miles from Auckland. Officers informed Captain Mercer that great difficulty was always experienced by the artillery in breaching the pas or fortified places occupied by the natives. So he had sections of pas made specially.

On 7 February 1863, H.M.S. *Orpheus*, 21 guns, was wrecked when she went aground at the entrance to the Manukau Harbour with many lives lost. One hundred and eighty-seven died out of a complement of 256 officers, men and boys. The survivors of the ship were conveyed to Auckland on board the *Miranda*. Dr. Mouatt V.C and Dr. Temple were in attendance to render the necessary surgical aid. John Pascoe, Chief Boatswain's mate on the *Orpheus* was one of those drowned. They brought his body back to be used as evidence at the resulting inquest. Afterwards at the funeral his body was placed on a Royal Artillery gun carriage drawn by six horses. The funeral was attended by many dignatories and Dr. Temple.

In March 1863, Captain Mercer was ordered to take his squadron down to Taranaki by sea, as hostilities were expected to break out there shortly. He was also to take four Armstrong 12-pounders with harnesses. At the time only four officers were with the battery: Captain Mercer, Lieutenant Pickard, Asst-Surgeon Temple, and Vetinary Surgeon Anderson. Around the 18 March, 50 men and horses left from Auckland to the Manukau harbour to embark for Taranaki, under Lieutenant Pickard. When they arrived at New Plymouth in Taranaki, the horses had to be hoisted overboard and towed on shore by men in surfboats. The second troop and guns followed a week later. Captain Mercer's troops were at once converted into a squadron of cavalry as a temporary measure in case of emergency. It was assumed that these men were used to horses.

With the Great South Road now completed, adequately served by transport, and with an instant telegraph communication installed, General Cameron was in a position if needed to carry war across the Mangatawhiri, the boundary of the King Country. (The "King Movement" was the title for the Waikato, Taupo and Bay of Plenty Tribes). During April and May, several reports reached the Governor from officers, settlers and friendly natives in the lower Waikato of increased feelings of hostility on the part of the Waikato Maoris.

The rainy season had now started and this made the roads so slippery that horses fell continually. On 4 June 1863, after a night march of 15 miles over difficult country, a force of about 600 men and three 12-pounder Armstrong guns under Lieutenant General Cameron, attacked a position taken up by natives on the left bank of the Katikara River, about 15 miles south of New Plymouth. As soon as it was light the entrenchments were stormed and taken.

About the end of June 1863, Captain Mercer received instructions to take up a position to shell some native entrenchments at Kaitake, on the lower ranges of Mount Egmont, seven miles from New Plymouth. War now seemed imminent as the Auckland militia was called up on 22 June. Maoris in South Auckland were ordered to take an oath of allegiance to the Queen and to give up their arms. Most ignored the edict.

At 4 a.m on 9 July 1863, the whole of the 65th Regiment, then in Albert Barracks, left for Drury on their way to the front. The next day they were followed by Captain Mercer's artillery battery with four 12-pounder Armstrong guns, four 24-pounder howitzers, and a nine pounder. On 11 July, Grey issued a virtual declaration of war, and the following day a small force of British troops crossed the Mangatawhiri – the Waikato Campaign had begun. The Mangatawhiri was considered by the Waikato Maori to be their northern boundary. They had warned the colonial forces that any military incursion across it would be regarded as a declaration of war. The British established three redoubts in close proximity at the northern end of the Koheroa Ridge, to hold 150 men each. Headquarters were now established at Queen's Redoubt. By early 1863, a metalled road had been completed to Havelock (Pokeno) where this large redoubt, capable of housing 450 men had been built.

So, redoubts were erected for the protection of Auckland; the bush was cut down for hundreds of yards on either side of the Great South Road; a Commissariat Transport Corps of nearly 1,000 men was raised; four regiments of Militia were recruited, chiefly in Australia and the South; and the strength of the Imperial forces was raised to 10,000 men. This meant the total force was about 25,000 to cope with the Maoris, who were never able to bring more than 600 men into the field.

On the 17th, Maoris were seen on the heights south of the Koheroa redoubts. Cameron ordered some 500 men to advance. This led to a series of skirmishes. Gradually the 400 Maori were forced to retreat, eventually fleeing the Whangamarino River. The engagement commenced at 11 a.m. and ended at 1 o'clock. Thirty Maori warriors fell; one officer and 11 British soldiers were injured, one mortally. The reason the troops lost so few men was probably due to the fact that the Maoris rarely took deliberate aim. The Maoris threw away their weapons, ammunition, food and clothing in order to make their escape. On 19 July, 300 men of the 65th Regiment marched from Drury to build a redoubt on high ground overlooking the river. This was afterwards named the "Alexandra Redoubt".

General Cameron decided to pay a flying visit to the reputed headquarters of the rebel natives at Paparata, about 15 miles away, and organised a large-scale expedition on 2 August. The main body of 700 troops moved from the Queen's Redoubt shortly after 7 p.m. The expedition was conducted with utmost secrecy and by night. The garrison remaining at the redoubt numbered around 300 men and officers, under the command of Colonel Mould, C.B.

When the various detachments of men arrived at the Boating Station on the Mangatawhiri Creek, at the terminus of the Great South Road, they boarded boats and landed at the base of the Koheroa bluff. In about one hour, the boats had brought over the last draft of men. At about 9.30 p.m., the detachment of the Royal Artillery, under the command of Captain Mercer and Lieutenant Pickard, consisting of 60 men and a full complement of non-commissioned officers, with two Armstrong guns, started from the rendezvous at Koheroa. The remainder of troops marched at 10.20 p.m. The column, headed by General Cameron, proceeded along in silence. The medical staff on the field consisted of Dr Mouatt, V.C., Deputy Inspector General; Surgeon Major Carte; Surgeon Peake, of the 10th Regiment; Assistant Surgeons Temple, R.A. and Hilston, of H.M.S. *Harrier*. The weather was favourable, and each man wore his blue fatigue coat and trousers, and carried 60 rounds of ammunition, and one day's provisions, besides his rifle and bayonet. The remainder of the ammunition was carried by pack horses.

An accident during the night deprived the expedition of one of the Armstrong guns. In several places the ridge was very narrow and the banks on either side were precipitous. The guns were drawn by bullocks, and about three miles from the Koheroa camp, the bullock team attached to the last gun approached too close to the right cliff. The gun and limber overturned and fell down into the ravine, breaking one wheel. The gun was retrieved and Lieutenant Pickard returned to the redoubt for a wheel. He was accompanied by four men, and returned an hour later and fixed the wheel. Subsequently Lieutenant Pickard was ordered to take the gun back to the camp.

After marching about nine miles the troops were halted for an hour on flat land at the brink of a swamp. Fog lay heavily over the swamp hampering visibility. Daylight broke as the troops approached Paparata. As the sun rose the fog became denser. A temporary bridge was soon laid and the troops crossed as detailed for the attack. The settlement was rushed but no natives were there. It was evident they had been fully aware of the attack, so the troops rushed up the road towards the upper settlement at the foot of the range. However, it was dense jungle, so the attack was led in single file but the Maoris failed to take advantage of their knowledge of the ground. Instead of taking up position on a higher level, protected by natural cover, they waited in the bush and fired their first volley from here. The first shot struck Private Thomas Karney of the 12th Regiment, inflicting dangerous wounds. The shot which struck him was fired within a few yards of him, but the man who fired was completely sheltered from sight. The troops immediately rushed into the opening and charged the position from where the shot had been fired. Not a native was visible, but their yells were audible in another direction indicating they had changed position to avoid the bullets of the troops. As the place was clearly untenable and the enemy had withdrawn, the general ordered a withdrawal.

They withdrew in single file through the jungle. The natives fired a few long-range shots and indulged in savage yelling and war dances. Gradually the troops moved off, and the Maoris began to come out of their hiding places. They let out volleys of fire indicating that they claimed the victory, but General Cameron had made a successful reconnaissance and knew the number of natives assembled at Paparata to be around 400. The troops arrived in camp at 3 o'clock after a very tiring march of around 30 miles.

The Maori force, which contested the Koheroa ridge, had first occupied the Te Teoteo's Pa, an old fortification at the end of a spur overlooking the confluence of the Whangamarino and Waikato Rivers. By 14 August, Cameron's troops had occupied the pa and developed a redoubt nearby – the Whangamarino Redoubt under Lieutenant Pickard. Beyond the Whangamarino was a swamp, impassable at this time of year, and the Maoris had collected in large numbers at the other extremity of the swamp, where they built entrenchments.

The Royal Artillery gunners and men of the 12th regiment set about making a track from Koheroa accessible for artillery. On 18 August, two 12-pounder Armstrong guns were brought up and placed in position below and south of the redoubt. The Artillery was ordered to annoy the Maoris at Meremere by firing at any that appeared, and at the canoes which brought their provisions. Another 12-pounder Armstrong was brought from Queen's Redoubt and all three guns were placed in a small battery.

On 29 October, two 40-pounder Armstrong guns arrived from Sydney on the *Pioneer*. They were positioned below the redoubts facing the next Maori position – Meremere – 2 kms to the south across the swamp, where the Maoris had developed a highly fortified position with around 1,100 men. On the morning of 31 October at about 2.30 a.m. Cameron embarked 600 men on his river fleet – the *Avon* and the *Pioneer*. These were two steamships purchased by the government. While the Maori position was bombarded by the 40-pounder gun, the *Avon* and *Pioneer* with barges in tow steamed past Meremere before daylight. They were hit but not harmed by musket fire from the Maoris. The gunboats in tow were cast off and the men landed as quickly as possible. Two 12-pounder Armstrongs and a naval 6-pounder Armstrong were landed and hauled to the top of the hill about 500 yards from the river, where a redoubt was commenced. This was later named "Mould's Redoubt", and was capable of holding 700 men. On 1 November, the troops came under fire. Incessant fire continued for about one hour, until the Maoris decamped at about 6 a.m. Outflanked, after a brief foray, the Maoris abandoned their position. On 1 November, the British occupied the abandoned pa and established a redoubt.

On 3 November, the troops commenced the redoubt for 200 men, which was occupied on the 11th by a detachment of three officers and 50 men of the 12th. The Maoris had expected to hold Meremere for some considerable time, but now there was free access by land to the Waikato country. The 65th (280 men) remained at Meremere, the garrison of which stood then at 780. The remainder, the Royal Artillery and 40th returned to Queen's.

RANGIRIRI

As early as May 1863, Colonel Mould reported from Lower Waikato that the Maoris were busy constructing earthworks at Rangiriri. On 18 November, General Cameron reconnoitred the Maori position at Rangiriri in order to plan his attack. The defence works consisted of a main line of entrenchments across the narrow isthmus dividing Lake Waikare from the Waikato River. This line had a double ditch backed by an earth parapet 21 feet high. At the centre it was strengthened by a formidable redoubt. Behind the main line, and at right angles to it, a series of rifle pits faced the river. General Cameron came to the conclusion that the defences might be taken in reverse by landing a force in the rear of the main entrenchment.

On the morning of 20 November 1863, General Cameron led his troops, two Armstrong 12-pounders drawn by bullocks, and a 6-pounder naval field gun drawn by sailors, at 7.00 a.m. from Meremere for Rangiriri, about 12 miles south. It took eight bullocks to pull each gun. Cameron had around 800 men with 500 more on board two river steamers. Half way to Rangiriri, 36 of the gunners were supplied with revolvers, and Captain Mercer was told that if there was any difficulty in the projected storming of the Maori encampment his men would be called upon to assist in the assault. The force which assembled on the north front of the Rangiriri ridge at 3 o'clock in the afternoon was made up as follows: Royal Navy 100 officers and men; 15 Royal Engineers; 54 Royal Artillery; 112 men of the 12th Regiment; 186 of the 14th Regiment; and 386 men of the 65th Regiment. The track they had followed led through several swamps, gullies and narrow ridges and resulted in a hot march.

The Maoris had thrown up a considerable line of earthworks across the isthmus between the swampy margins of Lake Waikare and the Waikato River. The fortification blocked the bullock track which led to the south. After they had evacuated their strongly entrenched position at Meremere, a considerable number of Maoris withdrew temporarily from the field, while the rest, with reinforcements, set to work fortifying their new position here. Unusually they failed to leave a way of escape open in the rear. They were also numerically too weak to defend the long line of fortification.

The British plan was to attack on two fronts at the same time. Firstly, a land attack on the front of the main position, but also an attack from steamers on the southern ridge. The *Pioneer* and *Avon* carried the headquarters of the 40th Regiment, and four armoured gunboats carried soldiers and sailors from Mangatawhiri. Troops from Meremere walked along the river bank.

The guns were placed about 600 yards from the centre of the Maori position, on rising ground. The Maoris began firing immediately, but without effect, except a few shots striking the wheels and gun-carriages.

At 3.30 p.m., just before the signal was given for the steamers to attack, the Maoris opened fire along the whole line but did not inflict any damage as they were out of range at 600 yards. The object of the artillery fire was to try to distract the natives so that the steamers could disembark troops. This took some considerable time. The attack had begun with an artillery bombardment at a range of about 700 yards. The three Armstrong guns shelled the Maori works for nearly two hours. The solid earthworks suffered little from this shelling, but many casualties were inflicted on the Maoris, crowded in their trenches and pits. After the assault was ordered the rapidity of fire increased. Guns were loaded as fast as they were being fired. This firing prevented the Maoris taking any aim at the advancing troops.

General Cameron ordered an assault on the Maori trenches, and the 65th Regiment was detailed. The leading company, under Lieutenant Toker, carried scaling-ladders and planks. They included a small detachment of Royal Engineers, under Captain Brooke. Three companies of the 65th followed, with the 14th in support. The storming party, with fixed bayonets at the charge, swept up the hill, and quickly forced the defenders out of the first line of entrenchments, but lost several men. The warriors fell back to defend the second line of rifle-pits, but this was also taken. The 40th Regiment, late in the afternoon, succeeded in landing from the steamers and attacked and captured a series of entrenchments on a spur above. Half the position was taken, and the Maoris tried to escape. Some fled to the Waikare Lake, where they were shot down by the 40th Regiment, others made it to a few canoes in the swamp. Two shells from the Armstrongs burst on the latter group, who ran back to join the others.

An attempt by the main body of the 65th and the 14th to storm the central redoubt failed because the ladders were too short to reach the top of the parapets. Some did reach the high rampart but were hurled back or shot down.

About one hour after the first assault, General Cameron asked Captain Henry Mercer, battery commander of "C" Battery, 4 Brigade, R.A. for some shells to be thrown by hand. Captain Mercer replied that Armstrong shell were unsuited for this purpose. He was then ordered to bring down his men to drive out the Maoris, who were still resisting. They were strongly entrenched, well armed and numerically superior to our troops. The night was rapidly settling in. All previous assaults, though gallantly made, had been repulsed with heavy loss, when Captain Mercer was selected, with 36 of his artillerymen to storm the stockade. He was described as:

> One of those brave, gallant, and God-fearing men who are an honour to our service, and to humanity itself. He had a presentiment that he would fall, but was prepared to die. He had been preparing for death for years, and it did not take him by surprise.

Leaving their position at the guns they crossed the more or less dead ground on the west and after crossing the captured line of earthworks approached from the rear. Scaling the parapets they fired their revolvers at the defenders inside, Lieutenant Pickard lying flat on the top and firing his revolver at all who faced him. They attempted to reach the top of the parapet, but only one or two succeeded in setting foot on it. They tried an attack, but failed as the men were not able to fight the natives at close quarters. Captain Mercer rolled backwards on the ground mortally wounded, struck by a bullet in the jaw, carrying away the lower part of his face. He rolled behind an earthwork out of reach of enemy fire and afterwards managed to crawl into a safe corner. Sergeant Major Hamilton reached the top and fired his revolver into the Maoris, but was forced back with a severe gunshot wound in the right arm. Four other non-commissioned officers and men were killed or wounded while trying to get into the Maori stronghold. Driver Culverwell, Captain Mercer's servant, ran to Mercer and was mortally wounded while doing so. Lieutenant Pickard, finding himself left alone on the parapet, descended and followed his Captain, and also succeeded in reaching the corner. The enemy fire was so deadly, that no one could attempt to reach him or any of the dead or wounded. The gunners were then engaged in blocking a narrow passage leading to the principle Maori stronghold,

Artillery Group. Temple: eighth from left standing. Pickard: third from left sitting. Mercer on right end standing

from which much loss had been inflicted on the troops. While this was open it prevented assistance being given to the wounded.

First one soldier advanced, then another, and another, but only to meet with a speedy death. It was at this moment that Assistant Surgeon William Temple learned that his friend Mercer, with whom he had trained at Woolwich, stood in need of his aid. In spite of being warned that to go to Mercer's aid was almost certain death, he sprang forward towards the opening. His progress was watched with breathless anxiety by the troops. Without weighing up his chances, and without hesitation, he reached the spot so fatal to others. The enemy's fire was redoubled as the Assistant Surgeon was enveloped in smoke. For a moment he disappeared in the smoke, and then was seen by Mercer's side trying to alleviate any suffering. He stooped when exposed to enemy fire, and the bullets passed harmlessly over his head. Together with Lieutenant Pickard, they exposed themselves to imminent danger in crossing the entrance to the Maori keep, at a point upon which the enemy were concentrating their fire, in order to render assistance to the wounded. Lieutenant Arthur Pickard, R.A. was the only other man brave enough to venture into the crossfire, and he went backwards and forwards to carry water to quench the thirst of his comrades.

Because of the need to fill the narrow entrance to allow the wounded to be evacuated before nightfall, a party of Royal Engineer sappers under Captain E. Brooke dug a trench to fill it up with planks and earth. This was finished with difficulty under fire at about 10 p.m. when Captain Mercer and the other wounded men were removed. Gunner Jas. Reid was wounded while assisting Dr. Temple to remove the wounded.

William Temple later wrote in his report:

> A heavy and deadly fire was kept up by the enemy through the opening during the whole of the evening and I may mention that between my crossing and Lieutenant Pickard's recrossing I saw one man shot dead and several were wounded through it.

In a letter home dated 21 November he wrote:

My own darling Nannie,

I wrote you a few lines this morning to tell you that I was alright, but I see that the "poor" Pioneer has not yet been able to get away. She started at half past 9 o'clock and ever since then she has been manoeuvring about in the river without being able to get more than half a mile. So I am going to give you a fuller account of our proceedings as I said before, we, i.e. the Artillery and two companies of the 40, left the Redoubt on Thursday and were taken up to the Queens – where we encamped for the night. Captain Brook and Dr. Spencer entertained us sumptuously.

Temple assisting his friend Mercer

We started next morning and got here about 3 p.m. and soon afterwards began to fire from our guns, several of our shells burst beautifully and no doubt did good execution among the enemy. A short time afterwards the 12th, 14th and 65th charged but the fire was so heavy and so well directed that our men were killed and wounded in great numbers.

I was still at the guns when I heard that a great number of the 65th were wounded on the left, so I took a couple of our stretchers with our men and had not gone 100 yards until I found Col. Austin badly wounded in his thigh, so I dressed him and got him carried back. While I was dressing him a shot struck one of my stretcher bearers just behind me, however, he was only slightly wounded. When I got back with Col. Austin, the General had just sent word that he wanted Mercer and his Gunners with swords and revolvers to charge so I went with them. We had hardly got in until our Sergeant Major came back to me with his poor wrist awfully shattered. I am afraid he will lose the hand. Then I went on again and found Culverwell mortally wounded, so I gave the poor fellow some rum and water. It was all I could do for him. Then I had to cross over a spare where all our men except Pickard and Gnr. Quinn were shot down. However I got the men to fire into the embrasure so as to cover me, if possible, and I bolted across without any greater inconvenience than having my left ear quite deaf from a gun going off at it as I was crossing. It has all gone now, however. When I got over I found poor Mercer very badly wounded through both jaws, Mr. Murphy, 12th, killed and about 11 other men killed and wounded in a little place not bigger than your old room in Emily Place. In this same place were Pickard, John (65th) Crawhall and Phillips, (12th) and five men able to fight, so you may guess we were well occupied.

After remaining there about an hour the General sent for Pickard who had to go back across the opening, so we got up the firing again on our side to cover him and fortunately he got over all right. We then got some shells and threw them over the parapet at the enemy and set fire to some whares (Maori word for houses) that were inside; we then got a trench dug and had our wounded carried across about 11 at night. Col. Manto and Captain Brook were engaged in making a mine, but the earth was not good and they had no fuse so they had to give it up. Everything was prepared to pick down the enemy's parapet and go in at them in the morning, so the troops settled down in the trenches for the night and Pickard and I went back to the guns and lay down and slept until daylight. We were called up about 2 to "stand to our arms" but it was a false alarm. After we had got everything in readiness, up went a white flag and the Maori gave in.

187 surrendered themselves prisoners. We have found 41 dead Maoris – and I dare say there are some more still. We buried 38 of our men yesterday and we have 83 wounded making in all about 121 casualties. It is the sharpest thing we have had yet and I should not be surprised if it would be the last. However, time will tell.

The steamer came up last night and I heard that Mercer was much better and likely to do well.

However, Captain Mercer lay there all night, resting his poor mangled head on the lifeless body of one of his brave gunners. He lived but three short days, dying at Queen's Redoubt on 25 November, aged 38, with his wife by his side. He had written her a note: " … they ordered me to storm the place, sword in hand, and my poor servant was killed by my side …".

General Cameron then ordered an assault by Captain Mayne of H.M.S. *Eclipse* with 90 sailors armed with rifles and cutlasses. Because the Maoris were firing from behind parapets and the soldiers could not get in, it was felt that a naval party, without rifles should attack. Once more they were thrown back, and dead and dying men lay in the ditch and ground in front of it. A few reached the top of the parapet. Midshipman Watkins was one of them; he fell back into the trench with a bullet through his head. Commander Mayne was severely wounded in the left hip. When this assault was also repelled, Commander Phillimore of the *Curacoa* and a party of seamen charged up the ditch and threw hand grenades into the redoubt. This attack also proved unsuccessful.

The officer commanding the Royal Engineers, Colonel Mould (William Temple's father-in-law) proposed mining, which was attempted before daybreak the next morning; but the fuse was damp, and refused to explode. They then advanced under cover, and affected a breach in the wall. On realising that their position was no longer tenable, the Maoris hoisted a white flag, and surrendered at dawn. It has been stated that the reason for the surrender was the lack of powder to continue the defence. The loss of the Maoris was about 45 killed, while the British losses amounted to six officers killed or died of wounds, and nine wounded; 40 men killed, and 80 wounded. William Thompson, the great chief of the rebellion, had escaped, with most of his followers. One hundred and three defenders had surrendered. The prisoners of war were escorted to the native church near the river; they were afterwards taken down the Waikato in the *Pioneer* and marched to Auckland.

The Royal Artillery at Rangiriri consisted of Captain Mercer (killed), Lieutenant Pickard, Assistant Surgeon Temple, 4 sergeants, 1 trumpeter, 46 men (3 killed – Martin, Culverwell, Kevan; 2 wounded), 54 in all. The official report in the Gazette of 30 November 1863 gives a total of 861 of the force marched up under General Cameron, but this does not include the men of the 40th who came up in boats (about 417).

Soon after the surrender, a large force of Maoris was seen near Paetai, on the south side of the Rangiriri stream. They were a body of reinforcements but they eventually retired to Ngaruawahia.

The command of the artillery devolved to Brevet Major Strover, of the 12th Brigade, R.A. The guns remained at Rangiriri for about six weeks, and the men were employed assisting the engineers making redoubts, landing places etc, and afterwards in making a road through a swamp on the right bank of the Waikato.

After more detailed reports of the battle had reached Auckland, serious criticisms of General Cameron arose in respect of his ordering Captain Mercer and his artillerymen from their guns into the Maori entrenchment – a hopeless position.

THE HIGHEST AWARD FOR BRAVERY

For his part at Rangiriri, William Temple was mentioned in Despatches from Lieutenant General Sir Duncan Cameron K.C.B. – Commanding the Forces in the Australian Colonies and in New Zealand – on 26 November 1863 as follows:

> Where the Royal Artillery displayed great daring and intrepidity in the assault on the Central redoubt. The enemy kept up a deadly fire through a narrow opening in the parapet of the redoubt, and prevented the wounded who were lying close to the work from being removed, amongst them Captain Mercer R.A. Assistant Surgeon Temple here performed an act of courage and devotion to his duty worthy of record, by passing this opening for the purpose of attending to the wounded, although the extreme danger of his doing so was pointed out to him; every man but one (Lieutenant Pickard) who had previously attempted to cross having been killed or wounded.

He was again mentioned in Despatches on 19 February 1864 (*London Gazette* 22821 p.772) and received the New Zealand Medal 1860–66.

He was, more importantly, recommended for the Victoria Cross, which was in the *London Gazette* 22896 on 23 September 1864, page 4552;

The citation read:

> Royal Artillery …
>   Assistant Surgeon William TEMPLE and Lieutenant Arthur Frederick PICKARD,
> Royal Artillery. Date of Acts of Bravery, November 20th, 1863.

For gallant conduct during the assault on the enemy's position at Rangiriri, in New Zealand, on the 20th November last, in exposing their lives to imminent danger, in crossing the entrance of the Maori keep, at a point upon which the enemy had concentrated their fire, with a view to render assistance to the wounded, and more especially to the late Captain Mercer, of the Royal Artillery. Lieutenant Pickard, it is stated, crossed, and recrossed the parapet, to procure water for the wounded, when none of the men could be induced to perform this service, the space over which he traversed being exposed to a cross-fire; and testimony is borne to the calmness displayed by him, and Assistant-Surgeon Temple, under the trying circumstances in which they were placed.

He was decorated with the V.C. by Lieutenant General Sir Duncan A. Cameron KCB at Albert Barracks, Auckland, New Zealand, on 31 December 1864. Also decorated on this occasion was W. G. N. Manley. A newspaper article reported the event as follows:

Victoria Crosses were presented to Assistant-surgeons MANLEY and TEMPLE, Royal Artillery, on Saturday last, in presence of the whole of the troops, in garrison, consisting of the Royal Artillery, Royal Engineers, Military Train and 14th Regiment. Precisely at 5 o'clock p.m. Lieut.-General Sir Duncan Cameron, K.C.B., rode into the Barrack-square, accompanied by his staff and heads of departments, and was received by the troops, who were drawn up in line, with a general salute. Upon a brief inspection the line was broke up, and three sides of a square formed, the General and his staff being in the centre. Assistant-surgeons Manley and Temple were called forward, when Colonel Carey read a letter from the Secretary of State for War, which contained instructions to the General as to the manner in which the decorations were to be presented, also setting forth the high estimation in which the Cross should be held by all ranks in her Majesty's service. He then read extracts from the London Gazette, which stated the acts of bravery for which the honours had been awarded: Dr. Manley, for volunteering to accompanying the storming party at the attack on the Gate

Pa, on the 29th April last, and assisting the late Commander out of the pa after he was mortally wounded, also stated to have been the last man to leave the pa after the repulse of the troops. Dr. Temple, for his gallant conduct at Rangiriri, on the 20th November last, in crossing and recrossing several times a point where the enemy had concentrated his fire, for the purpose of carrying water to the wounded, and to dress their wounds, but more especially for the manner in which he risked his life in crossing to the assistance of the late Captain Mercer, who was lying mortally wounded, having been shot down while crossing the point in question.

The General, in a few words, expressed his sense of their gallantry, and referred to Inspector-General of Hospitals Dr. MOUAT C.B., V.C., the head of the medical department in this island, who had earned in the Crimea the much prized distinction that he now had the pleasure

Temple's V.C. and New Zealand Medal

of conferring upon them. Three cheers for the officers, three for Manley and Temple, and three hearty ones for the General having been given, the troops were marched to their private parades and dismissed. A large number of spectators were on the ground, and were entertained by the fine band of the 14th Regiment playing some of their very best selections after the ceremony terminated.

There was some misguided concern by Sir Edward Lugard, the Permanent Under Secretary, that the award of the Victoria Cross was being cheapened, as indicated in the following extract from Michael Crook's book *The Evolution of the Victoria Cross*:

> For those who accepted the thinking that had led to the institution of the Cross, a quite different issue arose to exercise their minds. This was that the new award might be cheapened. This fear seems to have been very present with Sir Edward Lugard, the PUS at the time of the disturbances in New Zealand in the 1860s. When the award of the Cross to Leading Seaman Odgers was cited by the CO of the 65th Regiment as grounds for conferring the decoration on L/Cpl Ficrook 'as being the first man who entered the far more stubbornly defended position of Mahoetahi', Lugard's comment to the Secretary of State, Lord Herbert, who concurred with it, was 'I do not see sufficient grounds for granting the distinction – indeed the practice of giving it on every petty occasion lowers the character of the decoration'. This view was expressed in February 1861; three years later, in putting forward five further VC recommendations, again rising from events in New Zealand, Lugard's note to the new Secretary of State, Lord de Grey, in August 1864, read 'Approve? According to precedent these Officers and men are entitled to the Cross – but I regret to say it is losing its value in the Army, being looked upon in the light of a medal from the Royal Humane Society, instead of a reward for heroic bravery, in leading a forlorn hope, or other daring act, leading to important Military results.'

It may be of some interest to mention that the recommendations in question were in respect of Lieutenant Pickard, Assistant Surgeon Temple, Ensign Down, Drummer Stagpoole and Assistant Surgeon Manley, and all did in fact receive the Cross. In the following March he was expressing very similar views to Lord de Grey on the case of Major Heaphy:

> The Victoria Cross, I regret to say, is not what it was originally intended to be, owing to the extraordinary recommendations made by the Horse Guards for it in cases where a Humane Society Medal would have been appropriate …

THE END OF THE WAR

The defeat of the Maoris at Rangiriri opened up the route to the Waikato and was virtually the end of the war. The path to Tawhio's capital of Ngaruawhia lay open to the British forces and was duly captured on 9 December 1863. The British occupied the site of the Maori King's headquarters on the point between the confluence of the Waikato and Waipa Rivers, and established a small shipyard, a redoubt and a storage depot.

At the end of the month guns at Rangiriri were taken to pieces and embarked on board flat-bottomed boats, which took them to Rahuipokeka, about eight miles up the river. Here they were disembarked and taken up by steamer to Ngaruawhia, about 15 miles further up the Waikato, where the gunners spent time building bridges over creeks, and in foraging parties. Mounted artillery under Lieutenant Rait, R.A., also arrived in Ngaruawhia. Maori forces had withdrawn further south, leaving four months of fighting still ahead for the British before the Waikato was in their hands.

The guns were again dismantled around 24 January 1864 and sent up river by steamer. The gunners marched, and at Whata-Whata, about 12 miles from Ngaruawhia, the guns were landed and reassembled. On 27 January, three 12-pounders, each drawn by six bullocks, headed for Te Rore, about 12 miles south. They took two days to reach their destination. The ground was difficult, with narrow paths, and hurriedly made roads. At about 6 p.m. on the second day, the guns reached a creek about 30 feet wide, with soft low banks. Again the guns were dismantled and taken across a canoe, which acted as a bridge. They were then reassembled and taken on about three miles to the camp.

On 27 January, Colonel Williams, R.A., arrived to take command of the Royal Artillery in New Zealand. He arrived at Te Rore, where the headquarters of the army were posted, on the night of 28 January, and appointed Lieutenant Pickard acting adjutant. At dawn the previous day the field force had begun to advance overland. It numbered 2,183 personnel, supported by three 6-pounder Armstrong guns and 121 horsemen of the Royal Artillery, Colonial Defence forces and volunteer cavalry.

Grey offered peace on condition that all land and arms be surrendered. The terms were rejected and the Maori forces fell back to their third line of defence, which protected their key agricultural area at Rangioawhia, near Te Awamutu. Women and children had been sent there to escape the worst areas of fighting. On 21 February a night march was made to Rangioawhia, where an engagement took place the following day. Colonel Nixon's cavalry galloped into the camp surprising the remaining inhabitants. Twelve Maori died that morning, a further 12 taken prisoner, and 33 women and children detained. Colonel Nixon was also killed. The native entrenchments were taken by the 50th Regiment. While the natives were running in all directions to escape, they were charged by a mounted corps of Royal Artillery, under Lieutenant Rait, R.A. They did much damage, but one driver and one horse were killed, and three or four men and horses, including Lieutenant Rait's horse, were wounded during the charge. After the engagement, laden with food and loot, Cameron's forces withdrew to Te Awamutu.

The three 12-pounders of "C" Battery were sent on to Te Awamutu (two miles from Rangioawhia) from Te Rore, and one was placed in each redoubt built there. During the stay of the regiments at Te Awamutu, medical officers, including William Temple, served the garrison. Cameron had selected Te Awamutu, site of the Church Mission Society's mission station, as his frontier headquarters and winter camp. Within the triangle formed by the redoubts, buildings were erected or commandeered for the general staff, commissariat, artillery and engineers, as well as for a post office, bakery and general hospital. At its peak in 1864, some 4,000 military personnel lived there.

The natives now retired to Maungatautari, on the Waikato River, where they built strong entrenchments on a range of hills. The works were more formidable than any yet constructed, but by the beginning of April 1864, a reconnoitring party discovered that the position had been abandoned.

This was partly due to a heavy defeat the Maoris had suffered at Orakau, near Rangioawhia at the end of March, where they had withstood several British assaults. With a strength of little over 300 men, little food, water or ammunition, the Maoris built a small camp here. Brigadier General Carey, who was in command of the force at Te Awamutu, took all available manpower (1,200 troops) and marched on Orakau. They surrounded the Maoris one night, and after two assaults had failed, used a six-pounder to breach the palisade. One hundred hand grenades had been sent in boxes on pack ponies and they proved very useful. Sergeant Angus McKay of "C" Battery threw the hand grenades at great personal risk to himself, where they caused much damage. At 3.30 p.m. the Maoris made a daring escape, rushing out through a circle of troops which was less strongly guarded than the rest. They lost about half their number as they escaped into the swamps, creeks and ravines. The British hunted down and killed many of those who escaped, including women and the wounded. Lieutenant Rait led the mounted company of artillery drivers, who suffered few casualties. So, Orakau was taken on 2 April, 1864. Of the 300 Maoris, at least 160 died. Seventeen British soldiers were killed, and 52 wounded.

About the end of April, orders were received to send all the ordnance to Auckland, whence they proceeded to Taranaki where operations were now to be carried on. While this was happening, intelligence was received from Tauranga, a settlement on the east coast. This required the guns intended for Taranaki to be sent to Tauranga as quickly as possible. All was ready by 28 April. The Maori encampment was reconnoitred on 27 April. It was known as Gate Pa. Batteries were constructed during the night of 28 and morning of 29 April, while the 68th Regiment was sent round by a swamp on the right flank to prevent escape in that direction.

The batteries opened fire soon after daybreak, with hardly a shot being returned. After much shelling, an assault was ordered. The storming party consisted of the 43rd Regiment and the Royal Navy. As they arrived within shot of the breach made by the artillery, the Maoris opened fire. The storming party was eventually forced to retreat. By daybreak on the morning of 30 April, it was found that the natives had left during the night. It was discovered that the Maoris had been firing from underground pits almost completely covered by roofs of flax and earth. This made attacking them very difficult.

The 10-inch mortars and 32-pounder howitzers arrived at Tauranga by sea from Auckland a few days later. They were re-embarked at the end of May and taken back to Auckland.

The last occasion artillery was in action was at an engagement at Te Ranga, a few miles inland from Tauranga and Gate Pa. This occurred in June, where several rounds were fired during the attack and at the retreating Maoris afterwards. The troops were commanded by Colonel Greer, 68th Regiment.

By October 1865, the troops, mainly 65th, were withdrawn from the Waikato and Queen's Redoubt was evacuated. In the same month, the British troops still in New Zealand until affairs had quietened down started to leave for home. The 65th left that month and in April 1866 and at one or two monthly intervals after that, the other soldiers gradually left. With Maori resistance effectively eliminated, the government fixed the confiscation line, making the Punio River the frontier. The Crown confiscated virtually all of the Waikato heartland north of the Punio River, some 1.2 million acres: of this, 225,000 acres being designated native reserves and some 50,000 acres being returned to the tribes. About 150,000 acres were subdivided for military settlements and allocated to soldiers who had fought in the campaign.

Artillery Group with Temple on left

AFTER THE WAR

The regiment continued in New Zealand and William Temple and Anne attended the Military Race Ball in September 1864, as did Colonel and the Misses Mould.

Assistant Surgeon William Temple was based in Auckland and attended several Coroner's Inquests. In September 1864, he was called to give evidence at the inquest on the body of Sergeant Stewart, of the Royal Artillery, who was found dead in a gully behind the Albert Barracks on Saturday 3 September.

The inquest was held at the Wynyard Hotel before the Coroner T. M. Philson Esq. In his examination William Temple stated:

> I am an assistant-surgeon in the Royal Artillery, and am stationed at Auckland. I have no record that the deceased was ever on the sick list since he came out from England in March, 1861. This morning, at ten o'clock I was informed that he had been found dead. I went to the dead-house and saw his body. His clothes were wet and covered with mud. I did not observe any blood or marks of violence. I think he had been dead about twelve hours before I last saw him. At the desire of the jury I have now made a post mortem examination of his body – his head and neck were swollen and discoloured, but free from bruises and fractures. I found no marks of violence on the trunk or limbs … I think that death was occasioned by suffocation.

It was reported that the gully was about three to four feet from the surface where the deceased fell. The sides of the gully were "very precipitous and likely to cause considerable danger to persons walking there at night". The deceased was about 33 years old and left a widow and two children. The verdict was: "Found dead from suffocation in a gully situated between the Albert Barracks and Barrack Street, on Saturday September 3rd instant".

He was also involved in the case of Sarah Richards, who was supposed to have committed suicide by throwing herself into a well at the Albert Barracks in May 1865. This case was heard at the Wynyard Hotel before Mr Philson on 3 May.

Giving evidence on the 33-year-old married lady, Assistant Surgeon Temple reported:

> I was called to visit deceased about nine o'clock on Tuesday night. She was supposed to have jumped into the well. I saw the body brought up about 20 minutes after I got to the well. It was taken to the female hospital. She appeared to have been drowned. There was no pulse or respiration. There was a slight appearance of froth about the mouth and nostrils. I discovered no bruises; no bones were broken. I treated her by Dr. Marshall Hall's plan to restore respiration for an hour but without success. I think deceased was stunned by the fall, and never rose to the surface. She died from drowning. I have known deceased for two or three years. She was of intemperate habits. She was ill on Sunday last and came to me, when she smelt of drink. She had a swelled face from a bad tooth. She was not labouring under delirium tremens when I saw her last. I never suspected her to be of unsound mind. Her husband, on Monday, asked me to try and get her into the lunatic asylum, but I said I could not certify, as I had not seen anything to convince me she was insane.

The jury returned the following verdict:

> That deceased, not being of sound mind, lunatic and distracted, through the abuse of strong drink, on the 2nd May did drown herself in the large well in Albert Barracks. The jury earnestly call the attention of the military authorities to the open and unprotected state of the well aforesaid, into which a soldier some years ago fell and was drowned.

At the end of August 1865, a Ball was given by the non-commissioned officers and men of the Royal Engineers in a large room in the Albert Barracks, as a mark of respect to Major and Mrs Mould, preparatory to them leaving for England. The Ball was attended by Major and Mrs Mould, Colonel Mould C.B., the Misses Mould, Dr Temple and others. The band of the 14th Regiment provided the music for dancing into the early hours of the following morning.

On 18 April 1866, William Temple left Auckland for London on board the *Silver Eagle*. The captain was John Ross and she carried a cargo of kauri gum and jute. She cleared Cape Horn on 7 May and crossed the line on 1 June. She experienced unusually light easterly winds through the whole area of the south-east and north-east trades; from the Western Islands to the Channel north-east and east winds, with dense fogs. She arrived in London on 1 July. Also on board was the headquarters and six companies of the 43rd Regiment of Light Infantry, 390 men, 26 women, and 38 children, under the command of Lieutenant Colonel F. H. Synge, with "Assistant Surgeon Temple (wife and child), of the Royal Artillery, in medical charge". (Their first child Annie Georgina was born in Auckland on 18 August 1863.)

Temple spent some time in Ireland where his daughter Elizabeth Alice was born on 6 August 1866 and baptised at Monaghan. He was transferred to Medical Staff in June 1867. It was announced in the *London Gazette* 23267, dated 25 June 1867, that he had been transferred from the Royal Artillery to the Medical Staff to be Staff Assistant Surgeon. Just prior to this, he attended a Dinner held on 24 May 1867 in Willis's Rooms, King Street, St. James's, London. This was attended by all New Zealand officers now in the United Kingdom, with General Cameron presiding.

It was announced in October 1867 that he was to be Surgeon, Army Medical Department, attached to Woolwich Arsenal, from 1 November 1868. Here three more children were born – Mabel Eva (born 26 November 1868), Ethel Kate Murphy (born 25 September 1870) and William Arthur Mould (born 14 June 1872).

It was in 1861 that the first military hospital was established in Woolwich in the Royal Artillery Garrison Hospital. The Royal Herbert Hospital, Woolwich opened on 1 November 1865 and the first patients were transferred from the old Garrison Hospital within the Royal Artillery at Woolwich. From as early as 1727 the artillery appointed its own medical officers. This led to the establishment of a separate medical department with its own surgeon general. In the 1800s, a medical officer known as the Regimental Surgeon, with a warrant officer as his assistant surgeon was appointed to each regiment, which also provided a hospital. This regimental basis of appointment for Medical Officers continued until it was abolished in 1873. The Royal Army Medical Corps was established in 1898.

In 1871, the family were living in Woolwich at the Royal Arsenal. They had Mary Eveleigh, a Nurse; Charlotte Pager, Housemaid and Ann Simmons, Cook living with them.

On 18 October 1873, Temple was promoted Surgeon Major, based in Portsmouth, in charge of the Station Hospital at Portsea. This was a Military Hospital in Lion Terrace.

He then spent five years in Bengal from 19 December 1873 until 5 April 1879, with the Army Medical Department. Sometime before 1878, he served in Kashmir. Here, Reginald Cecil Temple was born on 13 August 1877 and his brother Bertram Henry Temple the following day. William returned home to serve in Southsea on 6 April 1879, where Frank Valiant Temple was born on 17 August 1879. The last of the children, Eleanor was born in 1880. The family is listed in the 1881 census as living at "Moray House". Waverley Grove, Portsea, Hants. William and Anne were living with their nine children from 9 months to 17 years in age. William's father-in-law lived at 2 Eastern Villas Road nearby. He stayed here until 21 September 1881, before returning to Bengal the following day. He was now a Lieutenant Colonel and returned as Secretary to the Surgeon General of the Indian Army Medical Services. On 10 April 1885, he was appointed Brigade Surgeon, and was very well spoken of by G.O.C. Rawalpindi Division. From 1886 to 1889, he was Honorary Surgeon to His Excellency the Viceroy in recognition of his services to India. He served on the Viceroy's Personal Medical Staff. His address in 1886 was Allan Bank, Simla. In 1858, the administration of India was transferred from the Honourable East India Company to the British Crown. From that date, the Head of the British administration in India had the title of Viceroy. This time William stayed in India for seven years until 28 March 1889. He retired on 1 November 1889.

In the 1891 census, his wife Anne was living with her brother in law, Edward Byrne, a retired Civil Engineer at 8 Cavendish Road, Portsea and in the Scotland Census William was living at 6 Teviot Place, McGhie Street, Hamilton with eldest daughter Annie G, now aged 27, and the four youngest children – Bertram, Reginald, Frank and Eleanor, all aged between 10 and 13.

However, by the 1901 census, William and Anne were living at 74 Alleyn Road, Dulwich. By now William was 67, his wife 10 years younger. Living with them was Annie Georgina, and Bertram Henry. *Who Was Who* listed his Recreations as: "takes an interest in photography, mechanical work, field sports etc". He had been among the earliest generation of photographers in New Zealand. His photos are retained in the Turnbull War Memorial Library in Wellington.

His wife Anne died on 9 January 1914, aged 70 at 7 South Parade, Southsea. She was buried on 13 January in Highland Road

Lieutenant Colonel Temple V.C.

Cemetery. William died on 13 February 1919 aged 85, after a long illness. He died at the home of his youngest daughter, Eleanor, Funchal, 4 Madeira Park, Tunbridge Wells, Kent. She lived here from 1914, when she bought the house from a Mrs. Smith, until 1929. She had married Arthur Thompson, a Colonel in the Gurkhas in 1902. William died from hypostatic pneumonia of five-days' duration, haemorrhage from the kidneys of two years duration and old age. His eldest daughter, Annie Georgina, was present at the death. His body was taken from Madeira Park to Portsmouth, where he was buried in the family grave with his wife. This is in Highland Road Cemetery, Southsea, Hants, Grave No. A. North wall, Row 12, Grave 31. He is one of nine V.C.s buried there. His estate had a gross value of £3,704 with net perpetuity of £3,651. He left his Victoria Cross, medals, family portraits, and certain silver and jewellery to his daughter. The medals together with his sword, military chest, iron chest, hat and gun are still in family hands in Northumberland, and 4 Madeira Park, Tunbridge Wells has been turned into apartments.

FAMILY MATTERS

William and Anne had nine children who survived out of 12 in all. Three died young – Beatrice, Amy and George. Elizabeth (Bessie) Temple married Major Hickman, Indian Army, and had six children. Mabel Eva Temple married Lieutenant Colonel Gerhart L'Honneux Sanders (then a Second Lieutenant). When he asked William Temple's permission to marry her, the ageing Colonel, all braid and waxed moustaches, expressed his consent by declaring "better for her to be your widow than my unwed daughter!"

Ethel Kate Morphy Temple married Lieutenant David Beames of the Indian Army in 1886 aged 17. She later emigrated to Canada with him to farm and had four sons. They were the inspiration for a play by Rudyard Kipling.

4 Madeira Park, Tunbridge Wells

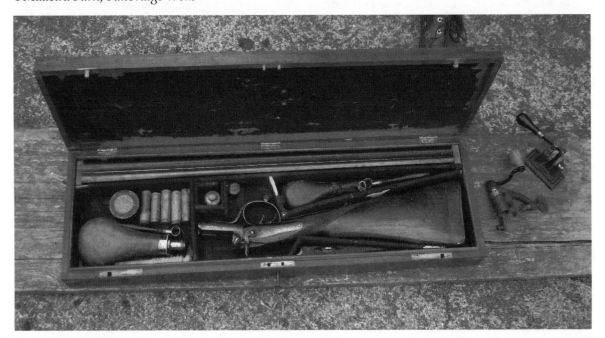

Temple's Shotgun

    William Arthur Mould Temple was commissioned in July 1893 and served as a captain in the 1st Battalion the Gloucestershire Regiment. He had been a prisoner of war in the Boer War, being captured at Farquhar's Farm on 30 October 1899 and later released. He married Rhoda Mary Hebe Hazleden and they had one daughter, Hazel Temple. He was wounded in the right lung at Koekuit, near Langemarck, Belgium on 21 October 1914 and died the next day at Poperinghe, No. 4 Clearing

Mabel Temple's Wedding. William Temple stands on the extreme right next to his wife

Hospital, aged 42. He was buried at Lijssenhoek Military Cemetery, Poperinghe.

Reginald Cecil Temple was born on 13 August 1877 at a tented Military Camp in Kashmir. He was first educated at Portsmouth Grammar School and joined the Royal Military College, Sandhurst on 1 September 1895. He became a Brevet Lieutenant Colonel in the Royal Marines Artillery during World War One. He later rose to be a Lieutenant General of the Royal Marines, Commander of the Bath (1923), O.B.E. (1919), and Chevalier Legion d'Honneur(1919). He also earned the Mons Star, Victory in Europe Medal, WW1 Medal, and in World War Two, the Defence Medal for Home Service with the L.D.V. (Home Guard) and the A.R.P. He was educated secondly at Dulwich College and entered the Royal Marine Artillery in 1895. In 1920, he married Zillah Edith Henderson (née Hunt). Reginald and Zillah had two sons. He became Assistant Adjutant General, Royal Marines, Eastney 1921–25, Colonel Commandant Depot Royal Marines, Deal 1925–27; Major General 1927; and Lieutenant General 1929. He was Royal

General Reginald Temple

Marine A.D.C. to King George V in 1926 and retired in 1930. He was awarded a pension for good and meritorious service. He died on 30 May 1959 at Fareham and was cremated. His wife died in Fareham on 5 February 1972.

Bertram Henry Temple was born in Kashmir and educated at Dulwich College. He was a Brevet Lieutenant Colonel in the Royal Marine Light Infantry, as was his brother Frank in the same regiment. He married Sarah Cecilia Rose, eldest daughter of Captain Hugo Beaumont Burnaby R.N. on 20 June 1905. They emigrated to Canada and he died in Vancouver, possibly of T.B. She died in 1924.

Frank Valiant Temple was educated at Portsmouth Grammar School and at Dulwich. Joining the Royal Marines Light Infantry on 1 September 1897, he became a Brevet Colonel and Temporary Brigadier General in the Royal Marines Light Infantry. In 1906, he married Evelyn Ellen daughter of James Fear Evans of Trouville, France, and they had one daughter – Betty Temple. He served in the First World War 1914–19, being awarded a C.M.G. on 3 June 1919. He was Paymaster at Chatham and retired in 1934. His address was 10 Tower Gardens, Hythe, Kent. He died on 3 April 1937.

MEMORIALS

William Temple's name is on the V.C. Roll of Honour at the Union Jack Club, Sandell Street, Waterloo, London SE1 8UJ.

* * * * *

A picture recording his V.C. action and portrait are in the Army Medical Directorate Officers Mess, Camberley, Surrey. They were transferred from the Victoria Cross Room, The Royal Army Medical Corps Headquarter Mess, Millbank when the site closed.

* * * * *

There is a Temple Way named after him in High Brooms, Tunbridge Wells, Kent.

* * * * *

A red and gold leaved tree is dedicated to William and 28 other members of the Royal Army Medical Corps at The National Memorial Arboretum, Alrewas, Staffordshire. His tree has a small red plaque dedicated to his V.C. at Rangiriri.

* * * * *

His name was on the Memorial Board at the Royal Artillery Chapel at Woolwich, which is no longer there.

* * * * *

Temple's Grave, Southsea

CHAPTER FOUR

⚘

A Gurkha Life –
The Story of Lieutenant John Duncan Grant 1877–1967

FOREWORD

Richard Snow has assiduously undertaken the task of documenting the lives of Tunbridge Wells V.C.s and I am naturally very proud that Lieutenant John Duncan Grant or "Uncle Jack" as he was known to us should be included among their number.

For a man of such outstanding valour, he was, in civilian life, extraordinarily kind and gentle and although I was only a small boy when I met him, this still left a deep impression on me. I remember the touching letter that he wrote thanking me for a Christmas card that I had made him at the age of six. The handwriting in the letter was very shaky but the sentiments were warm and heartfelt. I was terribly sad when he died a few weeks later and am only sorry that I no longer have in my possession this precious memento of him.

Like Lieutenant John Duncan Grant, I too went to Cheltenham College and had daily lessons in a classroom named after him (all old Cheltenham V.C.s shared this distinction). His portrait hung there too but I rather think the significance of all this was lost on me. He had been to Cheltenham some 80 years before me, but this did not prevent the headmaster unforgettably saying to me, "I hope you take after your uncle, my boy". It did not seem an unusual thing to say and sadly for both me and the headmaster I did not come close to following in his illustrious footsteps. I do not believe that many did.

Michael Turkheim
Great nephew of John Duncan Grant

INDIAN BEGINNINGS

John Duncan Grant was born on Friday 28 December 1877 in Roorkee, United Provinces, India. Roorkee was a significant station for the Royal Engineers who had their college there.

His father was Colonel Suene Grant who was a Royal Engineer. He was born on 23 March 1851 and like John attended Cheltenham College. He was first commissioned as a Lieutenant on 2 August 1871. He married Caroline Elizabeth Napper, who was born in India on 25 August 1851. Suene was posted to India where he served as Executive Engineer 4th Grade at the Department of Public Works, Military Works Branch. He was promoted Captain on 2 August 1883; Major on 3 November 1881; Lieutenant Colonel on 31 December 1896; and Colonel on 31 December 1900 and served as Chief Engineer of Sir Alfred Gaselee's Command in India. He was placed on half-pay on 31 December 1901, having completed five years as a Regimental Lieutenant Colonel.

Suene Grant

John's sister Eileen was born in India on 5 October 1889. By this time John had been sent to school in England. The 1901 census shows Suene and Caroline living with Eileen at 5 Jevington Gardens, Eastbourne. He retired on 23 March 1908, with an Indian Pension. By 1910, he had moved to 'Brinnington', King Edward Road, Minehead, Somerset where he lived until his death in 1919, aged 68.

Meanwhile John went to Manor House School, Hastings around 1886. Manor House was a Preparatory School in St. Mary's Terrace, Hastings. He left in 1890, joining the Junior Department in Teighmore House (Lower 4J) at Cheltenham College in May of that year. When he moved to the senior school he was in Cheltondale Boarding House, which has since been demolished. He was then in the Military Department of the School, which prepared boys for a career in the army. In his last term he was in the Upper Sixth and came 16 in his class of 24 (19 in mathematical subjects). He did not play in any of the College sports teams but he played hockey and rugby for his house in 1894 and 1895. He left in December 1895.

He then went on to attend the Royal Military Academy, Sandhurst in August 1896. At that time his father was a Major. John's rate of contribution was £40, which was a reduced annual fee as he was the son of an officer. There is no record of his achievements there. He was commissioned as a Second Lieutenant on 22 January 1898, and put on the Unattached List for promotion to the Indian Staff Corps, where he was assigned in 1899.

A Staff Corps for the Bengal, Madras and Bombay Armies (i.e. the Indian Army) had been set up in 1861. This was to provide officers for the native regiments, and for the staff and army departments. The Staff Corps was usually the prelude to a lifetime career in the Indian Army. In 1903, in order to avoid confusion the designation "Indian Staff Corps" as applied to officers on regimental duty was withdrawn and replaced by the more appropriate term "Indian Army".

On 23 March 1899, he joined the 30th (Punjab) Regiment of Bengal Infantry. On 22 April 1900, he was promoted Lieutenant. On 11 August, he transferred to 44th Gurkha (Rifle) Regiment of Bengal Infantry, which was renamed the 44th Gurkha Rifles in 1901. Between 1901 and 1906

Cheltondale Hockey Team 1894 (Grant sitting front, far left)

Gurkha Regiments were renumbered from 1–10 and redesignated as "Gurkha Rifles". So the 44th changed to 8th Gurkha Rifles in 1902 and 1st/8th Gurkha Rifles in 1907.

TIBET 1904

The Tibetan borders had been a cause of tension between Tibet and Britain since the 1880s. The Tibetans were unable to accept the two agreements between China, their nominal overlords, and Britain, which were concluded in 1890 and 1893. Letters from the Viceroy, Lord Curzon sent to the Dalai Lama in 1900 and 1901 had been ignored. Britain was concerned that the Russians might enter Tibet to influence the North East Frontier. This would provide Russia with a direct route to British India and break the chain of semi-independent, mountainous buffer-states which separated India from the empires to the north.

In July 1903, a commercial mission with a military escort consisting of 500 troops, under Colonel Francis Younghusband, was sent to negotiate with the Chinese and Tibetans at Khamba Jong, a tiny Tibetan village north of Sikkim. However, by November no Chinese or Tibetan delegates had arrived. The latter refused to co-operate and Colonel Younghusband withdrew to Siliguri, in Darjeeling District, where, after approval from London, a major force assembled, from 9 November 1903, with the intention of advancing to Gyantse, some 200 miles from Lhasa, and enforcing Tibetan co-operation. The 8th Gurkha Rifles, reinforced by three British Officers and two Gurkha Officers of 7th Gurkha Rifles were mobilized for service, and assembled at Siliguri on 20 November.

The force was fewer than 3,000 men strong, mostly Indian and Gurkha troops who would be used to the terrain, with some British Gunners, four companies of Royal Fusiliers and Maxim gun sections from the Norfolk Regiment and Royal Irish Rifles. Its transport column included thousands of coollies, as well as mules, bullocks, camels, buffaloes, ponies and yaks. It also had two zebrules – half donkey, half zebra – which were on 'troop-trials' and found to be useless, and at times used sheep as pack animals.

Amongst this expeditionary force drawn from the 8th Gurkhas and Royal Fusiliers was Lieutenant Grant. There were six companies of Gurkhas who were, on this occasion, to become

Gurkha cavalry. The men were not well versed in riding and kept falling off their horses. To make it easier they were given small packhorses rather than proper cavalry mounts so that they did not have so far to fall. The bridles did not fit and the girths were too long. Eventually some decent tackle was acquired, and a batch of more suitable horses were delivered. The men were given plenty of time to practice.

Tibet's government, guided by the Dalai Lama was understandably unhappy about the presence of a large acquisitive foreign power dispatching a military mission, and began marshalling its armed forces. They were fully aware that no help could be expected from the Chinese government, and so intended to use their arduous terrain and mountain-trained army to stop the British advance.

The British Army which left Gnatong in Sikkim on 11 December 1903, was well prepared for the coming conflict due to the lengthy time experienced in Indian border wars. The Chumbi Valley was the initial objective, which was achieved by 20 December after crossing the 134,500 ft. Jelap La Pass. Chumbi was occupied on the 15th and a flying column was despatched to take Phari Jong at the head of the valley. A garrison of 8th Gurkha Rifles was left there, commanded by Major G. R. Row. The remainder returned to Chumbi. The British were commanded by Brigadier General J. R. Macdonald. They then stopped for the winter in the border country, using the time to train the troops.

The Tibetan Army at this time was about 16,000 strong, together with able-bodied monks. They used swords, bows and arrows, matchlocks, and several thousand rifles.

The next three months were spent collecting supplies and trying to improve the roads with the entire force enduring the effects of high altitude and dreadful climatic conditions. Fifty degrees of frost was quite normal. On 24 March 1904, the advance commenced. A blizzard struck a supply column, causing 70 cases of snow blindness and the Gurkhas went 36 hours without food. It was so cold that rifle bolts froze in the breeches. Over 50 miles were covered before the first major obstacle at the pass of Guru, near Lake Bhan Tso, on 31 March. There are various versions of what happened here.

One version suggests a force of some 2,000 Tibetans blocked the way and refused to retire or surrender. Their General rode to meet Younghusband and Macdonald. However, he displayed his inexperience by not fortifying the western side of the pass, leaving his soldiers there exposed in plain view of his opponents. He hoped there would be no bloodshed, and appears to have ordered his men to extinguish the fuses on their muskets, the relighting of which is a lengthy and difficult operation. Macdonald would not accept the warnings of the Tibetan General and dispatched Sikh and Gurkha soldiers to disarm the Tibetan forces, who were unable to resist the advance due to their extinguished fuses, but still refused to surrender their arms. British accounts say that a brawl developed, and the Tibetan General became angry and shot a Sikh soldier in the face rather than give up his pistol. This prompted a violent response from the soldier's comrades which rapidly escalated the situation. The Tibetan account differs by claiming that the British tricked the General into extinguishing his troop's fuses and that once this was done the British opened fire first anyway.

A more authoritative version tells us that the Tibetans mustered a large army at Guru, a few miles beyond the Mission Camp at Tuna, which threatened to attack the Mission if it did not withdraw to Yatang. Every week the Tibetan camp was strengthened by new arrivals of armed men, until in March the Tibetan force numbered about 5,000 warriors, half of whom now blocked the road to Gyantse, and the other, a few miles off, the road to Lhasa.

On approaching the Tibetans no shots were fired. They were forcibly ejected from their entrenchments. On nearing the walls of Guru their leader (the Depon) rode out and told the British his men had orders not to fire, and that Macdonald and the Mission could approach Guru. As several Tibetans were seen fingering their loaded matchlocks Macdonald deemed it necessary to take their weapons off them and proceeded to do so. However, as the latter struggled to retain them, their leaders encouraged them to resist. The fuses on their matchlocks were already lit, and things looked threatening. Then a shot was fired. The angry Depon and some of his men were arguing with some

Sikh sepoys. When the Sikhs began to seize the loaded muskets, the Tibetans hustled the sepoys and began throwing stones at them. The Lhasa General then rushed forward and pulled a musket away from a Sikh and fired a revolver at him, blowing away his jaw. As soon as the shot was fired, as it was a signal for attack, the Tibetans shouted and fired point-blank, while others charged with their swords drawn. The British officers fired their revolvers back.

Within seconds, the sepoys began to retaliate. Under cover they fired into the enemy, which with the quick-firing Maxims, mowed down the Tibetans in a few minutes. Those that survived broke and fled.

Either way, the battle did not last long. It was all over in about ten minutes. Once disarmed, the Tibetans attempted to retreat, but became entangled with each other and the steep landscape. They were so close together that they were unable either to use their swords or to fire. The Sikh and Gurkha regiments fired on them, together with the British-manned Maxim guns. Despite this withering attack, the Tibetan forces fell back in good order holding off cavalry pursuit at bayonet point. A stand was made by some of them in Guru village, which was shelled and assaulted by the 8th Gurkha Rifles in fine style. Half a mile from the battlefield, the Tibetans reached shelter and were allowed to withdraw. Behind them, they left between 500 and 600 fatalities and 168 wounded. Their General was amongst the dead, and the whole of his personal escort, as well as five high-ranking Lhasa officials were killed. British losses were 12, including the unfortunate Sikh who had been shot in the face. Besides these, two or three officers and a number of men received bruises from the flat edge of the Tibetan swords. Some of the officers (including Major Dunlop) were wounded as well as Mr Edward Candler, the *Daily Mail* correspondent, who was unarmed. He received no fewer than 12 wounds.

Macdonald's troops attempted to pass through the fortified Lamdang or Red Idol Gorge on 9 April. On the 10th, the 8th Gurkha Rifles, commanded by Major G. R. Row, by a turning movement, outflanked a very strong position. The Gurkhas were ordered to scale the steep hillsides of the gorge and drive out the Tibetans, who were hiding high on the cliffs. This they began, but were soon lost in a blizzard, which cut off all communications. It was a long arduous climb by the 8th Gurkhas which enabled the 32nd Pioneers to be sent into the gorge. Several hours' later troops going into the pass were fired on until the storm lifted around noon. The Tibetans used 20 leather cannons. By then the Gurkhas had found their way to a position above the Tibetan troops, who were facing fire from both sides as Sikh soldiers moved up the hill. The Sikhs stormed the Tibetan position, killing many, though the officers restrained the men. The Tibetans retreated after fighting fanatically at close quarters. They came under intense fire from British artillery and retreated in good order, leaving behind 500 casualties. British losses were few. When the Tibetans fled, the Gurkhas found a large number of peasants hiding in caves in terror. They were assured that no harm would come to them.

The next day the British forces reached Gyantse, and the jong or fort was handed over without opposition. The jong was strongly built on a rock 600 feet high, in the middle of a richly cultivated plain. It was not occupied, however, as its water supply was outside and the perimeter inconveniently large for the occupation force. This consisted of six companies of infantry, including a double company of 8th Gurkha Rifles, two 7-pounder guns, 50 Mounted Infantry, and two Maxims – all under the command of Lieutenant Colonel Brander, 32nd Sikh Pioneers. The entrance gate of the jong was demolished, and the Mission occupied the hamlet of Chunglu, 1,500 yards from the fort. The main body returned to Chumbi and Phari, leaving a double company.

At the end of April, the Tibetans attempted to cut communications with Chumbi but were defeated at Karola by a force from Gyantse. Colonel Brander decided to attack a strong force of Tibetans established on the Karola, some 46 miles distant on the main road to Lhasa. Leaving 160 men at Gyantse as Mission escort, he marched with the remainder on 3 May. The enemy were strongly entrenched in well-constructed trenches. The 8th Gurkhas, under Major Row and Lieutenant Coleridge, had to climb 2,000 feet in driving snow. As soon as the flank was turned, the Tibetans vacated their position, which they had stubbornly held, and fled. They lost around 450 out of 3,000 men, many of whom were armed with breech-loading rifles, effective to 1,100 yards. The company of the 8th, in fighting at an altitude of over 18,000 feet above sea-level, probably hold the record for an action fought at such a height on foot.

The *New York Times* for 11 May 1904, states:

> Two English rifles were recaptured, one of which had been lost by Lieutenant Grant at Phari some months ago. It is noteworthy that superior arms and ammunition manufactured at Lhasa are being used by the enemy. The manufacture is rough but effective, and the range is about 1,000 yards.

At dawn on 5 May, the post at Gyantse was attacked by 800 Tibetans. A few succeeded in penetrating the enclosure, but they were repulsed with some 250 Tibetans killed or wounded. They had travelled some 50 miles, believing that practically the whole of the British escort had moved away on the 3rd. One young Gurkha recruit, Jitbahadur Gurung, who had six month's service, was acting as a gate sentry when he was set upon by 12 men. He defended himself so well that the enemy retreated, leaving three men dead. British losses were very small but several Mission servants were brutally murdered that night in Gyantse.

The *New York Times* for 11 May again states:

> The story of the attempted surprise on the morning of the 5th is most dramatic. The Tibetans actually gained the walls of the compounds. Their shouting betrayed their intention just in time for the defenders to take their positions, otherwise no doubt large numbers of the enemy would have surmounted the defences and the indiscriminate slaughter of those inside would have followed. The sick men in hospital insisted upon joining in the fighting, and the mission servants were valuable both in defense of the walls and the subsequent chase of the enemy.

Colonel Brander returned on 9 May. The jong had been occupied by a strong force of the enemy, who kept up a constant fire on the post. The *New York Times* states:

> The present situation is interesting. The Tibetans have strongly fortified Jong and open fire upon everyone approaching the town. Some hundreds have taken refuge in the monastery, which is strongly defended by Sangars, whence they have opened fire upon our troops. Persons of importance arrive daily at Jong, and Lhasa sends conscripts from monasteries and villages in a wide radius.

On 17 May, the Tibetans occupied a house about 500 yards from the mission post, and from here opened a vigorous fire. Two days later the 8th Gurkhas double company and two companies of the 32nd Pioneers assaulted and captured the house, afterwards known as "Gurkha Post". The capture of Tagu and Palla villages followed, the 8th again being engaged. Palla was important, for in the final stages of the assault on the jong, this village, about 800 yards south-east of the jong, was to be the starting place for the assault.

During this time, the main force at Chumbi was reinforced and prepared to advance. Tibetans were informed that if they did not start negotiations at Gyantse by 25 June the British would march on Lhasa, and on 12 June the main force moved out of Chumbi. They reached Kangma without incident on 22nd and halted a day while Colonel Hogge dispersed a force of 1,000 Tibetans who were holding a sangared position on the road which runs down from the Karola. The only incident of the march was a stand made by the enemy at a monastery named Niani, about four miles from Gyantse. The monastery was very strong, surrounded by a 40-foot high wall, which was eight-foot thick, with only two entrances. It was held by 800 Tibetans. The fight lasted from 10.00 a.m. to

2.00 p.m. but, after an assault by Pioneers, it surrendered with some 200 enemy casualties. The Mission escort co-operated in the assault from the east. Colonel Brander from Gyantse assisted by occupying the hills above the village. On 26 June, General Macdonald reached Gyantse with a column, and they were ineffectually bombarded from the Jong. The Mission post was relieved. With this column were two double companies of the 8th Gurkhas which had been left behind.

The *New York Times* for 6 July, stated that:

> The Tibetans obstinately held the villages, fighting with the ferocity of wild-cats caught in a trap. The initial assault was delivered by the Second Mounted Infantry and the 40th Pathans, who were later reinforced by the 23rd Pioneers. The Tibetans held their fire till the British troops were within a few hundred yards of them, but were unable to check the onward rush of the Pathans.
>
> The Tibetan houses and monasteries are full of small rooms and cellars, so that fighting took place in cellars in pitch darkness. Some of the Pathan officers discovered that the enemy would blaze off their rifles and matchlocks as soon as a doorway or trapdoor was darkened. They accordingly pushed their helmets in front of them, and the men did the same with their turbans, afterward rushing in immediately the Tibetans had fired. Finally after some assistance from shell fire, the Pathans and Mounted Infantry captured the monastery and villages on the right, Colonel Brander's party shooting down from the hills above a few Tibetans who fled. Meanwhile the 23rd Pioneers were engaged in clearing the villages on the left, where the resistance offered was just as obstinate. The Tibetans refused to leave the small houses, despite the fact that the British brought up guns and shelled them at a range of 300 yards.

Macdonald's intention now was to take the main Tibetan stronghold at Gyantse Jong. Once this was taken, the road to Lhasa would be opened. It overlooked British supply routes making it the primary target for Macdonald's army. Operations to clear the Gyantse valley of the enemy were commenced on 28 June. The Tibetans now concentrated on Tsechen Monastery, a very strong position at the end of a very steep hill. At 5 p.m. the 8th Gurkhas, 40th Pathans, 1st Sappers and Miners, well supported by guns of 7 Mounted Battery, R.G.A. succeeded in taking the stronghold. The Tibetans fought well, holding their ground until they were driven out at bayonet point. The capture of this position much disheartened the Tibetans. Communications between Gyantse Jong and Shigatse were cut off, and the Jong was now surrounded on three sides. British losses were minimal, but Captain Bliss, 8th Gurkha Rifles was wounded.

The enemy, concentrated around Gyantse Jong, was estimated at 6,000 strong, and they sent in a flag of truce. After futile negotiations hostilities were suspended until noon on 5 July. At 1.45 p.m. General Macdonald renewed rifle fire on the jong. He proposed to draw the Tibetan soldiers away from the walls of Gyantse Jong for several days before a siege. At 3.30 p.m. two guns, six companies of infantry, and one company of mounted infantry, were sent to make a feint on the monastery side of the jong. An artillery bombardment would create a breach which could then be stormed by the main force. Gurkha troops took several batteries in the vicinity by climbing vertical cliffs under fire, a feat they achieved. Some houses at the foot of the hill were occupied, held until dark, and left with fires burning. By 5 July the armistice had expired at noon, the enemy had been cleared and they were ready to assault the jong the following day. Shortly after midnight a force of twelve guns, twelve companies of infantry, one company of mounted infantry, and half a company of Sappers moved out in two columns to take up a position south east of Gyantse.

THE STORMING OF GYANTSE JONG

After negotiations broke down, the main attack on the jong was ordered for the morning of 6 July. Younghusband reported that:

The fortress to be attacked from our little post in the plain looked impregnable. It was built of solid masonry on a precipitous rock rising sheer out of the plain. It was held by at least double, and possibly treble, our own force, and they were armed, many hundreds of them, with Lhasa-made rifles, which carried over 1000 yards. In addition there were several guns mounted.

The main attack was carried out in two phases. The first of these involved the capture of the houses at the eastern foot of the hill. Three columns were then organised into two. The right-hand column was under Colonel Campbell of the 40th Pathans, and that on the left under Major Murray, 8th Gurkhas. This left column was composed of one double company 8th Gurkhas and one of Pioneers. At 3.30 a.m. these columns started from Palla Village (some 800 yards south east). The sky was clear, and the moonlight lit the advance for the enemy, who opened fire at about 300 yards. As soon as it was light the troops were able to find their way through the intricate mass of houses, and by 8 a.m. that part of the town south-west of the jong was taken.

The troops began to make good their position in the area thus won, but the real business had yet to be accomplished. The jong, with 5,000 or 6,000 Tibetans inside it, still had to be assaulted. During the morning the troops rested. At about 2 p.m. General Campbell, who was in charge of all the advanced troops in the town, sent back word to General Macdonald, who was in Palla Village, recommending that an assault should be made on the extreme east of the jong. To him, in his advanced position, immediately under the walls, it appeared that if our guns could make a breach in the wall itself an assault could be made. It would mean that the storming party would have a stiff, hazardous climb over the steepest part of the rock. General Macdonald agreed with this especially as the Tibetans now seemed exhausted and ordered the assault to be made at once.

At 3 p.m. General Macdonald ordered forward four companies of the reserve, directing the 10-pounder guns to concentrate their fire on the portion of the wall to be breached for the assault. This caused the Tibetans to redouble their fire, which was matched by our troops. The 10-pounder battery under Major Fuller did magnificent work. They were only 1000 yards from the point to be breached, and were able to place one shell after another in exactly the same spot. Heavy fire was directed at a point at the extreme east of the jong, 160 feet above the plain. The rampart slowly crumpled under the constant barrage of shells and bullets, the wind blowing away fragments of splintered stone creating a thick haze. Gradually the wall came tumbling down. A larger and larger gap was made, and by 4 p.m. a breach large enough for an assault had been achieved. The explosion of a magazine of Tibetan gunpowder helped in the operation, which must have killed many in the jong.

The heliograph flashed from post to post to signal the final assault. Major Fuller gave the order for rapid firing on the upper buildings. Maxim guns from three different directions rattled away. Then a small cluster of black figures, increasing in numbers, was seen, like a swarm of ants, making its way up the precipitous rock towards the breach. A cheer went up from all directions. The Tibetans were still firing and hurling down stones, causing our troops to redouble their fire.

This was phase two of the assault. Two companies (one double company) of the 8th and one company of the Royal Fusiliers had formed part of the general reserve behind Palla Village, and were detailed to make the final assault. The companies of the 8th were 'E' and 'C'. With 'E' Company were Major Baldwin, commanding, Lieutenants Grant and Humphreys. With 'C' were Captain G.L.S. Ward and Captain Bliss.

Lieutenant Grant and some of the leading men reached the foot of the breach. Very gradually he and the Gurkhas made their way up. First a few arrived under the breach, then more and more. Grant was seen leading his men straight for the opening. At that moment bugles rang out the 'cease-fire', so as not to place the storming party in any danger. The

Tibetans, too, stopped firing, leading to a silence. The Gurkhas and the Royal Fusiliers, who formed the storming party, streamed through the breach. They worked up from building to building. The advance had to be made in more or less single file, as the entrance was narrow and rocky. They had to crawl on hands and knees to the breach in the curtain. Hurled back more than once by stones, Lieutenant Grant and Havildar Karbir Pun, both wounded, succeeded in forcing an entrance. Showers of rock and stone were being hurled down by the Tibetans. As they neared the top, Lieutenant Grant fell back wounded. Havildar Pun fell down the rock some thirty feet. In spite of their injuries, they again attempted to scale the breach, and, with the aid of covering fire from the men below, successfully reached the top, where the Havildar shot one of the enemy. Grant was the first through, with the faithful Karbir Pun at his heels, their rifles clearing a path for them as they scrambled inside the jong. They were then followed by more officers and men. At last the troops were seen placing a Union Jack on the highest pinnacle of the jong. The Tibetans had fled and the jong was captured by 6 p.m. The success of the assault was largely due to Lieutenant Grant and Havildar Pun.

The *Pioneer* Newspaper of 8 July reported:

There is no more stirring story in the annals of Indian frontier warfare than that of the capture of Gyantse Fort, held by seven thousand Tibetans by a handful of British and Indian soldiers. The excitement of a long day culminated in a scaling of a breach in the walls of the jong by Lieutenant Grant, 8th Gurkhas, followed by a mixed company of Gurkhas and Fusiliers. We watched with bated breath these heroic men climb the cleft in the rock in the face of a hail of fire and torrents of stones hurled

Storming the Jong

on their heads by the frantic Tibetans. A stone struck Lieutenant Grant and swept him off his feet, one thought to certain death below, but he recovered himself wonderfully, and was the first man over the breach. As I write at dusk the battle is not quite over: one still hears fitful outbursts of musketry, but the jong is ours.

The same newspaper reported on 20 July from a despatch of 8th July:

Even a whole day after the event one writes under stress of a deep emotion. As on the triumphant evening so now, so many hours after the brain finds some difficulty in tracing incidents in their proper sequence. Our troops rolled out to the attack at two in the morning, and when the sun was setting blazing red against a dust storm gathering in the east the jong was won. Gurkhas and Fusiliers were cheering on the topmost tower. That is the supreme and ultimate fact which emerges out of the excitement of the day. Then wondering how the feat was accomplished, the picture of Grant and his Gurkhas, with our British Tommies hard at their heels, flashes vivid into the memory. From towers on right and left and beyond

Tibetan bullets were hurled into the cleft up which our soldiers were clinging and climbing. A persistent avalanche of stones was poured down upon them. Men swept off their feet were caught and held up by their comrades, and so the sinuous khaki line won its stubborn way to the breach and up to the tower on the pinnacle. And when the fight was won and we counted our losses another wonder! Only 37 men hit! There were numbers of others with bruises, with blood streaming over their faces and clothes from cuts with stones and scrapes from bullets, but only 37 are shown in the hospital return. One can only conceive that the sheer luck which has ever followed the British arms was with us in the taking of the jong.

The assaulting party was given twenty minutes breathing space under cover of the villages we held, and then that grim climb against death began. We could see the Tibetans running down from the upper towers and manning the sangars below. One of their chief powder magazines had blown up a short time before, but they were not dismayed. Our guns poured shrapnel into them over the heads of the climbing troops, but their riflemen stuck persistently to their loopholes while a special party rolled stones down the cleft, nor did the general bolt begin till the heroic Grant had scrambled over the breach. It was thus we won the jong.

In his account of the assault dated 28 February 1948, written for Colonel Huxford's *History of the 8th Gurkha Rifles 1824–1949* (Gale and Polden, 1952), Grant writes from memory and a few rather sketchy Diary entries, and two letters written the next day and early in August:

At 8p.m. on the 5th we returned to camp after having a demonstration to the west of the Jong and the Monastery.

At 11.30 the same evening we were off again to PALLA village, some 700 to 800 yards east of the Jong.

The three columns detailed for storming the houses at the foot of the Jong hill started off at 3.30 a.m. and had succeeded in their tasks well before midday. The left column was under Major Murray and I think Coleridge was with him. Subadar Major Kabiraj Karki's party actually got some fifty feet up the bare rock above the houses and near the Main Gate. They held on for two hours till 2 p.m. when they were recalled by General Macdonald.

E and C Companies and a Royal Fusilier company were detailed to carry out the final assault. Baldwin commanding E having no Company Officer, Humphreys, the Adjutant, and myself, the Quarter Master were attached. Ward commanding C had Bliss with him. It was decided that I was to go with the leading section, Humphries with the next and Baldwin with his two remaining sections. The Fusilier Company and C Company to be in immediate support.

At 2.30 p.m. we started off to cover the 600 yards or so to the houses captured by the right columns in the morning. We were greeted by missiles from the Jong jingals but only one man was hit.

On arrival at the cover of the houses we were met by Colonel Campbell, 40th Pathans commanding the attack and the ubiquitous Sheppard R.E., who proceeded to guide us through the houses and to break down some closed and barred doors to facilitate our exit. 'Bubble' or 'Squeak' under Luke, R.A., did a little enlarging of the breach already made in the curtain some 150 to 200 feet above us. All this final preparation took about half an hour. Sheppard wished us 'good luck'.

On emerging from the flat roofed houses we had to go up a very steep and stony slope and the Tibetans at once started heaving down rocks and stones. They also fired some Lhasa made Martinis. We were well covered by the fire of the Mountain Guns, but, unfortunately, we came into some of our own Machine Gun covering fire. Baldwin was shot clean through the calf though he did not realise it til he took his putties off in camp. So like 'Poor Old

Baldwin' as he would soliloquise! Some of the men, too, were hit by small bore bullets. I had an 'in and out' just behind the knee – a mere scratch.

Advancing up a just perceptible spur running down from northeasternmost bastion possibly better cover from fire and certainly somewhat better footing was obtained than in the shallow re-entrant straight below the breach where the shale and the rubble was a veritable moving landslide. We had to move up more or less in single file and a man knocked down or slipping was likely to take his 'follower' with him. It was on this spur that my orderly had his thigh badly smashed by a rock thrown from the bastion.

We had to get across to our left and it was then that E Company, under a very unpleasant shower of rocks and stones and, I think, a few of the small bore bullets referred to above, was temporarily held up a short way below the breach. However, with the arrival of about half of C Company and the cessation of our own distant covering fire the final successful bid was made, with the remainder of C and the Fusiliers in close support.

Quarter Master Havildar Karbir Pun, who had been wounded and had taken several tosses like many of us, was first in, shooting a Tibetan as he got level with the top of the breach. The remainder bolted but a lot, I was subsequently told, were accounted for in the buildings higher up.

Subadar Nawalsing, E Company set a very fine example throughout and the men too were grand.

The following is an entry in My Diary for 6 July:

Took up reserve position behind Palla bagh and village – remained behind village till 3.30 p.m. Attacking columns get home about 9 a.m. Shelling jong till about 3.30 p.m. E & C coys advance across maidan from Palla to villages (taken in morning at foot of jong hill) – after half hrs wait E Coy advanced on to breach. Casualties here 1 killed and 13 wounded including Baldwin, self, Nawalsing, Karbir Pun Al – whole of jong taken. G.O.C.'s congratulations to regt.

And on 10 October when back in Gyantse from Lhasa:

Hear Kabiraj, Nawalsing, Karbir, Jangir (Rana? I can't decipher) and Karkabir have got Order of Merit all for the Jong Day. First/ admitted to/ two 2nd Class. If the last two were with E Coy or C Coy on the 6th I must plead the passage of years (44 and a half) for not remembering. Also I am more than ashamed to have forgotten the name of my orderly (Ranbahadur?) who stuck to me like a leech till he was knocked out.

As there were clearly going to be no negotiations, despite the British victory, the advance on Lhasa started on 10 July and was unopposed. Younghusband took nearly 2,000 soldiers, including six companies of the 8th Gurkha Rifles: all those who were not needed to protect the road back to Sikkim. Lieutenant Grant was also involved. They crossed several fortified ambush points without incident. They had to traverse the Tsangpo River in native boats and ferry barges. They arrived in the Capital on 3 August, becoming the first Europeans, apart from a few missionaries and pilgrims, to visit the Tibetan capital. They discovered that the Dalai Lama and all the Tibetan officials had fled. Instead, Younghusband met the Chinese resident official, who escorted them into the City with his personal guard. Younghusband was at last able to negotiate and the Tibetans agreed to recognise the 1890 and 1893 agreements and not to enter into negotiations with foreign powers without British permission.

The British Mission left Lhasa on 23 September 1904, after a ceremonial presentation of gifts. Captured Tibetans were released without condition. In just six months the British had achieved all their objectives, losing just 202 men in action, and 411 to other causes. The Tibetans must have lost several thousand during 16 major and minor actions, including two battles.

By 15 November, the Gurkhas reached Shillong. The 8th were congratulated as they were involved in every action along the way. They received a splendid reception on return to Shillong, the Headquarters Station since 1867. The 1/8th celebrates 6 July as Gyantse Day.

A VICTORIA CROSS AND A WEDDING

John Duncan Grant was mentioned in Despatches on 13 December 1904, and awarded the V.C. in the *London Gazette* 27758, p.574, on 24 January 1905. In addition, Havildar Karbir Pun was recommended for the Indian Order of Merit, First Class (GO 957, 1904). "The Havildar really led", Grant modestly recalled 50 years later. However, it was not until 1911 that native officers and men became eligible for the supreme award of valour, which is why he received a lesser honour.

The Victoria Cross was the last one gazetted before the First World War, being the 522nd Cross won. (There was an interval of peace for exactly ten years before the next Victoria Cross was gained.) It was recommended by Lieutenant Colonel M. A. Kerr, Commanding Officer, 8th Gurkha Rifles and by Brigadier J. R. L. Macdonald, CB, RE, Officer Commanding the Tibet Mission Escort, who witnessed the deed.

The Citation reads as follows:

> On the occasion of the storming of the Gyantse Jong on 6 July, 1904, the storming Company, headed by Lieutenant Grant, on emerging from the cover of the village, had to advance up a bare, almost precipitous, rock-face, with little or no cover available, and under a heavy fire from the curtain, flanking towers on both sides of the curtain, and higher buildings higher up the Jong. Showers of rocks and stones were at the time being hurled down the hillside by the enemy from above. One man could only go up at a time, crawling on hands and knees, to the breach in the curtain.
>
> Lieutenant Grant, followed by Havildar Karbir Pun, 8th Gurkha Rifles, at once attempted to scale it, but on reaching near the top he was wounded, and hurled back, as was also the Havildar, who fell down the rock some thirty feet.
>
> Regardless of their injuries they again attempted to scale the breach, and, covered by the fire of the men below, were successful in their object, the Havildar shooting one of the enemy on gaining the top. The successful issue of the assault was very greatly due to the splendid example shown by Lieutenant Grant and Havildar Karbir Pun.
>
> The latter has been recommended for the Indian Order of Merit.

John Duncan Grant in 1905

Lieutenant Grant was presented with the V.C. by His Majesty, King Edward V11 at Buckingham Palace on 24 July 1905.

He then lived at 38 Drayton Gardens, London, S.W.10 and on 19 January 1907 married Kathleen Mary Freyer at All Saint's Church, Margaret Street, London. Kathleen had been born in India on 24 July 1884, and her father was a surgeon at the time of the wedding. On the Marriage Certificate it lists Lieutenant Grant's residence as the Bentinck Hotel, Margaret Street and Kathleen's as 27 Harley Street (her father's house).

John and Kathleen went on to have two children, Hugh Duncan Grant born 3 June 1908, and Madeline Grant who was born at Raniket, Upper Provinces, India on 28 May 1911. Hugh also went to Cheltenham College from 1922–1926. A School Testimonial for him stated that "he ended as a House Prefect, then going abroad to study French with a view to the Consular Service, via the 'Varsity'. A Sound and reliable fellow, who means business and has plenty of sense". He died in March 1988 and Madeline in March 1994.

Madeline Grant Passport Photo

Three days after the wedding on 22 January, he attained his captaincy. In 1908, he attended the Staff College at Quetta, Pakistan, passing out the following year. It had been difficult and expensive for British officers to return to England to attend the Staff College at Sandhurst, so Kitchener established a new one at Quetta. John Grant was appointed Staff Captain Bareilly Brigade/ Meerut Division on 9 February 1910. He then took leave from March to November 1910.

THE WAR YEARS

From 1910, the movements of John Duncan Grant do not follow those of the 8th Gurkha Rifles. From 8 November until 10 June 1911, he was appointed Staff Captain, India. He then became Brigade Major, 5th (Jhelum) Brigade, 2nd Rawalpindi Division from 11 June until 2 October, before being appointed General Staff Officer, 3rd Grade, New Zealand Military Forces between 3 October 1911 and 1 October 1914.

In October 1914, the Brigade was mobilised, and in November John went to Egypt joining the 11th Indian Division in December. Here he joined what was known as Expeditionary Force E, which consisted originally of only the Lucknow Brigade, but eventually became responsible for all Indian Forces in the Near East.

On 1 September 1915, John was appointed Brevet Major, and from 30 November until 13 January 1916, he served with the Indian Expeditionary Force in the Persian Gulf. He was appointed as Brigade Major, 35th Brigade/ 7th (Meerut) Division in Mesopotamia. The 7th Division landed at Basra on 31 December 1915, under Major General Sir George Younghusband, newly arrived from France. They were substantially reorganised, and took part in the attempt to relieve the besieged garrison of Kut al Amara.

Following the British defeat at the Battle of Ctesiphon in November 1915, and the humiliating withdrawal of troops to Kut al Amara, British Commander Sir Charles Townshend (heading the 6th Poona Division) found himself besieged by some 10,500 Turkish forces on 7 December.

So, he sent out urgent appeals for reinforcements. The regional British Commander-in-Chief Sir John Nixon assembled a relief force under General Aylmer, boosted by the arrival of three new Indian infantry divisions. They were hastily sent to the British forward base of Ali Gharbi, some 200 kilometres upriver from Nixon's Basra H.Q.

Aylmer set off with 19,000 troops, 46 guns, three monitors and two aircraft on 4 January 1916. They took the title of the Tigris Corps. His path was blocked by 22,500 Turkish troops and 72 guns under Commander Nur-Ud-Din at Sheikh Sa'ad, 15 km upriver from Ali Garbi and 32 km from Kut. On 6 January, Aylmer's forces launched an initial attack, which was repelled by the Turks, resulting in heavy British losses, another attack the following day also failed. The 7th was a humid day with thick mist following heavy rain. Without heavy artillery, the British were ordered again to attack entrenched positions. The attacking infantry were hit by concentrated crossfire. As they moved forward into heavy firing, the Turks counter-attacked and attempted to encircle on the right. The small British field artillery fought this danger off. By nightfall, the position remained stalemate. When they attacked again on the night of 8/9 January Aylmer was surprised to discover the Turkish trenches unoccupied. The Turkish forces had withdrawn overnight for reasons unknown. Since Nur-Ud-Din could not justify his decision to retreat he was summarily dismissed and replaced by Khalil Pasha.

Exhausted and dispirited, the British had suffered some 4,000 casualties during the engagement for no significant gain. Underequipped Field Ambulances struggled to cope – the Meerut Division had capacity to cope with 250 casualties, but there were thousands. More than 1,000 wounded men were still lying out in the open, eleven days after the fighting.

In January 1916, days were hot, foggy and humid and night was below freezing. It was a season of heavy rain, the ground was a quagmire and rivers were swollen. At dawn on 13 January, there was a thick mist. The Turkish Army now set up new and stronger defences along the banks of the Wadi River, about six miles upstream from Kut, through which the British would have to pass in order to reach Kut. This was a good defensive position, as it lay in front of a narrow strip of land called the Hanna Defile that lay between the river and the marshes.

Aylmer planned to surround the Turks, sending troops around to secure the area immediately behind the Turkish lines while simultaneously attacking with artillery from the front. The attack began in the early afternoon of the 13th, after being cancelled in the morning because of thick mist and a slow advance by artillery across the river. Meeting little opposition, at least at first, British infantry advanced in thin numbers: so thin indeed that in many places the British advanced directly past Turkish posts, exposing themselves to withering fire from behind. They had lost the intended element of surprise. Forced to deal with the unusual circumstances of having to defend from behind, the British advance rapidly slowed. Now aware of British plans Khalil's force swiftly redeployed from a north-south facing position to east-west to avoid being outflanked. By the time the attack was called off at the end of the day, his troops had gained control of the Wadi, and the Turks retained command of the Hanna Defile. The advance was small and 1,600 men were killed or wounded, including John Grant who was wounded.

The repulse of the British had given Khalil Pasha renewed confidence. Aylmer still needed to defeat the Turks to relieve Townshend. So on 16 January he launched a fresh attack at the Battle of Hanna. The attack began with an advance by 4,000 troops of 7th Division, preceded by short artillery bombardments at noon on 20 January and on the next morning. The only effect of this weak bombardment of 12,000 rounds was to warn Khalil of the forthcoming attack. As a consequence of this around 60 per cent of the attacking British force – advancing through a no man's land in 600 yards of water – was cut down by machine-guns and no ground was gained.

Intending to resume the attack the next day, General Aylmer called off the operations once he realised the critical condition of his force's injured and sick. The failed attack had resulted in a further 2,700 British casualties. Aylmer now realised the impossibility of the task to relieve Townshend. His force of less than 10,000 men was now outnumbered by at least five-to-one in the area. He was however ordered by new regional Commander-in-Chief, Sir Percival Lake, to try again at the Battle of Dujaila.

Trench warfare continued throughout February as the flooding season approached. Aylmer then devised a plan to cross the Tigris for a straightforward attack upon the Dujaila Redoubt, which held some 25,000 experienced troops, many of whom had fought at Gallipoli as well as along the Tigris. He wanted to await reinforcements from Gallipoli, but was overruled by Lake, who was wary of delaying while the floods increased in strength.

Aylmer ordered the bulk of his two divisions to march overnight in preparation for storming the Redoubt. In the meantime, Townshend was to attack Turkish forces from behind. The attack was put back from March 6 to 8 because of heavy rain. General Kemball led the main advance at 10.00 a.m. and by noon he was stopped around 700 metres short of the Redoubt. General Keary followed up with a second attack but missed a good opportunity to breach weakened areas of the Turkish line. Townshend decided to call off his planned attack from Kut once he realised that the morning's operation had failed.

Thereafter the attack fizzled out with the consequence that the British forces gained no ground having suffered a further 3,500 casualties. The Turks had lost 1200. Because of this latest failure Aylmer was recalled and replaced by George Gorringe on 12 March. One final attempt was made at the First Battle of Kut the following month. With its failure the fate of the garrison at Kut was sealed.

It was not until 29 April 1916, after nearly five months under siege that Townshend finally submitted, along with 10,000 of his men, in the largest single surrender of British troops up to that time. The garrison was practically starving, and most were, physically, in a dreadful condition. The British won back Kut in February 1917, on their way to the capture of Baghdad the following month.

John Duncan Grant was promoted to Major (*London Gazette* 5 May 1916) and then General Staff Officer 1, Army H.Q. India at Delhi from 27 June 1916 and was Mentioned in Despatches in the *London Gazette* on 19 October 1916. Some sources say he served in France and Belgium on the Western Front from 15 April to 5 July 1917, and that he was wounded in France. This has not been substantiated. In November 1915 there were only two Indian Cavalry Divisions, 3rd and 4th, in France. They were the only Indian troops there and during April–July 1917, both divisions were in reserve in the Peronne area though individual regiments sent detachments to the front line acting as infantry and they did see action. It is just possible that he visited the front line. He served in Delhi until June 1918.

On 4 June 1918, he was promoted Acting Lieutenant Colonel and Commandant of 3rd Battalion 11th Gurkha Rifles. The 11th Gurkha Rifles were formed in May 1918, with the 3rd Battalion raised at Baghdad on 26 May that year. A letter from his sister Eileen in January 1919 is addressed to Major J. D. Grant V.C., 3/11 Gurkha Rifles, Chaklala, India. She was serving at No. 6 Camp East A.P.0.4, with the British Expeditionary Force, where she had been for six weeks. She refers to him as "Jack" and she says, "I wonder what will happen to you now and if you will go back to the 8th – I suppose you would love to get some leave and come home". However, he went to Afghanistan in 1919 to the Third Afghan War.

The Third Afghan War was begun by Amir Amanullah, who had taken the throne in February 1919 after his father was murdered. He proclaimed a Jihad against Britain, and on 3 May, Afghan troops crossed the Indian border, and occupied Bagh. British Indian troops recaptured it on 11 May, pushing on into Afghanistan, while British bombers attacked Jalalabad and Kabul. Amanullah sued for peace on 31 May, with peace being proclaimed at the Treaty of Rawalpindi on 8 August. This reaffirmed Afghan independence. The treaty ended large British subsidies to the Afghan Government which had helped maintain Afghan neutrality during the First World War.

John Duncan Grant was Mentioned in Despatches on 1 November 1919. An Announcement was made by the India Office on 3 August 1920:

> The names of the undermentioned Officers ... have been brought to notice for distinguished
> service during the operations against AFGHANISTAN by General S.G.C. Monro, G.C.B.,

G.C.S.I., G.C.M.G., in his despatch dated 1st November 1919 (published in the supplement of the 'London Gazette' dated 15th March 1920):-
3rd Battalion, 11th Gurkha Rifles.
        GRANT, Major (Acting Lieutenant-Colonel) J.D., V.C., 2–8th Gurkha Rifles (attached)

Also in the Gazette of India for 10 January 1925, it was stated:

Major (acting LIEUTENANT-COLONEL) (now LIEUTENANT-COLONEL) J.D. GRANT, V.C., D.S.O., 8th Gurkha Rifles, attached, relinquishes his acting rank on ceasing to command a battalion, dated 5th Dec. 1919.

John's portrait by family member, Alice Grant

John standing on right, then William Eltringham (brother-in-law) with Madeline (John's daughter) next to him

AFTER 1920

On Saturday 26 June 1920, John attended the Afternoon Party for Victoria Cross Heroes held by King George V at Buckingham Palace. 324 V.C. recipients attended the Party, where the King was accompanied by the Queen and members of the Royal Family. The V.C. recipients assembled at Wellington Barracks, and marched to the garden of the Palace via Birdcage Walk, Horse Guards Parade and the Mall preceded by the Band of the Welsh Guards. The King inspected the V.C. recipients, who afterwards filed past His Majesty, and had the honour of being presented to the King and Queen.

On 3 August 1920, John was given temporary command of 3rd Battalion 11th Gurkha Rifles (from 2/8th Gurkha Rifles) in Waziristan for nine months. In the remote and rugged region of Waziristan in British India's north-west border with Afghanistan, mountain tribes of independent-minded Muslim fighters gave the British Army a difficult time for decades. The Waziristan Revolt of 1919–20 was sparked by the Afghan invasion of British India in 1919. Though the British quickly defeated the Afghans, the Waziri tribesmen gave colonial forces a very difficult time. Many Waziri tribesmen were veterans of the British-led and controlled Indian Army and used modern military tactics and Lee Enfield Rifles. The fighting lasted for 12 months with aircraft being used to suppress tribesmen in some raids.

On 10 September 1920, John was mentioned in the Gazette of India for his services in Waziristan and his appointment as Lieutenant Colonel from 1 February 1921 was in the Gazette of India on 6 May 1921. He was also appointed Commandant of 1/10th Gurkha Rifles from 21 September 1921, and joined the 1st Battalion at Chaman in Pakistan on the border with Afghanistan, This appointment followed a staff appointment.

In April 1921, John was designated commanding officer of 13th Rajputs but remained with 3/11 Gurkha Rifles. However the Indian Army List for 1 July shows him as 'leave ex India' from 29 June (until February 1922) and the 2nd i/c 13th Rajputs as Acting C.O. It seems unlikely that he took up the appointment, though he is listed under Indian Army lieutenant colonels as 13th Rajputs in April and December 1922. In 1922 the infantry regiments of the British Army were reorganised and all the Rajput regiments (with the exception of the 13th Rajput Infantry, which became the 10th Battalion of the 6th Rajputana Rifles) were amalgamated.

On 23 April 1921, when commanding 11th Gurkha Rifles, John was sent out from Ladha by H.Q. 9th Brigade with reinforcements to assist two convoys which had been attacked by 280 Mahsuds under Mahsud Malik (Musa Khan) near Piazha Raghza. A party from John's detachment, while occupying a hill in the vicinity, was successful in surprising a party of 50 Mahsuds and inflicting considerable casualties on them.

The *London Gazette* 32788, of 19 December 1922 announced the award of the Distinguished Service Order (D.S.O.) as follows:

> The King has been graciously pleased to approve of the undermentioned rewards for distinguished service rendered in the Field with the Waziristan Force, 1920–21. To be dated 23 October, 1921:-
>
> Awarded the Distinguished Service Order:
> Lt.-Col. John Duncan Grant, V.C., 13th Rajputs, I.A.

The Medal was presented on 1 June 1923.

On 28 December 1925, Lieutenant Colonel Grant returned to India, being appointed Assistant Adjutant General at Army H.Q., India until 1928. He was promoted Colonel and Deputy Director of Auxiliary and Territorial Forces (Assistant Adjutant General) India from 29 April 1928 until 1929. From 1920 the Auxiliary Force was the equivalent of the Territorial Army in England.

On 27 March 1929, Colonel Grant was transferred to the unemployed list, and he retired from the army on 4 June that year.

IN RETIREMENT

Colonel Grant is believed to have retired to Brighton and on 3 June 1929 (the day before he retired) received the Most Honourable Order of the Bath (CB) in the Birthday Honours. (*London Gazette* 33501 p. 3688):

> The King has been graciously pleased on the occasion of His Majesty's Birthday, to give orders, for the following promotions in, and appointments to, the Most Honourable Order of the Bath:-
> To be Ordinary Members of the Military Division of the Third Class, or Companions of the Most Honourable Order of the Bath.
> Colonel John Duncan Grant, V.C., D.S.O., Indian Army, Deputy Director, Auxiliary and Territorial Force, India.

John Fishing

On 9 November 1929, John Grant attended the V.C. Dinner in the Royal Gallery at the House of Lords, where he sat at Table 7 Seat 194. When the V.C.s arrived at the Houses of Parliament, the crowds had to be controlled by Cavalry, Mounted Police and Foot Police together with British Legion Stewards. They were met at the House of Lords by Admiral Sir Lionel Halsey – the Prince's Equerry. They next went into the Peers' Gallery and were issued with a menu card. At 8 p.m. it was announced that His Royal Highness the Prince of Wales was waiting to receive the guests, so they moved off in single file to be announced. They then passed into the Royal Gallery. All round the walls were oil paintings of past monarchs and a great archway under which was a huge Victoria Cross made of poppies and leaves by disabled ex-Servicemen.

After the dinner, Lord Jellicoe read an appeal by the British Legion which with the guests consent was to be signed by each V.C. present. This was an urgent appeal for funds to help all ex-servicemen, widows and orphans in distress, and for employers to find employment for 800,000 men who had fought for their country and were still without a job. This was received unanimously. On leaving the Dinner, the Prince presented each V.C. holder with a copy of the new British Legion Book. When the guests left the crowds outside were nearly as large as when they arrived.

On 15 June 1934, Colonel Grant attended the Gurkha Brigade Dinner at the Junior United Services Club, Pall Mall, London. In the same year he was appointed Colonel of the 10th Gurkha Rifles, a post he held until 1947.

On 28 December 1937 and 1938 his sixtieth and sixty-first birthdays were announced in the *Daily Telegraph* Today's Birthday Column.

Colonel Grant served in the London District Home Guard Command. The Home Guard was created in July 1940, from the Local Defence Volunteers, and was not entitled to use military ranks until February 1941.

In his passport issued on 26 June 1946 Colonel Grant is described as being 5ft 9ins tall, grey eyes, red hair and having a scar over his left eye.

In October 1949 His Majesty King George VI was most graciously pleased to approve that the additional title of Princess Mary's Own should in future be included in that of

Passport Photo

the 10th Gurkha Rifles, and that the regiment should henceforth be designated the 10th Princess Mary's Own Gurkha Rifles.

His Majesty approved the affiliation of the Royal Scots and the 10th Princess Mary's Own Gurkha Rifles in announcing Army Order 39 of 1950. At the insistence of H.R.H. the Princess Royal a ceremony to mark the Affiliation was held at Glencorse Barracks, near Edinburgh, on 4 April 1950.

The main part of this ceremony was the handing over of claymores presented by the Royal Scots to the regiment. The claymores were the gifts of Colonel Mackenzie, formerly Colonel of the Royal Scots and Brigadier Money of the Royal Scots. Colonel Mackenzie had been largely instrumental in bringing the long-cherished desire for affiliation to fruition.

In 1950, Colonel Grant attended the Regimental (10th Gurkhas) Luncheon Party in honour of H.R.H. Princess Mary, after the regiment became 'Princess Mary's Own' in London. He sat on Princess Mary's right.

On 26 June 1956, Colonel Grant took part in the Review of Holders of the Victoria Cross by H.M. The Queen in Hyde Park, London. In the "Peterborough" column of the *Daily Telegraph* for 29 June there was a piece headed "Old-Style Taxi Driver":

John with his Sister Eileen

Yesterday morning I was rung up by one of the V.C.s who had been at the Hyde Park Parade. After the parade he took a taxi home to Kensington. When he turned to pay the fare the taxi driver said: 'No, Sir. This is on me. I am an old soldier myself'. I promised not to divulge the V.C.s name, but he allows me to say that he won it as a Gurkha 50 years ago.

In retirement, Colonel Grant was living at 116 Cranmer Court, Sloane Avenue, London, SW3, and he was a member of the United Services Club.

He was also present at the annual dinner of the Gurkha Brigade Association held at the Savoy on 31 October 1960. The King of Nepal was present and he was met by Field Marshall Viscount Slim, President of the Association. It was reported in the *Daily Telegraph* for 1 November that "if Lord Slim was the most distinguished living Gurkha at last night's dinner, he was not the most senior in years.

There was Col. Grant, for instance, now in his 83rd year, who had won the V.C. during the Tibet campaign of 1904".

He missed a ceremony at Sandhurst on 4 May 1962 as he was abroad. That year he also missed the July Dinner of the Victoria Cross and George Cross Association at the Cafe Royal, Regent Street, London for the same reason. However, he was present at the fourth Dinner at the same venue on 16 July 1964.

Colonel Grant died at the Fraserley Nursing Home, 11 and 13 Park Road, Tunbridge Wells, Kent aged 89 on 20 February 1967. It is not known why he came to Tunbridge Wells. His Death

Family photo: Eileen, John's sister on left with her daughter Anne-Marie. John stands on right

Certificate states the cause of death as: a) bronchopneumonia b) cerebral arteriosclerosis and c) senility. He was cremated on 24 February at Tunbridge Wells Crematorium at a private funeral with no flowers and his ashes were thought to have been scattered in the Garden of Remembrance. (Ref 16-32-79.) There was no memorial to him there. The entry (9281) in the Register of Cremation lists his wife Kathleen's address as The Spa Hotel, Tunbridge Wells. It also tells us that the ashes were buried, and that the service was conducted by The Reverend Victor Beaton of St. Marks, Tunbridge Wells. It was reported in the *Daily Telegraph* that he left £5,034 net in his Will published on 13 May 1967. He was the oldest recipient of the Victoria Cross at the time of his death.

In his will dated 24 June 1956 he had requested that no one went into mourning. "I would like as cheap and simple a funeral as possible. No flowers 'by request'. If not cremated no headstone or curb just grass over the grave". With regard to his medals he instructed "should my son predecease my daughter then I would like her to decide what to do with my father's medals, my Uncle Arthur's medals, and my own. She might like to keep mine but here again I would not like them to go from the Grant family. Failing remaining in the family the R.U.S.I. or Cheltenham College might like them".

After he died, his widow Kathleen donated the £25 honorarium given annually to the widows of holders of the Victoria Cross to the Walter Walker Scholarship Fund for Gurkha Children. At some stage she moved into the Lady Mary Nursing Home, 6 Garden Road, Tunbridge Wells. This was a "convalescent, geriatric and medical home, with single rooms only" and had a large garden. It was run from 1970 by Mrs M. Moncur S.R.N. and the address was 6–10 Garden Road. It had previously been a Nursing Home under a Mrs. M. Bye before 1970. Kathleen was there in 1972/3 as evidenced by letters from her at that address. She died on 5 July 1975.

Her entry in the Register of Cremation at the Kent and Sussex Crematorium, Tunbridge Wells lists their son Hugh as living at Flat 3, 14 Hans Crescent, London SW1. The service was again conducted by Mr. Beaton. She is listed as being buried with her husband, but the location is unknown.

The Fraserley Nursing Home no longer exists. The buildings were knocked down and have been replaced by Pegasus Court Retirement Homes. On the opposite side of the road is a wooden seat with a small plaque that reads: "Presented by the Proprietors of FRASERLEY 11 Park Road August 1963".

John's children, as previously mentioned, were Hugh Duncan Grant (born 1908), who died in London in March 1988, and Madeline Bunty Grant (born 1911). At one time she lived at 22 Evelyn Mansions, Carlisle Place, London S.W. 1. She died on 31 March 1994. John's V.C. and medals passed first to his son, Hugh and when he died they were taken to Spink and Son Ltd. for probate valuation in 1988 by Madeline (£10,225), but their whereabouts are at present unknown. His nearest relatives are now Fleur and Michael Turkheim, great niece and great nephew. They tell me that John Duncan Grant was always known as "Uncle Jack".

John's Medal Entitlement was:

Madeline Grant

    V.C.
    C.B.
    D.S.O.
    Tibet Medal (1903–4)
      1 Clasp "Gyantse"
    1914–15 Star.
    British War Medal (1914–20)
    Victory Medal (1914–19)
    India General Service Medal (1908–35)
      3 Clasps:
      "Afghanistan NWF 1919"
      "Mahsud 1919–20"
      "Waziristan 1921–24"
    King G.V1 Coronation Medal (1937)
    QE11 Coronation Medal (1953).

TRIBUTES AND MEMORIALS

On 2 March 1967, D. Ashcroft M.A., Headmaster of Cheltenham College wrote to Hugh, John's son at 116 Cranmer Court in London:

Dear Mr Grant,

We were very sorry indeed, here at College, to read of your Father's death some days ago.

I expect you know that in the Centenary classroom block there are thirteen classrooms, each named after one of the College's V.C.'s. I am also writing because you might not be aware that we have a portrait of your Father; a large one, which was lent to us by him in 1957. It is not something which would readily hang in a private home, but we ought to remind you that we have it in our possession. The name of the artist we have not been able to decipher, and therefore I doubt if it has any great value which would have to be declared. Would you be so good as to let me know, at your convenience, what the family wishes are? We should naturally be very happy to retain it.

I would be glad if you would let your mother know that we have recorded with sadness the passing of a brave Cheltonian, and that we send you both our sympathies.

All the classrooms named after V.C. Winners are in the building still called New Block which was opened in 1939. There used to be a wooden plaque with the name above the door and a framed picture with the citation inside each room. Some of the pictures remain but the plaques have all vanished and the rooms are known mundanely by numbers. Room 7 is Grant's.

Unfortunately, the portrait was stolen from the College together with another that hung beside it some time ago. David Gibson, a local artist, was commissioned to paint copies of them both. The new one hangs outside the Registrar's Office.

John Grant's name is also on the Honours Board at the back of Big Classical, the original College schoolroom which is now used as a theatre. It bears the names of all Old Cheltonian winners of the Victoria Cross and other medals:

> JOHN DUNCAN GRANT
> Lieutenant, 8th Gurkha Rifles
> Gyantse Jong, Tibet, 6th July 1904

* * * * *

Photos of all 14 College V.C.s and a world map showing where the decorations were won is on permanent display in the library (Big Modern) at the College.

* * * * *

There is a Memorial Plaque to John at Quetta Staff College, Pakistan.

* * * * *

His name is on the V.C. Roll of Honour at the Union Jack Club, Sandell Street, Waterloo, London SE1 8UJ.

* * * * *

On 7 July 2009, a plaque was unveiled beneath a cherry tree at the Kent and Sussex Crematorium by Michael Turkheim, great nephew of John Duncan Grant. It is on the grass area to the right just inside the entrance.

The simple ceremony was attended by Michael and Fleur Turkheim; Councillor Leonard Price, the Mayor of Tunbridge Wells; Major Shivu Limbu, Gurkha Major 2RGR; two Gurkha soldiers, Piper and Bugler from the Gurkha Regiment; Ian Beavis from the Tunbridge Wells Museum; various Borough councillors; Keith Hetherington (local historian); Mick Ilston, Registrar from the Crematorium; and the author.

The Plaque at Tunbridge Wells Crematorium

Michael and Fleur Turkheim at the V.C. Grove, Dunorlan Park, Tunbridge Wells

CHAPTER FIVE

Salesman Hero of Ypres –
The Story of Captain Douglas Walter Belcher 1889–1953

FOREWORD

Unfortunately, I do not remember my grandfather before he became ill, so although we visited periodically (and enjoyed his wife's lovely chocolate cake) I never had a conversation with him, so could not claim to know him. We knew some details of his First World War experiences, but not the full story as so meticulously researched by Richard Snow. It has made us search our memories and look again at the reminders from that time – the huge album of newspaper cuttings compiled by a neighbour, the monumental black clock, rose bowl, sword, and illuminated address presented to him, also his framed copy of Kipling's poem "If" and the black metal box in which my mother keeps her bank statements, with "Capt. D. W. Belcher V.C". painted on the lid. All these were earned in those horrific hours with his team in 1915, leading to fame, which he felt undeserved, and yet was probably the highlight of his life. I would like to think that in the same circumstances we would react in the same way. I am sure my late father, Francis would have done.

Virginia Roberts
Granddaughter

FROM BIRTH TO WARING AND GILLOW

Douglas Walter Belcher was born at 2 Park Villas, Arlington Road, Surbiton, Surrey on 15 July 1889. His father was Walter Harry Belcher (born 1857) who married Emily Taylor (born 1853) in Kingston-on-Thames in 1884. His father was a linen draper in business at 101 Brighton Road, Surbiton which he continued for around 20 years retiring around 1912. Douglas had one brother Cecil George Belcher who was born in 1891.

2 Park Villas, Surbiton

Douglas was baptised at St. Andrews Church, Surbiton on 18 August 1889. His early education was in a private school in Brighton Road, kept by a Mrs Burgess. When he was 11 years old he went to Tiffin School, Kingston-on-Thames where he proved an apt pupil. Even at that age, he was keen on playing at soldiers and organising martial displays and expeditions among his school friends.

He was very fit as a youngster and was very keen on rowing, cycling, tennis and cricket. The latter was his favourite sport and he was a popular and valued member of the Surbiton United and Ditton Hill Cricket Clubs. He was a particularly good rifle shot, and a boy chorister at St. Mary's Church, Surbiton.

He was engaged for some time after leaving Tiffin in 1905 in his father's drapery business, and then he was employed as a clerk by J. Randall Porter M.A. of Surbiton. By the time he was 18 he was living at 17 Brighton Road, Surbiton.

He then joined the Antiques Department of Waring and Gillow, Oxford Street, London, English furniture manufacturers who were formed in 1897. Each morning he caught the same train up from Surbiton to Waterloo. He enjoyed shooting on their rifle range.

A customer wrote to the "Weekly Dispatch". while he was there, describing him as a smart young man who described each piece of furniture with a story about its background:

> He seemed to regard each of the antiques in his charge with so much interest and could make them all so attractive to a buyer.
>
> He was, I noticed, of middle height, very erect, obviously muscular, and in the pink of condition and training. Rather an unusual man, I thought, to be selling antique furniture and talking about it 'like a book'. After I had bought a sideboard, the young man led me to his desk on the side of which was a card with his name: Mr D.W. Belcher, in neat print. After he had booked my order I said to him: 'How do you manage to have such a healthy tan and keep yourself in such condition? You look as if you led an outdoor life'.
>
> 'No,' he answered, 'I have been here for three years, and before then I was in the counting house for three years. I get out of doors all I can when I am not working. Every morning I have a bathe in the Thames at Surbiton, where I live, and generally swim across the river and back. But most of my time is spent in the Territorials. I have been in the Queen Victoria's Rifles for eight or nine years, and that all helps to keep me fairly fit'.

TO WAR WITH THE TERRITORIAL FORCE

In 1906, aged 17, Douglas enlisted in the Volunteer Force in the Cyclist Volunteer Corps. He joined the 26th Middlesex (Cyclist) Battalion which was formed in 1888. Various Rifle Volunteer Corps formed cyclist sections as scouts in 1885.

On 23 April 1908, he transferred to the 1/25th (County of London) Cyclist Battalion and then the 9th (County of London) Battalion, the London Regiment (Queen Victoria's Rifles). While with them, he won a silver cup for shooting in 1912.

In April 1913, he enlisted in the 1/5th (City of London) Battalion, the London Regiment (London Rifle Brigade). His address was given as 6 St. Andrews Road, Surbiton. Because it was below strength, there were plenty of men clamouring to join, and vacancies were swiftly filled. Douglas was one of 60 officers, N.C.O.s and men of the regiment who took part in the famous march from the Duke of York's Column, London to Brighton Aquarium. This took place on 19/20 April 1914. The men in full kit accomplished the journey in 14 hours 23 minutes for 52.5 miles through the night. This established a new record for the distance for forced marching under service conditions.

A local paper reported:

> All the men finished, not a man was carried a yard and they never broke their formation
> between halts. Yet these lads had only received six weeks training, most of it in the last three
> weeks. On arrival in Brighton they had not the bearing of men who had walked all night;
> their ranks were firm; their alignment correct, their tread regular. Only their deeply flushed
> faces, dust covered legs and here and there a collar thrown open, gave evidence of the long
> journey.

The London Rifle Brigade was affiliated to the Rifle Brigade and wore black buttons and shoulder titles. Their headquarters was Bunhill Row, London and on 15 August 1914, the Battalion was asked if it would register for foreign service by the commanding officer, Lord Cairns. He said that the regiment had always claimed to be one of the best in the force and that now was the time to prove it. The London Rifle Brigade was the first battalion in the brigade to agree to serve abroad, but most reckoned the fighting would be over by Christmas. The Brigade spent some weeks training at Bisley and then marched via Reigate to East Grinstead arriving there on 10 September, they stayed until the 16th, when they marched to Camp Hill, Crowborough, Sussex.

At the outbreak of war Mr S. J. Waring, a director of Waring and Gillow made personal appeals for recruits to the employees of his company in London, Liverpool, Manchester and Lancaster, with the result that between 400 and 500 enlisted. Douglas volunteered for foreign service and went to France as a Lance Sergeant (No. 9539) in November 1914. He joined "O" Company of the 1st Battalion. He landed with the London Rifle Brigade on board the *Chyebassa* from Southampton at Le Havre on 5 November. His weight was 10 stone 7 pounds, which went up to over 13 stone after he won the V.C.

Since the battles of the Marne in September, the front had shifted from France to Flanders as each side had sought to manoeuvre round the other's exposed wing. So the German and Anglo-French forces steadily worked their way northwards to the Channel coast. In the process, the Germans set out to consolidate their position in Belgium. Ghent, Bruges and Ostend had fallen, and the Belgian Government had fled to France. In October, French and British troops had occupied Ypres.

Once in France the London Rifle Brigade joined 11th Brigade, 4th Division, serving with them in the trenches at Ploegsteert or "Plugstreet".

When they arrived at General Headquarters at St.Omer on 7 November, the Brigade had not even been expected, and consequently no arrangements had been made for the night. After waiting three hours on the train, they were able to march off to a dismal, dirty old artillery barracks. The train consisted of 50 vehicles and carried 848 all ranks, with 22 vehicles, two machine-guns and 68 horses. The following day they marched three and a half miles to a large unfurnished convent, with no water, heat or light. They spent most days training by trench digging or artillery formation regardless of the weather.

On 20 November, Brigadier General Hunter Weston came and addressed the officers about the 11th Infantry Brigade, which he commanded, and to which the London Rifle Brigade were attached. He pointed out that half-companies were to be attached to Regular Battalions for a spell in the trenches. As soon as they had proved themselves, half-companies were to be placed in the line intact, and later whole companies.

During the night of 20/21 November, the first men of the old "E" and "O" Companies moved up through Ploegsteert Wood and entered the trenches on the eastern side. The regiment arrived in Ploegsteert village on 22 November. This was just behind the line, and they were billeted in the village. The village is at the very south of the area associated with Ypres. Half the Battalion proceeded to the trenches. When they moved into Ploegsteert there was a good deal of frost, and many men suffered from it, particularly in their feet. This was followed by rain, which made the trenches very muddy and heavy. They were to stay in the area until 17 April 1915.

Trench training continued until 18 December. Platoons and whole companies were gradually attached to the Regulars. When they were not actually in the line, they spent their days carrying out fatigues of various kinds. A support line in the wood was created and renamed Bunhill Row. During this time the Battalion gained various nicknames including "London Fatigue party" and "Fatigue Fifth".

The 11th Infantry Brigade was comprised of the following Battalions: 1st Somerset Light Infantry, 1st East Lancashire Regiment, 1st Hampshire Regiment, and 1st Rifle Brigade.

On 18 December, the Brigade made an attack in front of Ploegsteert Wood to clear its edges. They also wanted to establish a line. The Somerset Light Infantry and Rifle Brigade attacked, with the London Rifle Brigade in support. The weather was appalling, and the ground difficult. However, they managed to clear the wood.

The London Rifle Brigade was not needed to continue the attack. This was their first experience of artillery fire. Two half-companies were engaged in assisting, while the rest of the Battalion spent a miserable night in the marshes in the wood. Each of the four companies was attached to one of the Regular Battalions – "A" to the East Lancs., "B" to the Somerset Light Infantry, "C" to the Hants. and "D" to the Rifle Brigade.

On 23 December, everyone received a card from their Majesties and an embossed tin box from Princess Mary containing a card, a pipe and tobacco or cigarettes, and many Christmas cards from the G.O.C. and others were circulated.

Men from the Brigade took part in the famous Christmas Truce. Several informal truces took place along the trench-lines of northern France and Belgium. The Germans had brought Christmas trees into their trenches and dugouts and had decorated some parts of the parapets. They began by placing candles on trees, and singing Christmas carols, most notably 'Stille Nacht' (Silent Night). The British then responded by singing English carols.

First contacts were made on Christmas Eve, as the opposing trenches were not far apart. However, it was Christmas day that the truce really took effect. It followed a particularly cold and misty dawn. Officers followed their men out into no man's land in small groups of three or four, so that the trenches were always manned. By and large, the truce was taken as an opportunity to meet, to shake hands, to show family photos and to exchange small items of food and tobacco.

A private of the London Rifle Brigade wrote:

> Soon after dusk on the 24th the Germans put up lanterns on top of their trenches and started singing; and their shooting practically ceased. Firing ceased on both sides, and both Germans and English ventured out on top of their trenches. After day-break on Christmas Day small parties on both sides ventured out in front of their trenches, all unarmed, and we heard that a German officer came over and promised that they would not fire if we did not.

Apparently during the morning small parties of Germans and English fraternised between the trenches, and when I and some of our pals strolled up from the reserve trenches after dinner, we found a crowd of some 100 Tommies of each nationality having a regular mother's meeting between the trenches. We found our enemies to be Saxons.

One of the Germans had been a waiter at the Savoy, and another a West End barber's assistant. Talk and souvenirs were exchanged. There are those who did not appreciate this cessation of hostilities, even on Christmas Day!

Rifleman Oswald Tilley summed up feelings when he wrote to his parents on the 27th: "Just you think that while you were eating your turkey etc, I was out talking and shaking hands with the very men I had been trying to kill a few hours before. It was astonishing!"

General Sir Horace Smith-Dorrien requested particulars of those units and officers who took part, with a view to disciplinary action. In the event, no action was taken against any unit or officer.

Between the 27th and 31st the weather turned wet with rain, sleet and storm. There was still a friendly mood in some areas for several days and there was little firing, although open fraternisation gradually died away. Many of the men suffered with trench feet from the cold and wet and a good many of them went sick. On New Year's Eve, there was a certain amount of singing and exchanging of messages, but no truce as such. The truce ended as it had begun, by mutual agreement.

In January 1915, it was felt that the Rifles were now hardened soldiers, and from their 2nd Battalion at home were being regularly fed with drafts of trained men. They were allocated a line of trenches to hold, and as one of them said, "we are no end proud of getting a proper job to do on our own, exactly the same as the Regulars".

The Brigade was taken out of the trenches in preparation for it taking over a part of the line in its own right. The Battalion's disposition was – one company in the front trench, one in London Farm and its environs, one in reserve in Ploegsteert, and one company resting, washing and cleaning billets in Armentieres. Each company spent three days in each place. On 1 February, the first large draft arrived from home – six N.C.O.s and 145 men.

Working parties were detailed to attend to wiring, using the pumps and advising on drainage of the trenches etc. Another group was sent to build shelters in the trenches. The latter group were under Lance Corporal Dodds until he received a commission. Then Douglas Belcher took over his work. During this period, and until the Battalion left the wood, this party did excellent work.

This was a period of "standing by", but after three days in the East Lancashire's trenches in front of the Convent, the Battalion took over the centre section in the wood on the 21 March.

On 21 March, the Battalion took over the trenches which had been manned by the Somersets. Douglas Belcher together with Lance Corporals E. F. Rice and Stransom, who were the heads of the building and wiring parties were attached to Battalion Headquarters, but the men of these parties were returned to their companies for duty.

Between 21 March and 17 April, the section was held with these three companies in the wood, and the fourth in reserve in the village. Other battalions of the 11th Brigade went to rest on the 16th, with the London Rifle Brigade coming out on the last day. The Battalion's introduction to warfare had been muddy rather than bloody.

Holy Communion was celebrated on Easter Sunday, with the Bishop of London, Senior Chaplain to the regiment, during his visit to the front. He came to Ploegsteert on 3 April and also consecrated the Battalion's graveyard in the village.

By 17 April, two battalions had been withdrawn to Steenwerck, and the 4th Division had its first period of rest since the Retreat. It was the first rest for the London Rifle Brigade since its arrival in the firing line five months before, and the first time the 11th Brigade had been out of line for a rest since August 1914.

Orders were received on the 23rd to be ready to move at an hour's notice. The Second Battle of Ypres was the first time the Germans used poison gas on a large scale on the Western Front. The battle included the Battle of St. Julien (24 April–4 May 1915). The London Rifle Brigade entrained at mid-day on the 24th, spending the night in billets outside Poperinghe, moving off at 5.30 a.m. next morning to the outskirts of Vlamertinghe. They stopped there until 6 p.m., parading with the rest of the Brigade to go into the Salient.

The 11th Brigade was ordered on the night of the 25th to join up the left of the 28th Division with the right of the 10th Brigade, and so relieve the Canadians, who were holding out in the area of St. Julian. However, there appeared to be gaps in this line. Two officers from each battalion (including Captain Husey and Lieutenant Johnston of the London Rifle Brigade) were sent up in advance but were unable to find any available information, except for the fact that there was apparently a gap.

During the night, the Hants joined up with the 28th Division, prolonging the line nearly to the junction of the Zonnebeke – St Julian and Ypres – Passchendale roads. This left a gap of around 1,000 yards between its left and the remainder of the Brigade. The London Rifle Brigade, being in support, were ordered to dig in 600 yards southeast of Fortuin. They reached this position at 1.45 a.m. For the rest of the day and for the next week, the Battalion was heavily shelled, suffering a number of casualties, mainly from enfilade fire.

Early in the afternoon a company was ordered to take up position ensuring the gap would be joined up between the Somerset Light Infantry and the Hants. However, it proved impossible to move men by day, and the Hants left could not be found, so the whole Battalion was ordered to move into the gap at dusk. They dug in for a second night. On the night of the 28th the Rifle Brigade finally joined up with the Hants, meaning the line was once more continuous.

The London Rifle Brigade moved up on the 29th to relieve the 4th East Yorks. The Battalion was to remain in these trenches undergoing infantry attacks and intense shellfire for the next four violent days. At about 5 p.m. on 2 May, the Germans advanced, under cover of heavy shell fire and gas. They moved from the ridge beyond the Haanebeke stream into dead ground on the near side of the stream, and dug in some 3,900 yards away.

London Rifle Brigade casualties were heavy, especially on the right, where there was more open ground. The Battalion was affected by gas for about ten minutes, but the wind dispersed it before any real damage was done. The Germans too suffered heavy casualties during their advance. This was mainly from two rifle companies on the right. The London Rifle Brigade on the right brought heavy fire on the enemy with excellent results. By 6.30 p.m. active fighting had ceased, but sniping and machine-gun fire continued until dark. The men were exhausted and reinforcements were brought up.

At 8.25 p.m. the following report was sent to Brigade:

> Situation quieter. Fear casualties very heavy, will report later. All supports now in trench. Improbable that we can hold length of trench without assistance. Men have had no sleep for seven nights. This, with the incessant shelling, has told on them. Germans are entrenching nearer to us, opposite our centre. No.3 Company which is there hopes that it did good execution on them. Can you send any Very lights?

With help from two companies of the 4th Yorks and one company of the East Lancs, which was also attached to the Battalion, the damage to the trenches was almost all repaired during the night, and all wounded evacuated.

On 3 May, there was intermittent shelling all day. By 9 a.m. two of the Battalion machine-guns had been knocked out. The line was readjusted, and the entire brigade retired without further casualties. On the 4th the actual withdrawal started at 12.45 a.m., commencing from the right. It was timed so they would reach Wieltje at 1.45 a.m. Casualties during the period 25 April to 4 May were 16 officers and 392 other ranks.

Between 4 and 8 May time was spent at various places in woods behind Vlamertinghe resting, reorganising, and dealing with build-ups of mail. On the 9th the Battalion moved early in the morning to the grounds of the chateau at Vlamertinghe. That night and the following one they dug in on the east of the canal on the north of La Brique. They moved up to the canal bank on the 11th. On the 12th the London Rifle Brigade relieved the Dublins on a section of the front line, on the extreme right of the 4th Division, with a cavalry division on its immediate right. They had been ordered to send a minimum of 150 men and also to occupy the three defended posts east of Wieltje village, with a garrison of 20 men in each. The remainder of the London Rifle Brigade and its headquarters were to be from the right of Essex Farm to St. Jean-Wieltje Road.

The Battalion was about 290-strong in the line that night. No. 1 Company and one platoon of No. 2 Company moved up to the Wieltje-St. Jean Road to a point near the top of a rise. Their object was to reach the front line avoiding heavy casualties, as they were spotted relieving some troops on the left, and the Germans were firing their machine-guns constantly sweeping the front line. When they managed to reach the trenches they found them in a terrible state – wide, shallow and partially blown in. The platoon on the extreme left was isolated, where around 30 feet of trench had been knocked flat, but on the extreme right, touching the road, conditions were a little better. It also rained throughout the day.

HOLDING THE BREASTWORK – 13 MAY 1915

Sir John French's despatch reads:

> On the 13th May the heaviest bombardment yet experienced broke out at 4.30 a.m., and continued with little intermission throughout the day … the 5th London Regiment, despite very heavy casualties, maintained their position unfalteringly.

"A" and part of "B" Companies were in the front line. "C" Company garrisoned three fortified supporting points. The rest of "B" Company and "D" Company were in support. Shelling on the Battalion's sector had begun at 4 a.m. Half an hour later telegraph communications with the front line were severed, so runners had to be used. At 6.40 a.m. a brigade message was received to the effect that the 11th Brigade line was to be held at all costs. It was not until about 8 a.m. that the front line was reinforced. The distance between the front line and the supports was about 900 yards. The machine-gun that covered the approach to the road was knocked out during the morning. This left an undefended gap of about 30 yards between the right of the London Rifle Brigade and a small piece of trench on the right of the Wieltje Road held by Sergeant Belcher and half a dozen men.

The 11th Brigade front was held by two companies of the 1/5th (City of London) Battalion, the London Regiment, the 1st East Lancs., 1st Rifle Brigade, 1st Hampshires and, joining up with French troops, the 1st Somerset Light Infantry.

It was a day of biting north winds and torrential rain, turning the trenches into a quagmire. The infantry on the left of the cavalry were fiercely attacked, but managed to hold their own.

In the early afternoon a gun team, with machine-guns and ammunition came up to replace the one that had been knocked out earlier. By now the front line was becoming a shambles, as the gap on the left had become much wider, and communication with the platoon on the extreme left was almost impossible. The enemy sent forward, in front of the London Rifle Brigade, a line of skirmishers, who were shot down but at great cost to the garrison, which suffered many fatal casualties.

They first held a trench near Shell-Trap Farm and, with their left resting on the hamlet of Fortuin, suffered a huge bombardment, losing 117 men from shell-fire in a single day. Yet when the German infantry attacked in the dark they wiped out all the attackers.

A message came through at midday from Battalion headquarters:

> The left regiment of the 2nd Cavalry Brigade has been very much cut up by the shell-fire, and its trenches practically destroyed. The remnants of the regiment retired. There is thus a gap of about 300 yards between my next regiment and your right. It is impossible to hold

this gap thoroughly as we cannot dig trenches owing to machine-gun fire. Two squadrons are doing their best to occupy the gap by holding the shell holes. I have asked them to try and get in touch with your right. Will you let me know how the right of your battalion is situated?

For 300 yards the line held by the 2nd Cavalry Brigade had broken, and left the 11th Infantry Brigade with its right in the air and nothing but Sergeant Belcher's post to protect its flank.

Lance Sergeant Belcher was a section commander in one of two 1 London Rifle Brigade companies in the front line, where shells were falling at the rate of over 100 a minute. Belcher, with the remnants of his section, together with other members of 1 London Rifle Brigade, 18 men in total, held a small section of trench, less than 40 yards long, south of the Wieltje-St.Julien Road. On either side it was completely cut off from the rest of the line, and the enemy, realising its strategic importance, were making it a target for particularly violent fire. Shells were dropping all around as they crouched beneath the woefully inadequate protection of the sand-bagged parapet. Now and again a high-explosive shell would shower them with mud. They had reached the trench at 3 a.m. amid a hail of German shells. "We were being shelled to blazes". Belcher said. The ground was torn up every few yards and "looked as if a giant had been over it with a cinder shifter". Gradually the heavy bombardment took its toll, but Belcher's men continued to fire on the Germans, who were within 200 yards. Rifles were jamming with the mud or becoming too hot to hold, but they stayed in their position, while others in nearby trenches withdrew. Belcher's face became very serious when the message was delivered from the troops on his right that their position was untenable and that they were going to retire. Although his comrades in the other part of the line were actually retiring, and advised him to do the same, he refused. Belcher had his full share of anxiety. He was not in the least afraid, although he realised that the awful shelling would soon place the whole party out of action. Belcher had received orders to hold the trench. "I knew I was in for a hot thing," he said. "The breastwork, which was only about 35 yards long, was not only cut-off from the division on each side, but was nearer the Germans and a target for their fire".

Belcher encouraged his men, "Come on lads," he'd say, "Give the blighters hell! Let's show 'em what we're made of!" Sandbags were blown in by the hostile guns and the violent and continuous bombardment went on until Belcher was left with only eight of his men and two hussars, whom he had picked up. Belcher knew the disastrous consequences if they quit. He gave the order to stand firm. "It's up to us," he shouted above the din. "Let's stick it out". He sent back a brief message: "Troops on my right retiring, I am holding on". The reply came back: "Good," it ran. "Hold on".

As the breastwork in their trench became almost useless, Belcher decided to occupy an adjacent vacant trench. With only five men remaining, they changed trenches. A few minutes later the trench they had vacated was demolished. Showers of earth and splinters rained about Belcher as he dashed to the neighbouring trench where his four men awaited him, but miraculously he escaped being hit. They held the German army at bay, for every time the enemy collected for an attack, Belcher ordered rapid fire. The Germans were only from 150–200 yards away but, by maintaining a bold and skilful front, and by using so quick and deadly a fire that the breastwork seemed fully manned, they completely outwitted the advancing Germans. They had no intention of giving-in, and skipped about dodging the enemy's fire. The rifles became impossible to hold through constant firing; the answering shells caused showers of dust that half-blinded them. They remained in position for over nine hours, firing at the enemy, until they were finally relieved. Belcher only had a graze on his chin and a shrapnel rent in his cap. He would have died rather than give in, once having declared, "I am holding on".

The following N.C.O.s and riflemen were with Sergeant Belcher:
Lance Corporals H. J. C. Rowe and J. H. Wheatley (wounded), Riflemen H. G. Buck (wounded); C. M. Evans, G. W. Freeman (killed), H. Parker, H. W. Rowe, R. S. Weeks (wounded). Lance Corporal Rowe and Rifleman Buck were awarded Military Medals for their gallantry.

In an interview in the *Surbiton Times* on 10th July, Belcher said that the barricade was about 35 yards long. By holding it his party kept in touch with the right and left of the broken front, and they also protected an important road. He remarked:

> It was an awful place – It had been shelled four days before we went to it, and it was absolutely unrecognisable when we came away. It was blown to bits. When the troops on my right had withdrawn we shifted along a bit and, directly we had due to a high-explosive shell blew the whole thing in where we had just previously been standing, so I think it was a very good move on our part, don't you?

They had held a key position. Without them the road was clear for the Germans to break through our front by the Wieltje and make a flank attack on the 4th Division. They had held the Wieltje road in the most critical phase of the battle, and saved a British Division from a disastrous flank attack.

When he reported to his commanding officer, Belcher was greeted with: "Congratulations on a brilliant performance. You saved the situation, sergeant". Belcher made light of the situation and said in a letter to a friend: "It was a bit saucy wasn't it? Five men – three wounded – holding up the Germans!" He laughingly said, "But I must have looked a picture. What with the drizzling rain, blood oozing from the graze on my chin, and a four-day growth of beard on my face!"

A fellow-member of the London Rifle Brigade paid tribute to Belcher:

> I happened to be near Sergeant Belcher when he distinguished himself, and I marvel how he ever came back. I think he accomplished what not one man in a thousand would have done, and absolutely stuck on for death or glory.

Graham Williams, who came through unwounded, later wrote that the cavalry on Belcher's right flank, "trained professional soldiers had broken, while the LRB, 'Saturday afternoon soldiers' never for one moment thought of leaving their position, in spite of having suffered the same shelling".

The relieving party set to work repairing the damaged trench, and their fresh fire, in greatly increased volume, led to the Germans abandoning their attack. The shelling did not stop until 6 p.m. and it wasn't until later in the evening that the Battalion was withdrawn to the second line, when two companies of the King's Own came up to relieve them. The Battalion moved back during the night to support trenches.

On 14 May evening the Battalion moved into the trenches in front of La Brique, which it had dug less than a week before. The men were totally exhausted as they had been on the go for over three weeks, and for the last ten days the little sleep they obtained was out in the open. The following day they moved further forward into the second line, and two companies of the 6th Battalion Northumberland Fusiliers were attached to it. After being withdrawn to the canal bank on the 16th, orders were given that the London Rifle Brigade was to be withdrawn and sent to General Headquarters. The Battalion marched to Vlamertinghe to be billeted there. On the 20th the Divisional Commander inspected the Battalion, expressing his deep appreciation of everything it had achieved since 25 April. It then boarded motor-buses to proceed to General Headquarters.

Thus the London Rifle Brigade left the 4th Division after six months. The Brigade, Divisional, and Corps Commanders all personally thanked the Battalion for the work it had done, and congratulated it on its achievements under the most trying circumstances. Even more appreciated were the farewell letters from the Battalions of the 11th Brigade, showing that they really felt the Brigade to have become part of their Regular Brigade.

The London Rifle Brigade arrived at Tatinghem, enjoying ten days' complete rest with perfect weather. The strength of the Battalion was 19 officers and 344 other ranks of which ten per cent had come over from France on 5 November 1914. On 1 June, three battalions marched into St. Omer and amalgamated for works on lines of communications. This meant the handing over of all active service equipment, and all transport.

Headquarters, and those not employed at different railheads, remained at St. Omer, first in the Artillery barracks, and from 1 July under canvas.

Some years later a poem commemorated Belcher's feat. The author is unknown:

> The right supports were falling back
> Before the Germans' fierce attack,
> And everything was looking black,
> For hope had nearly gone,
> When Belcher got his message through
> "In spite of what the foe may do
> I still am holding on'".
> There were but six brave fighters there.
> The honour and the risk to share,
> To outward seeming far from fair
> Or good to look upon;
> Yet wounds and death appalled them not,
> 'Twas theirs to guard the danger spot,
> And *win* by holding on.
> So may we all of British race
> Each in his own appointed place,
> The darkest hour of conflict face,
> Till hope's tomorrow dawn:
> Though ranks be thinned' of help bereft,
> What battered remnant still is left
> Will still be holding on.

A HERO RETURNS

In mid-June Sergeant Belcher was granted the V.C. for his gallant work on the 13th and the following telegrams were exchanged:

> To O.C., L.R.B. and Officers, N.C.O.s and Riflemen, I beg to send on behalf of the 1st Battalion Queen Victoria's Rifles serving at the front our most hearty congratulations to Lce- Sergt. D.W. Belcher upon being awarded the V.C. and for the honour he has brought thereby to himself and the distinguished regiment he belongs to. All Q.V.R.s send our best wishes and good luck to all the L.R.B. Yours sincerely, V.W.F. Dickins, Lieut.-Col.

> To the Officer Commanding, Officers, N.C.O.s and Riflemen Q.V.R. On behalf of the Officers, N.C.O.'s and Riflemen of the London Rifle Brigade I wish to thank you for your letter of congratulation on Lce-Sergt. Belcher being awarded the V.C. If the Press is correct in stating that Lce-Sergt. Belcher used to be in your regiment, we do not grudge you the reflected glory. The best of luck to you all. Arthur S. Bates, Commanding L.R.B.

Belcher was gazetted for his Victoria Cross on 23 June 1915 (page 6115, No. 29202):

> On the early morning of 13th May, 1915, when in charge of a portion of an advanced breastwork south of the Wieltje – St. Julien Road, during a fierce and continuous bombardment by the enemy, which frequently blew in the breastwork, Lance-Sergeant

Belcher with a mere handful of men elected to remain and endeavour to hold his position after the troops near him had been withdrawn. By his skill and great gallantry he maintained his position during the day, opening rapid fire on the enemy, who were only 150 to 200 yards distant, whenever he saw them collecting for an attack. There is little doubt that the bold front shown by Lance-Sergeant Belcher prevented the enemy breaking through on the Wieltje Road, and averted an attack on the flank of one of our Divisions.

He was decorated with the V.C. by H.M. King George V at Buckingham Palace on 12 July 1915. With a hearty handshake the King said: "It gives me great pleasure to decorate you with the Victoria Cross for the conspicuous valour you have shown".

On that day the following appeared in an extract from Battalion Orders, as quoted in the Battalion War Diary: "The commanding officer wishes to congratulate Sergeant Belcher on the most distinguished honour he, and the Bn. have received by the honour of the Victoria Cross for his gallant conduct on May 13th". The orders also named the eight men who were with Belcher.

A movement, headed by the Chairman of the District Council, Mr S. Kavanagh J.P., the Clerk, Mr F. W. Wood and several of Belcher's friends was started in Surbiton to present a public testimonial to Sergeant Belcher. "The pence of the poor will therefore be as welcome as the cheque of the rich". Money could be paid into the fund at the District Council Offices or to a local bank. News that he had been awarded the V.C. spread like wildfire around Surbiton, for there was not a more popular individual in the district. His parents still resided in the locality even though they had retired from business three years earlier.

He became the first territorial soldier holding a non-commissioned rank to be awarded a V.C. during the First World War. His mother told a Daily Express reporter in June:

> Douglas was home on 72 hours leave only a very short time ago. He went to the front last November, as a private in the London Rifle Brigade, and, with the exception of the short leave I mentioned, he has been there ever since. Although we knew he had distinguished himself, and that he had been recommended for a medal of some sort, we had no idea it was to be the V.C. My son was unwilling to discuss the affair at all, saying, I remember, when someone present at his first meal home tried to get him to talk about it, 'oh, let's get on with the tea, shall we?' Even as a child he was quite fearless. He is, and always has been, the best of sons.

She told a *Surrey Comet* reporter that she first heard the news through a London reporter who called her and asked if he could have one of "Dug's" photographs. She knew he had been recommended for the Distinguished Conduct Medal, but the fact that he had been awarded the Victoria Cross came as a big surprise.

When she was asked how the news affected her, she laughingly remarked:

> Oh dear, I don't know what I did. I was so excited, and completely carried away. Very naturally my husband and I are very proud of the distinction our son has gained. My husband says he wishes he could have been with 'Dug' when he won the Victoria Cross, but of course that was impossible, for he is too old, and another thing, he is an invalid.

He had obtained leave from the front and arrived at his home in St. Andrew's Road, Surbiton tired and travel-weary after his journey from the trenches. The Surrey Comet also reports that a young woman travelled in the same railway carriage and eyed him curiously. She, too, got out at Surbiton, and walking from the station plucked up courage to say, "Excuse me, are you not Sergeant Belcher, the Victoria Cross man?" Belcher admitted he was, and received her congratulations.

He had written to say that his parents might expect him home any day. When he arrived he looked tanned and tough and as fit as a fiddle after the strenuous time he had experienced in the trenches. He arrived home in his khaki uniform he had been wearing on active service, and carrying his knapsack and trusty rifle. He spent his brief leave with his parents, and visiting many friends, two of whom drove him from place to place. He also managed to fit in a sitting with a local photographer.

Mr and Mrs Belcher had been inundated with congratulations upon the high honour their son had gained. They included a congratulatory address from the Chairman and Board of the Early Closing Association in honour of a shop assistant winning the highest honour. This took place at Anderton's Hotel, Fleet Street, London on 28 June.

Belcher on leave in June 1915

On the motion of Mr. John Bodger J.P., resolutions were unanimously passed expressing the pride and gratification of the board that the V.C., had, for the first time in the nation's history, been awarded to two shop assistants – Lance Sergeant Belcher and Lance Corporal Edw. Dwyer (1st East Surrey Regiment), and directed that the congratulations of the board be forwarded to these two soldiers and their parents, and trusted that 'the life of so brave a soldier may long be spared'.

Sergeant O'Leary, Lance Corporal Dwyer and Belcher – Three V.C. Heroes

On Wednesday 7 July, Belcher and several companions visited the Kingston Empire to witness a performance. They booked in the circle, but the manager made a private box available. During the evening a cordial greeting to the Surbiton V.C. was thrown in bold letters on the screen, and the theatre orchestra dashed into the lilting strains of "For he's a jolly good fellow". When the lights went up and Sergeant Belcher was "discovered" seated in the box, the audience broke into wild cheering. After the performance some of his admirers endeavoured to "chair" him, but, leaving by a private exit, he boarded a tramcar to his home and so escaped them.

The *Surrey Comet* describes the homecoming at Surbiton on 12 July after his V.C. presentation:

Belcher welcomed home in 1915

Sergeant Belcher, wreathed in smiles and wearing his coveted decoration, reached Surbiton in a motor car shortly after 7 o'clock. He had been expected back by train, and a large crowd collected in the station yard to give him a hearty welcome home. The 'toot-toot' of the motor horn and the cry 'we've got Belcher' soon caused the car to be surrounded, and when it had come to a standstill a lady, stepping out of the crowd, presented the Victoria Cross hero with a bouquet. Sergeant Belcher attempted to acknowledge the rousing reception he received, but his voice could not be heard for the continuous cheering, and so, after much handshaking and many congratulations, the party proceeded up St. Mark's Hill to the District Council offices.

The monthly meeting of the Council had just terminated when Sergeant Belcher was ushered into the oak-panelled chamber. He was given a place of honour on the rostrum, on the left of the Chairman. When the applause which heralded Sergeant Belcher's entry had subsided, Mr Kavanagh, on behalf of the Council and the official staff, complimented Sergeant Belcher on the courageous act that had gained for him the Victoria Cross. A resolution expressing the Council's appreciation of the services he had rendered to his country, and the distinction he had won was to be inscribed on vellum and presented to him, the Chairman said.

Sergeant Belcher, in acknowledging the ovation, modestly remarked that he did only what any other Sergeant in the London Rifle Brigade would have done in similar circumstances. Happily his act had very fortunate results. He cordially thanked the Council for the reception accorded him. On leaving the Council buildings he obligingly consented to sign a number of autograph books which were thrust into his hands, and then, still smiling and unperturbed by the demonstration, he re-entered the car, and with his friends paid a visit to Kingston, his progress through the streets of Surbiton and the neighbouring borough being quite a triumphal journey.

On Tuesday 13th the large hall at Tiffin Boys' School was gaily decorated with Union Jacks and other flags and completely filled with Tiffinians, past and present as a mark of appreciation of the honour he has won for himself and the school where he was educated.

Deafening cheers were raised by the boys as the VC hero was escorted to the platform by the Headmaster (Mr C. J. Grist M.A.) and the Mayor of Kingston (Alderman C. H. Burge).

Mr Grist, in addressing Sgt. Belcher, V.C., said there was no introduction necessary in his old school. Doubtless he had received many greetings, but he could never have a more heartfelt and sincere one than that accorded to him at Tiffin School. The decoration he wore had upon it a word dear to the heart of all boys, "Valour". The volume of cheering came from the lungs, but the sentiment was shown from the hearts.

Mr Grist continuing, said they wanted to give Sergt. Belcher some tangible token of the esteem they had for him, and had consulted his mother in order to select a suitable Gift, and their choice had been a handsome black marble clock, with a brass plate bearing the inscription, 'Presented to Lance-Sergt. Douglas W. Belcher, V.C., by the masters and boys of Tiffin School, July 1915'. Loud and prolonged cheering marked the actual presentation.

Sergt. Belcher was delighted with his reception, but confessed to being a little confused. He said: 'I don't know what to say. I am very glad to be in the dear old school again. Really, I have done no more than any other Sergeant in the London Rifle Brigade would have done, or any Old Tiffinian, either. I cannot say any more'.

After the Mayor had added his congratulations, Mr A.E. Rayment, 'one of the oldest of the old boys' added a few words of congratulation, and after further cheering for the hero, the Mayor, and the Master, the gathering terminated with the singing of the National Anthem.

Belcher signing autographs

Sergeant Belcher's seven days' leave expired on the 14th, but the War Office granted him a week's extension until 21 July.

The *Weekly Dispatch* printed a story telling how the card bearing his name Mr D. W. Belcher was still fixed to his desk in the antique department at Waring and Gillow. It was shown to the reporter with immense pride by Mr J. A. Jack, under whom Mr Belcher worked. It had never been moved, although Mr Belcher had not been at the desk for nearly eleven months.

'Douglas Belcher was a steady slogger at his work here, and you never met a man with less swank,' said Mr Jack. 'He was so quiet and unpretentious that just after he had offered his services for the front someone said to me, 'Fancy Belcher going'. I replied 'I never thought he would do anything else'. Practically everyone here knew him because he was in the office for three years before he came to this department, and was doing work which brought him personally into touch with all the members of the staff. So you can imagine the state of excitement we have all been in since we heard the news. He is the first Territorial not an officer to win the V.C.

He was here a few days ago on a very short leave, but unfortunately I was away. I had a letter from him this morning saying 'I particularly wanted to see you.' I had an awfully nice letter from the old colonel of the brigade.

A few weeks ago we heard from Lieutenant Wallis that Mr Belcher's name had been sent in for mention in Sir John French's despatches, and that he might even receive the VC. You can imagine our disappointment when we searched the long list of nearly 4,000 names published in the despatches the other day and found that his name was not there.

On Saturday 17 July he was presented with an illuminated address, a silver rose bowl and a purse of gold by his former employees, Waring and Gillow, with over 3,000 employees attending a ceremony in his honour at the company premises at White City. Here they made tents and manufactured aeroplane parts for the war. He received a stirring ovation. "The country owes its freedom, its happiness, and its riches to men like you, and will ever remain grateful to them," said Mrs S. J. Waring in making the presentation. Replying to Mrs Waring's speech, Belcher replied that he often thought of his old firm when at the front, saying, "sometimes we'd see the old vans at the front, and we'd think of home and London and all that". He ended his remarks by appealing for more recruits: "I'm glad to see you all again, but I don't want to go back without a few more recruits with me," he concluded, "we want men at the front – and still more men".

Mrs Waring presents the Silver Rose Bowl

When asked which of the many attentions he received was the most embarrassing, he replied that nothing made him "feel such a fool" as a long and fervent handshake from a member of the opposite sex, who persisted in gazing into his eyes all the time that she held his hand. It made him feel as if he must burst into tears, or use strong language. He also confessed to being made quite miserable by kindly folk who pressed cigars upon him and insisted upon him starting to smoke in their presence in order to hear if the weed is to his liking. Until he joined the army he had not smoked cigars, and he wasn't altogether happy with any but the mildest sort.

On Wednesday 21 July, his last day of leave, he received his public testimonial in Surbiton. It had been decided that the testimonial should take the form of an army service revolver, suitably inscribed, and a purse of money. Donations quickly began to pour in, and were expected to reach £100 in a limited amount of time.

The Illuminated Address from Waring and Gillow

Waring and Gillow Ladies Welcome their Hero

The *Surrey Comet* continues:

As a preliminary to the presentation, which was made on the Victoria recreation ground in Balaclava Road, a street procession was arranged. It was formed up at the fountain at Tolworth under the experienced direction of Major B. Parmeter, who rendered valuable service as chief marshall. Soldiers and civilians and representatives of various local patriotic organisations joined forces in the procession, which was about half a mile in length. A start was made soon after half-past two o'clock, the way being led by a mounted police patrol. Then came the excellent band belonging to the depot of the East Surrey Regiment, at Kingston. Behind them, four deep, marched with erect carriage a contingent of the 10th Royal Fusiliers, and on their heels came the men of the 3/3rd Home Counties Field Ambulance. R.A.M.C.(T.) with their mascot. Next followed the local detachments of the 2nd Batt. Surrey Volunteer Training Corps, and then came the bugle band of the London Rifle Brigade. Preceding the artistically decorated motor car lent by Mr Stephen Kavanagh, in which Surbiton's hero was seated in company with Mr Kavanagh, Mr Wood and Major Macauley, marched a guard of honour composed of about one hundred men of the London Rifle Brigade, a number of whom are home recovering from wounds received at the Front. Then came the members of the testimonial committee, and bringing up the rear was a strong contingent of local Boy Scouts and the Surbiton section of the Kingston and District Fire Brigade, mounted on their engines, with their brightly burnished helmets glittering in the powerful rays of the sun.

The entire course, from Tolworth to lower Surbiton, was thickly lined with people, and all along the route a brave display of bunting was made. Hats and handkerchiefs were waved and lusty cheers broke from the throats of the assembled throng as Sergt. Belcher, wearing his khaki uniform with the Victoria Cross pinned on his breast, drove past all radiant with smiles, and many people strove to grip the hand of the plucky soldier. It was a happy thought on the part of the executive committee to arrange for the procession to pass down St. Andrew's Road, for it is there that the gallant hero's parents reside.

There must have been between two and three thousand people on the Victoria recreation ground when the procession entered by the Victoria Avenue gate and made its way to the platform erected hard by the railway embankment. The presentation had been timed for half-past three, and there being a wait of ten minutes the several Press photographers in attendance had abundant opportunities of 'snapping' Sergt. Belcher and those with him. This ordeal over, the principals made their way to the platform, and from this point of vantage the surging crowd furnished an impressive spectacle, with their faces upturned in an endeavour to catch a glimpse of the Surbiton V.C.

When the cheering had subsided, Mr Kavanagh addressing the assembly, explained that endeavours had been made to obtain a longer extension of leave for Sergt. Belcher, but it could not be arranged. They had met there that afternoon, said Mr Kavanagh, to do honour to Sergt. Belcher, who, by his bravery and devotion to duty, had won the Victoria Cross. Sergt. Belcher being a Surbiton man, they were all the more pleased at the high distinction he had gained. (Cheers.) The purse he was to be presented with was not quite full, but it was the intention of the committee to keep the fund open until the last day of July, to give those who had not subscribed an opportunity of doing so. (Applause.)

Amid a fresh outburst of cheering, Mr Kavanagh asked Sergt. Belcher to accept the purse of notes and the Army service revolver. The latter bore the inscription 'presented to Sergt. D.W. Belcher,V.C., London Rifle Brigade, by the inhabitants of Surbiton, July 21, 1915,' and the Chairman facetiously remarked that he hoped Sergt. Belcher would use it with good effect.

Belcher replied: I really don't know what to say. (Laughter.) I only know that I thank you all very much for the very generous gift I have received. I am very proud at this moment to be a Surbitonian and I am jolly glad to see you all here. (Cheers.) I am very proud to be in the London Rifle Brigade. With regard to what I did I think it was only what any other Sergeant of the London Rifle Brigade would have done under similar circumstances. I am only too pleased to see them all again, and I shall be glad to be back amongst the rest of them once more. (Cheers.) I am glad to have had the opportunity of coming back to Surbiton again and to be on the ground where I used to play cricket and made a few ducks. (Laughter.) Thank you all very much indeed. I can't say more than that. (Cheers.).

After Lieutenant-Colonel Treeby addressed the meeting, the Rt. Hon. George Cave M.P. arrived and was called upon to speak. He said he was:

> …glad to have arrived in time to assist in honouring Sergt. Belcher. They were all proud of their Surrey V.C. They knew how the call came to him. They were proud of him and his men, and they were proud that he was a Surrey man and a Surbiton man. (Cheers.) He received his education at Tiffin Boys' School. (Applause.) He was 'one of them', and they knew he would do the right thing if the chance presented itself. (Cheers.) Sergt. Belcher had told them that any sergeant of the London Rifle Brigade would have done the same as he did. He (the speaker) was glad to believe that was true, but the call came to Sergt. Belcher, and he embraced the opportunity, and it was right that they should do him honour. (Cheers.) Sergt. Belcher was returning to the front that night. He (the Rt. Hon. George Cave) tried to get him a little more leave, but he received a letter from Sergt. Belcher's commanding officer saying he could not spare him any longer. So he had to go back. Out at the Front the work might be hard and long, but Sergt. Belcher would remember the day in England when he was honoured by his friends and neighbours. (Cheers.) The Rt. Hon. George Cave concluded by wishing Sergt. Belcher 'Good luck, God speed, and a safe return'.
>
> In proposing a vote of thanks to the Rt. Hon. George Cave for his attendance, Canon Potter said that Surbiton was tremendously proud of Sergt. Belcher V.C., and he would say for Tiffin Boys' School what any of the masters would have said, had one been present that afternoon, how proud the school was of its old pupil. Sergt. Belcher was returning to the Front that night, and he hoped all present would say 'God bless him and keep him and make him faithful to the great causes of his country and his God.' The Rev. A. E. Beavan seconded the vote, which was carried with acclamation. The throng then broke into the lilting refrain of 'He's a jolly good fellow'; the band played the National Anthem, and Sergt. Belcher was driven away from the ground on the Surbiton fire-engine.
>
> A large crowd assembled in the vicinity of Sergt. Belcher's residence to cheer him off when he left Surbiton early the same evening. He drove to London in a motor-car, accompanied by his fiancée, and some male friends, to catch the 7 o'clock train from Victoria, but on his arrival at that station he found that the troop train had left before the time he had been notified it would start. There was no help for it but to return to Surbiton, which he did, but before coming away he duly reported himself to an officer who was on the railway platform. Sergt. Belcher spent Thursday morning in Surbiton, and commenced his journey back to France early in the afternoon.

A Family Photo July 1915

COMMISSIONED AND SECONDED

On 11 August, the Composite Battalion was resolved into its component units again. Early in September it became an open secret that a British offensive was due shortly and the use of gas on a large scale was said to be going to form a feature of the attack. On 2 October, the London Rifle Brigade was transferred from Lines of Communication to G.H.Q. Troops, and marched to Blendeques. Here they spent 23 days and included a period of training before being sent back to the Front.

By now the Brigade was attached to the 8th Brigade under Brigadier General J. D. Maclachan, and formed part of the 3rd Division. They were moved by motor-bus in pouring rain and relieved the Honourable Artillery Company. The billets were very cramped and the weather was very wet. Training continued with inspections until 23 November. The Battalion then marched to Poperinghe where they stayed until 12 December and they tried to get the trenches, which were in a shocking state, into some

Douglas Belcher V.C.

sort of shape. They had relieved the Liverpool Scottish in the front line. The Battalion was in the trenches during an abortive gas attack on 19 December, but was not affected by the gas, which passed just behind it. The Battalion was in line again from 28 December until 4 January 1916, when the Battalion was put in reserve. From 1–8 February the Battalion marched from trenches to rest, and back into reserve. It was attached to three different brigades.

On 8 February, the Brigade received orders to join the 169th Infantry Brigade which was then being formed. The Brigade formed part of the 56th Division, which was in the VI Corps. The Brigade continued training until 27 February when it marched in a snowstorm to Ergnies and went into billets. On 22 March, after six days rest, they marched to the village of Magnacourt sur Cance, where the inhabitants were hostile because they objected to military occupation of their stables and barns. However they remained there throughout April training in the morning and playing games in the afternoon. On 7 May the Brigade marched to Halloy and went into huts there, joining the VII Corps. After various period in trenches, the tour ended on the night of 29 May when they were relieved by the Queen Victoria's Rifles.

On 1 July, the first day of the Battle of the Somme, the London Rifle Brigade, as part of 56th Division, was ordered to attack at Gommecourt, one of the strongest parts of the German line, in an effort to divert German artillery from British attacks further south. Gommecourt Park was the most westerly point of the German position, forming a very sharp salient. The Park was in a thick wood with the village behind. The idea was for 56th Division to attack on the south side of the wood, and the 46th to the north, joining up with the 56th in the village and establishing a line in the German trenches cutting off the German garrison in the park. The whole attack was a feint, keeping the Germans occupied, while the great attack on the Somme was launched. The London Rifle Brigade attacked on the left of the Division and the Queen Victoria's Rifles on their right.

The attack was started at 7.30 a.m., and in spite of casualties, the German lines were reached. The situation began to look critical at about mid-day and the Brigade was attacked more and more by bombers and snipers resulting in a number of casualties. Hundreds of Germans surrendered but many escaped. By the evening the final withdrawal took place. The Battalion lost that day in killed, wounded and missing 83 per cent of the officers who went into action and 70 per cent of the N.C.O.s and men. The nights of the 1st and 2nd were taken up with bringing in the wounded. On the 2nd at about noon, the remnant of the Battalion was ordered to withdraw and remain in reserve trenches. The Battalion then marched to billets in St. Amand and the next two days were spent in bathing, cleaning up and recovering.

By early October, the fighting for the London Rifle Brigade in the Somme district was over and by November spells of light work were carried out in the trenches. Intervals were used for resting, cleaning up and training.

On 10 November 1916, Douglas Belcher was commissioned as a Second Lieutenant in 3/9th Battalion, the London Regiment (Queen Victoria's Rifles). The 3/9th was formed in Tadworth in 1915 and supplied drafts to 1/9th and 2/9th Battalions.

During this time Madame Tussaud's added waxwork models of Sergeant Belcher, Sergeant O'Leary and Lance Corporal Dwyer V.C. Every one of the chief celebrities of the war had a replica in the exhibition. This and many others were destroyed by a raging fire caused by an electrical fault on 18 March 1925. Fire gutted two floors of the building, destroying not only almost all the waxwork figures and their costumes, but priceless furnishings, paintings and relics too.

On 31 January 1917, Douglas married Emily Frances Luxford (born 1896) at St. Mark's Church, Surbiton, where he had been a boy chorister. Her parents also lived in Surbiton. Her father Sidney Wynn Luxford was a Fruiterer and he was married twice. Mr J. A. Jack of the Southern Company of the London National Guard, Manager of the antique department of Waring and Gillow, was best man.

They had two sons. The elder, Francis Douglas Belcher was born on 31 December 1917. He attended Skinners School, Tunbridge Wells in the 1930s. Leaving 1933, he was encouraged to

Douglas and Emily

join the army as a boy soldier at Chepstow, reaching at least the rank of WO2 (Warrant Officer) in the Royal Army Service Corps and later WO1 R.E.M.E. He was granted the British Empire Medal in 1945. Their second son, Brian Wynn Belcher was born on 15 February 1926 at Claygate, Surrey. He went to Masonic School and became a builder.

On 18 October 1918, Douglas was seconded to the Indian Army from the Territorial Forces on probation with seniority as a Lieutenant backdated to 10 November 1917. On 2 November he was attached to 1/6th Gurkha Rifles at Abbottabad, India, where his family were able to join him. Abbottabad was the base depot of the regiment. That month the Battalion marched into Abbottabad along a route lined by cheering members of the garrison. They had spent a year in Persia, providing support to the Persian Army.

On 10th November 1920, Douglas was promoted Captain, Indian Army, and in 1921 was a company commander in Mesopotamia during the Arab rising. In January 1922, he was attached to 5th Battalion, 70th Burma Rifles at Meikhla on the Indian Army List. While he was with the Indian Army, he gained a good knowledge of the language.

On 19th July 1922, he retired with ill health from the Indian Army with gratuity under the provisions of a Royal Warrant dated 25 April 1922.

He suffered with bad health after the war brought on by his experiences and found it difficult to hold down a job and make ends meet. He continued to live in Surbiton and Claygate for a while, and in 1922 worked for a Cigar merchant for a short time before breaking down. He was then re-employed in the antiques department at Waring and Gillow until ill health forced his retirement. As he was quoted in the Sunday Dispatch of 24 May 1931:

> … then had a breakdown and a year or so after went to work for a firm in its antique department, but I had not been in the new job long before my health went again, and the doctors told me that I had to get an open-air life or things were going to be serious.
>
> I went to Tunbridge Wells where my wife had been struggling to run our present business to help keep the home going. We hadn't any capital – my health had done away with that – but we managed to keep things going. She worked hard in the shop and I went on the round.

THE TUNBRIDGE WELLS YEARS

So the family moved to Tunbridge Wells around 1927, in which year Douglas was elected Chairman of the Tunbridge Wells Branch of the British Legion and later President of the band. He also later founded the local branch of the Old Contemptibles Association in 1932, which was named "Belcher V.C. Branch" in his honour. He also became its President.

The Old Contemptibles Association was founded in June 1925, and there were 178 branches in the United Kingdom and 14 overseas branches. They were the veterans of the British Expeditionary Force sent to France in 1914, so named because of a German reference to the contemptible little army facing them.

Douglas developed neurasthenia (lassitude, irritability, lack of concentration, worry and hypochondria), while his wife ran a fruiterer and florists shop at 69 Calverley Road, Tunbridge

Wells. The motivation for the shop came from Emily, who did not care for life as the wife of an army officer. The shop had previously been a fruiterers owned by Mr C. F. Ellis. Emily's father ran a chain of fruit shops in Kingston, Surbiton and Weybridge. It is quite probable that the shop in Tunbridge Wells became available in 1927 just at the time when Douglas felt he needed a different sort of life. He went to work assisting his wife in the shop, and spent 18 months delivering fruit and vegetables on his bicycle. He also had a costers barrow in the town on market days, which his son Francis helped to run. However, his heart wasn't really in it. His heart was still in the army. He was given money to pay bills and went off and bought pictures instead. He played the piano when he was supposed to be doing the accounts.

Mrs Belcher told the *Sunday Dispatch:*

Douglas Belcher

> When he came here to help me with the business he went out getting orders and delivering vegetables on a push-bicycle … For 18 months he rode it, sometimes as much as ten miles out of town. Then a kind friend gave us a motor-van. Business improved and we were able to have assistance in the shop. It has been a tough time for him, but he's putting a bold face on it.

69 Calverley Road today

On Saturday 9 November 1929, Douglas Belcher attended the V.C. Dinner given by the Prince of Wales at the Royal Gallery of the House of Lords. He sat at Table 4, Seat 107. "The thought that it was a great honour to represent my Regiment was uppermost in my mind," Douglas told the Kent and Sussex Courier. "I also felt it was a great privilege to represent the town of Tunbridge Wells". He said that perhaps it was the most wonderful experience of his life. There were 321 V.C.s present. His Souvenir programme was personally autographed by the Prince afterwards.

In March 1933, he was a guest of honour at the first dinner of the Tunbridge Wells and District Branch of the South African War Veterans' Association at the Royal Mount Ephraim Hotel. He marvelled at the fact that this Association had a membership of 48, but had only been established six months. His branch of the Old Contemptibles had a membership of 50, but had been going for a year.

One of the suppliers to the shop was Reginald Larkin, who came to the shop with produce grown on his family farm nearby. He had been badly wounded in the war, and could only do light manual work. Douglas's son Brian remembers as a small boy seeing this man "with a stiff leg leaving the shop and climbing onto a four wheeled horsecart and cracking a whip to encourage the horse up Calverley Road". In October 1933, the shop was sold.

In December 1933, a presentation was made to Captain Belcher by the local branch of the Royal British Legion. He had been its chairman for six years and had proved an able counsellor. He was given a case containing two pipes, the gift of the Executive Committee. The presentation was made by Major J. B. Elliott, the President. The latter said he was sorry to be losing Captain Belcher, particularly as it was through ill health. Captain Belcher, in acknowledgement, said he was leaving Tunbridge Wells with regret. He would always be deeply interested in the branch's progress.

With the shop in Tunbridge Wells sold, Douglas, Emily, Brian and Reginald, together with Emily's widowed mother, Louisa Luxford all moved to Westhorpe, Suffolk. It was thought sensible to move to a new area. They moved to Westhorpe Old Rectory, where his son Brian, then aged seven, remembers his father helping run the poultry farm and building poultry houses to use in the meadow:

> This was the first time that I recall him (Reginald Larkin) living with us as a family. I think the purchase of the Old Rectory was with his money. He had an army pension for his wounds and he had saved this money since the war. He also had a small share from his family's farm.

Louisa Luxford had a large ground floor room, and she provided an Austin car for Douglas to use. Sometime later Louisa and Douglas left and returned to Louisa's home, possibly 34 Woodbines Avenue, Kingston where Douglas lodged with her for a while. The Luxfords owned many commercial properties at different times – 17 commercial and at least six houses rented or owned in the Kingston/ Surbiton area between 1901 and her death in 1947.

In February 1935, Captain Belcher was elected an Honorary Life Member of the Old Tiffinian Association, and he attended a meeting of members that month 'who gave him a rousing welcome, and, at their request, presented a photograph of himself.' The photo was hung at the Association's Headquarters at the boys' school, London Road, Kingston and was inscribed:

> Capt. Douglas Belcher, The Old Tiffinian V.C., Ypres, May 13th, 1915.

At the end of May 1935, Belcher helped arrange a visit to Chessington Zoo for 450 children of St. Mark's School, Surbiton. This was a special jubilee outing and they were taken in coaches for the afternoon.

In June 1935, Captain Belcher presented prizes with Sergeant Hamilton V.C. to winners at the annual sports and fete organised by the Dittons branch of the British Legion at Long Ditton, Surrey.

By 1934, his health improved and in February 1935 he petitioned for divorce, which was heard in the Divorce Court on 7 October. He petitioned for a decree nisi against his wife, which was not defended. Mr Justice Bucknill granted Captain Belcher a decree nisi and gave him the custody of his sons, then aged seventeen and nine.

In October 1937, he was working as a clerk-commissionaire in a city firm of chartered accountants. The clerks never called him "Belcher". He was always addressed as "Mr. Belcher" or "Captain". By then he was living in Villiers Avenue, Surbiton. He confessed to only ever having worn his V.C. twice – apart from British Legion parades when he lived in Tunbridge Wells. The first time was when it was pinned on. He kept it hidden away in the bank.

In June 1938, he led the procession at a Torchlight Tattoo held at the Memorial Sports Ground, Redhill, Surrey. The Tattoo was held from 30 June until 2 July. It included a parade of Standards of all ex-Servicemen's organisations, including a considerable number of British Legion Standards.

Appropriate music and marches were played by the Band of H.M. Irish Guards for this item, which was performed entirely by ex-Service men. Emily took Brian from the Royal Masonic School at Bushey to see this.

On 30 October he was present at the 18th annual Ypres Memorial Service on Horse Guards Parade. He was pictured with two other V.C. winners, Sergeant W. C. Boulter and Lance Corporal A. Wilcox.

Belcher, Boulter and Wilcox at the Ypres Commemoration Service

REJOINED THE ARMY AND REMARRIED

In April 1939, Douglas attended the 25th Anniversary Dinner of the Brighton March. Forty-two attended at Brigade H.Q., Bunhill Row. On 24 May 1939, Douglas enlisted at the age of 50 in the London Rifle Brigade National Defence Company with the rank of private, having relinquished the rank of captain on enlistment into the army. "I joined up in the Territorial ranks to be with some old friends in the London Rifle Brigade. I hope I may get commissioned again, but as it is I think I am doing a useful job".

In February 1940, he was promoted to platoon sergeant. It is believed he may been invalided out of the army following a bad fall at Woolwich Barracks, and granted the rank of captain on discharge. However the family have no knowledge of a fall. The Surrey Comet of 9 August 1941 stated: "a bad fall at Woolwich Barracks caused him to be invalided out of the service in May, but now, after passing a medical board examination, he is awaiting an army appointment for further service during the war".

On 5 August 1941, he was married to Gertrude Elizabeth Brine at St. Ethelburga's Church, Bishopsgate, London. A guard of honour was formed by members of Captain Belcher's old regiment, The London Rifle Brigade, and the National Defence Corps. On 26 August 1941, he rejoined the army with Service Number 188583 and reverted to the rank of lieutenant at his own request while employed with the Royal Army Pay Corps "during the present emergency". He was employed on Prisoner of War duties from 1941–43. On 12 August 1943, he was restored to the rank of captain on ceasing to be employed. In April 1945 he and Gertrude lived at 11, Alwyne Mansion, Wimbledon until he had a stroke and returned to Claygate until his death.

On 8 June 1946, he attended the Victory Day Celebration Parade in Whitehall and Dinner and Reception at the Dorchester. The latter was provided for holders of the V.C. by the Directors of the News of the World. A Military Parade past the Royal Family – King George VI, Queen Elizabeth, Queen Mary, Princess Elizabeth and Princess Margaret, with Churchill and various dignatories, formed the centre piece. There were crowds in Trafalgar Square day and night to mark the celebrations commemorating the end of the Second World War. There were ships illuminated on the Thames and a grand firework display.

His son Brian recalls:

> My father attended our wedding in September 1948, and I recall hearing him say that he had a minor stroke while watching a cricket match (a sport he used to play and liked). Subsequently he had a series of strokes and became bedridden. Douglas and Gertrude moved to the ground floor of the Claygate property, which was still in the family. The people who were renting it agreed to move upstairs.

Douglas died at his home – Tera, 16 Rythe Road, Claygate, Surrey on Wednesday 3 June 1953, aged 63 years and 11 months. (The house had been purchased by Louisa Luxford for Douglas and Emily when they came out of the army. It was then rented out until Douglas needed it in later years.) This was the day after the Queen's Coronation. His funeral took place on 19 June at 3.00 p.m. He had a military funeral which included a "slow march" from Rythe Road to Holy Trinity Church, where he was buried. In his will he left £1,702. His wife, Gertrude died on 14 March 1967 and is also buried at Claygate.

Some years later the local British Legion received an anonymous letter deploring the dilapidated state of his last resting place. The Legion traced his surviving son Brian, who had lived in Suffolk for many years. They arranged for it to be repaired and the headstone was restored, and the lettering redone. The British Legion had a member who was a stonemason. Brian paid for a new headstone so it was not a burden on their funds and for the grave to be properly tended.

The Grave of Douglas Belcher V.C.   *The Headstone on Belcher's Grave*

In March 1956 his elder son Francis wrote to the *Soldier Magazine*:

> My late father won the Victoria Cross while serving with the London Rifle Brigade in World War One. He left me his medals and I would like to present his Victoria Cross to a regimental museum so that it can always occupy a place of honour. Can SOLDIER put me in touch with the person to whom the medal should be handed? WO 11 F. Belcher , BEM, REME, Parsons Barracks, Aldershot.
> *This reader has been referred to the curator of the Rifle Brigade Museum of Winchester.

The Medals are now held by the Royal Green Jackets Museum in Winchester.
Douglas's medal entitlement was:

Victoria Cross
1914–15 Star
British War Medal (1914–20)
Victory Medal (1914–19)
King George VI Coronation Medal (1937)
Queen Elizabeth 11 Coronation Medal (1953).

MASONRY AND MEMORIALS

Douglas Belcher was a very enthusiastic and well respected Freemason. He was initiated into the Arts and Crafts Lodge, Number 3387, meeting at Freemasons Hall, London on 4 March 1916, then being passed on 5 April 1916, and Raised on 6 May. At the time he was a 26-year-old Lieutenant. His membership ceased in 1931.

He was a Petitioner (Founder Member) of the Hazara Lodge, Number 4159, Club Abbottabad, Hazara in the Punjab, India when it was founded on 13 July 1920. He served as Junior Warden and resigned 31 October 1922 presumably on leaving India. In November 1937 he joined the London Rifle Brigade Lodge, Number 1962, meeting in Mark Masons' Hall, London. At that time he was 48 and serving as a clerk with Waring and Gillow. He did not hold any office in this Lodge. He retained membership until his death.

On 27 April 1945, he became a joining member of the Lodge of Amity, Number 171, Freemasons' Hall, London giving his address as Wimbledon and his occupation as Civil Servant. He did not take any office, resigning on 13 November 1949.

Because of the Indian independence, Hazara Lodge, Number 4159, was transferred on 6 November 1947 to Freemasons' Hall, London from the District Grand Lodge of the Punjab. He rejoined the Lodge on 6 April 1948 at the age of 59, and was Worshipful Master from June 1948. In March 1951 he was elected an Honorary Member.

Although he was a pupil at Tiffin School and therefore qualified to join the Tiffinian Lodge 3530, he did not join. However Tiffinian Lodge designed and funded a plaque to his memory and this was unveiled in the Tiffin School Hall on 10 November 2006. At the unveiling on that day was his 90-year-old daughter-in-law, his granddaughter and his great-grandson. His granddaughter, Mary Luxford laid a wreath on behalf of her father.

The plaque reads:

> To Commemorate the Award of
> THE VICTORIA CROSS
> To
> Lance Sergeant
> DOUGLAS WALTER BELCHER
> 5th Battalion. The London Regiment
> For his skill and great gallantry
> In the Second Battle of Ypres Belgium
> 13 May 1915
> This Salute to an Old Boy of the School is presented by the Tiffinian Lodge

At the end of January 2006, a display about the history of the V.C., highlighting recipients with Surrey connections was held at the Local and Family History Centre in Ewell Library. It was open for four weeks and coincided with the 150th Anniversary of the Victoria Cross.

* * * * *

Belcher's portrait appears on one of the Gallaher Ltd. Cigarette Cards (No. 44) – Great War Series 2 1915 – Victoria Cross Heroes. There were 25 cards in each Series. There were 8 series all WW1.

* * * * *

He is commemorated on the Rifle Brigade's Roll of Fame on the north wall of the Nave, close to the West Door in Winchester Cathedral.

* * * * *

His photo hangs in the Union Jack Club, Sandell Street, Waterloo, London SE1 8UJ and his name is on the V.C. Roll of Honour.

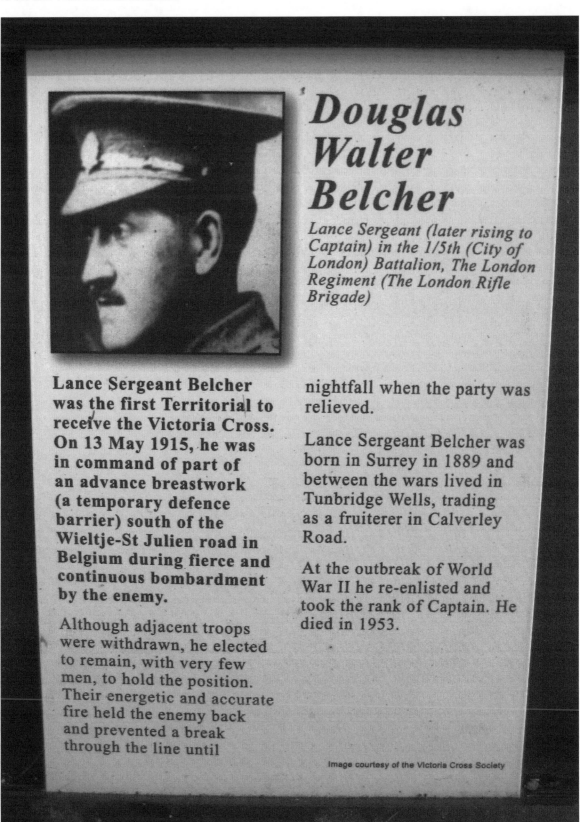

Douglas Walter Belcher

Lance Sergeant (later rising to Captain) in the 1/5th (City of London) Battalion, The London Regiment (The London Rifle Brigade)

Lance Sergeant Belcher was the first Territorial to receive the Victoria Cross. On 13 May 1915, he was in command of part of an advance breastwork (a temporary defence barrier) south of the Wieltje-St Julien road in Belgium during fierce and continuous bombardment by the enemy.

Although adjacent troops were withdrawn, he elected to remain, with very few men, to hold the position. Their energetic and accurate fire held the enemy back and prevented a break through the line until nightfall when the party was relieved.

Lance Sergeant Belcher was born in Surrey in 1889 and between the wars lived in Tunbridge Wells, trading as a fruiterer in Calverley Road.

At the outbreak of World War II he re-enlisted and took the rank of Captain. He died in 1953.

Image courtesy of the Victoria Cross Society

Belcher's Write-up in the Victoria Cross Grove, Dunorlan Park, Tunbridge Wells

CHAPTER SIX

From Army Chaplain to Modest Rector –
The Story of Rev. William Robert Fountaine Addison 1883–
1962

FOREWORD

As a child I have very fond memories of my Uncle Will. My older sister Helen and I used to visit Will when he was at Bulford Camp. I remember that he was very kind and used to buy us sweets. I remember his warm sense of humour.

We both used to attend his services on Sundays - I recall that Helen and I used to giggle behind the pews! I also remember that Uncle Will always preached a sermon with plenty of humour!

By 1939 I had left home and at the outbreak of the Second World War joined the WRAC as an ambulance driver. I did meet Uncle Will quite some time later at a family funeral at Brookwood Cemetery when he remarked that I "still looked as beautiful as ever!"

He was only the second man in Holy Orders to win the Victoria Cross during the First World War. After a meritorious career as an army chaplain he spent twenty years as a rector in Norfolk.

I am delighted and proud to be able to write a few words to add to Richard Snow's research on a brave and wonderful member of the family.

Betty Milne, niece of Marjorie Addison.

I met Will Addison before I left England as a child. He was married to my grandfather's sister Marjorie. He was a kind man who seemed to love children. He came here to Canada (my home now) in 1905 I think with another man. They took up a grant in Manitoba with the intent to farm. However the weather was unusually cold and after two years of struggle he gave it up. He went into the British Columbia forests to work as a lumberjack. A very brave thing to do in itself in those days. While working there he was called to God and he then returned to England to enter the Church.

Barbara Cullen, great niece of Marjorie Addison

THE ADDISON FAMILY

When William Robert Fountaine Addison was born in 1883, his unusual middle name, Fountaine, came from his great grandfather's wife. His great grandfather, William Addison, born 1767 in Dinsdale, County Durham, married twice. His first wife was Mary Fountaine, whom he married on 22 April 1800. After she died, sometime before 1818 he married Lucy Rattray. William was rector of St. George, Middleton-one-Row, County Durham. He died on 31 May 1837 in Clifton, Bristol. Lucy died in 1851. William and Lucy had five children – the eldest son, William Fountaine Addison became curate of St. Giles Church, Reading before becoming canon of Gibraltar in 1869 and vicar of Ossett, Yorkshire in 1877. In 1851, he married Sarah Ellen Elizabeth Grylls at Newton Abbot in Devon. They had at least two children. William Fountaine Addison died in 1893.

William Grylls Addison was the eldest son of William and Sarah, and was born in 1853 at Dorchester, Oxfordshire. He was a landscape painter and water colourist. He had exhibitions between 1880 and 1900 at The Dudley Gallery, The Royal Glasgow Institute of Fine Arts, The Walker Art Gallery, Liverpool, Manchester City Art Gallery, The Royal Society of British Artists, The Royal Institute of Painters and The Royal Academy. In 1880, he married Alice Knight at Sevenoaks, Kent and they lived in London from 1880 until 1883.

In 1883, the Addison family moved to Chapel Terrace, North Warnborough, Odiham, Hampshire. It was here that the eldest son, William Robert Fountaine Addison was born on 18 September 1838. He was not born in Cranbrook, Kent as many sources state. The birth was registered on 13 October and the name Fountaine was entered after registration. His brothers and sisters were all born in North Warnborough. Charles Rattray Addison was born in the September quarter of 1885. Philip Francis Addison, born in the March quarter 1888, served as a Private with the 1st/5th Battalion, Buffs (East Kent Regiment). He was killed in action in Mesopotamia on 24 February 1917. He was buried in Amara War Cemetery, Mesopotamia in Plot XXIX Row B.

William's birthplace, Odiham, Hants.

Lancelot Joseph Addison, whose birth was registered during the December quarter of 1891, emigrated to New Zealand and joined the Canterbury Regiment, New Zealand Expeditionary Forces. He was killed in action at Gallipoli on 7 August 1915 and was commemorated on the Chunuk Bair (New Zealand) Memorial. Both Philip Francis and Lancelot Joseph are remembered on the War Memorial in St. Dunstan's Church, Cranbrook, Kent. The last of William's brothers was John Humphrey Addison, whose birth was registered during the June quarter of 1893. No more is known of him. There were also two sisters. Mary Addison, whose birth and death were sadly registered during the March quarter of 1887. The second was Ella Rosamund Addison, whose birth was registered during the December quarter of 1889. Ella, who died a spinster in Oakwood Hospital, Maidstone on 30 April 1967, aged 77 is buried in Golford Cemetery, Cranbrook. Her simple headstone rests under a tree in the cemetery in Plot Q42. The Cemetery is past the Cranbrook Windmill on the right, opposite Dulwich College Preparatory School.

In 1896, William Grylls Addison and his family moved to Etchinghill House, Gore Lane, Goudhurst, Kent where William continued to paint and exhibit.

Sadly, in 1904 William Grylls Addison took his own life. The Kent and Sussex Courier of 7 October 1904 reported on an inquest held at Etchinghill House by Mr C. Duncan Murton, Coroner for the Cranbrook district:

Etchinghill House

Master Philip Addison, son of the deceased, said on the previous morning he came downstairs to breakfast, and as his father had not arrived he called out to him. Not receiving any reply, witness went up to the bedroom, and found his father lying in bed with an awful cut across his throat. Witness called his sister, Miss Dorothy Addison, whose room was just opposite, and afterwards went for Major-General Fitz Hugh, a neighbour, who immediately came to his house. Witness saw his father about ten minutes to nine on Thursday evening, when he appeared as usual. Nothing had been said by the deceased to lead the family to suppose that he would take his own life.

Major-General Alfred Fitz Hugh deposed that he found the deceased lying in bed with a terrible cut across his throat. There was a razor on one side of the body, and a small hand mirror on the other side, both being covered with blood. On a chest of drawers at the head of the bed was a candlestick, the candle in which had been allowed to burn right out. The deceased was quite dead, and was lying in a composed position. Witness was with the deceased on Thursday afternoon for about a quarter of an hour, and then noticed that he seemed in an extremely depressed condition.

Miss Dorothy Addison said she last saw her father alive on Thursday evening at about half past ten, just before going to bed. She did not notice anything peculiar in his manner, and thought he seemed very well.

Dr. G.H. Mapleton, of Goudhurst, stated that when he arrived Mr Addison was quite dead. The wound in the throat was of such a nature that it would cause almost instantaneous death. In his opinion the cut was self inflicted.

Dr. Thomas Joyce of Cranbrook, said he had been the medical attendant of Mr Addison and his family during the nine years they had been in Goudhurst. The deceased had had

145

The Rose Walk, Finchcocks, Goudhurst after the original drawing by Wm.G. Addison

several attacks of melancholia, from which he had completely recovered. The last attack began about a fortnight before his death. Deceased complained of absolute sleeplessness, and inability to do justice to his work. He had arranged for an exhibition of his pictures at the Dore Gallery, in London, for the first week in October, but was unable to complete his pictures by that time. By the advice of witness, deceased arranged with the manager of the Dore Gallery that the exhibition should be postponed. Mr Addison was intensely worried,

3 West Terrace, Cranbrook

FAMILY PHOTOGRAPHS
1 9 0 3 - 1 9 1 2

William Addison, 1903

William and his sister, Ella Addison, Cranbrook, 1907

William, as lumberjack, 1907

William, lunchtime in a pub, at Chelsham, Surrey, 1908

Marjorie, Hill Cottage, Caterham, 1908

Marjorie in fencing kit, 1908

Marjorie shows off new clothes, 1908

Marjorie, 1909

William Addison at Bickleigh Vale, near Plymouth, 1909

William Addison on the Mewstone Rock, Wembury Bay, Devon, 1911

Dorothy Wallis, Marjorie's sister-in-law, with William Addison, on shore of River Yealm, summer 1912

and could at times, scarcely speak without tears, but there was nothing in his condition that could warrant his being placed under control. Mrs Addison had only just left home.

The jury returned a verdict of Suicide during temporary insanity.

William died on 30 September 1904 and was buried on 4 October in the graveyard at St. Mary's Church, Goudhurst.

After his death Alice moved to Cranbrook, Kent and lived at 3, West Terrace. She died over 30 years later on 3 March 1938 in Cranbrook. She was in her 88th year and was described by the Kent and Sussex Courier as a "delightful personality". She was a vice-president of the Cranbrook Badminton Club, and a keen supporter of the Town Band, and the local Operatic and Dramatic Society, whose shows she invariably attended.

She was buried with her husband at St. Mary's, Goudhurst on 5 March 1938. Her son, the Rev. W. R. F. Addison V.C., Chaplain to the Forces, officiated.

AN ARMY CHAPLAIN

So, William Robert Fountaine Addison was born on 18 September 1883 in North Warnborough, near Odiham, Hants. He attended Robert May's Grammar School, West Street, Odiham in 1892. Then the family moved to Goudhurst in 1896 where William attended Horsmonden Village School.

William's Birth Certificate

After the death of his father in 1904, William migrated to Canada and spent some time working initially as a farmer and then for two or three years as a lumberjack in a lumber camp in British Columbia. While there he acquired a taste for playing poker. Having worked hard in Canada, in 1909 he returned to England and studied farming in Devon. His brothers had, in the meantime, emigrated to Australasia.

William, in the meantime, had made up his mind to enter the Church, and saved up enough money to go to College. From 1911–1913 he attended Sarum Theological College, Salisbury, Wiltshire. In the 1911 census he is listed as a "student for holy orders" and the address is given as

Galva, Plympton. In May 1913, he was ordained in Salisbury Cathedral and appointed curate of St. Edmund's. He was at the same time assistant chaplain to the Church Lads' Brigade.

He was an extremely popular man in Salisbury. The *Daily Sketch* of 27 September 1916 said:

> Work of the hardest kind never came amiss to him – he revelled in it as a pleasure. But he worked for a purpose. His heart and ambition were wrapped up in the Church, and he resolved to take orders. After years of sheer hard toiling (in Canada) he collected sufficient funds to return to England, and entered the Theological College at Salisbury as a student. He was ordained, and received his first curacy at St. Edmund's Church, where he remained until the war called him.

Canon Morrice, Rector of St. Edmund's was quoted as saying:

> His experience in a lumber camp and of Colonial life caused him to mix with men of all kinds; and it was this experience that made him seek ordination that he might give himself more fully to the work of keeping men and boys from ruin and winning them to better things.
>
> This was the kind of work which was nearest his heart, and, this being so, it was natural that he should be much interested in the Church Lads' Brigade, of which he was assistant Chaplain.
>
> He was most regular at their parades, was zealous in gaining recruits, and most assiduous in his efforts to interest the lads.
>
> But he threw himself heartily into all the work of the parish and his geniality made him a welcome visitor in the homes of rich and poor alike. We were very sorry to lose him from the parish, but we recognised that he would make an excellent Forces Chaplain.

A friend said:

> He's a jolly nice fellow: anybody could get on with him. But he spent most of his time with the boys. He was a prodigious worker, and would often sit up until two and three in the morning writing – and always to help somebody or something or other.

Addison with his Church Lads' Brigade

In addition to his curacy and his involvement in the Church Lads' Brigade, he was editor of Sarum St. Edmunds Parish Church magazine.

> What spare time he had was devoted to his favourite hobby of bird-nesting. And Mrs. Burt, his landlady, often found his bed empty of a morning. 'I never worried', she told the Daily Sketch, 'I knew he was out bird-nesting'.

In conversation with Mr Sainsbury, a friend, the *Daily Sketch* learned that, in addition to being a worker, he was a great sportsman, and that boxing was his favourite pastime.

When the War came, William was commissioned in the Royal Army Chaplains Department as a 4th Class Temporary Chaplain. The four Classes were: 4th Class: Captain; 3rd Class: Major;

2nd Class: Lieutenant Colonel; 1st Class: Colonel. He was attached to the 38th Infantry Brigade, 13th Division, which included the 6th Battalion, The King's Own Royal Lancaster Regiment. His commission was dated 22 September 1915. He was then promoted captain.

In August 1914, when the British Expeditionary Force sailed for France the Department was still only small comprising just over 1900 commissioned chaplains so there was no difficulty in providing the 65 required. By the time the war ended there were nearly 3,500. They only carried a Bible, Prayer Book and probably sweets and cigarettes for the troops. They had only their faith to protect them, not rifle or revolver. In early 1915, the British Government resolved to ease Turkish pressure on the Russians on the Caucasus front by seizing control of the Dardanelles channel, the Gallipoli peninsular, and then Istanbul. From there pressure could be brought on Austria-Hungary, forcing the central Powers to divert troops from the Western Front.

By the end of July 1915, it had become clear that the original plan for taking the Gallipoli peninsular had failed. To achieve it another landing with fresh forces was necessary and the point chosen was Suvla Bay – a few miles north of Anzac Cove. As part of the Gallipoli Campaign, landings were made on 6 and 7 August 1915 at Suvla Bay, with 20,000 troops being set down with little Turkish opposition. William Addison was sent out as chaplain on 29 September. Commander-in-Chief Sir Ian Hamilton failed to obtain adequate reinforcements and was removed from command in October 1915, to be replaced by Sir Charles Monro, who recommended evacuation, which was approved by Lord Kitchener on 15 November 1915. The successful evacuation of 105,000 men and 300 guns from Anzac Cove and Suvla Bay was successfully conducted from 10–20 December 1915. On 9 January 1916, the last of the Allied troops were withdrawn.

MESOPOTAMIA

The Mesopotamian campaign was fought in the Middle Eastern theatre of the Great War between the Allied Powers represented by the British Empire, consisting mainly of troops from the Indian Empire, and the Central Powers, mainly from the Ottoman Empire. Shortly after the European War started, the British sent a military force to protect Abadan, which had one of the world's earliest oil refineries. The oilfields near the Persian Gulf were essential to Britain's oil supply. The Ottoman Fourth Army was also located in this region. After various naval activities, Great Britain and France declared war on the Ottoman Empire on 5 November 1914. Mesopotamia was a low priority for the Ottomans so they placed portions of the 38th Division at the mouth of Shatt-al-Arab. The rest of the defensive force was stationed in Basra.

After the British successfully occupied Basra on 22 November, and some other minor victories, General Sir John Nixon was sent in April 1915 to take command. He ordered Charles Vere Ferrers Townshend to advance to Kut or even to Baghdad if possible. Townshend advanced up the Tigris River. Because they advanced rapidly, the Ottomans were worried about the possible fall of Baghdad. On 22 November 1915, Townshend fought a battle at Ctesiphon, a town 25 miles south of Baghdad. The conflict lasted five days, ending as a stalemate, with both sides retreating from the battlefield. Townshend retreated to Kut-al-Amara, where he halted and fortified his position. But by 3 December, the British were encircled. The siege of Kut began on 7 December. From the British point of view, defending Kut as opposed to retreating to Basra was a mistake since Kut was isolated, and therefore could not be resupplied. New fortified positions were established by the Ottomans down river to prevent any attempt to rescue Townshend. Townshend suggested an attempt to break out but this was initially rejected by Sir John Nixon, however he quickly relented. Nixon, under the command of General Aylmer established a relief force. General Aylmer made three major attempts to break the siege, but was rebuffed on each occasion.

Following this General Nixon was replaced by General Lake. British forces received small quantities of supplies from the air, but these were not enough to feed the garrison. Between January and March 1916, both Townshend and Aylmer launched several attacks in an attempt to break the siege. These included Sheikh Sa'ad, The Battle of the Wadi, and the Battle of Hanna all in January.

This was followed on 8 March by an attack on the Dujaila Redoubt, resulting in 4,000 deaths. All these attempts did not succeed and their costs were heavy. Food and hopes were running out for Townshend in Kut. Disease was spreading very rapidly and could not be cured.

After the battles of Hanna and Dujaila both sides were reinforced. Major General Sir Frederick Stanley Maude's 13th Infantry Division joined the fight. This unit had distinguished itself in the Gallipoli campaign, but had suffered 6,000 casualties there. Although replacements brought them back to full strength of 10,500 men, they were not battle tested. With reinforcements the Tigris Corps numbered 30,357 men, 127 guns, 11 aircraft and 4 gunboats.

Turkish Commander Khalil Pasha secured reserves from Baghdad. He commanded roughly the same number as the Tigris Corps, but he had only 88 guns. The Turks were dug in at Hanna, at Fallahiyeh, some three miles behind Hanna, and at Sanna-i-Yat, three miles beyond that.

This then is the background before the arrival of the 6th Battalion King's Own Royal Lancaster Regiment, to be joined by Captain William Addison. He was among 1,000 British infantry men and 500 field and horse artillery who were due to arrive in Basra from England on the 14 February. On 12 February 1916, the 13th Division began to move from Egypt to Mesopotamia. They landed at Basra on 27 February, and were told they were to join the relief column. They left Basra on 2 March, landing at Orah on 7th. On 10 March, they left for Sheik Sa'ad, where they spent some weeks' night training. Around the 20th, they left again for Orah, where they landed that night to prepare for the dash to Kut. They were told they must get through at all costs to relieve General Townshend.

On 12 March, General Aylmer was dismissed and replaced by General George Gorringe. The relief attempt by Gorringe is usually referred to as the First Battle of Kut. The British Empire forces numbered about 30,000 soldiers, roughly equal to the Ottomans. The battle began at dawn on 5 April. The 13th Division assaulted Turkish trenches on the left bank of the Tigris at Hanna and Fallahiyeh. Hoping to catch the Turks by surprise, Gorringe had ordered the initial assault by the infantry alone. Only after the first Turkish trenches had been taken would the artillery fire commence.

The Turks were aware of the British preparations, and when the British Infantry crept forward they found the Turks had abandoned the first trench line at Hanna during the night. The 6th King's Own Royal Lancaster Regiment and 13th Division went over the top and captured the first line of trenches called Umel Hamel at 5 a.m. The 13th Division bore the brunt of the losses that day, suffering almost 2,000 casualties with little ground gained.

They then advanced seven miles during the day and at about 3 p.m. started to dig in. The trenches were dug by about 5.30 when they made ready to attack the Fallahiyeh redoubt. At 6.30 they moved forward for the attack an hour later. Fallahiyeh was captured but with heavy losses, the Division had 1868 casualties.

The following day the regiment bivouacked all day in the open and had a roll call. That morning Gorringe had brought up the 7th Division to relieve the 13th and move against the Turkish defences at Sanna-i-Yat. They mounted three separate attacks but gained only 500 yards. Mail was received by the 13th Division and sent on the 7th, and on the 8th they assembled to move against the Turks again. They left at about 8.30 and marched all night towards the front line at Sanna-i-Yat hoping to surprise the Turks. However they

The Reverend William Addison

were surprised instead and the attack was unsuccessful so they dug in within 200 yards of the Turks position. The Division had found themselves facing three well-equipped Turkish trench lines in the darkness of the early hours of Sunday the 9 April. Suddenly they found themselves illuminated by the light of the Turkish flares but it was too late to call off the operation and the attack went ahead. Rifle and machine-gun fire ploughed into the attackers and very few men reached the Turkish lines.

On 9 April Townshend received a wire from the British Headquarters:

> The 13th Division tried to assault the position at dawn. Turks discovered advance when leading troops were within 100 yards and manned trenches in force, opening very heavy fire. Division failed to reach enemy's fire trench and is dug in, its nearest detachments being within 300 yards of enemy's position. At present they are reorganising, evacuating wounded and resting.

The 13th Division had only advanced to the first Turkish trenches and were to suffer 1,807 casualties. They failed because there were no troops following up the attack in support. Five Victoria Crosses were later awarded for valour that day, including William Addison. In the two actions at Fallahiyeh and Sanna-i-Yat, the 13th Division sustained 46 per cent casualties of actual troops engaged. The Division were eventually relieved at 10 p.m. by the 7th Division.

The adjutant, Captain Pennefather wrote:

> It was after the attack had failed and while troops were trying to dig in under intense machine-gun fire, that the Rev. W.R.F. Addison, the C. of E. Chaplain attached to the Battalion, gained the Victoria Cross for his unceasing attention to the wounded throughout the whole morning under incessant fire on perfectly flat ground within 400 yards of the Turks. I saw him myself, having been wounded early in the morning.

William Addison had been following up, encouraging and assisting the medical teams and stretcher bearers. He took his life in both hands, and went out across no man's land to attend to a wounded soldier. In spite of murderous Turkish fire, he survived, and carried the wounded soldier to the cover of a trench. He then repeated this suicidal act by going back again several times to bind up the wounds of other men, and help them to the same cover, all the time under heavy rifle and machine-gun fire. His unaided efforts, his splendid example, and utter disregard of personal danger, encouraged the stretcher-bearers to join him in going forward under fire to collect more of the wounded.

A summary in the war diary of the 13th Division (WO95/5147) noted on the 9th: "During the fight and in addition to the officers, the Chaplains and Medical detachments, including the stretcher bearers particularly distinguished themselves by their splendid work".

As his Victoria Cross citation said:

> For most conspicuous bravery. He carried a wounded man to the cover of a trench, and assisted several others to the same cover, after binding up their wounds under heavy rifle fire and machine-gun fire. In addition to these unaided efforts, by his splendid example and utter disregard of personal danger, encouraged the stretcher-bearers to go forward under heavy fire and collect the wounded.

This appeared in the *London Gazette*, 26 September 1916, number 29765, p. 9417. He became the second man in holy orders to win the highest military award for bravery during the war.

As the *South Norfolk News* reported in an article by Steve Snelling on 31 March 1983:

> William Addison could hear the pitiful wailing of the wounded above the rattle of machine gun fire. Their cries and screams sang out over the bloody, barren battlefield at Sanna-i-Yat.

Moments earlier they had left their trenches, a long thin line of khaki, confident of breaching the Turkish defences barring the road to besieged Kut.

Now, they lay, torn to shreds, in no-man's land. And it didn't seem likely that any man could help them. The front line stretcher bearers were pinned down by the scything fire.

Addison, a 32-year-old chaplain fourth class attached to the King's Own Royal Lancaster Regiment, knew all of that. A veteran of little more than 12 months' service, he had seen enough fighting in the muddied Mesopotamian campaign to know that survival for battlefield wounded hinged on their receiving immediate treatment.

Suddenly something inside him made him clamber over the parapet into no-man's land.

Battle-weary soldiers, the tattered remnants of the shattered 13th Division, watched incredulously as the small, wiry chaplain darted from shell-hole to shell-hole.

By now the hazy grey early morning sky was clear. The Turks had a perfect view of the dusty, desert wilderness that was no-man's land. They fired at anything that moved.

The man who had been ordered to stay out of the front line bore a charmed life. Incredibly, Addison reached the nearest wounded man unharmed.

Again and again he braved the storm of lead to bring in desperately wounded men. Some time on that awful day Addison was himself severely wounded in the leg.

But he hardly seemed to notice it. When the Turkish infantry mounted their own counter-attack, he coolly went on with his self-appointed task.

It is even said that when officer casualties reached threatening proportions, the gallant padre took charge of the depleted defenders and beat off the assault with machine guns and grenades.

His action on that grimmest of days earned him a severe reprimand for disobeying orders and straying into the front line. It also won him the Victoria Cross.

William Addison was convinced that he had been protected and guided through that terrible ordeal by a greater force than man.

Years later in a rare moment, he talked of that conviction. 'I felt,' he said, 'that I was not alone but that I had someone with me. And something inside me told me that what I was doing was the right thing.'

On 10 April, the 6th King's Own Royal Lancaster Regiment bivouacked in the rain and towards evening they had a Thanksgiving Service conducted by Captain Addison, who had been recommended for bravery. On the 11th, the Battalion went on outpost duty and at midnight there was a great thunderstorm. The following day they moved towards Essen Redoubts but were put in reserve at Abu-Romain-Mounds. The East and South Lancashire Regiments took the front line of trenches.

Gorringe then transferred his main effort to the other bank of the Tigris where heavy rains had cut the road to Kut. On 12 April at a cost of 400 casualties, the 3rd Division gained a lodgement, but heavy rain delayed exploitation.

On 15 April, when Townshend reported that food supplies at Kut would be exhausted by the 29th, Gorringe's men stormed the forward Turkish outposts at Bait Asia on the

Carrying a Wounded Man

south bank. Two days later, the 3rd Division drove a salient into the Turkish defences there and Gurkha troops captured two Turkish guns. But Khalil was able to concentrate 10,000 men there and mounted five counter attacks that night, retaking the salient at a cost of 4,000 casualties. British and Indian losses were 1600 men and 15 machine-guns taken.

154

With 5,000 reinforcements delayed from Basra, on 22 April, Gorringe mounted a final effort, this time against Sanna-i-Yat. Following artillery bombardment, several thousand men of 7th Division attacked. Although the Turks evacuated their first two trench lines, they then counter attacked in force and inflicted 1283 casualties.

A telegram from headquarters read: "22nd April, 7.50 p.m. Much regret that the attack on Sanna-i-Yat position this morning was repulsed. Gorringe, however, will not relax his efforts".

Between 5 and 23 April the Tigris Corps sustained just under 10,000 casualties. From January to April the losses were 23,000.

With the Kut garrison now on minimal rations, Gorringe called off the effort. After a siege which lasted 143 days, Major General Charles Townshend surrendered. An announcement from the War Office in London blamed shortage of supplies and said resistance was conducted with "gallantry and fortitude". The news caused dismay. For a British force to lay down its arms was without precedent in the war. General Gorringe's relief force was in fact only 20 miles away, but proved incapable of fighting a way through the Turkish cordon. British and Indian troops suffered greatly from intense winter cold and lack of supplies.

Royal Navy river steamers failed to break the blockade and one boat, the Junlar, fell into enemy hands. For the first time an air drop was tried. British aeroplanes made desperate attempts to supply the besieged Division but the food that was delivered was not enough. Surrender talks began two days earlier, and then the white flag was hoisted on the 29 April. More than 8,000 British and Indian troops went into captivity. Red Cross boats went up the river to bring the sick and wounded back from Kut while an armistice was declared until the boats returned on 1 May. The siege of Kut was an important Turkish victory. The British government on the other hand was forced to pour more resources into Mesopotamia.

Seventy per cent of the British and 50 per cent of the Indian troops died of disease or at the hands of the Turkish guards during captivity. Townshend himself was taken to the Island of Malki on the Sea of Marmara, to sit out the war in luxury.

Nearly all the British commanders involved in the failure to rescue Townshend were removed from command. The British Army underwent a major overhaul. A new commander, Lieutenant General Sir Frederick Stanley Maude was given the job of restoring Britain's military reputation. He spent the rest of 1916 rebuilding his army.

From 9 May the 6th Battalion the King's Own Royal Lancaster Regiment relieved the North Lancs and spent the next eight days in the trenches, before being relieved by the Norfolk Regiment, the Dorsets and Ghurkhas and native infantry. On the 18th, General Maude told the regiment that the Turks had evacuated the trenches at Essen that morning. They were in need of water and the weather was very hot again.

On 20 September, the 6th Battalion commenced the march from Sheik Sa'ad to Armara, a distance of 98.5 miles. On 25 October, Colonel McNaughton of the 12th Lancers took command of the 6th Bn. King's Own Royal Lancaster Regiment.

On 19 October 1916, The Reverend William Addison was mentioned in Despatches, and received two more mentions later. On 5 November 1916, he was presented with his Victoria Cross ribbon along with three others from the Division by Lieutenant General F. S. Maude at Amara. All the 13th Division were present. He wrote in one of his letters:

> The parade was a fine one and the Division looked magnificent. It is extraordinary how the men have picked up during the last few weeks, and they looked not only clean and smart, but they stepped briskly and looked healthy. It was a red-letter day in the Division, for I fancy that there are not many – if any – that can say they have had four V.C.s presented on the same day.

On 25 November, the 39 and 40 Brigades left Armara for Sheik Sa'ad, and the 6th Battalion followed on 4 December on board the PS8 50, one of the largest boats on the Tigris. They arrived in Sheik Sa'ad the following day and pitched camp. The 6th brought the first rain since April. It had been very hot and in his last letter to Mrs Burt, his Salisbury landlady, Captain Addison wrote:

> I often wish I was back at St. Edmund's but really I like the life out here. By the way, I can eat anything now, and not a bit faddy. It is fearfully hot here – 120 deg. in the shade, and the shade is only a tent.

On 7 December, the 6th Battalion struck camp and moved off at about 9.30 a.m., marching a distance of eight miles, the first four being very dusty. On the 14th they dug themselves in, after hearing a bombardment in the direction of Sanna-i-Yat early that morning.

The British launched their new campaign on 13 December 1916. The British had some 50,000 well trained and well equipped troops: the Indian 111 Corps also called the Tigris Corps. The Ottoman forces were smaller, perhaps around 25,000 strong under the command of Khalil Pasha.

Charles Palmer of the 6th King's Own Royal Lancaster Regiment wrote in his diary on 15 December:

> We prepare to move at 9a.m. and leave our redoubts but we have only marched about 800 yards when the first shot of the day is fired, and one or two big guns also open fire on us. We go a bit further in artillery formation but as the rifle fire gets more rapid and nearer we extend into skirmishing order, no. 1, 2, 3 companies being the front line, no.4 company being in reserve all day. After advancing another 500 yards we all dig in and the Turkish guns continue to shell us but it is evident that young Johnny Turk is in a bad way for guns. I only heard about 4. One of them being a 5–9 Howitzer which was firing big dirty black shells and he had the range of no. 1–2 company to an inch and considering the numbers of shells they sent over we had very few casualties. It was here that Captain Saunders of no. 1 company, one of the best officers in the Battalion was wounded, a bullet wound in the abdomen. I also saw our Chaplain Rev Capt. Addison (V.C.) wounded in the right hand but he would not leave the Battalion, he came from the firing line and helped the doctor. Capt. Freake Evans, captain of my company was also badly wounded in the back. About 4.30 p.m. the orders came to prepare to advance and we all dumped our packs, the stretcher bearers dumping theirs with no.4 company. We then made an advance of another 900 yards and I do not think it could have been done cooler on parade. All the way we were under heavy shell and rifle fire, I think our total casualties were about 85. We dug in again about 12 midnight, we have a very good trench about 6 feet deep.

By the 17th, they were three miles in front of Kut, and on 24 December 1916, the regiment had a Church Parade with Captain Addison offering up a prayer for Captain Saunders who had died. The *Daily Sketch* for Wednesday 27 September 1916 had reported that he had had one narrow escape during his humane work:

> It was at a burial service on the field. He was reading the service by means of an electric torch, when a bullet from a sniper's rifle knocked his hat off. Several other shots followed, but Mr. Addison went on with the service in the dark.

Charles Palmer reported that Christmas Day rations were "1lb. Bread, one tin of bully, tea, butter, one slice of cake, 1lb. tin of pudding between a platoon".

In January 1917, Maude's 150,000 troops set out from the regional command headquarters at Basra to launch the offensive that would culminate in the recapture of Kut on 24 February. They proceeded cautiously, advancing on both sides of the Tigris River. Progress was slow but sure, on account of heavy rain and an overriding concern to minimalise casualties. It took a full two months to clear the west bank of resistance below Kut. The Ottoman forces contested a fortified place called the Khadairi Bend which the British captured after two weeks of siege work (6 January to 19 January 1917). On 7 January, the rain stopped, and for two days the Turkish trenches were heavily bombarded and raids carried out on the Turkish front line at Sanna-i-Yat. They then had to force the Turks out of a strong defensive line along the Hai River. This took a further two weeks from 25 January till 4 February.

Charles Palmer's Diary for 3 February reads:

> We move off at 1.30 a.m. across the Shat-el-Hai and march about 7 miles when we bivouac in the open. Just before dawn we are told we are in reserve to the 39th and 40th Brigades. Towards noon we hear that the 39th and 40th Brigade while skirmishing have run up against a strong Turkish position and got a dose of the Turks shell fire. They have a few casualties including the Colonel who was acting Brigadier General commanding our brigade. We rest till after tea when we get ready to move at 5.30 a.m. and about this time no.2 platoon comes in. They have been on the march and they tell us it is full of geese, ducks and hares but as we have not got sporting guns we give them a miss. Our next day's rations come up and out of 100lbs of biscuits 50lbs are mouldy. Towards 7 o'clock we move off and march about a mile to our right flank where we form up and unload our mules and bivouac for the night. We then get issued with one blanket and an oil-sheet and our orders are to turn in for the night, but we must be ready to move off again at 5.30 a.m. We get word here that the 14th Division have captured the first and second line of Turkish trenches, the Devon's, Hants, Ghurkhas being in action, so we now turn in. It is some time before we settle down as our long range guns are going all night long.

On 9 February, he wrote:

> We are roused at 5am. The cooks have been up early and have tea and porridge for us. We also have a rum issue, 3 spoonfuls each, and at 6.30 am we move up the communication trench towards the firing line. About ten minutes before the attack a chum remarked that it was the 9th of February. Also that our previous big attack by the Battalion had been on the 9th of April (1916), the 9th of August (1915), and had been unsuccessful. Would this be successful or not, we had not long to wait. About 9am the word came to get ready and the bombardment started.
>
> Hardly had the first line gone over before it was plain to see that the strength of the Turks had been underestimated. They open out such a rapid fire that it was evident that they had been waiting for us. Capt. Addison was wounded in the thigh in trying to get to the wounded. The Turks made desperate attempts to capture the position making about 7 counter attacks but our bombs and machine gun and rifle fire simply riddled them and the more that came the more we killed.

Another Ottoman position called Dahra bend was taken on 16 February. Finally, the British recaptured Kut on 24 February 1917 in the Second Battle of Kut.

The local Ottoman commander, Karabekir Bey, did not let his army become trapped in Kut as General Townshend had been in the previous year. But his forces were ground down by the constant battles and defeats – only 2,500 remained after Kut fell. These linked up with the Baghdad garrison of some 10,000.

After three days' worth of supplies had been accumulated, Maude continued his march towards Baghdad. Khalil Pasha stationed The Turkish 6th Army some 35 miles to the south of the city, near the junction of the Tigris with the Diyala River. In the absence of significant reserves, the Turks were vastly outnumbered. Maude's troops reached the Diyala on 8 March, mounting their first assault the next morning, which the Turks successfully repelled. After struggling to cross the fast-moving river, Maude decided to try further north. Alerted by German aircraft, Khalil Pasha sent the bulk of his forces to meet the Allied forces. He left behind a single regiment to hold the original defensive position at the Diyala, which was quickly and decisively crushed by the Allied forces with a sudden attack on 10 March. Stunned, Pasha ordered his troops to retreat. By the end of the day, the evacuation of Baghdad was underway.

The Ottoman authorities had ordered the evacuation of Baghdad at 8 p.m. on 10 March. But the situation was rapidly moving beyond Khalil's control. The British captured Baghdad without a fight on 11th March 1917. Some 9,000 Ottoman troops were caught in the confusion and became prisoners of the British. After marching more than 100 miles in 15 days, they entered the city to cheers from the 140,000 occupants.

Charles Palmer's Diary for 11 March reads:

> Reveille at 5.30, march off at 6.15am and after advancing about a mile we stop for 1 hour. Then we learn that the Turks have flown from Baghdad and we go forward and take the city, entering about 9.30 am amid great rejoicing of the inhabitants who came and kissed our feet. After marching up to the ambassador's house we learn that the arabs are looting in another part of the city so we get the order to fix bayonets and charge them. We then march through the city and bivouac 2 miles the other side and get down for the night after a good days march.

Once Baghdad was occupied, the Indo-British cavalry pressed onward along the left bank of the Tigris, and reached a point 30 miles upstream from Baghdad in less than 24 hours. The remnants of the Turkish Divisions were overtaken by infantry on 14 March. While all this was happening a second strong Indo-British force pursued the second Turkish army that was retreating up the Diyala River. They were defeated and fled back over the river on 29 March.

Such was the superiority of British means of movement that, even in the terrible summer heat, General Maude was able to speed his forces across the desert effectively. On 8 July, he proceeded up the Euphrates from Feluja, arriving within striking distance of Ramadie, where there were strong Turkish entrenchments. William Addison returned home in July.

The way was ready for Sir Stanley Maude to advance on Ramadie, where he won a resounding victory on 29 September to be followed by victory at Tekrit on 5 November before his tragic death at Baghdad on 18th November. He died of cholera. He was succeeded by Lieutenant General Sir William R. Marshall, who promptly set to work to drive the Turks still farther away from Baghdad.

By 5 December, he had forced them back as far as Kifri, about 150 miles from the city, but the winter conditions prevented any further operations until the spring of 1918. The British resumed the offensive in February 1918 capturing Hit and Khan al Baghdad in March, and Kifri in April.

On 29 April the net was closed around the 2nd Turkish Division along the stream by Tuz Khurmatli. Lancashire troops broke into the enemy's right flank and compelled them to abandon Tuz. With few losses to the British troops, the battle was won in three hours, leaving only fugitive Turk remnants to be overtaken on the Kirkuk road. Kirkuk and Altun Keupri were taken, before Sir William Marshall drew his chasing force slowly backward, leaving the latter places to the enemy, and concentrating on the Tuz region, where he had taken 3,000 prisoners, 16 guns, 28 machine-guns, and a large amount of military stores.

At about this time Sir William Marshall's forces were considerably diminished by the urgent need for reinforcements in France and Flanders. However by now Mesopotamia had been almost entirely won, and little more than strong military police work was required to guard it. The spring and summer of 1918 was used to aid the recovery of the area.

It was not until October that the main body of the Mesopotamian Expeditionary Force came into action again in a final battle on the Tigris. On 7 October Sir William Marshall took the offensive. He made a direct attack up the Tigris. It wasn't until 23 October that the Turks abandoned their great stronghold in the gorge during the night. Brigadier General Lewin took Kirkuk again.

Turkish forces on the left bank of the Tigris retreated across a bridge they had prepared at El Humr. By 30 October the Turks surrendered, and Marshall led his troops to Mosul, which he entered unopposed on 3 November. Thus ended a campaign that lasted four years. Some 114,000 square miles of territory had been captured, and 45,000 prisoners and 250 guns been taken.

In 1918, Mesopotamia assumed its modern name of Iraq, under a British mandate, and imperial forces remained garrisoned there to subdue dissident tribesmen.

By 31 December 1918, all areas north of Kirkuk had been evacuated. On 11 January 1919, the 13th Division – by now only some 12,000 strong – began to move south to Armara, and disbandment of the Division proceeded there during February 1919. The 13th Division, the only wholly British Division to have served in Mesopotamia, ceased to exist on 17 March 1919. During the war it had suffered 12,656 killed, wounded and missing.

HOME FROM THE WAR

On 5 November 1916, William Addison was awarded the Cross of the Order of St. George 4th Class (Rus.), conferred by His Imperial Majesty the Emperor of Russia, vide p.4725 of *London Gazette* No. 30070, dated 15 May 1917. (Listed without citation.)

This was Russia's highest exclusively military Order, instituted in 1769, which came to be considered among the most prestigious military awards in the world. It was awarded to officers and generals for special gallantry. Before membership of the Order could be granted, a candidate's case had to be investigated by a council composed of Knights of the Order.

The highest class was rarely awarded. Normally a person initially received the fourth class, and would gradually be promoted to higher classes for subsequent acts of bravery. The 4th Class was silver and worn as a badge on the left breast.

During a period of leave from Mesopotamia, William married Marjorie Helen Katrine Wallis, who was born at Godstone, Surrey in 1888. She was the daughter of W. E. Wallis of Caterham. They were married by Rev. J. Bell, Vicar at Christ Church, Brighton, Sussex on 19 July 1917.

Addison in uniform

William Addison received a presentation in Cranbrook on his return from active service and honeymoon on Wednesday 1 August 1917, which took place in Queen Elizabeth's School. This was to mark the occasion of his return to England and marriage. A troop of local Boy Scouts formed a guard of honour.

The Kent and Sussex Courier reported that:

> There was a very crowded and distinguished attendance, and a guard of honour was formed by the Cranbrook Platoon K.R.V. (Kent Reserve Volunteers), under Lieut. T.B. Cheesman, and the 1st Cranbrook Troop of B.P. Scouts, under the charge of Scoutmaster Miss. E. Winch. Canon Bell (The Vicar), in an excellent speech, referred to the pleasure felt to do honour, to meet and to welcome their hero, and to ask his acceptance of a present as a mark of their appreciation.
>
> Canon Bell then stated he had asked somebody more distinguished to make the presentation without success, reading letters from the Bishop of Croydon, The Marquis

Camden, Mr. F.S.W. Cornwallis and General Wilkinson, Commander of the Home Counties Reserve Brigade, who regretted their absence, but who, one and all, bore testimony to Mr. Addison's distinguished service. Dr. Thos. Joyce, Chairman of the Cranbrook Parish Council, also spoke in eloquent terms, in the course of which he said that the fire of patriotism burnt brightly in Mr. Addison's family, the other brothers leaving good situations to serve their country and another brother also fighting at the front at the present time. Of those three, two had already given their lives for their country. Canon Bell then made the presentation (a handsome illuminated address and a cheque), the address taking the following form:-

Presented to the Rev. Wm. Robert Fountaine Addison, Chaplain of His Majesty's Forces, V.C., Companion of the Russian Military Order of St. George, by his friends and neighbours of the Cranbrook district on the occasion of his homecoming from Mesopotamia in July, 1917, to mark their great admiration for his most conspicuous bravery, his splendid example, and his utter disregard of personal danger in rescuing the wounded on the field of battle. They all beg his acceptance of the accompanying cheque, and add their prayers for his future happiness and success in his sacred calling.

Addison addressed the crowd saying 'Officers, N.C.O.s and men of the Cranbrook Platoon, I compliment you on your smart appearance. I trust you will not be called on to do active defence duty and trust the war may soon be over, when you will feel that you have done your best to make men patriotic at home'.

Mr Addison warmly expressed his acknowledgements. It had been a tremendous surprise to him to find so much interest taken in him. For his own part he thought he had done nothing. He described in a very interesting manner his work, from his landing in Suvla Bay on September 29, 1915 to his return home in July from Mesopotamia, where he had been wounded. He had the pleasure while at Baghdad of presenting 36 men (part of a larger number reduced by wounds and death) for Confirmation by the Bishop of Nagpurwhe, and thought it was a very good number indeed and he also paid high testimony to the gallant defence of Kut by General Townsend and the splendid behaviour of the County Regiment in action (The Buffs).

Canon Bell then thanked Mr Henry Neve for organising the event, and Rev. C.F. Pierce, Headmaster of the School. He regretted that two of Mr Addison's brothers, who were educated at the School, could not have given Mr Addison a welcome. The event terminated with the National Anthem.

On 3 August, he was presented with his Victoria Cross by King George V at Buckingham Palace. Also decorated with the V.C. on that occasion was R. V. Moon.

William Addison was also present at another ceremony later in the same year in the rectory gardens of St. Edmund's, Salisbury. Guests included the Mayor and the St. Edmund's Company of the Church Lads' Brigade together with their bugle band. An Australian band was also in attendance. When Addison and his wife arrived there were loud cheers; the chaplain was wearing his uniform with his two medals together with two gold stripes denoting wounds received. Several speeches were made and he was then presented with a cheque, mainly contributed to by the congregation of St. Edmund's. In his reply Addison briefly outlined his links with Salisbury and gave a brief

Addison Cigarette Card – Series 6 of Gallagher Cards, Great War Series, Victoria Cross Heroes

The Addisons at Bulford Camp, 1920

account of his time in the army working as a chaplain at Suvla Bay and the subsequent evacuation, the Mesopotamia Campaign and the winning of his V.C. He said that later, after the troops had been fighting, he held a service and nearly every man attended from all denominations. After his speech he was called upon to present stripes to several members of the Church Lads' Brigade.

After his return from the war, he was given permanent chaplaincy to the Forces. On 26 June 1920, he attended the V.C. Garden Party at Buckingham Palace given by H.M. King George V. His Majesty was accompanied by the Queen and other Members of the Royal Family.

The Victoria Cross recipients assembled at Wellington Barracks, and marched to the Garden of the Palace via Birdcage Walk, Horse Guards Parade and the Mall preceded by the Band of the Welsh Guards. The King inspected the V.C. recipients, who afterwards filed past His Majesty, and had the honour of being presented to the King and Queen.

On November 11, William Addison was privileged to be part of the V.C. Guard of Honour for the internment of the Unknown Soldier at Westminster Abbey. The remains of the unidentified "British" soldier were brought back from the battle areas of Aisne, Arras, the Somme and Ypres. During the service the nave was lined by 100 holders of the Victoria Cross. William Addison also attended the Ceremony at the Cenotaph on Armistice Day.

From 1920–23 Padre Addison was Chief Chaplain to the Forces at Bulford Camp on Salisbury Plain. He was then posted to Aldershot, Hants from 1923–25. In January 1925 he was promoted Chaplain of the Forces 3rd Class and posted to Malta. Here he was based at Christ Church Garrison Church, Pembroke Barracks. At the time it only consisted of a Church Room, which had been handed over to the War Department in 1921. It was used for voluntary services by the men based at the barracks, but it only accommodated about 60 people, and was therefore too small for Parade Services which were held in the nearby St. Andrew's gymnasium.

Padre Addison spent 1926 in Khartoum, before carrying out a tour of duty with the Shanghai Defence Force in 1927. This Force was formed on 22 January 1927 in London. Together with Japan, The United States, France and Italy, Britain despatched a substantial force of 20,000 from Britain, Malta and India. After 1928, this Force was reduced gradually, although the British did not finally leave Shanghai until 1939.

He returned to England in 1929 and was posted to Shorncliffe Garrison, Kent. On Saturday 9 November 1929, he attended the Victoria Cross Reunion Dinner in the Royal Gallery, the House of Lords, London given by the British Legion. This event was hosted by The Prince of Wales, and 319 V.C. Holders attended. Rev. Addison sat on Table 6, seat

Chaplain to the Forces

166, between Sergeant Henry Cator V.C., and Sergeant Edward Mott V.C., DCM.

In 1930, he was posted to Shoeburyness Garrison, Essex, where he stayed until June 1931. An article in the *Southend Times* dated 22 May 1931 states:

> The Rev. W.R.F. Addison, V.C., chaplain to the forces, is leaving Shoeburyness, on June 12th, to take up duties as chaplain to the forces at Tidworth Garrison. He will be greatly missed, as he is one of the most popular parsons to have been at Shoeburyness for years with the troops. He is a most fluent preacher. He has preached the Gospel all over the world and on active service where he gained his Victoria Cross. He is well known outside the Garrison for his preaching, as he has preached at St. Mary's (Prittlewell), All Saints' (Southend), St. Andrew's (Westcliff), and opened the Southend British Legion Fayre.

On 3 May 1932 William Addison was promoted Chaplain to the Forces 2nd Class and posted to Bulford Camp. In November, he was appointed Senior Chaplain to the Forces, and the following year officiated at Salisbury Plain "Royal Engineers' Week" at the Camp. More than 50 veterans paraded in the square to accompany the 3rd Divisional Royal Engineers to Bulford Garrison Church. They attended a service at which the Padre Addison preached, before a march-past. Also during the year he conducted a service to dedicate a new West window, the gift of officers of the Royal Artillery, Royal Engineers and Royal Army Service Corps, stationed at Bulford from 1929–33.

In August 1934, William Addison attended Salisbury City Petty Sessions. The Salisbury Journal reported on 31 August:

> MONDAY – Before the Mayor (Mr. E.J. Case), the Deputy-Mayor (Mr. G. Hancock), Mr F. H. Wort. Mr G. Nicholson and Mrs J. L. Lovibond.
>
> CONFLICT OF EVIDENCE – The Rev. William Robert Fountain Addison, V.C., S.C.F., Senior Chaplains' Quarters, Bulford Camp, was summoned for causing a car of which he was in charge to remain at rest on the junction of New Street and High Street in such a position as to be likely to cause danger to other persons using the road, on August 16.- He pleaded not guilty.
>
> He was fined £1 with 5 shillings costs.

Padre William Addison V.C.

In early November 1934, Padre Addison was posted to Bordon as Senior Chaplain to the Forces, succeeding the Rev. D.B.L. Foster. On 16 October 1935, he attended the annual dinner of the Royal Army Chaplains' Department at the Junior United Services Club. He tried to attend these annual dinners when he could. In November 1935, he addressed a united memorial service at East Grinstead Parish Church. In his address he said: "This isn't a funeral service. It is one of absolute joy in reminding us of the splendid and wonderful example of those who laid down their lives". The service was preceded by a church parade organised by the British Legion.

In August 1938, Padre Addison retired from army service as a Chaplain after more than 20 years' service, and having lived in 21 different houses.

COLTISHALL

Now in his fifties, William Addison became Rector of Coltishall with Great Hautbois in Norfolk in 1938, where he stayed for 20 years.

John Cryer of Coltishall remembers him:

> I was only two when he arrived but later came into contact with him probably more than most as my grandfather, with whom we were living, was headmaster of Coltishall School. There were visits to the 'Rectory' for tea when an awestruck child actually had the V.C. in his hand! Later, with other boys, there were frequent visits with results of bird-nesting forays and when we were shown how to start our own collections. The high spot was always the chance to browse his magnificent collections of eggs and butterflies. All very illegal now, but for me, the start of an interest in wildlife that continues. He was a very nice and worthy man.

Geoff Williams also remembers:

> I came to live in Coltishall in July 1939 when my parents moved here from Hampshire. Mr and Mrs Addison and their two teenage sons, Bill and John, were living in the Rectory on Rectory Road. I remember being in church on 3 September 1939 when Mr Addison announced the outbreak of war from the pulpit, having been handed a message following the radio announcement by the Prime Minister at 11a.m. Shortly afterwards Mr Addison rejoined the army as a chaplain and the Rectory was requisitioned by the army. On 14 January 1942 he was appointed Deputy Assistant Chaplain-General of South Wales. On 12 May 1942, he again retired from the army and returned to Coltishall. He officiated at my wedding on 29 September 1954 and also at the christenings of my sons in 1956 and 1958 – by this time he was rather shaky and unable to hold the baby himself. As my father was one of the church wardens, we knew the Addison family quite well and were always proud of the fact that our rector had been awarded the V.C.

On 13 July 1939, he assisted Miss E. Flowerdew (a sister of the late Gordon Flowerdew V.C.) to open a garden fête at Caltofts, Harleston on the Norfolk-Suffolk border. This was held in aid of British Legion funds. William Addison said that

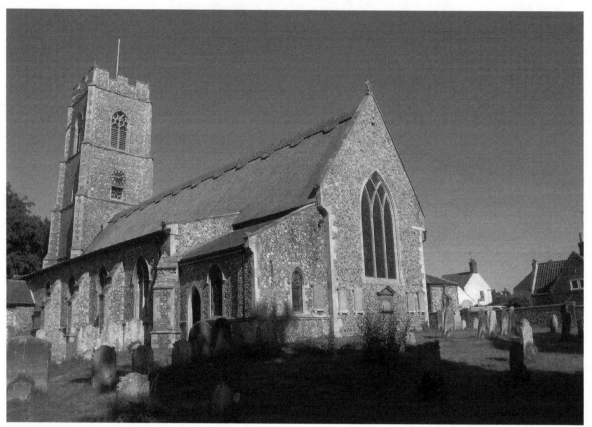

Coltishall Church of St. John the Baptist

after the terror of the war and the many hardships undergone, there was a great need for brotherhood and comradeship. He thought that if the work of the Legion was carried on in its true spirit of brotherhood, men of other nations, who fought in the Great War, might, through the efforts of the Legion, join with them in that great object.

Addison in 1951 or 1952

During his time in south Wales one parishioner, Ivan Williamson, stated in a local newspaper article: "He was a real man's man, far more at ease in men's company than with women … unlike some parsons he was very down to earth. He used to swear sometimes, but that didn't make him any the worse … he was very strict about church laws".

He made it a rule to visit every house in the parish at least once a year. He took his pastoral duties extremely seriously, but he was also passionate about the game of cricket. After the war he rebuilt the Horstead and District Cricket Club, which had lapsed, and often acted "as a most fair and strict impartial umpire". He rarely missed a match, and the Rectory was only a short walk away.

In 1947, he preached in Westminster Abbey. He became Rural Dean of Ingworth in 1948 and was also chaplain to the district branch of the British Legion, treasurer of the football club, and chairman of the bowls team of "The Good Companions". He was also interested in collecting butterflies, and he

Joan Wallis, William and Marjorie, with Barbara and and Sue (Marjorie's great nieces,) in 1952

discovered a large tortoiseshell not previously seen in the Belaugh meadows. He was also a keen birdwatcher and fisherman, particularly on Blickling Reach.

In 1953, he signed a Trust Deed with the Trustees of the William Fox Juvenile Society for the educational and vocational advancement of children resident in Coltishall and Horstead.

On Monday 25 June 1956, he attended the Service of Thanksgiving marking the centenary of the Victoria Cross in Westminster Abbey. The Archbishop of Canterbury spoke to the vast congregation. After the Service the 300 V.C. holders, with their relatives, went to Westminster Hall. The Prime Minister was there and the V.C.s and guests had tea as guests of the government in the House of Commons. They were made to feel very welcome.

The following day a Review of Holders of the Victoria Cross was held at Hyde Park, attended by Her Majesty Queen Elizabeth the Second. The commander of the Parade was Lieutenant General, the Lord Freyburg V.C. The V.C. holders had assembled at Wellington Barracks, where they were driven to Hyde Park. The weather was perfect. After marching past the Queen, they marched off to music by the R.A.F. Central Band.

Mr W. F. Knight, Coltishall village verger and shoemaker in 1956 admitted that he had only heard William Addison mention the V.C. twice. Once was when he was explaining why he had been asked to conduct an Armistice Service and the other occasion was when an American parent asked him to include his decoration in his signature on a baptismal certificate. He described William Addison as small, quiet, neat and orderly in speech and in the organisation of his life. His duties in the parish and deanery came first. He always appeared to be a very fragile man, and former church warden, Bill Stibbons, recalled that he was "thin and frail, nothing like what you'd expect a hero to look like". Walter Allen, church organist for over 20 years, described him thus: "he seemed to be all bone. You couldn't have imagined that he had the physical strength to go out and rescue wounded and dying men".

The *Beccles and Bungay Journal* of 23 June 1956 stated that outside the church, he meets his parishioners in many different spheres. In addition to duties previously mentioned he was President

On Retirement

The Rector of Coltishall

of the local cricket club and village umpire. Forty years after he won his V.C. he said: "I have always believed in humanity, but I have always believed that the great hope for humanity was a belief in the Creator".

He retired as Rector of Coltishall and Great Hautbois in September 1958. The people of the village met in a packed Church Room to say goodbye on 12 September. He was presented with a cheque for £111 and a book inscribed with the names of nearly 300 donors. The presentation was made by Mr W. J. Allen, the church organist, who said he thought he had heard some 1500 sermons by the Rector and "had been struck by his intense sincerity, by his sense of humour and by the vividness of the pictures he drew from his widely travelled life".

Mr Allen paid tribute to the way Mrs Addison had supported her husband in his ministry and said that the presentation was a small token of the village's appreciation of their services. In his reply, Mr Addison said that he very much regretted that so few people attended their lovely church.

At a meeting of the Horstead and District Cricket Club in the Church Room, he was thanked for his role as President, umpire and general adviser. The oldest playing member, Mr. P. Harmer, on behalf of the members of the club, presented Mr Addison with a lamp and 50 shillings being the balance of the donations. He paid tribute to the services given to the club by Mr Addison. Mr F. Roy, who presided, described Mr Addison as a most fair and strictly impartial umpire. Mr Addison expressed his thanks.

FREEMASONRY

Padre Addison, like many V.C. holders, was a staunch Freemason. He was initiated on 14 November 1923 into the Aldershot Camp Lodge, Number 1331, Passed on 17 December 1923, and Raised on 14 May 1924. He resigned on 10 October 1938, but probably rejoined about 1940, and then finally resigned in 1942. In Malta he joined the Lodge of Saint John and Saint Paul, Number 349. He was also exalted into Royal Arch Masonry in the William Kingston Chapter, Number 407, Valletta, probably in 1925. He went on to Shanghai in 1927, but remained a member of 349 until 1930. He joined the Tuscan Lodge, Number 1027. He resigned in 1928, upon returning to England.

In 1946, he became a joining member of Suffield Holy Royal Arch Chapter, Number 1808, which meets at Aylsham, a few miles north of Coltishall. On 4 May 1949 the Boileau Lodge, Number 6862 was consecrated, and William Addison was one of the Founders and the first Senior Warden of the

Lodge. Suffield Lodge was the sponsoring Lodge for Boileau. The following year he was installed as Worshipful Master, and remained a member until into the sixties, by which time he had retired from Coltishall Parish. He served as Provincial Grand Chaplain from May 1951 to May 1953, an office which has been held by "gentlemen of the cloth" from time immemorial, except for a short period some years ago. The Provincial Grand Master at the time was the Lord Bishop of Norwich, Bishop Herbert, a friend of the King and a leading Freemason.

At William's Installation Meeting one of the guests was Harry Cator, who like Addison, had earned the Victoria Cross in the First World War, and in recognition of this he was seated beside William at the dinner following. The presence of two V.C.s at a Lodge meeting in Norfolk remains unique.

In 1958, William retired to St. Leonards-on-Sea, Sussex, where his wife Marjorie died, and was buried at Brookwood, Surrey. He was by then a very sick man. The ravages of Parkinson's disease had reduced a naturally thin frame to skeletal proportions. A succession of operations did little to stop the decline. Feeble and growing weaker by the day, he knew he was dying, but he showed no hint of fear. From his home he had written to his former organist, Walter Allen who said: "He told me how he looked forward to death, to being with his master and reunited with his wife. There was no hint of fear in his words. I don't think he knew the meaning of the word".

William Addison died on Sunday 7 January 1962 in a Hastings Nursing Home aged 78. His address up until then was Flat 2, 13 Albert Road, Bexhill-on-Sea. A Service of Thanksgiving was held at St. Barnabas' Church, Bexhill on 11 January at 11 a.m, conducted by the Vicar (The Reverend Dr. Box). Interment followed in the family grave in Brookwood Cemetery, near Woking, Surrey (220346 Plot 22) at 2.30 p.m.

A memorial service was held at Coltishall parish church led by the Ven. Robert Meiklejohn and during his address he stated that the late rector's life fell into two parts. "First there was his distinguished service as an Army chaplain up to 1938 and then secondly when he became Rector of Coltishall and gave simple, unostentatious, unassuming and devoted service to that church and people". Many sections of village life were represented in the congregation which filled the church. Muffled touches were rung on the church bells by Buxton bellringers. Those present included robed clergy of the deanery, members of the Parochial Church Council, the choir, Sunday school, Mothers' Union, Women's Institute, Parish Council, The Coltishall and District and North Walsham and District branches of the British Legion, the managers and teaching staffs of the county primary and infants' schools, Good Companions' Club, the former cricket club, the football club, the Ernest Hines Marl Lodge of Freemasons and a representative of the Chaplain General and Royal Army Chaplains' Department.

Bill Addison, his eldest son said: "I don't think he ever felt any problems in being a soldier and a man of the cloth. He had a robust religion – a simple, straightforward belief in what was right and wrong. He was a countryman at heart". Walter Allen reckoned he was "a gentleman, a very human man who always put people before himself. You couldn't be anything but proud of being in his company. He loved people, and he loved helping people. He was just the sort of person to be a parson. He was one of the greatest people I have ever met".

The grave was restored in 2007, as the memorial was badly weathered and the wording had become barely readable.

PORTRAITS, DESKS, ROADS AND MEDALS
William Addison's Medal entitlement was:

> Victoria Cross
> 1914–15 Star
> British War Medal (1914–20)
> Victory Medal (1914–19) + MiD Oakleaf

War Medal (1939–45)
King George V1 Coronation Medal (1937)
Queen Elizabeth 11 Coronation Medal (1953)
Order of St. George (4th Class) (Russia)

In February 1983 his eldest son, Bill loaned his father's medals to the National Army Museum. He did this because he was afraid of having them stolen. For years the V.C., Russian Order of St. George and campaign medals had occupied pride of place in his living room. But the dramatic rise in value of the V.C. forced him into action. He explained to the *South Norfolk News* that:

> these medals were being sold for £25,000 or more and quite frankly I took fright. The more they are worth, the bigger target they are for thieves. I felt I had to do something to reduce the risk of theft. And the idea of lending them to the National Army Museum on a permanent basis seemed the ideal solution. It meant that they were safe and it gave the public a chance to enjoy them just as much as I had.

The V.C. was the first one to be won by a Chaplain to be presented to the Museum. A Museum spokesman told the *South Norfolk News*: "We are very, very delighted to have it. The whole group is an extremely interesting one".

The Medals have recently been returned to his son, so are no longer with the National Army Museum.

* * * * *

At Robert May's School in Odiham his portrait hangs in the school reception alongside a certificate about his V.C. The portrait was commissioned by the Chairman of the School Governors at his own expense in 1919. The artist is unknown.

* * * * *

Addison Gardens in Odiham are named after him. In the 1980s two roads on a small estate were named after former Robert May's Grammar School pupils who received V.C.s, the other being Manley James. This is one of three roads that bear Addison's name. The others are Addison Close, Coltishall and Addison Road in High Brooms, Tunbridge Wells. In Coltishall the Old Rectory stood behind what is today Addison Close in St. John's Close. Modern houses have been built on the site of the old Rectory.

Addison Close, Coltishall

The Addison Room in Cranbrook

On Thursday 26 April 2007, the Mayor of Tunbridge Wells, Councillor Ron Weedon, hosted a road naming ceremony at Barratt Kent's new homes development at Connaught Park, Sandhurst Road, High Brooms, Tunbridge Wells. Five roads were named after local V.C.s including "Addison Road".

* * * * *

Addison's portrait appears on one of Series 6 of Gallagher Cigarette Cards- Great War Series- Victoria Cross Heroes. They issued eight series, all First World War, with 25 cards in each series.

* * * * *

His portrait, name plaque and details of his action appear in the Addison V.C. Room which is next to the Information Centre, formerly the Old Fire Station in Cranbrook, Kent. A parishioner brought Addison V.C. to the attention of the Parish Council in about 2006, and they decided to name the room after him. His name also appears on the Cranbrook Muster Roll of the men of Cranbrook who fought in the Great War.

* * * * *

In Coltishall his name is included on the board under the patronage of the Norwich Diocese, Vicar 1938–58, and a prayer desk with brass plate commemorates him. There were two pictures of him in the vestry, the first of him in the army as a chaplain and the second was taken at the vestry door of St. John's Church.

* * * * *

The Addison Prayer Desk, Coltishall

His name is also on the V.C. Roll of Honour at the Union Jack Club, Sandell Street, Waterloo, London SE1 8UJ.

CHAPTER SEVEN

A Finer Man Never Breathed – The Story of
Acting Captain Eric Stuart Dougall 1886–1918

FOREWORD

I know a lot more about Eric than I did before! Richard Snow's researches are a substantial effort, which all seem comprehensive and correct. In his letters Eric writes in so unconcerned a fashion – I suppose typical of men of the time, not mentioning the terrible situations in which they found themselves, presumably because they were aware those at home would not understand, nor did they wish to alarm them, and because they had been brought up to face horrors with insouciance.

Lucian Warwick-Haller, cousin twice removed of Eric Dougall

Briefly, my memories were from my father, Charles Geoffrey Harker (1906–1956) cousin to Eric. As he died in 1956 when I was ten, my memories of the story of Eric are that he was upheld to me as an example of outstanding duty and sacrifice, but also of his exhilaration and commitment at serving his country. For me it is important that these histories are remembered and honoured as widely as possible, not just lost in Family History archives. Thank you for all your efforts in this direction.

Alison Harker, cousin once removed of Eric Dougall

EARLY YEARS AT TONBRIDGE AND CAMBRIDGE

Eric Stuart Dougall was born on 13 April 1886 in Tunbridge Wells, Kent. His father, Andrew Dougall, M.Inst. C.E. was an Engineer and General Manager with the "Tunbridge Wells Gas Company". Eric's mother was Emily Elizabeth Dougall (née Harker) from Hull. Andrew and Emily were married in Hull on 31 August 1882, and they lived at Brookside, Upper Grosvenor Road, Tunbridge Wells. Brookside was next to Clifton Road, just after 228 Upper Grosvenor Road. This would now be at the end of Upper Grosvenor Road (Gas Works end). Although it is no longer there it would be close to the Gas Works site.

Tunbridge Wells Gas Works

Andrew was Engineer to the Company from 1881 until ill health forced him to step down in 1917, after 36 years. In 1901, he had become General Manager. The 1901 Census showed Andrew, aged 44 and Elizabeth his wife, aged 43, at Brookside together with Eric aged 14 and his daughters, Ellen 16 and Kathleen 8, all born in Tunbridge Wells. In 1902–3, he was elected first President of the United Institution, preceding which he had taken a very prominent part in the work of bringing about unity in the gas industry. He also became Honorary Auditor of the Southern District Association of Gas Engineers and Managers. Many people outside Tunbridge Wells were indebted to him for advice tendered in a consultative capacity. He was a fervent church goer and a leader among the young in the church, and a valuable counsel in his business and the various Societies in the town.

Eric was their only son, but they had two daughters – Ellen Mary who was born around 1884 (died 11 March 1953) and Kathleen Jerrett Dougall born 1892 (died 25 February 1969). Eric attended Grove House School, Tunbridge Wells from 1895–99. The school, on the present-day Christchurch site, was founded in 1845 and described as a Collegiate School. "Pupils were instructed in subjects necessary to qualify them for professional or commercial pursuits". In 1884, a local Prospectus stated: "House and School large, and in state of thorough repair". The Principal was William Webber.

In September 1899, Eric went to Tonbridge School as a Day Boy. They were divided into two Houses. He was appointed a House Praepostor for Day Boys "A" House in June 1904 and a School Praepostor in May 1905. He was in the Engineering Sixth from September 1903 and in July 1904 won the Engineering Sixth Mathematics Prize, and was awarded the Judd Leaving Exhibition of £75 for four years.

In December 1903, he was in the 2nd XV and was Captain in 1904, and in the Cadet Corps he was promoted Sergeant in January 1905. Though he was not a sprinter, he was a good runner, and in April 1904 he was third in the one-mile race, losing out narrowly on second to Layton. On 25 March 1905, he won the first Cross Country Run, substituted in that year for the old Steeplechases on the Marshes with their exciting water jumps. The race was about six miles and Dougall's time was 33 minutes. There were 90 runners in teams of ten from each House. After leading along the London Road for about quarter of a mile, the course branched off into fields to the back of Hildenborough, and eventually came out into the Shipbourne Road at Cage Green Farm. The winning post was outside the school gates in the High Street.

The weather was fine for the School Sports and there was a large crowd on the London Road Grounds on Saturday 1 April 1905. The report in the *Tonbridgian* for April 1905 reports on the mile race:

> For the first two laps Hemmant made the running for Dougall, who hereupon came to the front, and was not again caught up; he won easily, thirty yards in front of Bigg-Wither. Had he had someone to pace him in the third and fourth laps his time might have been even better.

Dougall wins the Cross Country Run at Tonbridge School

Dougall won in 4 minutes 49 minutes 49 seconds, and "finished apparently perfectly fresh". In the half-mile, which was won by G. M. Devenish in 2 minutes 8 seconds, he was beaten in the sprint after a great race:

> Hemmant led at first, but after the first lap he was passed by Dougall, who kept his place until the last 100 yards, when Devenish, who was running a splendid race, sprinted past him and finished in an excellent time.

Wright secured the Individual Points Cup with 25 points, Dougall being second with 19.

In his last term G. G. Nelson and he were both such good candidates for Mr. Buckmaster's Mechanical Drawing Prize that each received a Prize. Eric won an Open Natural Science Exhibition at Pembroke College, Cambridge, leaving Tonbridge in June 1905. He had originally intended to read for the Mathematical Tripos but in the event switched to Mechanical Sciences (Engineering). He was first in the three-mile race in the Cambridge University freshmen's sports. He was also running for Cambridge University Hare and Hounds and was chosen as reserve for the Varsity match against Oxford. In 1906 he was second in the one-mile race against Oxford, having made the pace for A. R. Welsh, who won for Cambridge. He was also third in the three-mile race in the Cambridge University Sports, and won the mile, and quarter-mile races in the Pembroke College Sports. By December that year he was running for Cambridge and was chosen to represent Cambridge in the annual Varsity cross country race winning his half-blue. He finished fifth and was third Cambridge scorer. In April 1907 he won the half-mile race in the University Sports. He won his "full Blue" as first string for Cambridge in the Inter-Varsity Sports half-mile, finishing second, being beaten by only a yard by P. S. Darling of Oxford. Rounding the final turn he began to make up ground, and with ten yards to go drew level, only for his opponent to summon up a desperate rally: Dougall just failed to snatch victory as they both lunged for the tape. By December 1907 he was Secretary of the Cambridge University Athletic Club. In 1908 he again represented Cambridge in the mile in the Inter-Varsity Sports, finishing second.

He graduated with a Third in the Mechanical Science Tripos in 1908. He became an Engineer with the Mersey Docks and Harbour Board. He trained under Mr A. G. Lyster, Chief Engineer. He became known here as a Rugby Footballer. He was present when, during the Great Dock Strike, to the grave concern of the Dock Authorities, four days before some important sailings were due, the stokers downed tools. Without hesitation Dougall, with some of his friends, took the job on. Down he went into the grimy holds and there he stayed, working through until the task was accomplished and the ships had sailed. The stokers just scowled on him.

In an undated letter to his cousin Gwyneth, sent from 17 Kimberley Street Liverpool, he states that "these rooms are quite comfortable and the landlady is a nice old thing for that class of person, she looks after me well and keeps the rooms clean, which is a great thing". He goes on to tell her about life in the docks:

> Usually I have to get up at 6 o'clock in the morning – think of that! – but the last week or two there has not been enough work on hand to keep the men going all day so work has not started until 9 o'clock. I get off at 5 o'clock in the evening and have an hour for lunch in the middle of the day. If you paid me a visit in the workshops I don't suppose you would recognise your 'Uncle' Eric in the grimy figure in blue overalls covered in dirt from head to foot. I have to work just like the ordinary workman the only difference being that I don't get any money on Saturdays while they do. I went to see a ship launched on Monday. You would have enjoyed seeing it – it was a great big one over 400 ft-long dash into the water while all the men who had helped to build it cheered and let off fireworks. I got on it and hoped to stay there while it was launched but a nasty man turned me off at the last minute.

He remained there until 1912 and in March sailed for Bombay to take up a position as Assistant Engineer to the Bombay Port Trust and three years later was placed on the permanent staff. Soon after the outbreak of war, being unable to come home, in 1914 he joined the Bombay Light Horse, where he was promoted to lance corporal.

In a letter to his cousin Gwyneth in Hornsea, Yorkshire dated 16 April 1915 he writes on Royal Bombay Yacht Club headed paper:

> I am always a very bad hand at answering letters but I think I have beaten all records in my slackness in replying to your very charming one received so long ago. It was in 1908 the last time I was in Hornsea just before I went over to Liverpool seven years ago! I am wondering how old you are now. You must have been about 9 then which makes you sixteen now. Is that anything like correct? If you had sent a photo of yourself I should have been able to judge but left to memory I imagine you as a small and wild child with a lot of fair hair and two long legs while you are probably a grave and sedate young lady. Hence I must be careful what I say.
>
> I am very fed up with being stuck out here and don't feel much of a hero to be doing nothing towards the war, except drill, while all my friends are fighting and many unfortunately dying. However it seems inevitable and I have got more or less used to it now although at first I was very restless. I don't know when I shall get home again; it all depends upon the length of the war. So far I have just completed 5 years but am very fit and well in spite of Bombay being not exactly a health resort at the best of times. I thoroughly enjoy the life. It seems more free and easy than at home and there are some very nice people here.

Also, all the men I have to work with are excellent fellows and that goes a long way towards making life worth living. The work itself is strenuous and I start at 7 a.m. and do not finish until 5.30 p.m. but it is all interesting.

Later, in 1915, he was able to take leave of absence and sail for England to apply for a commission.

OFF TO THE WAR

Eric returned to the United Kingdom in January 1916 and enlisted in "B" Reserve Brigade of the Royal Horse Artillery (Regt. No. 127027) on 21 February. He had already lodged an application for a commission in the artillery, engineers and infantry on 14 February. The Royal Horse Artillery was armed with light, mobile, horse-drawn guns that in theory provided firepower in support of the cavalry and in practice supplemented the Royal Field Artillery.After training as a cadet at St. John's Wood Eric was posted on 1 March to 3rd B Reserve Brigade, Royal Field Artillery (R.F.A.) at Exeter. On the 14 April he re-applied for a commission, this time exclusively for the artillery. On 22 April 1916, he wrote to his cousin Gwyneth from Brookside, Tunbridge Wells:

> I have just returned home for a weekend and have been trying to answer the many letters I owe, first and foremost of which come yours and Hewart's [her brother]. Please forgive me for being so long about it but I really have been hard at it lately.
>
> My address is 'B' Reserve Brigade R.H.A., St. John's Wood Barracks, London N.W. and I am one of about 200 fellows who are being trained with a view to commissions in the Artillery. It is a very strenuous course and from "Reveille" at 6 am until 7.30 p.m. we do not have a minute to ourselves and after that we are supposed to study in the evening. I usually find myself going to sleep when I sit down to a book in the evening. I have done two months now and do not get quite so much of the dirty work, stables etc, as I did but have to do another 3 months before I get a chance of a commission. It seems a long time but the training is very technical and cannot be done all at once. When I do get gazetted I hope to join a battery fairly quickly and I shall be jolly annoyed if the war is over before I can get out there. It would be too bad after coming such a long way to join.
>
> It is very nice being so near London and I often manage to get home on a Saturday or Sunday afternoon for a few hours. Also London is so central that I have managed to meet quite a lot of old friends in my spare moments.
>
> Last weekend I spent on guard striding up and down the main entrance with a drawn sword trying to look fierce. Not a very pleasant way to spend a weekend but fortunately it does not come very often.

On 2 July Eric was granted a commission as a Second Lieutenant in the Royal Field Artillery (Special Reserve), leaving for France that month. The Royal Field Artillery was the most numerous arm of the artillery, the horse-drawn R.F.A. was responsible for the medium calibre guns and howitzers, deployed close to the front line and was reasonably mobile.

Eric joined the 19th Divisional Ammunition Column in the field on 28 July, serving in France and Flanders, where he was appointed Group Intelligence Officer. The Brigade Ammunition Column numbered 158 heads, commanded by a captain. Its job was to bring ammunition and other supplies to the battery positions from divisional dumps. So Eric arrived in the thick of things to join 19th Division, who had been in France since July 1915. The 19th Division was part of the Fourth Army under General Sir Henry Rawlinson on the Western Front. Eric had not been present at the Battle of Albert in early July or at the attacks on High Wood, which took place just before he arrived.

He would have arrived at the time of the Battle of Pozières Ridge. This was the next target of advance for the British on the Albert-Bapaume Road. This village was on top of a slope leading to a main ridge, and this was in the centre of the British section of the Somme battlefield. It was critical

Leaving Tunbridge Wells for France.

for German defences, as it formed an outpost to the second defensive trench system. The attack was preceded by a three-day bombardment. It took many weeks of hard fighting to advance up the road towards Pozières, and the village and ridge was eventually taken by the 1st Australian Division, part of Gough's Reserve Army. After Pozières was taken on 23 July, it became a focus of attention for the Germans, who determined to retake it at all costs. From the 25 July they battled to retake it and from 25 July artillery joined in. On the 26th the British joined in to help secure Pozières. The battle of Pozières Ridge was fought between 25 July and 3 September. The fighting was mainly in the areas around Pozières itself. In the early days of August the British gained further successes, taking positions north-west of Pozières, between Bazentin-Le-Petit and Martinpuich, and to the west of Guillemont. On 18 August a steady push was made all along the front line from Thiepval to the Somme, and the Leipzig redoubt was captured after an artillery bombardment.

On the 8 September, Eric transferred to 88th Brigade, Royal Field Artillery. On 29 September General Sir Douglas Haig began plans for an attack using the Third, Fourth and Reserve Armies, with the ultimate objective of taking Cambrai, more than 20 miles distant. By the 30th, the British front line was in front of the village of Le Sars. Across the Ancre the villages of Beaumont Hamel and Beaucourt remained in German hands. The focus of the battle now moved to the Ancre.

The Battle of the Ancre Heights began on 1 October 1916. Lieutenant Gough's Reserve Army (which included 19th Division) finally managed to break out of the positions it had occupied since the start of the Somme fighting on 1 July, and Gough wanted to keep up the offensive above the River Ancre. It was the Canadian Corps, under Lieutenant General Sir Julian Byng, which was heavily involved in the battle.

At 3.15 p.m. on 1 October, the Canadians once again tried to take Regina Trench along a front of more than 1 km. Artillery had bombarded the Trench, but the 4th and 5th Canadian Mounted Rifles came up against uncut barbed wire defences, and fierce German machine-gun fire. Casualties were high, and the incessant rain made it impossible to continue.

The second phase began at 4.50 a.m. on 8 October. Eight Canadian battalions renewed the attack on Regina Trench. The artillery had failed to cause much damage and the Canadians met heavy resistance. Few objectives were achieved with heavy casualties. The final phase began on 21 October, and the Trench was quickly captured. On 24th they were unsuccessful in another attempt. On 30 October Gough's Reserve Army was renamed the Fifth Army, and they took up the weight of the main advance. Then on the night of 10–11 November British and Canadian forces began a final assault on the last part of the Regina Trench. This was completed in a couple of hours, thanks to a successful artillery bombardment.

The Fifth Army attack was renewed north of the Ancre on 13 November, when it became the Battle of the Ancre, an engagement which lasted until 19 November and finally brought the Somme battles to an end. Mud, rain, the growing cold and fatigue were finally taking their toll. Attacks continued and shortly the objectives of the Fourth Army Front were taken. On the Fifth Army front Regina Trench and the Thiepval Ridge were taken by mid-November. The objectives for the second phase of the Battle of the Ancre were Serre, Beaumont Hamel, St.- Pierre-Divion and Grandcourt. Gough had at his disposal all the artillery that could be spared from Third and Fourth Armies, as well as 52 tanks. He split the attack into three phases. The first was an advance to capture the Beaumont Hamel Valley and the ridge of Serre. The second was to proceed round to the eastern edge of Serre itself, and the final attack would be up the Ancre Valley to Beaucourt.

The first attack began just before dawn on the 13th: Beaumont Hamel was reached by 10.30 a.m., and by mid-afternoon the village was taken. The advance then continued towards Serre. Beaucourt fell on the 14th, with 600 Germans taken prisoner that day. To the north, efforts were less successful. The 3rd Division and 31st Division were expected to take the village of Serre but their attack failed. On the night of 17 November snow fell, which combined with the mud was intolerable. Gough was keen to press on. On 18 November, No. 2 Corps was ordered to head for the village of Grandcourt and the river. No. V Corps were to secure the remainder of Redan Ridge. Neither attack succeeded. Shortly after this Gough called off the Battle of the Ancre, and the Battle of the Somme effectively ended. The weather had proved the final decision-maker. The troops now settled down to endure winter on the Somme in which the weather was the common enemy.

The winter of 1916–17 was very harsh and the soldiers suffered in wet, freezing trenches. Eric Dougall took leave in England from 6–15 December. However the fighting continued along the Western Front and casualty figures continued to mount. The morale of the British troops was still good despite the losses at the Somme. Eric kept two little pocket diaries for 1917 and 1918. He writes in his Diary for 3 January: "Breakfasted with 49th and moved into our very damp mess. The men spent the day digging themselves shelters and getting the guns into action". From 9 to 12 January he records "Bombarded all day. Night firing from 10–2 a.m". The artillery was growing in power and expertise, and ammunition failures were becoming fewer. In February, Eric was suffering. He recalls in his Diary on the 13th that it was a "pretty rotten day with fever". The following day he "took 9 a.m. parade feeling like nothing on earth and then retired to bed". He remained there until the 17th.

On 10 March, he records: "Took two limbers to Beauquesne to fetch guns from mobile workshop but could only get one. Padre joined us". The following day: "went to Beauquesne. Took the other gun to Decoches to our new billet". On 31 March he records: "Horse show and inspection by General Plumer". The following day 1 April "rode into Calais with Herzog and La Barte. Lunched at Hotel. Got back about 3p.m".

Eric's brigade then moved to the Ypres Sector and in May 1917 he was promoted to Acting Captain as second-in-command of his battery A/88th Brigade R.F.A. On 10 May he records: "Battery was shelled in the morning. Thomas Scofield and Mossop hit. Shelled heavily in afternoon". On the 26th "reconnoitre at night and got badly shelled", and on the 27th: "shelling near camp. Had one man hit (Ward)". The following day: "Working all day on position. Moved our camp there in afternoon and had some trouble getting the cooks cart up at night owing to shell fire on the roads".

He was now to win the Military Cross for his bravery during the Battle of Messines. On 5 June he records: "watched a jolly good raid in the afternoon". The battle began on 7 June 1917 when the British Second Army under the command of General Herbert Plumer launched an offensive near the village of Messines in West Flanders, Belgium. The target was a ridge running north from Messines village past Wytschaete village which created a natural stronghold southeast of Ypres. This would give the British control of important strategic ground.

British X Corps was on the northern edge of the sector. The IX Corps including the 19th Division were in the centre, and 2nd Anzac Corps to the southeast. In the week before the assault, some 2,200 artillery guns bombarded the German trenches with around three to four million shells. This destroyed nearly 90 per cent of the German field-gun positions. At 2.50 a.m. the artillery bombardment ceased. Twenty minutes later 19 mines were detonated, killing around 10,000 Germans and destroying the town itself. It is said that the sound of the explosion was heard and felt in London. It created the largest man-made detonation using conventional explosives in history. At the same time artillery fire resumed. This totally disrupted the German defences and allowed troops to quickly carry out their objectives.

After this first phase, more than 40 batteries of artillery were brought forward to support the second phase. Bombardment continued for some hours until the reserve divisions, supported by tanks moved forward and secured the second line of objectives. This offensive had secured the southern end of the Ypres Salient in preparation for further offensives.

Eric's Diary for 7 June, when he won his M.C. (Military Cross) reads: "Attack 3.10 a.m. Followed up with wire to find objective but failed to register batteries owing to faulty wire. Returned to battery at night".

As already mentioned Eric won the Military Cross for his actions during the battle. This was gazetted in the *London Gazette* No. 30251, page 8808, dated 25 August 1917. The citation reads:

> For conspicuous gallantry and devotion to duty as Group Intelligence Officer and F.O.O. he took up a succession of observation posts in advanced and exposed positions from which he successfully maintained communication with headquarters. He was slightly wounded but remained at duty, and has frequently performed work requiring initiative under heavy fire with great coolness and gallantry. (F.O.O. = Forward Observation Officer.)

The wound he received to his face Eric described as a mere scratch. His Diary for 7 July records: "Heard I had the M.C. at night. Three men killed and two wounded at B's position and A shelled out". On the 9th he records: "Went off to Hazebrooke with Clive in motor ambulance at 1 p.m. Entrained at 4 p.m. and reached Boulogne at 10.45 p.m. Stayed at Louve Hotel". He was granted leave in England from 10 to 19 July, when he visited home and then Malvern.

On 31 July, seven weeks after the taking of the Messines–Wyteschaete Ridge, the Third Battle of Ypres began. The objectives were to clear the Belgian coast and the capture of Roulers, a vital railway centre. But first they needed to occupy the German-held ridges which dominated Ypres. Gough's troops attacked three times in August – at Pilckem Ridge, at Langemarck, and along the Menin Road.

On 2 August, Eric wrote to his cousin Gwyneth:

> I am a rotter for not answering your letter for such a long time. I shall almost begin to think I have done something if I receive any more letters of congratulations like yours. As a matter of fact between you and me I did absolutely nothing and feel ashamed of myself in consequence.
>
> Had a very good leave and enjoyed the quiet time. Coming back was not so pleasant but I have been so busy since that I have had no time to think of anything. The major has gone away for a month, so I have the cares of the battery on my shoulders. It is interesting work but rather worrying at times with my limited experience of the army.

On 12 August Eric records: "Rode into Hazebrook with Campbell and found it almost deserted because of shelling. Dined quietly at 45, Rue de la Gare". From the end of August Plumer's Second Army was appointed to lead the advance to Passchendaele, with Gough's Fifth Army protecting the flanks. Rain turned the area into a quagmire, severely impeding subsequent British attacks. By the end of August, despite heavy casualties, little progress had been made. Plumer's Army went in to attack on the Menin Road Ridge on 20 September.

Preparations during the first three weeks of the month coincided with good weather. In the new battle plan the role of the artillery was paramount. The British artillery was becoming a much better-trained and more integrated force. Plumer had 1,295 guns – a gun to every five yards. The preliminary bombardment had started on 31 August and intensified daily culminating in a two-day bombardment prior to the offensive.

At 5.40 a.m., 65,000 troops advanced on an eight-mile front and quickly overran enemy outposts. By midday the four attacking divisions on the Gheluvelt Plateau were on their final objectives. They consolidated their positions in anticipation of expected German counter-attacks. These were dispersed between noon and 7.30 p.m. by accurate British barrages. By the evening the forward slopes of the Gheluvelt Plateau were secured, although the following days saw further fierce counter-attacks. The Second Army lost 9,000 men killed, wounded or missing, and the Fifth Army around 11,000.

The next phase of the Second Army's advance up the Plateau was planned for 26 September. Once again British artillery barrages swept the German positions, with fresh assault troops being called forward. This time 1 Anzac Corps was to secure the key objective of Polygon Wood. The infantry attacked at 5.50 a.m. on 26 September on a front of nearly five miles, with an effective bombardment in support. They quickly overran the German defenders, and secured the important "Butte" position. The final objective, just beyond the eastern edge of the wood was secured by 9.45 a.m. By mid-morning most objectives had been gained. Counter-attacks were repelled by British barrages, causing heavy German casualties. Operations were called off by 3 October as the Second Army had completed the second phase of its advance across the Gheluvelt Plateau very quickly, though with heavy losses. The five British and two Australian divisions lost 15,375 men killed, wounded and missing.

Following these successes, it was decided to proceed with the third phase of Plumer's plan, an attack by 1 and 2 Anzac at Broodseinde on 4 October. It was preceded by intermittent barrages from 27 September instead of a continuous bombardment. Supported by British divisions, this time from four corps, they attacked and captured the village of Broodseinde. This battle resulted in another 8,000 casualties, but the Second Army now stood within reach of the Passchendaele position. This limited advance had been costly and by evening the rain set in once again, transforming the battleground into a quagmire.

Haig, now Field Marshall, decided to press on, encouraged by the high number of German casualties and reports of low German morale. He was determined to secure the Passchendaele Ridge. The main assault would be led by Plumer's Second Army, supported by Fifth Army formations to the north. However the weather was appalling and hampered preparations and any offensive. On the evening of 8 October assault troops laboured to the start line on an eight-mile attack frontage. At 5.20 a.m. on the 9th exhausted and under strength British and Australian troops took part in the Battle of Poelcapelle. However because of the conditions and a ragged and inaccurate barrage, and the determined fire of German machine-guns, forward movement ceased at 9.30 a.m. Around midday fierce German resistance forced the British to withdraw. Despite considerable casualties amounting to 9,000, practically none of the day's objectives were attained.

Field Marshall Haig agreed that the next attack to take Passchendaele should be made on Friday 12 October. For the First Battle of Passchendaele, the Second Army's 2 Anzac Corps made the main thrust, supported on the right by 1 Anzac Corps and on the left by five British divisions. However the artillery were unable to get forward; guns and ammunition supplies were deep in mud. The infantry struggling in the mud had no cover and the barrages failed to happen. Inadequate artillery support was key to subsequent failure. Men, trapped by dense barbed wire were cruelly shot down by machine-gun fire. British casualties were severe and they failed to attain their objective.

Field Marshall Haig was determined to take Passchendaele. General Arthur Currie's Canadian Corps was called up to replace the tired 2 Anzac Corps and spearhead the attack. The first assault on 26 October was made in pouring rain. The Canadians pushed forward as the Second Battle of Passchendaele began. Supporting flank operations by British infantry divisions proved costly failures.

Eric was on leave from 21 October until 1 November, so missed much of the early engagement. On his return he wrote to his cousin Gwyneth again:

Yes, I had a topping time on leave quite one of the best I have had. We were altogether at home and I also had some very choice days in London seeing old friends from India and elsewhere. I thoroughly enjoyed it all, but am quite settled down again.

Let's hope it will be all over before another winter and I shall be back to a nice warm climate again. I <u>don't</u> like the cold and mud of this beastly country.

Write again when you feel inclined for I love getting letters though I am not much use at writing them.

The Canadians again attacked at 5.50 a.m. on the 30th, accompanied by the fire of 420 guns. After a heavy barrage, they reached the outskirts of Passchendaele, but found it deserted. They withdrew as the fighting intensified. Following extensive British bombardments, the 2nd Canadian Division took the village on 6 November, gaining all its objectives but losing many casualties. For the next three days the Canadians consolidated their hold on the Passchendaele position. On 10 November they beat off a heavy German counter-attack. The Second Battle of Passchendaele, and the Third Battle of Ypres officially ended. The entire battle cost the Allies in Second and Fifth Armies a total of nearly 250,000 casualties of all types. The exact German total is unclear but can be numbered in the hundreds of thousands.

It was due to the lack of available reserves as much as the dreadful weather, atrocious battlefield conditions and continued stubborn resistance that the Third Battle of Ypres ground to a halt. In over three and a half months fighting, the Allied Forces had advanced around five miles.

On 19 November Eric "heard I was going on an overseas course". On 26th he proceeded via Shoeburyness to Salisbury before returning to France via Boulogne on Boxing Day. He was back at Baupaume by 7.30 p.m. on the 30th.

BATTERY COMMANDER AT MESSINES

By the end of 1917 following three years of trench fighting on the Western Front, both Allies and German armies were exhausted. After the immense number of casualties suffered at Passchendaele, Prime Minister Lloyd George refused to provide extra manpower for the cause. Thus the period from January to mid-March 1918 was one of the quietest of the whole war.

Eric Dougall was appointed Lieutenant on 7 January 1918 and his 1918 Diary reveals the quietness of the first few months. On 15 February he recalls: "Rode to Neuville and caught a bus at 8a.m. to Bray Sur Somme to witness a tank display. Drove to Bapaume for lunch". On 6 March: "Rode up to guns after breakfast and stayed to lunch. A lovely day. Moved into our new position at Havrincourt Chateau grounds". On the 13th: "Good visibility in morning. Did some effectual sniping at Huns in the open. Relieved 12 noon".

Germany was building up its strength over this time until they launched a bombardment on the early morning of 21 March which lasted for several hours. They used gas, rifle and machine-gun fire accompanied by artillery. This was the

Leaving for the Western Front

largest bombardment ever seen on the Western Front and launched the first phase of the Battle of the Somme. Allied troops, horses, transport and guns took heavy casualties. This was followed by an infantry assault in heavy mist. Most of the British forward positions were overwhelmed and nearly all of the British front line fell that morning. Thus began the Battle of St. Quentin. By the close of the first day the Germans had broken through the British first and second lines of defence along a quarter of the whole line attacked. Large parts of the Fifth Army were falling back. Gough had to order his troops to retreat, in spite of fighting back.

Eric's Diary on that day tells us: "Heavy strafe in morning. Went up to battery to ascertain situation and then ran 12 loads of ammunition. Another 12 in afternoon and took up limbers at night to withdrawn guns to rear position".

Eric Dougall

The following day the British continued to fall back, with the fog continuing until the afternoon. There followed a number of separate isolated engagements. The Third Army was able to hold ferocious German assaults in the Battle Zone until mid-afternoon when its centre was forced back producing scenes of disarray on the Bapaume-Cambrai road. The situation became dire for the Fifth Army and the retreat was in danger of becoming a rout. Within 48 hours the Germans had penetrated up to ten miles behind the British lines.

Eric's Diary records: "Wagon line routine in morning. Rode up to see route to defence position taking some N.C.O.s. Took limbers up at night and moved battery. Just got back to Ypres when orders came to move wagon line to Haplincourt".

Facing an unprecedented disaster all available troops were hastily thrown into action on 23 March to bolster the failing Fifth Army but they were not able to prevent the German infantry swarming over the Somme. Bitter fighting took place over open country. Almost 40 miles had been breached in the British line and the Fifth and Third Armies became separated. By now the German infantry had incurred heavy casualties and were starting to show signs of battle weariness. Field Marshall Haig ordered the construction of new rear defence lines on which to hold the expected continued German onslaught.

Eric recalls in his Diary for the 23rd: "Col. came round with orders to move guns to behind Barastre. Wagon Line near Le Transloy. Limbers stood by all night and moved guns back at dawn".

More ground was lost on the 24 March, Palm Sunday. By nightfall the British had lost the line of the Somme. The right of the Third Army repeatedly gave up ground as it tried in vain to maintain contact with the Fifth Army's endless retreats. Eric recalls: "A bad day for Brigade. Lost nearly all guns near Flers. Took transport through and eventually landed up the other side of Albert in early morning". That evening after enduring unceasing shelling, Bapaume was evacuated.

During the night elements of the right of the Third Army completed a long and confused retreat to occupy a new line. Renewed German onslaughts continued through the next day. By now gaps appeared in the defensive lines. Eric tells us: "Marched to Vardencourt for lunch and then on to Hedauville, Varenne, and eventually spent night in cemetery at Toutencourt". On the 26th Gough was "to delay the enemy as long as possible without being so involved as to make retirement impossible", and Eric recorded: "Got off early. Rode on to Valde Marson and heard that Brigade were at Herissart. Got there just in time for a Conference. The major found us later and we got a decent billet. I slept in forage at wagon line".

On 27 March "Marched to Marieux and camped for night in wood". On the 28th, "Went billeting for Bde. and after much trouble got fixed up at Berteaucourt. Good billets so had topping sleep". On the 31st, Easter Sunday, "Marched from Berteaucourt to Boubers-Sur-Canche. Lovely day and made a march of it bivouing in time for tea. Good billets".

On the 1 April, Eric "rode over to Pt. Houvin in afternoon to see about entraining. Entrained in evening". The next day "Detrained at Godewaersvelde and had breakfast at Trois Roi. Marched to camp near Bailleul and found town deserted. Slade and I viewed it after lunch". On 3 April "Came into action near Messines taking over from 16th A.F.A". Then the following day "too misty to do any firing. Walked up to O.P. after lunch".

In what was possibly his last letter, written in pale ink on a small piece of paper which was never sent, though probably intended for Gwyneth, Eric wrote:

> We have dug a hole in the ground and live in it with a tarpaulin which leaks disgracefully over the top. The first one we had was destroyed by a shell which landed on it and blew a lot of the Major's kit to blazes and annoyed him slightly. Last night I was up behind the front line with a working party converting an old shell hole into an observation post. We have most exciting times trying to see our targets. We have to crawl along from shell hole to shell hole hoping that snipers will not see us and that the shells will miss us. I find it a most exhilarating occupation.
>
> Goodbye for the present and excuse a short note. At present I have absolutely not a sheet of notepaper or an envelope so I shall have to wait until some arrive. Mother said some time ago that she was sending something in a parcel.
>
> Much love to yourself and Uncle and Aunt,
>
> Yours ever,
>
> Eric

On 3 April, following an Allied Conference, Lloyd George told Field Marshall Haig that Sir Hubert Gough must go following the poor performance of the Fifth Army. When the German offensive on the Somme opened on 21 March, Eric's battery was right at the point of the salient on the Cambrai front and being the last to withdraw from that area, retired fighting over the approximate line Ribecourt-Trescault-Bus-Le Transloy-Courcelette.

On the 4th Eric took over command of his battery. By the 5th the Allied line had been severely dented, but the German Army was running out of supplies. Gough had been replaced by Sir Henry Rawlinson and the Fifth Army was made the Reserve Army.

On the 7th "went down to group O.P. in Messines in morning and did some shooting from O.P. in afternoon. Very good visibility. Saw one of our planes hit direct by A.A. fire. Slade lost for the night". The following day "rode down to wagon line for lunch with Hall. Tea at wagon line and rode back to battery. Found Slade had turned up safe and sound".

By nightfall on 9 April the First Army had been driven back some three miles to the line of the River Lys.

On the 10 April, Eric performed supreme gallantry at the Battle of Messines. Three divisions of IX Corps were involved – 9th, 19th and 25th. The British resistance was helped by the artillery of the 19th and 9th Divisions, and the three Army brigades with the 25th. The guns not only remained in action until the infantry were pressed back in line with them, but the artillery officers undertook to keep the guns in action as long as the infantry remained. In his Diary Eric simply says: "Hun attacked. Fought guns all day till 7p.m. and then got them all out to behind Wytschaete. Moved to Klein Vierstraat".

His citation (*London Gazette* 30726 p.6571 4 June) for his posthumous V.C. gives more detail:

Lt. (A./Capt) Eric Stuart Dougall, M.C., late R.F.A. (S.R.)

Captain Dougall maintained his guns in action from early morning throughout a heavy concentration of gas and high-explosive shell. Finding that he could not clear the crest, owing to the withdrawal of our line, Captain Dougall ran his guns on to the top of the ridge to fire over open sights. By this time our infantry had been pressed back in line with the guns. Captain Dougall at once assumed command of the situation, rallied and organised the infantry, supplied them with Lewis guns, and armed as many gunners as he could spare with rifles. With these he formed a line in front of his battery, which during this period was harassing the advancing enemy with a rapid rate of fire. Although exposed to both rifle and machine-gun fire, this officer fearlessly walked about as though on parade, calmly giving orders and encouraging everybody. He inspired the infantry with his assurance that 'so long as you stick to your trenches I will keep my guns here'. This line was maintained throughout the day, thereby delaying the enemy's advance for over 12 hours. In the evening, having expended all ammunition, the battery received orders to withdraw. This was done by man-handling the guns over a distance of about 800 yards of shell-cratered country, an almost impossible feat considering the ground and the intense machine-gun fire. Owing to Captain Dougall's personality and skilful leadership throughout this trying day, there is no doubt that a serious breach in the line was averted.

His Diary for 11 April reads: "Walked up to Wytschaete with young Tovey in afternoon". The 12th "Moved from Klein Vierstraat to behind Kemmel at dusk. Spent night in a farmhouse. The last entry in his Diary is for 13th April, the day before he was killed: "Moved 2 guns to top of Kemmel after lunch and at dusk moved the other 3 up. Wall and self dozed all night in front of a fire in a Corps Observers tent".

Four days after his V.C. action Eric Dougall was killed by a shell splinter on the left side of the neck when directing the fire of his battery near Kemmel. He was killed instantly. This was the day after his 32nd birthday. He was buried in the village of Westoutre, at the British Cemetery. This is just behind Kemmel Hill, and some seven miles south-west of Ypres. He has a special memorial which means that he is buried there, but the exact location is unknown.

His promotion to Acting Major as from 4 April appeared in the *London Gazette* of 1 June, but was not recorded in the announcement of the award of the Victoria Cross, which appeared in the Gazette of 4 June.

FAMILY AND TRIBUTES

The following are extracts from some of the letters received by Eric's father, Andrew Dougall, who was now living at 13 Mount Ephraim Road. Ill health had forced him to retire from his job with the Tunbridge Wells Gas Company in January 1917.

The Adjutant of the Brigade wrote:

Throughout the time that I have spent with him, and it is some two years now, I have never met a man more popular amongst his brother officers or more

Captain Dougall

respected amongst his men than your son. A finer man never breathed, and his place in the Brigade can never be filled. He was in command of his battery at the time of his death and for the past week had been performing most gallant work.

The Major who had for long commanded the Battery:

I thought the world of him. He was quite fearless and a most determined officer, equally popular with officers and men. He was always cheerful under the most trying circumstances, very unselfish and always ready to do a job of work for other people. He was a wonderful person to have in a Battery, as, apart from being such a fine soldier, he was a charming companion and the mess was never dull so long as he was there to keep up the spirits … The Colonel thought quite as much of him as I did, and he was often selected for difficult and dangerous work on account of his great courage and determination.

The Chaplain of the Brigade:

Seldom have I met an officer who commanded such unbound devotion from his men and unqualified admiration from his brother officers, and I always considered that in him was found the most perfect example of a 'man' in the highest sense of the term. I understand that several days before his death he had been specially recommended for his coolness and presence of mind in a very trying position, when he rallied the infantry who had fallen back on his guns, and inspired them with a confidence that enabled them to attack and beat back the enemy.

The Colonel O.C. of the Brigade:

What I have read today in The Times gives but a faint idea of what his loss means to his battery and to the brigade. I have numerous splendid fellows in my brigade, but I have never known a man gain more quickly or more lastingly the confidence, admiration and affection of his comrades.

His superb unassuming gallantry was only one of the many qualities that won our admiration, and his memory will always be an inspiration to those who served under him.

Always cool and steadfast under any circumstances, it was perhaps a few days before his death that, under circumstances of the greatest difficulty and danger, his splendid qualities were given their fullest expression. This gallant performance of Dougall and his detachments will always be one of the proudest recollections of his battery and his brigade, and, though there are indeed few of us who can hope to emulate him, the example he has set us will assuredly in the days to come bring out what is best in each one of us.

In his will the administration was left to his father, and his effects were listed as £1,337 11s. 8d. As his father died in March 1919, administration of the will passed to Dougall's mother and sisters.

At the end of the Tunbridge Wells Town Council Meeting on 5 June 1918, the Mayor (Alderman R. Vaughan Gower M.B.E.) said he

wished to refer to the great honour done to the town by Temporary Captain Dougall, to whom the King had been pleased to approve of the award of the Victoria Cross. Captain Dougall, who had unfortunately made the supreme sacrifice, was the son of one of the most respected townsmen, Mr A. Dougall, for many years Manager of the Tunbridge Wells Gas Company. The members of the Council would agree with him that they were proud that such a man should have been a citizen of the Borough, and they also deeply regretted that he had not survived to wear the decoration which had been so worthily bestowed upon him by His Majesty. He would like to move that the Town Clerk be requested to write a letter to Captain Dougall's father expressing their pleasure at the honour his son had bestowed upon the town, and expressing great regret that he had not survived, together with their condolences with the father and relatives of the gallant officer. He also moved that the report appearing in The Times be entered on the minutes of the Council. This was carried upstanding and in silence.

On Sunday 9 June the Rev. Ernest Dowsett gave an address at the Children's Service at Mount Pleasant Congregational Church, using the Victoria Cross as his subject, and paying tribute to Eric Dougall. He said:

> I want the Victoria Cross to speak to us. I want it to interpret the spirit of our gallant fellow-townsman, Major Dougall, who one memorable day this spring, averted a break in the British line, delayed the enemy's advance for twelve hours, saved his guns, and won the V.C. … that was the character of the man Tunbridge Wells honours today.
>
> You can read it in all the letters from the officers in his Brigade. 'Cheerful, unselfish and always ready to do a job for other people,' that is what they say of him. Major Dougall was a man who grew restless under any form of praise. He carried a valorous heart in modest, unassuming guise. When honours came to him he took them, then he hid them! He would hide the memory of that brave day with his guns if he could. But his country will not let him hide it. His country has honoured him with the coveted decoration.
>
> We speak of brave men as 'lion-hearted', and Major Dougall was lion-hearted when his great day came at the Front. The enemy had pressed our infantry back into line with his guns. Cool as on parade, and with great determination and courage, he rallied the men, supplied them with Lewis guns, armed the gunners with rifles and formed a line in front of his Battery with the memorable challenge: So long as you stick to the trenches I will keep here with my guns. And there they stood all through the day. Major Dougall calmly giving orders in a deluge of fire, and putting heart into everybody. And it was only when the ammunition was spent that the Battery received orders to withdraw, and the guns, under the most difficult circumstances, were saved.

King George V wrote a letter to his father dated 10 June 1918:

> It is a matter of sincere regret to me that the death of Lieutenant (Acting Captain) Eric Stuart Dougall, M.C., Special Reserve, attached 'A' Battery, 88th Brigade, R.F.A., deprived me of the pride of personally conferring upon him the Victoria Cross, the greatest of all rewards for valour and devotion to duty.

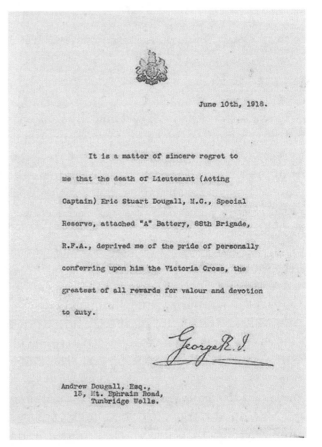

June 10th, 1918.

It is a matter of sincere regret to me that the death of Lieutenant (Acting Captain) Eric Stuart Dougall, M.C., Special Reserve, attached "A" Battery, 88th Brigade, R.F.A., deprived me of the pride of personally conferring upon him the Victoria Cross, the greatest of all rewards for valour and devotion to duty.

George R.I.

Andrew Dougall, Esq.,
15, Mt. Ephraim Road,
Tunbridge Wells.

The King's Letter

The King's letter was accompanied by a letter from the Colonel, Assistant Military Secretary at the War Office:

Sir,

I am direct to transmit the enclosed letter from His Majesty the King, and to ask if you will be so good as to inform me whether you would desire to attend at Buckingham Palace to receive the Victoria Cross awarded to your late Son, Lieutenant (Acting Captain) Eric Stuart Dougall, M.C., Special Reserve attached 'A' Battery, 88th Brigade Royal Field Artillery, or whether you would prefer that the decoration be transmitted to you.

In the event of your being desirous of attending personally for presentation by the King, instructions will be sent you later as to the hour and date on which presentation will be made by His Majesty.

On 9 July Emily, Eric's mother wrote to Mr William Sheldon Hadley, Master at Pembroke College, Cambridge:

Dear Mr Hadley,

My husband is not equal to much writing at present and wishes me to thank you for your sympathy in the loss of our dear son, also for your interest in his military achievements and the honour since awarded him. His death will be a life-long sorrow to us, but we have been comforted by many letters such as yours, testifying to the esteem and affection he inspired wherever he went. I remember how much he appreciated the kindness and friendship of Mrs Hadley and yourself when he was at Pembroke, and on his return from India to take a commission he regretted there was no opportunity to re-visit Cambridge, as he longed to do.

With united kind regards,
Yours very sincerely,
Emily E. Dougall.

Eric's sister Ellen Mary Dougall went to a private ceremony at Buckingham Palace on 10 July to receive the Victoria Cross and Military Cross from the King, as her father had been forced to retire through ill health and her mother was also ill. Private Henry James Nicholas was also decorated with the V.C. then.

On 26 March 1919, Eric's father, Andrew died at 13 Mount Ephraim Road, Tunbridge Wells. He had worked for Tunbridge Wells Gas Company for 36 years. He was buried at the Borough Cemetery. This followed a service at the Congregational Church, Mount Pleasant. Many local Gas Company representatives attended the funeral. The family mourners were: Mr. J. Stewart Dougall, Boston; Mr James Dougall, Westcliff-on-Sea (brothers); and Mr. Alfred Harker, F.R.S., St. John's College, Cambridge (brother-in-law). He is buried in the Borough Cemetery in Grave B1 288.

Dougall Family Grave, Tunbridge Wells

The following appeared in *The Times* on 14 April 1919:

> DOUGALL - In proud and cherished memory of Eric Stuart Dougall ("Sandy") V.C., M.C.,
> Major, R.F.A., killed in action on Mont Kemmel, 14th April, 1918.

His wife, Emily moved from 13 Mount Ephraim Road to 22 Dudley Road, Tunbridge Wells in May 1919. On 11 February 1923 the Tunbridge Wells War Memorial was unveiled. Mrs Dougall travelled from her Bayswater home (18a Richmond Road) to lay the first wreath as a fitting tribute to her brave son.

Tunbridge Wells War Memorial

Emily later lived at 16a Loudoun Road, St. John's Wood, London and died on 9 October 1936 and was buried alongside her husband in Tunbridge Wells.

From 1950 to 53 Eric's sisters, Kathleen and Ellen lived at Flat 3, Somerville Gardens, Tunbridge Wells. By 1955 Kathleen was on her own, and from 1959 until 1963 she was at 5b Molyneux Park Road, Tunbridge Wells. On 25 June 1956, she attended the service in Westminster Abbey to mark the centenary of the Victoria Cross. The following day she watched the special Royal Review in Hyde Park. "It was most impressive," she said, "and extremely well done. I felt really proud to be there." Eric's V.C. was displayed at the V.C. Centenary Exhibition at Marlborough House from 15 June until 7 July.

Kathleen died on 25 February 1969. On 14 March 1969 a letter was sent from Buss, Stone and Co, Solicitors, 2 and 3 The Priory, Tunbridge Wells to the Bursar of Pembroke College, Cambridge concerning the winding up of her estate:

> Clause 5 of her Will – I give free of duty to the Master and Fellows of Pembroke College,
> Cambridge the Victoria Cross and Military Cross awarded to my late brother Eric Stuart
> Dougall which are deposited in my box with Lloyds Bank Limited, Mount Pleasant,
> Tunbridge Wells aforesaid.

Eric Dougall's two diaries from 1917 and 1918, which he meticulously maintained during the war were also given, together with his New Testament. Both are pocket diaries. The 1917 one was "with the compliments of Stone and Co. Ltd, Fire Brick Works, Epsom, nr. Ewell, Surrey". His 1918 Diary was a Charles Letts and Co. Diary and Notebook signed by E. S. Dougall, who gave his address as A/88 R.F.A. BEF France. His New Testament is inscribed "E. S. Dougall, Brookside, Tunbridge Wells with love and best wishes from E. E. D. (his mother) Sunday, July 23 1916." In the front it contains Lord Roberts's Message to the Troops:

> 25th Aug. 1914. I ask you to put your trust in God. He will watch over you and strengthen you. You will find in this little Book guidance when you are in health, comfort when you are in sickness, and strength when you are in adversity.

In July 1991 a letter was received by James Scholes, Mayor of Tunbridge Wells from Mrs Betty Watson, Perth, Australia:

Kathleen Dougall and Friends

I am writing to you to ask your help in finding any relative of Eric Dougall as I have in my possession a letter written by him within a few days of his death to my father, who had been the padre and a very dear friend. There is also a letter from his mother acknowledging a

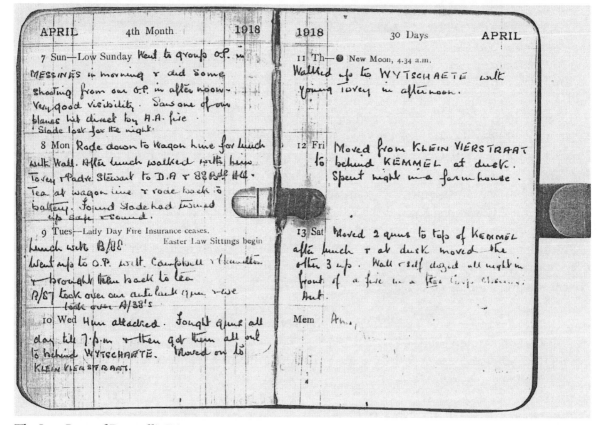

The Last Page of Dougall's Diary

letter of sympathy from my father … I know he was an only son but he may have had a sister. Should there be no relatives, I wonder if you know where his V.C. is kept as I think it would be fitting for these letters to be with it. The letters have been cherished by my father and me.

Mr Scholes then passed it to the *Focus* Newspaper. "It's a very interesting story about what may well be our most famous V.C., and I would like to appeal to local people for help in seeing if there are any living relatives and in trying to find the Victoria Cross itself". It appears that no one came forward at the time.

The following entry appeared in a Spink's Sale catalogue dated 28 April 1993:

> 518. 1. A group to Major E. S. Dougall, V.C., M.C., Royal Field Artillery.
>   (a) Military Cross George V Issue.
>   (b & c) War and Victory Medals (Major). With five related badges and buttons.
> 2. A group to E. M. Dougall, V.A.D. (presumably the "Miss Dougall" who received Major Dougall's V.C. from the King's hands)
>   (a & b) War and Victory Medals (V.A.D.)
>   (c) B.R.C.S. War Service 1914–18. With a badge of the Women's Advertising Club Of London. Generally about extremely fine (12) £2500

It is believed £3000 was raised, but it remains a mystery about the Military Cross as that was already held by Pembroke College, Cambridge. In 1996 it is believed the same medal set was sold for £2900 against a reserve price of £2500.

Eric's Medal entitlement was:
  Victoria Cross
  Military Cross
  British War Medal (1914–20)
  The Victory Medal (1914–19).

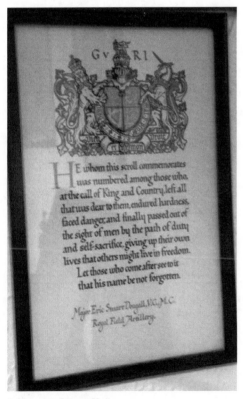

Memorial Scroll

HE WILL BE REMEMBERED

Eric Dougall's name is on a brass plaque in St. Thomas's Cathedral, Bombay, India.

* * * * *

He is proudly remembered on a joint memorial for Liverpool Cricket Club and Liverpool (Rugby) Football Club. He was a 1st XV Player during his years in Liverpool working at the Mersey Docks and Harbour Board. A lounge of the cricket club at Aigburth Road, Aigburth, Liverpool bears his name (and another lounge that of Noel Chavasse V.C., a contemporary of Dougall's, who won the 100 yards for Oxford in 1907). These refurbished lounges were opened in December 1986 and pictures of their citations are also displayed, together with framed portrait photos and a short biography.

* * * * *

His name appears on the Tonbridge School War Memorial. Following two general meetings of

Tonbridgians and friends of the school, held in 1917 and 1918, a Committee of Management, with full powers, was appointed to erect a structural monument to provide for the education at Tonbridge of sons of Old Tonbridgians and of Masters who gave their lives in the Great War. An appeal for subscriptions collected over £12,250. The structural memorial in the Chapel, dedicated by Bishop Russell Wakefield and unveiled by Major General Sir W. Edmund Ironside on 10 October 1925 was erected at a cost of little over £6,000.

Eric's name also appears on a slate plaque with other V.Cs in a cloister outside the school Library.

The Slate Plaque, Tonbridge School

* * * * *

He is remembered on the Pembroke College War Memorial in the Chapel Cloisters at Pembroke College, Cambridge. His name appears under the date of his matriculation – 1905.

* * * * *

His name appears on the Tunbridge Wells War Memorial.

* * * * *

On Thursday 26 April 2007, the Mayor of Tunbridge Wells, Councillor Ron Weedon, hosted a road naming ceremony at Barratt Kent's new homes development at Connaught Park, Sandhurst Road, High Brooms, Tunbridge Wells. Five roads were named after local V.C.s including "Dougall Close".

Dougall Close, High Brooms, Tunbridge Wells

* * * * *

His name is also on the V.C. Roll of Honour at the Union Jack Club, Sandell Street, Waterloo, London SE1 8UJ.

CHAPTER EIGHT

A Canadian Scot on the Western Front – The Story of Lieutenant Colonel William Hew Clark-Kennedy 1879–1961

FOREWORD

William was a very modest man and horrified by any public display, but equally of course, a man of steel who stood no nonsense. A good man to follow, a bad one to cross.

Lieutenant Colonel A. J. C. Clark-Kennedy, senior male cousin

A DISTINGUISHED FAMILY

William Hew Clark-Kennedy's father was Alexander William Maxwell Clark-Kennedy, who was born on 26 September 1851 at Rochester, Kent. He was educated at Eton and became a Lieutenant in the Coldstream Guards on 31 March 1870, and Captain on 15 April 1874. In 1868 he wrote "The Birds of Berkshire and Buckinghamshire: a contribution to the history of the two counties". His nickname was "Spats". He was promoted to Captain in 1874 and retired from the Army. On 4 February 1875, he married the Hon. Lettice Lucy Hewitt (born in Dublin around 1853), at St. Anne's, Meen Glas, County Donegal, Ireland.

Alexander and Lettice went on to have six sons and two daughters. Besides their house in London they rented another in Dorset (Henbury House, Sturminster Marshall). They came to Knockgray, Carsphairn, Castle Douglas, Kircudbrightshire, Scotland, the family home since 1704 for fishing and shooting holidays.

Alexander was author of several works on science, travel and poems. He was appointed J.P. and Deputy Lieutenant of the Stewartry of Kirkcudbright and J.P. for Dorset and Dumfriesshire. His appointments were: Fellow of the Linnaean Society, Fellow of the Royal Geographic Society, Fellow of the Zoological Society, Fellow of the Society of Antiquaries and Fellow of the Society of Antiquaries of Scotland. By 1891 the family had moved to 72 Eaton Place, St. George's, Hanover Square, London but he died at their next house at 11 Eccleston Square, London on 21 December 1894.

After his death Lettice moved up to Knockgray with her children and the London house was sold along with her husband's collections of bird and natural history specimens, weapons and sporting trophies, and their house in Dorset was also given up. To accommodate her large family she added a new wing with three further bedrooms and a bathroom to the back of Knockgray and it remained her home for the next 43 years until her death.

She died on 13 August 1939 and was duly buried beside her husband on the Craig of Knockgray. Knockgray was once more rented out for nearly 30 years.

The burial ground on Craig of Knockgray contains Alexander and Lettice's graves and three of their children. The other crosses are of two sons killed in action in France (Archibald Douglas Hewitt) and Palestine (Alexander Kenelm), and the two who died in South Africa and Canada (John William James and William Hew).

This, then, is the family background to William. His senior male cousin, Lieutenant Colonel Alexander John Clark-Kennedy, M.C. succeeded to the baronetcy of Knockgray. He was born on 12 March 1918 and was educated at Radley and the Royal Military College, Sandhurst. He commanded the 12th Lancers in 1938 and served in the Second World War, 1939–45. He was awarded the M.C. in 1940, was mentioned twice in Despatches, and was wounded. He served in France, the Western Desert, North Africa and Italy, and afterwards in Palestine, Malaya and Cyprus. He married on 7 July 1951, Pamela May Watson, daughter of Captain Henry Gilbert Watson, M.C., of Worthy Lands, Trebetherick, Cornwall and has two sons, Alexander Hugh Clark born 28 September 1952 and Andrew Charles Clark, born 10 December 1955. He was Company Commander and Master of the Sandhurst Foxhounds, R.M.A. Sandhurst, 1955–57. He was Commanding Officer, 12th Lancers and 1st Commanding Officer, 9th/12th Lancers on amalgamation. He retired in 1966, and has done much for the community around Knockgray including having rescued the damaged church bell when it was in danger of being carried away as a souvenir, by people who had found it in a midden. It is now back in the church. He refers to William as "Willie".

FROM SCOTLAND TO SOUTH AFRICA

William Hew Clark-Kennedy was born on 3 March 1879 (although on his Attestation Papers for the Army he gave his date of birth as 3 March 1880). He was born at Dunskey House, Portpatrick, near Castle Douglas, Wigtownshire, Scotland. This was a holiday home on the coast, which the family rented, while on holiday from Knockgray.

At Knockgray around 1890. L to R.: Lettice Lucy (mother), Leopold James (Brother), the gamekeeper's daughter, Lettice Eleanor (sister), Alice Arthur (sister), William Hew, John William James (brother)

By 1891 the family had moved to London, and was resident at 72 Eaton Place, St George Hanover Square, Knightsbridge. From 1891–1893 William attended St. Andrew's School, Southborough, Tunbridge Wells in Kent. The building (a large Victorian mansion) was built in 1870 and was then known as Southborough New Hall. It became a Preparatory School in 1891, so William was one of the first pupils. The building had an imposing front flanked by two wings. It fronted London Road stretching from Pinewood Court to Hythe Close and the land at the rear covered an area from the back of the Park Road Gardens to beyond the Bell Pub.

The estate passed from the ownership of Mr (later Sir) Frederick Bourne to Reverend Reginald Bull and his wife Agnes in 1891 for use as a school. Rev. Bull had two or three Assistant Masters, together with a full staff, matron and domestic staff. The school had its own Chapel, where the organist was also organist of St. Thomas' Church. The old stables were converted into a gymnasium. There were a number of playing fields behind the school, together with a swimming pool. The school thrived until 1919, when the south wing was gutted by a fire on the night of 8 February. At that time there were around 35 pupils. The school then settled at Yewhurst, near Forest Row. The Southborough property was sold off. After the Second World War the north wing temporarily housed council tenants until better accommodation could be found for them, and it was finally demolished in 1970.

William moved on to Westminster School, London which he entered on 19 January, 1893 with his brother Leopold. He stayed until July 1896. Unfortunately the school has no records to show how he performed there. He then joined the Standard Life Insurance Company as a Clerk in the London (West End) Office from 1896 until 1899. But in 1899 William's life took a turn in another direction, and his military ancestry came to the fore. He volunteered to serve in South Africa.

Relationships between the Boers, descendants of the original Dutch settlers in South Africa, and the British had been going downhill for some years. The British Government was wary of the Boer tendency to move into areas they considered properly theirs. The tensions between the two sides exploded into war in October 1899. At the start of the war the British were naturally inferior

St. Andrew's School, Southborough

in terms of numbers, weaponry and intimate knowledge of the terrain. Soon after the outbreak of the South African War in 1899, the War Office was finding it difficult to provide reinforcements, particularly mounted troops. The week of 10 – 17 December 1899 was a black one. In the space of seven days three separate actions at Sturmberg, Magersfontein and Colenso resulted in defeats. The total loss amounted to about 3,000 men and 12 guns. The Marquis of Lansdowne proposed calling on the Yeomanry Cavalry to help meet the shortfall. At the end of 1899 the government decided it needed a mounted infantry force, "The Imperial Yeomanry", for service in South Africa, and it needed to seek to recruit a limited number of mid-upper-class English volunteers. The response throughout the country was fast and overwhelming, with the offices of the Imperial Yeomanry Committee in London being besieged by volunteers wishing to enlist. The idea of volunteering for the Imperial Yeomanry appealed to young men's sporting instincts. In a short time 8,000 men of every class were enlisted.

So The Imperial Yeomanry was created by Royal Warrant on 24 December 1899. It was decided that the men should be dressed in neutral coloured Norfolk woollen jackets, breeches and gaiters, laced boots and felt hats. Each man was told to bring his own horse, clothing, saddlery etc. The government provided arms, ammunition and camp equipment. The Yeomanry made up the bulk of the new force, but the remainder were eager volunteers, including many important social and political figures. A large proportion of the men came from stately homes and gentlemen's clubs. This is hardly surprising as the recruits were expected to be able to ride and shoot. Some units consisted entirely of men of wealth and authority and these were independently raised but attached to the Imperial Yeomanry. One was Paget's Horse, which William joined as a trooper. They were made up of a "pretty average collection of young men of good social position and public-school education – a gentleman corps". Major George Thomas Cavendish Paget gained the rank of Major in the service of the Imperial Yeomanry. He fought in the war in Paget's Horse, which he raised. The Imperial Yeomanry was wealthy and was able to acquire better quality equipment and horses than those provided by the Army. Although there were supposedly strict requirements, many volunteers were accepted with substandard horsemanship or marksmanship, but they had plenty of time to train while waiting to embark for South Africa. Before they left the new recruits were given 2–3 months' basic training as mounted infantry at various district centres.

Thus William joined the Army to serve in the Imperial Yeomanry and sailed for South Africa. He enlisted as trooper 13008 in the 51st Company, 19th Battalion Imperial Yeomanry (Paget's Horse). The 19th Battalion also consisted of 52nd, 68th and 73rd Companies of Paget's Horse. Over 50 per cent of the original contingent was of middle and upper classes. The 51st Company was raised in 1900 and transferred in 1902 to 12th Battalion. The first contingent of recruits consisted of 550 officers, 10,371 men with 20 battalions and four companies, and arrived in South Africa between February and April 1900. William arrived in South Africa on 4 April 1900. Once in the Cape the men were sent 5 miles to Maitland Camp, which was understaffed and had poor facilities and where conditions were not good.

The Imperial Yeomanry became active on 5 April 1900, when the 3rd and 10th Battalions fought Boer volunteers led by Count de Villebois-Mareuil at Boshof. Following a number of tactical errors, the Boers were surrounded. The Count was killed, with the Yeomanry suffering only three casualties. On 27 May the 13th Battalion arrived at Lindley and were ambushed by the Boers. Led by Lieutenant Colonel Basil Spragge, the 13th decided to fight until help arrived. But help came too late and one officer and 16 men were killed and 400 captured.

After this disaster, the Imperial Yeomanry rode hundreds of miles across the Veldt, but saw very few Boers. Morale was low as the number of deaths and diseases increased. During the end of the year there were some small victories and in September 1900, the City Imperial Volunteers were returned to England, but not the Imperial Yeomanry. This had a bad effect on morale, and only one third of the force continued. By June and July of 1901, all of the first recruits returned home, except those who re-enlisted. William became a Lance Corporal in 1901 and 10 September the *London Gazette* (27353) tells us he was a Corporal with Paget's Horse, also known as the Rhodesian Horse during the South African War. He took part in this war which was also referred to as the Boer War and saw action at Cape Colony until 31 May 1902. He was Mentioned in Despatches on 29 November 1900, and received the Queen's Medal with four clasps. He was in the Orange Free State from 28 February 1900 until 31 May 1902, and was finally discharged in 1902. The climate in South Africa did not agree with him.

CANADA AND THE GREAT WAR

William returned from the war in South Africa to his job in London at the Standard Life Assurance Company, no doubt with many heroic stories. In 1902, he went to Canada as Secretary and Second Officer of the Standard Life Assurance Company, later becoming the Assistant Manager, Canada. He was based in Montreal. He stayed in this post until 1909. It appears that it became the principle duty of the Secretary to assist the Manager with the supervision of the Company's investments and mortgages. William joined the Canadian Militia almost on his return enlisting as a Second Lieutenant with the 5th Regiment Royal Highlanders of Canada as a reservist. The 5th, who were formed on 31 January 1862, had since 1904 been affiliated to the famous Black Watch.

He became very much a part of the social scene in Montreal. He was one of the main organisers of the fashionable St. Andrew's Ball of 1913 in which the Duke and Duchess of Connaught were the guests of honour. The Duke was Governor-General of Canada. The *Montreal Gazette* tells us that it was "one of the most brilliant social events ever held in Montreal, and was characterised by some excellent Scottish reels and other Highland dances which this officer did much to promote!"

William was a Freemason, and his Mother Lodge was the Saint Paul's Lodge, Number 12 of the Canadian Constitution, meeting in Montreal. The minutes of their meeting on 8 March 1910 state:

> A letter was read from Bro W.H. Clark-Kennedy asking for his Demit: he having been transferred by his Company to Johannesburg, S.A. His dues being paid, the W.M. granted his request expressing his regrets at the loss of our energetic Secretary; stating that as he is remaining on the Benevolent Fund his Demit is not required, and instructing that he be so notified.

He represented the Standard Life Assurance Company as Secretary in South Africa. The Head Office had moved from Cape Town to Johannesburg, under E. S. Kimber. He spent a few years there before coming back to Canada before the outbreak of the First World War. When, on the evening of 4 August 1914, war was declared between Great Britain and Germany the response was immediate throughout the British Empire. The people of Canada were determined to lead the way. Up until now there had been some militia regiments, and a small regular force. They provided the base for a new armed force to be raised. Parliament resolved that it should raise an expeditionary force of 22,000 men for despatch to Europe. But with the enthusiasm of the huge numbers of volunteers who came forward, an army of 33,000 men was raised in a few weeks. The various regiments were assembled at a newly created camp, Valcartier, outside Quebec. Men of the 5th Royal Highlanders of Canada were quick to respond to the call, and they departed for Valcartier on the evening of 24 August. The Battalion was 1,017 strong. A very large proportion of the men, like William, were born in Britain, young men who had gone out to Canada, lived there for some years, and, at the first call to arms, had volunteered to return and fight for the land of their birth

On his return to Canada, William married Kate Reford on 5 September 1914. Kate was the only daughter of Robert Reford of Drummond Street, Montreal. They were married while he was still in training at Valcartier military training camp, Quebec City, preparing for the Great War. As many as possible of the officers of the 13th attended the wedding.

William introduces Kate to his Mother and one of his Sisters at Knockgray

On 23 September William had enlisted in the Royal Highlanders of Canada in Montreal, and went to France with the 13th Battalion (Montreal Royal Highlanders), Canadian Expeditionary Force. The Militia units were under strength at the outbreak of war so it was decided to enroll volunteers in 260 new, full-strength battalions consisting of 1,000 men each. These battalions were known as the Canadian Expeditionary Force (C.E.F.). The various units at Valcartier were shuffled and reshuffled to form the 1st Canadian Division. The 13th Battalion found itself one of the four battalions constituting the 3rd Infantry Brigade, under the command of Colonel R. E. W. Turner, V.C., D.S.O. William held the rank of Captain, and was a company commander.

His Attestation Paper for the Canadian Overseas Expeditionary Force gives his home address as 260 Drummond Street, Montreal. His height was 5ft 9½, with a 34-inch chest. His complexion is listed as "Fair", his eyes as "Blue" and hair as "Brown". He had a birth mark on the left side of his back, and his Religion is listed as C.of E. [Church of England].

The government spared no expense in equipping their troops. By the end of September the Expeditionary Force was ready. On 26 September the 13th Battalion marched from Valcartier Training Camp for Quebec. There they embarked on H.M.S. *Alaunia*, of the Cunard Line. Their departure from Canada on the 30th was a well-kept secret, until early in October a report was circulated in England that they had landed in Southampton. However the report was untrue, and on 14 October they arrived in Plymouth.

Their basic training was carried out on Salisbury Plain, Wiltshire. On 22 October, the 13th was reorganised into a "double company" battalion. This meant the battalion consisted of four companies instead of eight. The command of No. 4 Company was given to William. The young recruits expected to sail for France after a couple of weeks, but they undertook hard training first, which continued well into February. Most of the troops were kept under canvas into the New Year, as huts had not been completed owing to a shortage of labour. It was an exceptionally wet winter, and the camp soon turned into a sea of mud. It was very boring for the troops in these conditions, and it did not help that they were fourteen miles from the nearest town.

The King visited the camp on 4 November, accompanied by the Queen, Lord Kitchener, and Lord Roberts. They were greeted with great enthusiasm. On 10 February the Battalion left the camp via Amesbury Station bound for Avonmouth, where they boarded the S.S. *Novian*. The *Novian* sailed at dawn on 12 February, and after a rough crossing arrived at St. Nazaire on the 15th. Following on the heels of a strong advance party, under William's command, the Battalion disembarked from the *Novian* and lined up on the dock. They then went by train to Hazebrouck, where they arrived at 6.30 p.m. on 19 February. The men were stiff after the rail journey but then marched seven miles to Flêtre. At Caestra Captain Clark-Kennedy met the Battalion, and the march to Flêtre was continued under his guidance.

They spent four days and five nights at Flêtre preparing for the trenches. At 8 a.m. on 23 February the Battalion marched from Flêtre to Armentières. There they were attached for instructional purposes to the 16th British Infantry Brigade, who were holding a line of trenches on both sides of the Lille road, about three miles south-east of the town.

On the 24th, two Companies of Royal Highlanders went into the line that night for their first tour of instruction. The next day No. 3 Company and No. 4 Company, under William, were given a similar short tour of instruction.

In early March it was felt that the Canadian Division were ready to take over a section of the line. They were to relieve the 7th British Division, bringing them into the line in a position extending roughly in a north-east direction from the Sailly-Fromelles road to the Touquet-Bridoux road. This took place on 6 March. On the night of 9 March the Battalion was relieved and marched back to billets at Point de la Justice, in Divisional Reserve. On 13 March they did another three days in the trenches gaining good experience, before proceeding to billets in Rue du Bois, where they were rested.

On the afternoon of the 26th the Battalion marched to reserve billets, seven miles away at Estaires, where they undertook eleven days of training in drill and route marching. On 7 April they marched 16 miles to Terdeghem, a village near the town of Cassel. On the 10th they were inspected by General Sir H. Smith-Dorrien, G.O.C. of the Second British Army, of which the Canadian Division was now a part. He told them that they were soon to proceed to a lively part of the line.

On 15 April the Battalion began marching towards the Ypres Salient. It was here where the Allied line followed the canal bulging eastward around the town of Ypres, Belgium. North of the Salient were the Belgians. Two French Divisions covered the northern part of the Salient itself, while the Canadians with one division covered the eastern part, with two British divisions. At Ypres St. John three Companies went into billets as Brigade Reserve, No. 4 Company and William proceeding to St. Julien as brigade support. They spent three days here making preparations for taking over part of the line.

On the night of 21 April, the 13th Battalion moved up to the line, taking over a series of trenches from 14th Battalion, Royal Montreal Regiment. The next day the Canadian Division held a line, 4,250 yards in length, extending in a north-west direction from the Ypres-Roulers railway to a point some 50 yards beyond the Ypres-Poelcapelle Road. The extreme left of the line was held by the 13th Battalion. The right section of the front was held by No. 4 Company under Captain Clark-Kennedy.

They soon realised their trenches were not strong enough, mainly made up with thin sand bags. The Germans were 50–70 yards away showing little sign of activity. At about 3 p.m. there was a terrific bombardment on the Canadian line and on the French line to the left. This fell on the trenches immediately behind the front line. After two hours of shelling, the Germans launched a great wave of chlorine gas, which was new to this type of warfare. This was unexpected and the Allies had no protection against it.

The Germans had planned to use gas for several weeks but had to wait until the wind became favourable. It never came until Thursday 22 April, when they decided to take advantage of a south-easterly wind blowing towards the French part of the line, north of Ypres. At Langemark the Allied line was continued by men of the Canadian Division under General Alderson. The gas fell on the trenches to the Canadian's left, so elements of the 13th received a whiff of it. The Germans had reckoned that if the French were broken north of Ypres the line of the Canadians could be turned and then Ypres would be captured easily.

When the gas came the position of the Canadian Division was one of extreme peril. They were holding the line with two brigades in the trenches, and the third in reserve. The 3rd Brigade had joined on with the French line at Poelcapelle. Brigadier General Turner of the 3rd Brigade ordered up his 3rd Battalion as soon as the attack started, and Canadian Artillery was sent to help the French. At about 5pm, Captain Clark-Kennedy of No. 4 Company returned to the front line after a daring expedition, as a result of which he got through to Brigade Headquarters. He brought back with him orders instructing the men to evacuate the line they were then holding and take up a new line. So they buried the dead and evacuated the wounded.

The gas had caused a considerable gap, through which the Germans moved forward. At about 6 p.m. a salvo from a battery in the rear made four direct hits on the Highlanders' trenches, causing about 12 casualties. The Germans, having broken through the French ranks, swung towards the Canadians' flank and were heading towards St. Julien. Here they met and defeated Number 3 Company with two platoons. It had been decided to evacuate previous positions and occupy a new line about 300 yards in the rear, before reinforcements arrived, enabling them to move forward again. Rifle fire poured in on the Battalion from three sides and the German shelling was heavy and effective. The men were short of food, water and ammunition. However the Highlanders bravely resisted. It was at first thought that the Canadians had been driven back, but four hours afterwards at 8.25 p.m., Brigadier General Turner reported that the line still held.

At 10 p.m. the 13th started to move, and almost immediately the Germans launched a series of fierce attacks from the front, rear and left flanks. The retreat was slow as they were carrying the wounded, but they held off the attacks. During the night of the 23rd Transport brought up rations, ammunition and water from Ypres. Soon after daybreak the Germans again used gas, and the 13th had to fall back. Finally a line was reached where the retreat was ended and orders issued to "stand fast". All day the Battalion held this line under heavy fire. At about 3 p.m. they received news that help was on its way. Until this arrived, Captain Clark-Kennedy, with Lieutenants Lindsay and MacTier and a small party maintained contact with the Germans. At dusk several battalions of British troops came up and passed through the weary Canadian lines. This meant the 13th spent the night in reserve trenches south of Wieltje, withdrawing about one mile to near Potijze the next morning.

At one point during the battle on the 24 April, Captain Clark-Kennedy was incorrectly reported killed (Casualty List 43). He was knocked over three times by shells, the third time being completely buried and rendered unconscious. The men on either side of him were killed. He eventually managed to dig himself out, although the enemy was close by. He managed to return to his own lines with valuable information. On the 1 May the casualty report was cancelled and he was reported to be alive and well. For his courage he was later awarded the French Croix de Guerre with Bronze Palm by the French Government.

Sunday 25th was spent here and that night the Battalion was ordered to La Breque. At about 2 a.m. on the 26th they were then ordered to retire across the Yser Canal to Brielen, some miles away. There they had a brief rest before being ordered forward once more to support an attack near La Brique. Having done this they moved to a point south of Wieltje, where they dug in. 27 April was spent under shell-fire from three directions. On the night of the 29th the Battalion moved forward about a mile to support an attack by the French, where they suffered a number of casualties. Early in the morning of 4 May the Highlanders moved back to a position near Vlamertinghe and at 7.30 p.m. they left the Ypres Salient and marched, together with the other Battalions of the 3rd Brigade to billets south of Bailleul. The 13th Battalion lost 12 officers and 454 other ranks at the Second Battle of Ypres, nearly half its fighting strength.

The actions during the 6 days between 24 and 30 April are officially known as the Battle of St. Julien. The significance of the Canadian effort lies in their determined stand during the first three days of the battle. The War Office announced "The Canadians had many casualties but their gallantry and determination undoubtedly saved the situation". This, then, was the first time a former colonial force (Canadians) pushed back a major European power (Germans) on European soil.

AWARDED THE D.S.O.

Lieutenant Colonel Loomis started to rebuild his unit, reckoning that after their achievements the Canadians would soon be called on again. A small draft of N.C.O.s and men arrived from England. On 9 May General Alderson visited the Battalion and addressed the officers and men, and three days later General Sir Horace Dorrien-Smith spoke only to a small group of officers, as all the companies were away on a route march. News also came from Scotland that the Black Watch were adding to their recruiting posters the phrase, "with which is allied the 13th Canadian Battalion, R.H.C".

On 9 May, Sir John French had attacked the German front in order to try and secure positions on the Vimy and Aubers Ridges. The British attack, the Battle of Aubers Ridge consisted of several days bitter fighting. The Germans were driven back but refused to be beaten. Following the lull, the attack was now to restart with the Canadian Division involved.

On the 13th, the Battalion headed south, and marched all night until they arrived at 2.30 a.m. at billets near Robecq. A Company inspection was carried out on the 15th and new equipment issued.

The Royal Highlanders resumed their march on 16 May. On the 17th, they occupied reserve trenches at Le Touret and after being shelled moved back to billets in Essars. At 5 a.m. on 19th they advanced to Le Touret again and spent a few hours in muddy ditches before moving to trenches in a hamlet known as Indian Village. While some men were used to strengthen their position, others buried the dead from the previous British line.

Other Battalions of 3rd Brigade took over a section of the front and became heavily engaged. On 18 May two companies of 14th Royal Montreal Regiment and two companies of 16th Canadian Scottish attacked towards the boundaries of an orchard at La Quinque Rue. This was heavily defended by Germans. On 20 May orders were issued for an attack on an area known as the Orchard. Two companies of 16th Canadian Scottish and two companies of the 15th (48th Highlanders) were ordered to assault the Orchard and a position extending to the right at 7.45 p.m. After the attack, the 13th Royal Highlanders of Canada were ordered to take over the positions, consolidate and hold them. So the 13th advanced from Indian Village at 7 p.m. – the companies were commanded by Captains K. M. Perry, E. M. Sellon, S. B. Lindsay and W. H. Clark-Kennedy, all of whom had fought at Ypres. Because they were advancing on open ground they advanced in single file. It was not long before the enemy opened fire with shrapnel. Coming up La Quinque Rue the Battalion was hit and many men fell. The 13th pushed up towards the Orchard, so that the 16th Battalion could launch their attack, pushing the Germans back. Once the assault had achieved its objective, the companies of the 13th took over. No. 4 Company, in support, relieved a Company of the 16th in shallow trenches to the left of the Orchard. Further left was a Territorial Battalion of the Black Watch, occupying front line trenches. Captain Clark-Kennedy visited the Battalion and gave orders to close a long gap between their front and the left of No. 3 Company's front in the Orchard.

All this time the enemy responded with heavy rifle and machine gun fire. All day on 21 May the enemy kept the Orchard under heavy fire inflicting considerable losses. In the afternoon, they counter-attacked but the Highlanders had little trouble beating them back. That night the Germans set fire to a large hay-stack in no man's land opposite No. 2 and 3 Companies. During the night of 22 May after two tiring days and nights, the 13th was relieved by the 3rd Battalion, and they marched to billets at Essars in thunder, lightning and pouring rain. Four days were spent here and the Battalion reported 10 officers and 170 other ranks as casualties.

The Battle of Festubert was coming to an end. Attacks by British and Canadian units continued for a few days, but it became evident that the operation as a whole had proved expensive. Despite having captured Festubert itself, the Allied Forces had advanced less than a kilometre. The British had suffered some 16,000 casualties during the action. Aubers Ridge was not yet in British hands. So on 25 May Sir John French ordered a withdrawal. The Royal Highlanders left billets in Essars, and moved up to relieve trenches between Rue L'Epinette and Rue du Bois. Two days later they relieved the 14th Battalion in the front line.

On their first night on the front line a wounded German was noticed lying in front of No. 4 Company's trenches. A stretcher-bearer of the 14th Battalion immediately volunteered to venture out and bring the wounded man in. While doing this he was fatally wounded as were two stretcher-bearers of the 13th who went to his assistance. Captain Clark-Kennedy and two of his men came to the rescue. They leapt over the parapet, reached the wounded, and brought all four safely in without further casualties.

On the night of the 31st the Highlanders were relieved by the 2nd Gordons of the 20th British Brigade. The 13th proceeded to Hinges, where they spent five days in billets, carrying out platoon drills and company route marches. Captain Clark-Kennedy attended 3rd Field Ambulance on 2 June with a back injury. On 5 June Lieutenant Colonel Loomis and other officers reconnoitred a reserve position at Givenchy north of the canal, which on the following day the Highlanders took over from the 5th Canadian Battalion. On the 9th, the Battalion moved up and relieved the Royal Montreal Regiment in the front line. The following night, the 4th Canadian Battalion relieved the 13th who returned to billets at Essars, where they had ten days of fine weather. More route marching, company training and battalion training were undertaken.

On 22 June , the Highlanders relieved the 10th Canadian Battalion in the front line in Givenchy for two days. They were bombarded by trench mortars, rifle grenades and hand bombs. Once again they were relieved by 2nd and 6th Gordons before returning to Essen, spending two days drilling and repairing equipment.

The Canadian Division left Essen at 10.35 p.m. on 26 June. The 13th Battalion marched all night until they reached billets at La Brecque, near Bailleul, where they spent the next two days. 1 July being Dominion Day was a half holiday. A football match was organised between two halves of the Regiment, and a sports programme was introduced. On 3 July, the Battalion was to occupy a position from Ploegstreet Wood (facing Warreton) to Wulverghem (opposite Messines). On the 5th, the Highlanders relieved the 1st Canadian Battalion in support, and at 8 p.m. on the 9th, the 13th Battalion relieved the 14th Battalion on the front line. On the 14th, the Royal Montreal Regiment took over the front and the 13th proceeded to billets in the Piggeries (previously used as the name suggests!)

On the 21st, the 4th Canadian Battalion relieved the 13th who proceeded to Divisional Reserve. During the next week they assisted the Engineers. From 6.30 p.m. on 21 August, the Battalion found themselves in the front line for four more days. They patrolled No Man's Land and gained a lot of valuable information. They were then relieved by 1st and 3rd Canadian Battalion.

Meanwhile Captain Clark-Kennedy received the news of his appointment as Temporary Major in the *London Gazette* on 17 July. He left the 13th on 17 September 1915 to take up a post on the Staff of the 3rd Brigade. He took leave from 3 to 31 December. It was announced in the *London Gazette* on 4 January 1916 (29427) that he was to be Staff Captain and transferred from 13th Battalion on reduction of establishment.

On 14 January 1916, it appeared in the *London Gazette* (29438) that he had been awarded the Distinguished Service Order (D.S.O.). The 13th Battalion heard the news on the 19th, and they were delighted as they still regarded him as their own. Thus he became attached for duty with the

William and his Wife, Kate

3rd Infantry Brigade H.Q. Third Brigade consisted of 13th (Royal Highlanders) Battalion; 14th (Royal Montreal Regiment) Battalion; 15th (48th Highlanders) Battalion; and 16th (Canadian Scottish) Battalion.

The *London Gazette* for 28 March 1916 page 3445 announced his award of the Croix de Guerre by the President of the French Republic. (29528):

> The President of the French Republic has bestowed the decoration 'Croix de Guerre' on the undermentioned Officers, Non-commissioned Officers and Men, in recognition of their distinguished service during the Campaign:-
>
> Major William Hew Clark-Kennedy, D.S.O., 3rd Canadian Infantry, Brigade Headquarters.

It was announced on 18 June that he was to be General Staff Officer (3rd Grade) with the 2nd Canadian Division. This meant he would cease to be attached as Staff Captain to the 3rd Canadian Infantry Brigade. The 2nd Canadian Division consisted of 4th, 5th and 6th Canadian Brigades, and Pioneers. Major Clark-Kennedy was next present at the Battle of Flers-Courcelette, part of the Somme offensive. At the beginning of September 1916, the Canadian Corps of four divisions moved to the Somme and took over from the Australians around Pozières.

It was General Haig's wish that the Canadians should have a chance to settle in before taking part in the Somme offensive. A G.H.Q. directive on 19 August had announced that there would be a strong offensive attack about mid-September, using "fresh forces and all available resources". This was the role for which the Canadian Corps had been sent for. While the 2nd and 3rd Canadian Divisions prepared for the battle, the 1st Division held the whole of the corps front. The Canadian Corps, attacking on the Reserve Army's right flank with two divisions on a 2,200 yard front, was to advance in a single movement. The 2nd Division's objectives were the defences in front of Courcelette. On the left the 3rd Division was to provide flank protection. Less than an hour after the 2nd Division reached its objective, the 4th and 6th Brigades were to establish posts at the south end of Courcelette along a sunken road. On the 15th, the 2nd and 3rd Divisions were on the extreme left for the assault on the Germans third line of defences and successfully captured Courcelette after two days. At the beginning of the Somme battles in July, Courcelette was a village well within

German-held territory. It was not until mid-September that the British had reached it. The battle was fought on a wide front and involved the first use of tanks. General Haig had decided to unveil a new weapon called the tank – six of the 49 available were allocated to the Canadian 2nd Division.

On 18 September, it was announced that Major Clark-Kennedy was to be Brigade Major with 5th Brigade from October, and he duly took up his duties on 3 October. Fifth Brigade consisted of 22nd (Canadien Français) Battalion; 24th (Victoria Rifles) Battalion; 25th (Nova Scotia) Battalion and 26th (New Brunswick) Battalion.

For the next two months, Canadian units fought almost continuously between Courcelette and Grandcourt, capturing formidable German positions such as Regina Trench. On 17 October, the 1st, 2nd and 3rd Divisions were rotated out of the line and partly replaced by the Canadian 4th. By 4 November, the 4th Canadian Division had pushed 700 yards beyond Regina. It was not until 9/10 November in bitterly cold weather that the Canadian gunners delivered a powerful blow to the Germans still defending Regina Trench. At midnight on 10/11 November, the assault began and by 2.20 a.m. the trench was in Canadian hands. The 4th Canadian Division then rejoined the Canadian Corps at Vimy Ridge. The Canadians lost 24,000 casualties on the Somme – making it the greatest place of Canadian sacrifice from either World War. Courcelette was Canada's main battlefield on the Somme in 1916 – 8,500 Canadian soldiers died here between September and November 1916.

There were no further advances that year. Autumn rains turned the battlefield into one huge bog bringing the offensive to a halt.

William Clark-Kennedy

FORWARD WITH 5th BRIGADE

The winter of 1916–17 was for the Canada Corps a period free from any major operations. It meant that there was time to recover, carry out training and take stock, while still holding the line. From 20 March onwards, in preparing for their next operation, the Canadians raided enemy lines each night. However this proved to be costly with some 1,400 casualties over two weeks. However it allowed them to gain valuable information about the strengths and weaknesses of the Germans.

The British operations that begun on 9 April are known collectively as the Battles of Arras. The opening phase (9–14 April) consisted of the First Battle of the Scarpe, an attack on that river by the Third Army; and the Battle of Vimy Ridge, a simultaneous attack on the adjoining four miles of front by the Canadian Corps and certain formations of the First Army. While the main task of the Canadian Corps was to form a strong defensive line for the Third Army's efforts, the Vimy operation was a significant landmark. The 7 km. Ridge overlooked Lens to the north, Douai to the east and Arras to the south. It was tactically one of the prime features on the Western Front. The Canadians knew that the Germans were unlikely to want to give it up without a fight. Preparations were put in hand for a southern attack, which General Byng, British Commander of the Canadian Corps, would lead. All four Canadian divisions would attack together for the first time, supplemented by the 5th British Division of the 1st Corps together with Canadian and British heavy artillery in support. General Byng was able to transform the exhausted Canadian divisions on the Somme into a remarkable attacking force. He was to become Governor-General of Canada after the war.

The crest of the Ridge was formed by Hill 135 and Hill 145, two miles north-west. Opposite the Canadian right was a gradual descent from Hill 135 to the headwaters of the Scarpe, north-west of Arras. There were just a few villages to break up the open country. The Canadians carefully planned and rehearsed their attack. The infantry were given specialist roles as machine gunners, riflemen and grenade-throwers. In the week before the battle, Canadian and British artillery pounded the Germans on the Ridge.

The Canadian attack was to be on a front of 7,000 yards, the centre being opposite Vimy village, on the east of the Ridge. The four divisions of the Canadian Corps, arranged in numerical order from right to left, were to assault simultaneously at 5.30 a.m., each with two brigades. The 1st and 2nd Divisions assisted by the British 13th Infantry Brigade on the left would then employ their reserve brigades against the remaining objectives. It was expected that the whole of the eastern escarpment could be in Canadian hands by 1.18 p.m.

All units were in position on 9 April by 4.00 a.m. and promptly at 5.30 a.m. on Easter Monday, the attack on Vimy Ridge opened with the roar of the 983 guns and mortars in support. This neutralised a large proportion of the enemy's guns. The ground over which the Canadians had to advance was particularly difficult, with mud, shell-holes, and old trenches and mine craters. In the right centre of attack were four battalions of 2nd Division, including the 24th and 26th Battalions of the 5th Brigade under Brigadier General A. H. Macdonell.

Within 30 minutes of the assault on 9 April, the Canadian 1st Division had succeeded in capturing the German front line position in spite of a snowstorm. Within a further half an hour the 2nd line had also fallen into Canadian hands. With the entire Ridge under Allied control by 12 April (when Hill 145, the highest feature fell) the operation was judged a spectacular success. This was the single most successful Allied advance on the Western Front to date. Hill 145, where the Vimy monument now stands, was captured in a frontal bayonet attack against machine-gun positions. The Ridge then remained in Allied hands for the remainder of the war.

Canadian troops earned a reputation as formidable, effective troops because of this stunning success. However it was a victory at a terrible cost, with more than 10,000 killed and wounded. The Germans suffered 20,000 casualties.

Meanwhile the struggle for the Passchendaele Ridge went on. On 7 July, the First Army notified the Canadian Corps of orders received from Sir Douglas Haig to capture Lens with a view to threatening an advance on Lille from the south. Lens was dominated from the north by Hill 70 and from the south by Sallaumines Hill. On 15 August, the Canadian Army Corps attacked the Germans around Lens. The Battle of Hill 70 took place near the French city of Lens involving the Canadians under General Arthur Currie and British I Corps (6th Division and 46th Division), and the defending German units of the 7th and 185th Infantry Divisions and the 4th Guards Infantry Division.

Before dawn on the 15th the Canadians went over the top, thrusting into Lens on their left, storming over Hill 70 on their centre, and taking Bois Rase and part of Bois Hugo on their left. Hill 70 was a feature rising only 15 feet above the surrounding terrain, and located north of Lens. The Canadian operation was a diversionary attack to relieve pressure on Lens itself. The two industrial suburbs of Cité St. Emile and Cité St. Laurent were captured. The Canadians at one stage penetrated nearly a mile into the German defences. The capture of Hill 70 proved relatively straightforward. The victors were able to shelter in great concrete dug-outs from which the enemy had been driven out.

The Canadians had taken the Hill and dug in. The Germans were ordered to retake Hill 70 at any cost. The advanced forces of the Canadians were first attacked by the 4th Prussian Guard Division. The Canadians allowed them to come close and then turned every available gun on them. When the Canadian Infantry went over the top, they swept down the eastern slopes of Hill 70, bayoneting some 700 Germans, and continued into western parts of the Cité. By the end of the morning, the Canadians occupied the high ground overlooking Lens, and the rest of their objectives were achieved by the end of the following day.

In the afternoon of 16 August a counter-offensive was launched by the Germans. At 6 p.m. the Germans attacked along the entire Canadian front line above Lens. Several attacks were repulsed. The Germans used mustard gas and flamethrowers, but were beaten back each time at enormous cost. In the evening of 18 August, a great gas-shell bombardment engulfed the Canadians. Ten thousand storm-troopers were repulsed by the Canadian riflemen and machine gunners. A further attempt was made to breach the southern flank of Hill 70, together with a northern thrust. There was also a full assault along the eastern front at 1.30am. The Canadians faced fierce fighting on all three sides of Hill 70, but again they kept the Germans at bay. After breaking the German counter-attacking force the Canadians once more attacked the weakened enemy early in the morning of 21 August. They pressed on to the German positions by the Cité St. Elizabeth, north of Lens. They managed to crawl through the barbed wire, climb the parapets and clear part of the long trench. They also passed into Lens from the south-western and western sides.

All day on 23 August, General Currie's two divisions attacked the Green Crassier, a weed-grown slag heap by the great railway yard of Lens. The Canadians gained a foothold in this stronghold and held it against counter-attacks. But things changed on the 24th as strong enemy groups supported by fire from artillery, trench mortars and machine-guns, repeatedly counter-attacked the Crassier from all sides. The Canadians fought back bravely but in the end bombs ran out and ammunition ran low. By late afternoon the Germans had recaptured it. However by this time it was estimated that the Canadians had defeated six German divisions. By the end of the battle, the Canadian Corps had suffered nearly 9,200 casualties, during the period 15–25 August.

By the morning of 23 August, the 3rd Division had relieved the 1st and 2nd on Hill 70. The last few days of August, all September and the beginning of October were relatively quiet, and devoted to preparations for a further offensive. The eyes of the Canadians now turned northwards where before many weeks passed they would be engaged in another battle.

The Third Battle of Ypres began on 31 July 1917. Early in October, with strategic objectives still in German hands and the British forces reaching the point of exhaustion, Haig decided on one more thrust. The Canadian Corps were ordered to relieve the decimated Anzac forces in the Ypres sector and prepare for the capture of Passchendaele. The Canadians part in the Third Battle of Ypres was restricted to the last part, known as Passchendaele. This was a village near the town of Ypres in West Flanders, Belgium. At and around Passchendaele was the highest ground on the ridge, looking down across the sweep of plains where the enemy was situated. The Canadian involvement was in the 2nd Battle of Passchendaele, which took place between 26 October and 10 November. Two divisions of the Canadian Corps were moved into the line. The Canadians by now had the reputation of being the best shock troops in the Allied Armies. They were recognised by all as having the physique, the stamina, the initiative and the confidence between officers and men. The Canadian Commander, Sir Arthur Currie, was reluctant to commit the Canadians to useless slaughter at Passchendaele. The plan was to drive a hole in the German lines, advance to the Belgian

William Clark-Kennedy

coast and capture the German submarine bases there. They moved into line during the middle of the month, and the battle began on 26 October with 20,000 men of the 3rd and 4th Canadian Divisions advancing up the hills of the salient. It cost the Allies 12,000 casualties for a gain of a few hundred yards. On 30 October with two British divisions, the Canadians began the attack on Passchendaele itself. They gained the ruined outskirts of the village during a violent rainstorm and held on bravely for five days. By the time reinforcements from the 1st and 2nd Canadian Divisions arrived on 6 November, four fifths of two Canadian divisions had been lost. The Germans still surrounded the area, so a limited attack on the 6th by the remainder of the 3rd Division's troops allowed the 1st Division to gain some ground.

Major Clark-Kennedy, in the War Diary of the 5th Canadian Infantry Brigade, states that it was the 2nd Canadian Division who were ordered to attack and capture the village with the 1st Division attacking on the north. The 2nd Division's attack was carried out by the 5th Canadian Infantry Brigade (he was Brigade Major) on the right and the 6th Canadian Infantry Brigade on the left, the 4th Canadian Infantry Brigade being held in Divisional Reserve. He reports that on the night of 5/6 November the 26th Battalion moved into their assembly area on the northern portion of the 5th Brigade front, establishing Battalion Headquarters at Hillside Farm, while the 24th Battalion continued to hold the line. The 25th Battalion moved up in support, the 22nd Battalion remaining in reserve.

The assault had begun at 6 a.m. with 36th Battalion advancing to attack. The whole of the 5th Brigade objectives were gained on schedule by 6.58 a.m., and consolidation commenced. By 10.00 a.m. the ground won by the Brigade had been well consolidated and the men were reported to be in high spirits. Rifles, ammunition etc., were still clean in spite of the mud. The supply of ammunition was more than adequate. The machine-gun barrage was perfect, and according to reports from prisoners, caused the enemy heavy casualties. At an early hour the village of Passchendaele was captured, and by midday all objectives had been gained. A few days before, the Germans had been ordered to hold Passchendaele at all costs, and if lost it must be recaptured at all costs.

The night of the 6th/7th and the day of 7 November were fairly quiet and allowed further consolidation. The following night the 5th Brigade extended their front to the north and took over the whole of the 2nd Canadian Divisional front, relieving the 6th Canadian Infantry Brigade. The 25th Battalion relieved the 24th and 26th Battalions and the 22nd Battalion relieved Units of the 5th Brigade. The relief was completed by 3 a.m. in spite of heavy hostile artillery fire. The enemy continued to shell Support areas on the 8th, and on the night of 8th/9th the 5th Canadian Infantry Brigade was relieved by the 4th Canadian Infantry Brigade. The Brigade H.Q. moved to Convent, Ypres. The 9th was spent re-organising and salvaging equipment. No. 22 Battalion helped with the wounded and carrying rations to the front. During the operation the Brigade captured five officers and 200 other ranks.

On 10 November the 1st Division took Hill 52, a low rise on which Passchendaele was situated on. A further attack by the 2nd Division the same day drove the Germans from the slopes to the east of the town. The Germans were unable to stand the onslaught. The high ground was now firmly under Allied control.

The majority of the battle had been fought in thick mud, on largely reclaimed marshland. Even the new tanks got bogged down. The Germans were well-entrenched. More than any other battle, Passchendaele came to symbolise the horrific nature of the First World War and the uselessness of the tactics employed. Sixteen thousand Canadians were lost in the intense final assault between 26 October and 10 November. Nine Canadian soldiers gained the Victoria Cross in recognition of their efforts at Passchendaele. The following March and April resulted in the Germans regaining almost all the ground gained at Passchendaele, in about three days.

It is interesting to note what Major Clark-Kennedy says in the 5th Canadian Infantry Brigade War Diary. His report dated 16 November 1917, states:

PASSCHENDAELE remains in our hands without any serious attempt of the Germans, so far, to retake it and this victory means that every piece of elevated ground in this war area is now commanded by our guns. PASSCHENDAELE also commands HOUTHULST Forest, which is in the process of being encircled. The capture of PASSCHENDAELE and other Ridges is symbolical of much larger strategical conception, for the development whereof their recovery from the enemy is an essential prelude. Their capture is the first and probably the far most difficult step. The worst work is over and the enemy must either recover ground – which he is unlikely to be able to do – or submit to domination which no troops could endure for any length of time. But the measure of our successes in FLANDERS, is not only to be estimated by the value of important positions taken. It is to be found also in the declining strength of the enemy's defence and diminished vigour of his counter attacks. He no longer meets an attack with an immediate counter-offensive, and operations since 20th September bear evidence of the gradual decline of German morale and gradual exhaustion. This is not surprising, considering his long succession of reverses and gigantic efforts to avert defeat by piling division on division.

During the last three months, 68 German Divisions have been through the mill in FLANDERS. Of these, 14 were put in during September. In October, 19 fresh divisions were added. Such was the state of the German reserves that 20 divisions had to be subjected to a second grinding, while two underwent that process for a third time. Thus, counting those which re-appeared after having been renovated, our troops in FLANDERS met and defeated during the last 3 months, 90 German Divisions among the best the German Army can provide.

By November 14, the Canadians, having done what was asked of them, retired back to the Vimy Region. Their positions were taken over by the British troops. With this battle behind them, the Canadians would take up their positions by Arras/Vimy/Lens and prepare to take on the final German defences of the Siegfried Line and in fact, lead the final assault that would bring the war to a close.

1918 AND TOWARDS AMIENS

On 3 November 1917, Major Clark-Kennedy relinquished his role as Brigade Major of the 5th Brigade to return to regimental duty. He was Mentioned in Despatches in the *London Gazette* of 25 December (L.G. 30448), and two days later it was announced that he was to be Lieutenant Colonel in command of the 24th Battalion Quebec Regiment (Victoria Rifles). This would take effect from 3 March 1918 and was announced in the *London Gazette* on 15 February 1918. (L.G. 30532).

The Canadians, who had been holding seven miles around Lens, at the right of the First Army's line, had not been involved in any fighting during March and April 1918. The Canadian Corps had three divisions in the line, with the 2nd Division, including Lieutenant Colonel Clark-Kennedy, in the Corps training area at Auchel, eight miles west of Bethune. The Canadians were holding Lens and Vimy Ridge, which were the gateways to important collieries and key centres of communication. So the first few months of 1918 were spent completing trenches, wire entanglements and machine-gun emplacements.

On 23 March, the 2nd Canadian Division was ordered into G.H.Q. reserve in the Mont St. Eloi area. By the 25th, the Corps was holding a 17,000 yard front with only two divisions – 3rd and 4th. On the 26th orders came which detached the remaining two divisions from General Currie's command and sent his Corps H.Q. into reserve. The Canadian sector was to be taken over by the two adjacent British Corps. On 27th, the 1st and 2nd Canadian Divisions were placed in General Byng's Third Army south of Arras – the former with 17 Corps, astride the Arras-Cambrai road, and the 2nd on its immediate right in the Neuville-Vitasse sector of 6th Corps front.

On 8 April, the Canadian Corps held a line of approximately 16,000 yards with three divisions. General Currie ordered that the 2nd Canadian Division, then holding some 6,000 yards of the

William Clark-Kennedy

Third Army's line, should revert to his command as a reserve. But the 2nd Division did not rejoin the Corps until 1 July. General Currie insisted that his four divisions should only fight together as a Corps, thus missing out on battles in March and April. During the first week of May, the Canadian Corps were relieved by five divisions of the 17th and 18th British Corps. Dominion Day brought a welcome break in training. The 2nd Canadian Division was relieved by the 3rd Division after 92 days continuously in the line. Nearly 50,000 Canadian soldiers of all ranks gathered on a fine day at Ticques, a small village 14 miles west of Arras to watch or compete in a Sports Day, and the day ended with a Concert Revue.

Lieutenant Colonel Clark-Kennedy, meanwhile, was mentioned in Despatches on 31 May (L.G. 30448). On 3 June, it was gazetted in the *London Gazette* (30716) that he had been awarded the C.M.G. (Companion of the Order of St. Michael and St. George):

> The KING has been graciously pleased, on the occasion of His Majesty's Birthday, to give directions for the following promotion in, and appointments to, the Most Distinguished Order of Saint Michael and Saint George, for services rendered in connection with Military Operations in France and Flanders. Dated 3 June 1918:
>
> To be Additional Members of the Third Class, or Companions, of the said Most Distinguished Order:- CANADIAN FORCE.
>
> Lt.-Col. William Hew Clark-Kennedy, D.S.O., Quebec Regt.

On 24 June, Clark-Kennedy took two weeks leave in the United Kingdom until 12 July.

The Canadian Corps' long period of rest and training came to an end on 15 July when it relieved 17 Corps in the line. On the 18th, the 2nd Canadian Division was withdrawn into G.H.Q. reserve in readiness for the attack threatening the Second Army in Flanders. Since the start of the German offensive in March, the Canadians had suffered over 9,000 casualties. Of these 5,690 had been sustained up to the time when the Corps withdrew into reserve (7 May). There were 3,998 casualties between 8 May and 7 August inclusive. On 22 July, General Currie held a conference of divisional commanders, and a week later he informed them of forthcoming offensive operations to be undertaken by the Canadian Corps on the 4th Army front.

Next day the Corps began to move secretly to a concentration area west of Amiens. They were sent to be placed alongside the Australians. Success depended first on the secrecy and the speed with which the Canadians were moved, and then on staff arrangements for moving into action all the infantry, cavalry, tanks and armoured cars. This was conducted skilfully. The men and their trains hid by day and moved by night to an unknown destination, which neither the Germans' aerial scouts nor their espionage agents could trace. They arrived in darkness, south-east of Amiens, at the end of the first week in August, and were positioned by Gentilles Wood. Though the Canadian's guns were in position for nearly three days, not one fired a shot. This was to prevent the enemy from becoming suspicious. So the Allies successfully moved the four Infantry Divisions of the Canadian Corps to Amiens without them being detected by the Germans. A detachment from the Corps of two infantry battalions, a wireless unit and a casualty clearing station had been sent to the front near Ypres to bluff the Germans that the entire Corps was moving north to Flanders.

The need to free the Paris-Amiens Railway, which was subject to frequent enemy artillery attack, as was Amiens itself, was one of the major aims of the operation. The Germans, who had been expecting an attack in the north in Flanders, were taken by surprise by the Amiens offensive. The well-planned attack, which began in foggy weather at 4.20 a.m. on 8 August, was made by the 4th Army along a 14-mile front. The barrage opened with the firing of more than 900 guns and the infantry pressing forward. The main blow was to be struck by the Canadians in the centre. Opposing them were the German Second Army (von der Marwitz) and the right of the German Eighteenth Army (von Hutier).

General Henry Rawlinson in command of 4th Army employed nine divisions supported by 400 tanks in the initial assault. Each of the assaulting Canadian divisions was allotted a battalion of 42 fighting tanks from the British 4th Tank Brigade (The 4th Division, in reserve, received a 36-tank battalion). General Currie placed the 1st Division in the Centre, with the 2nd Division on its left and the 3rd Division on its right. The Battle of Amiens was the opening phase of the Allied offensive later known as the Hundred Days Offensive that eventually led to the end of the First World War. While there were great successes, there was no time to lose to maintain momentum. The initial attack provided the maximum shock of surprise, and south of the Somme the troops of the Australian and Canadian Corps rapidly overran and overwhelmed the German forward divisions. The attack was totally unexpected, and when the infantry rushed into action, followed by the tanks, the enemy was taken by complete surprise. The attack resumed at 8.20 prompt.

The advance of the 2nd Canadian Division on the Corps left on the 8 August took place over more favourable ground than that assigned to the rest of the Corps. The Divisional Commander, Major General Sir Henry Burstall, planned to use in order the 4th, 5th and 6th Brigades in successive phases of the advance. The mist prevented tanks from giving initial support, but within half an hour they were on their way, and helped to take out the enemy's machine-guns.

The main opposition met by the 24th Battalion, on the Brigade left, and the 26th on the right, still came from a small number of machine-gun posts. It took longer to clear Pieuret Wood and Snipe Copse, east and south-east of Marcelcave, than it did to secure Wiencourt, the first of two villages in 5th Brigade's path. The 5th Brigade reached its objective around 2.15 p.m. Although the day's operations by the 4th Army had attained somewhat less than complete success, the enemy suffered its greatest defeat since the start of the war. The German line had been thrown back as much as eight miles in the Canadian sector alone. The 4th Army's casualties were approximately 8,800, Canadian casualties totalled 3,868. The Canadian Corps were credited with capturing 5,033 prisoners and 161 guns. During the "Black day of the German Army" battle-weary troops had, at various points, fled from the front, and entire units had disintegrated.

During the fighting on 8 August and throughout the following night the Germans had quickly brought up seven divisions from reserve, with further formations on their way. On 9 August, the 4th

Army was ordered to push forward to a line directly northward opposite the Canadian sector. To reach it required an advance of nine miles on the Army right. Plans were completed for the 1st and 2nd Divisions to attack at 5 p.m. on a front of one brigade each, but this was later postponed until 10 a.m. on the 9th. However further delays meant that it was past 1.00 p.m. before any advance began. The 5th Brigade, attacking with the 22nd and 25th Battalions, was met by a hail of machine-gun bullets, making an advance over the open ground impossible. Instead small scouting parties worked their way forward along ditches and sunken roads to outflank the enemy posts and take them with enfilade fire. Soon after 3.00 p.m. the 5th Brigade, joined at last by its tanks was continuing eastward on Meharicourt. Within the hour the 29th Battalion had driven the Germans from a sugar factory 1,000 yards to the east. The 27th and 28th Battalions then went into the lead. Helped by its tanks, the 5th Brigade quickened its pace. Shortly before 5.00 p.m., Meharicourt was captured by the 22nd Battalion. Both the 1st and 2nd Divisions, which had halted on a line 500 yards east of Meharicourt, pushed posts well forward during the night.

On this second day of the battle, the Canadians had made advances of up to four miles – there had been too much delay and countermanding of orders. Canadian casualties for 9th August numbered 2,574. The enemy was still re-enforcing his front. On the 10th the renewed advance was set for 9.30 a.m. The 4th Division relieved the 1st and 2nd Divisions in the left half of the Corps sector.

As a general offensive, the Battle of Amiens ended on 11 August. The battle is remembered for its effects on both sides' morale and the extent of surrendering German forces. Amiens was one of the first major battles involving armoured warfare and marked the end of trench warfare on the Western Front. The 4th Army's offensive was to be discontinued until it had the support of all available artillery and an increased number of tanks. During the night of 11–12 August the 2nd and 3rd Divisions came back into line. By 12th August the 4th Army had taken 21,000 prisoners at a cost of 20,000 casualties.

The next eight days saw no large-scale fighting on the Allied front. On 16 August, as the French launched an attack on Goyencourt, two miles from Roye, General Currie ordered the Canadian 1st Division to push forward to Fresnoy-les-Roye and La Chavatte, with the 2nd Division assisting on the left. Chavatte was not secured until the 17th and attempts to reach Fresnoy were abandoned.

Between 8 and 13 August, the Corps had defeated elements of 15 German divisions, completely routing four. By the 20th it had penetrated up to 14 miles and had liberated 27 villages. These successes had been gained at a cost of 11,822 Canadian casualties (8–20 August), 9,074 being incurred on the four opening days of the offensive. On the night of 19–20 August the 2nd Canadian Division began moving northward by bus and train to rejoin the First Army in the Arras sector, followed the next night by the 3rd Division.

HEROISM AT THE BATTLE OF THE SCARPE

The success of the Amiens offensive convinced Sir Douglas Haig that the time had come for an all-out effort against the Germans. From 20 to 26 August, the French and British made some progress. But it was not until the 26th that an expansion of the battle into the First Army's sector brought the Canadian Corps back into action. Back under the command of General Horne east of Arras, the Canadian Corps was confronted by a series of strong defensive positions which the enemy held in depth. Immediately in front of the Canadians were the old British trenches lost in the German offensive of March 1918, and to the east lay the enemy's former front line. This was backed up, two miles east of Monchy, by the so-called Fresnes-Rouvroy line. Another mile east, the approaches to Cambrai were blocked by the strongest position of all – the Drocourt-Quéant line, which, extending northward from the Hindenburg Line at Quéant, had been constructed by the Germans to prevent any Allied advance into the Douai plain. Further east was the unfinished Canal du Nord, connecting the Somme with the Sensée Canal.

On 22 August, General Currie outlined plans for an attack eastward astride the Arras-Cambrai road. The Canadians were to force the Drocourt-Quéant line south of the Scarpe and advance to the line of the Canal du Nord. The Germans had one of the strongest defensive positions on the Western Front. The front taken over by the 2nd and 3rd Canadian Divisions extended from Neuville-Vitasse north to the River Scarpe, and the 1st and 4th Canadian Divisions did not arrive until 25 and 28 August respectively.

General Currie's plan was for simultaneous attacks by the British Division on the left, the 3rd Canadian Division between the Scarpe and the Cambrai road, and the 2nd on the right. They were to secure a north-south line just west of Monchy-le-Preux. The attack began at 3 a.m. on Monday 26 August with an artillery and machine-gun barrage. The 2nd Division attacking south of the road made fine progress. Advances were quick and the Germans were taken by surprise by the early start. In the middle of the morning the 2nd Division, which had been attacking eastward, was ordered to move its axis of advance to the south-east, and to capture the high ground south-east of Wancourt. This was carried out by the 8th Brigade with some success.

General Currie's orders for the next day directed both Canadian divisions to attack in two stages to break through the Fresnes-Rouvroy line. The 2nd Division was to secure the ground on its front lying between the Cojeul and the Sensée River, two miles beyond. Then having captured the villages of Cherisy and Vis-en-Artois in the Sensée Valley, advance a further 200 yards to the east. By nightfall, Monchy and the ground 1,000 yards to the rear were in Canadian hands. Heavy rain fell during the night of 26th–27th. Owing to the late arrival of 5th Brigade, the 2nd Division did not start operations until 10.00. The 18th Battalion occupied Vis-en-Artois without much trouble, but ran into very heavy and destructive enemy fire at the Sensée. Further south the 5th Brigade, advancing down the western slope of Wancourt Tower Ridge, received support from tanks and machine-guns. On the right the 26th Battalion was over the Sensée by noon, and shortly afterwards the 24th and 22nd Battalions, having captured Cherisy, crossed above and below the village. They met heavy resistance on the far bank and the 2nd Division was ordered to make good its line along the Sensée's east bank as well as securing the bridge on the Arras-Cambrai road. The proposed

William with Brigadier General J. MacBrien

relief of the 2nd and 3rd Canadian Divisions was postponed, and both were to continue the advance on 28th to breach the Fresnes-Rouvroy line and capture Cagnicourt, Dury and Etaing.

The fighting on the 28th, a warm and bright day, was very bitter and with heavy losses. A fine effort was made by the 2nd Canadian Division in the general direction of Cagnicourt. They attacked at 12.30 p.m., with the 5th Brigade carrying the major part of the operation. In spite of the determination of all ranks to take the Fresnes-Rouvroy line, the obstacle of uncut wire covered by intense machine-gun fire proved too much for the exhausted troops. Although the 22nd and 24th Battalions breached the German front line during the afternoon, a counter-attack at about 9 p.m. forced them back almost to their starting line.

Casualties for the day were heavy, and brought the total reported by the 2nd and 3rd Divisions in the three days fighting to 254 officers and 5,547 other ranks. The 22nd Battalion had lost all its officers, and the 24th Battalion was also hard hit. The total strength of the 22nd Battalion before the assault on Cherisy was about 650 men, plus 23 officers. Thirty-six hours later all the officers had been killed or wounded and only 39 men survived, commanded then by a sergeant-major. The 24th and other units of 5th Brigade had been almost totally destroyed with 24th Battalion suffering over 630 casualties during August. Lieutenant Colonel William Clark-Kennedy, the 24th's C.O., amalgamated the remnants of both battalions, and in spite of a serious wound, continued to direct his forces against the German lines.

His story runs over the 27 and 28 August. As the central unit in the attack, his battalion became the focal point of enemy shelling and machine-gun fire that inflicted heavy casualties, particularly to officers and platoon leaders. The battalion had become momentarily disorganised and the advance was in danger of slowing to a halt. He rallied and inspired his troops, setting an outstanding example by personally leading squads against the enemy machine-gun nests to put them out of action. Had it not been for his initiative in rallying and inspiring his troops, the attack might have failed then and there. The German machine-guns simply had to be overcome or else. He maintained control of his entire battalion at all times and enabled the Brigade to keep moving forward as a whole and meet its objectives, reaching the maze of trenches west of Cherisy and Cherisy Village, crossing the Sensée River, and occupying the Occident Trench in front of the barbed wire defences protecting the Fresnes-Rouvroy line. He continued to encourage his men under heavy fire well into the night, while at the same time sending concise field situation reports back to Brigade and Division H.Q. He marched up and down in front of his battalion's position, constantly encouraging his men.

On the following day (28th) he again demonstrated his leadership and gallantry in the attack on the Fresnes-Rouvroy line itself and the Upton Wood. At midday the attack of the 24th Battalion encountered bitter artillery and machine-gun resistance. The casualties in the early stages of the advance included Lieutenant Colonel Clark-Kennedy, who fell with a shattered leg. Although badly wounded in the leg, in intense pain and bleeding profusely, he refused to be evacuated from the battlefield. He set up his command post in a shell hole and continued to direct his battalion. Knowledge of the situation was brought back to Brigade H.Q. by Sergeant J. N. Swift, who reported that the unit was definitely held up some 200 yards short of the first objective. Sergeant Swift added that the casualties had been severe but that the commanding officer, though badly injured and quite unable to move, was in touch with the situation and was carrying out his duties to the full extent that circumstances would permit. Realising that his exhausted troops could advance no further, Clark-Kennedy established a strong defensive line to prevent loss to the enemy of important ground gained and from which it was possible for the relieving troops to continue the advance. He held his position for five hours. Only then, at 5.30 p.m., realising that the situation had stabilized on his front, did he allow stretcher-bearers to carry him from the field to a dressing station in order to have his wounds attended to. It was for this action that he was to be awarded the Victoria Cross.

He was reported from base "wounded" with a gunshot wound in the right leg, and was admitted to No.3 General Hospital, Le Treport, which was used as such from 26 November 1914 until 17

March 1919. His medical report stated "Bullet entered over the antero-internal surface of the head of R. Tibia three-quarters of an inch below the joint. Exit slightly lower just external to Patellar Tuberosity". On September 3 he was transferred to P.O.W. Hospital for Officers, Marylebone, London. An X-ray on 5 September showed a fracture of the upper one-third tibia which did not appear to involve the joint. This was treated by a Thomas splint. On the 13th he moved again to I.O.D.E. Canadian Red Cross Hospital, Hyde Park Place before being discharged on 18 October. The medical report stated "General condition good. Scars of entrance and exit well healed. Fracture has knit solidly in good position. There is slight oedema of the R. knee and of the leg below. The scar of exit external to the Patellar Tuberosity is slightly depressed. There is no pain nor tenderness. He uses crutches. Condition otherwise normal. Recommendation – one month's sick leave, during which to attend I.O.D.E. Hospital for outdoor treatment, where he had been receiving massage from the staff". The Medical Board Report for 19 November stated that his condition had greatly improved during the past month, and that he would be fit for service in a further month. He was then on leave from 18 November until 26 November, when he rejoined the 24th.

Meanwhile, in response to a significant advance by the British First Army, the Germans were ordered to withdraw along a 55-mile front. They came under further pressure as the Anzacs advanced across the Somme on 30–31 August, taking Peronne and Mont St Quentin. Between 26 August and 2 September, in hard continuous fighting, the Canadian Corps fought strong German positions until they reached the heavily fortified line of the Canal du Nord. Near Quéant, on the northern flank, the Canadian Corps broke through on 2 September. Assisted by 15 tanks from the British Tank Corps, they successfully crossed the formidable barrier. A breakthrough of the German defences had been fully achieved. Victory was not far off. In these unfavourable circumstances the Germans, who had suffered heavy losses, were forced, on 3 September, to retire to the Hindenburg Line. This was their starting point in the March offensive, bringing the whole operation to a close. By 10th September the Allies had closed up to the new line.

Early in October Cambrai was captured in one of the bloodiest battles of the war. The enemy was badly shaken by the Allied victories in September and early October. When the Canadian Corps exchanged places with 22nd Corps during the second week in October, it found itself north of the Scarpe. The 2nd Canadian Division on the evening of 11 October formed General Currie's right flank above Iwuy. By 16 October, the Germans began their retreat. The Canadians now found themselves acting as liberators. They occupied more than a dozen towns and villages on 18 October, and the following day they took more than 40 communities. During the night of the 19–20 October the 2nd Division went into reserve. On 27 October, General Horne called his commanders to discuss the capture of Valenciennes and Mont Houy and these were secured by 2 November. They crossed into Belgium and renewed the advance by the British Armies towards the German frontier. On 10 November, Mons was captured, after which there was virtually no fighting.

Although the signing of the Armistice on 11 November brought an end to the fighting, new duties took over. Several months were to pass before they returned to Canada. The enemy had a week in which to prepare to withdraw across the Rhine. In 1914, the Germans had taken barely three weeks to throw a million and a half men across the frontier, and their enlarged armies had to retire at least as fast as they came.

Immediately after the conclusion of hostilities the Canadian Corps concentrated on the forthcoming march to the Rhine. From the British First Army, the Canadian Corps under Sir Arthur Currie was appointed to march from Mons, and proceed towards Huy, on the Meuse, on the way to Bonn. The 3rd Division was centred on Mons, the 2nd on its right, with the 1st and 4th in the rear west and south-west.

On Sunday 17 November, a day of thanksgiving, representatives of Canadian units attended special church services in Mons, and the next day began the march to the Rhine. The 2nd Division headed towards Bonn, clearing up as they went. With bayonets fixed and flags flying, the leading troops crossed the German frontier at 9.00 a.m. on 4 December, the 1st Division at Petit Thier and the 2nd at Beho. Bonn was occupied by the Canadians on 8 December, when a small force of cavalry entered the town and held the Rhine Bridge. Then on 12 December, Sir Arthur Currie was accorded the distinction of taking the Salute in honour of Canadian achievements. The next day the infantry including the 2nd Canadian Division crossed the river in heavy rain. Once across the Rhine the Canadian units marched to assigned towns and villages, where comfortable billets awaited them. They were assigned the ground on the east bank of the Rhine, including Bonn. Sport and educational facilities were provided.

The Canadians occupation role continued well into the New Year. Troops began to leave for Belgium on 5 January 1919. The 1st Division completed its move on 18 January, and the next day the relief of 2nd Division began. They went to the neighbourhood of Auvelais, 10 miles west of Namur. They were kept occupied with physical fitness, educational classes and recreation. Divisional Commanders had to ensure that every soldier was fully documented before embarking from France. During January, a Canadian Embarkation Camp, holding 6,000 men, was set up at Le Havre through which all units returned to England. Transfer of 1st Division commenced on 19 March, with 2nd and 4th Divisions following. Corps troops went to camps at Seaford, Ripon, Shorncliffe, Purfleet and Sunningdale.

The troops then embarked for Canada. Two-thirds of the force reached home within five months, and most were home within one year. Around 50,000 troops were moved each month, and the Canadian Corps were returned by units. They were greeted by grateful and enthusiastic crowds in cities and villages across Canada. Canada began the war with one division of citizen soldiers under the command of a British General, and ended with a superb fighting force. For a nation of eight million people Canada's war effort was incredible. A total of 619,686 men and women served in Canadian forces, and of these 66,655 gave their lives and another 172,950 were wounded. Nearly one in ten of all Canadians who fought in the war never returned.

Meanwhile Lieutenant Colonel Clark-Kennedy had returned to duty with the 24th on 26 November 1918. He returned to France with a friend who was also in the 24th, Tom Courtenay. They had both been wounded in the same campaign. Tom named his older daughter after his respected friend and commanding officer, Lieutenant Colonel Clark-Kennedy.

On 14 December Clark-Kennedy was awarded the Victoria Cross LG 31067 p.14773:

> For most conspicuous bravery, initiative and skillful leading on the 27th and 28th August, 1918, when in command of his battalion. On the 27th he led his battalion with great bravery and skill from Crow and Aigrette trenches in front of Wancourt to the attack on the Fresnes-Rouvroy line. From the outset the brigade, of which the 24th Battalion was a central unit, came under very heavy shell and machine-gun fire, suffering many casualties, especially amongst leaders. Units became partially disorganised and the advance was checked. Appreciating the vital importance to the brigade front of a lead by the centre, and undismayed by annihilating fire, Lt.-Col. Clark-Kennedy, by sheer personality and initiative, inspired his men and led them forward. On several occasions he set an outstanding example by leading parties straight at the machine-gun nests which were holding up the advance and overcame these obstacles.
>
> By controlling the direction of neighbouring units and collecting men who had lost their leaders, he rendered valuable services in strengthening the line, and enabled the whole brigade front to move forward.
>
> By the afternoon, very largely due to the determined leadership of this officer and disregard for his own life, his battalion, despite their heavy losses, had made good the maze of trenches west of Cherisy and Cherisy Village, had crossed the Sensée River bed, and had occupied Occident Trench in front of the heavy fire of the Fresnes-Rouvroy line; under continuous fire he then went up and down his line until far into the night, improving the position, giving wonderful encouragement to his men, and sent back very clear reports.

On the next day he again showed valorous leadership in the attack on the Fresnes-Rouvroy line and Upton Wood. Though severely wounded soon after the start he refused aid, and dragged himself to a shell-hole, from which he could observe. Realising that his exhausted troops could advance no further he established a strong line of defence and thereby prevented the loss of most important ground. Despite intense pain and serious loss of blood he refused to be evacuated for over five hours, by which time he had established the line in a position from which it was possible for the relieving troops to continue the advance.

It is impossible to overestimate the results achieved by the valour and leadership of this officer.

The local *Dumfries and Galloway Standard* for 21 December 1918 recalls William's return home:

The quaint and picturesque village of Carsphairn, which nestles at the foot of the lofty Cairnsmuir, was the scene of a happy function on Tuesday evening. It leaked out that Lieutenant-Colonel Wm. Hew Clark-Kennedy, V.C., 24th Battalion Quebec Regiment, would arrive home at Knockgray about 6 p.m., and the villagers were not loathe to bestir themselves to give the gallant Colonel a hearty welcome to celebrate his chivalrous courage on the field of battle, which earned for him the soldier's highest award. The Union Jack fluttered at the village flagstaff and a bonfire was lit at the 'preachin' knowe'. A streamer of flags and Japanese lanterns stretched across the village street.

The motor which conveyed Colonel and Mrs Clark-Kennedy halted under the streamer of flags.

The Rev. G. F. A. Macnaughton, parish minister, on behalf of the community, welcomed Lieutenant-Colonel Clark-Kennedy home, heartily and gratefully, and congratulated the hero on the distinction he had gained and the honour he had brought to his native place. Cheers were lustily given for Lieutenant-Colonel and Mrs Clark-Kennedy.

Colonel Clark-Kennedy sincerely thanked those present for the kindly welcome they had given him.

On 31 December he was mentioned in Despatches L.G. 31089. On 11 January 1919, he was awarded a Bar to his D.S.O. London Gazette 31119. "For great gallantry in action during which the battalion under his command reached the objectives allotted to it. On several occasions, at great risk, he personally directed the capture of strong points obstinately defended by the enemy. The success which his battalion obtained in these actions was due in no small degree to the example, courage and resourcefulness of its commander".

He arrived back in France for duty with the 2nd Division on 13 January 1919, and on the 15th was attached to H.Q. 5th Canadian Infantry Brigade. On 20 February, he ceased to be attached on returning to England and was posted to 2 R.D. South Ripon. Two days later he was taken on strength at the Quebec Regimental Depot. On 1 March he was decorated with the V.C., C.M.G., D.S.O. and Bar by King George V in the Ballroom at Buckingham Palace. He sailed to Canada on 28 March 1919 and was struck off strength on general demobilisation on 7 April 1919.

AFTER THE WAR

William returned to Canada and Kate, his wife. He returned to work for the Standard Life Assurance Company and was appointed Brevet Lieutenant Colonel, Corps Reserve Canadian Militia.

He returned to the United Kingdom on a number of occasions. In 1923, while at Knockgray, he unveiled the Carsphairn War Memorial, which lies just south of the village, and is made of local stone.

He attended the V.C. Dinner in the Royal Gallery at the House of Lords on 9 November 1929. A total of 319 V.C. holders attended the event. William was placed at Table 5 Seat 161. He sat between Brigadier General Wallace Wright V.C. and Sergeant John O'Neil V.C.

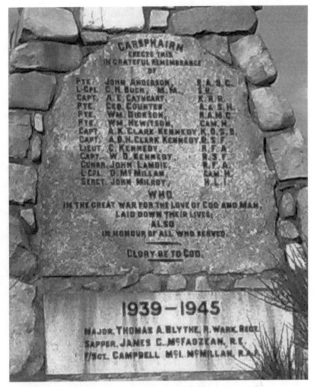

Carsphairn War Memorial Unveiled on 8th *The Names on the War Memorial, Carsphairn*
April 1923

In 1937, he was awarded the George VI Coronation Medal and in 1939 he was presented to their Majesties on the Royal Visit to Canada. In 1940 he was appointed Honorary Lieutenant Colonel of the 3rd Battalion, Black Watch (Royal Highland Regiment).

From 1922–1924, he was President of St. Andrew's Society of Montreal. This Society was organised in 1835 with the principal purpose being to assist persons of Scottish birth or descent, who are in need. Also to grant educational aid to qualified students of Scottish ancestry by means of bursaries and scholarships.

He eventually became Manager of Standard Life for Canada and he retained a close interest in the fortunes of the South African Branch and of the Colony in consequence of his experiences there. In 1943, he was appointed Chairman of the Guardian Assurance Company of Canada, being made a director in 1927. He was also chairman of the advisory board of the Guardian-Caledonian group of insurance companies.

In the *Overseas History of the Standard Life Assurance Company* by G. A. S. Norman, published in 1958, it states:

> The fine war record of one family must be unique and, as far as 'W.H'. was concerned, the Directors quite rightly felt that his well-deserved honours reflected upon the Canadian Branch and upon the whole Company. On resuming his life at Montreal Clark Kennedy brought the same determination to bear upon his civilian duties with such good effect as to create a new achievement by bringing the total new business in 1920 to the then magnificent total of £734,000. On this occasion Clark Kennedy, with characteristic modesty, attributed all the success to the enthusiasm and energy of his Staff and Field Force. Although the high total of 1920, was not quite maintained, the Branch entered upon a series of excellent new business figures during the succeeding years.
>
> In 1922, there occurred in Montreal a calamity which tested the powers of the Manager in another direction demanding quick and decisive action. On the morning of 7th February a disastrous fire broke out in the basement of the Company's fine building in St. James' Street.

The fire started at 5 o'clock and gained a hold so quickly that only two and a half hours later the building was a total loss. Fortunately the safes and vaults withstood the flames so admirably that nothing there was destroyed. All records and documents of value had been preserved. So speedily did Clark Kennedy get things in going order again that by the next day temporary office had been secured in the McGill Building, not far from the scene of destruction, and he cheerfully cabled across, 'Business as usual'.

The Company remained housed in the McGill Building until 1926 when the office was moved to 231, St James Street, later renumbered 391, and twelve years later leased offices in the Bank of Nova Scotia's Building at 437, St James Street West, but having occupied their own building for so many years in former times, it was long considered that the Company should seek new quarters when an opportunity arose for securing suitable premises. Such an opportunity came in 1946 when the present building at 1245, Sherbrooke Street was purchased.

William at Standard Life

The long experience of Clark Kennedy gives him a claim to be chosen as personifying the 'Old Guard' to which he often made reference and he will, I am sure, be happy to be identified with so many who served the Canadian Branch during and before his period of service. There is indeed no one, save the great Ramsey, who can lay claim to so long an active association with the Company in Canada and, as he is still active in the capacity of a senior director of the Canadian Board, his term of service has already lasted over sixty-two years.

As Manager he continued to guide, with industry and efficiency, the destinies of the Canadian Branch right up to 1946, watching and advising his staff in their various duties. In 1943, during the late war when his time for retirement had been reached, he was appointed a member of the Canadian Board while retaining, for the time being, his position of Manager.

To have, therefore, one such as Clark Kennedy, who has participated in so many of the events connected with the past history of the Company in Canada from the beginning of the century, is to have a rich store of experience at the disposal of all who care to draw upon it. The last of the 'Old Guard' is there as a guarantee that the great traditions built up in the past will be maintained by the new.

In November 1945, Clark-Kennedy retired from the assurance industry after 50 years of involvement, although he retained his directorship. In retirement he lived in Montreal, but visited London in 1956 for the V.C. Centenary celebrations. He took part in the Centenary Review of V.C. Holders, which took place on Tuesday 26 June 1956. Two hundred and ninety-nine holders of the V.C. marched past the Queen in Hyde Park. In total, in addition to the V.C., he held C.M.G. (1919), D.S.O. and Bar (1916, 1919), ED. This was the Efficiency Decoration which was instituted on 17 October 1930 and was awarded to Territorial Army (U.K.), the Indian Volunteer Forces and the Colonial Auxillary Forces. He also had the Queen's South Africa Medal with clasps, Cape Colony, Orange Free State, Transvaal, South Africa 1901; Croix de Guerre avec Palme (France) (1915); 1914/15 Star; British War Medal 1914–20; and Victory Medal 1914–19 with Mentioned-

William Clark-Kennedy's Grave. Montreal

in-Despatches oakleaf. He also held the Coronation Medal (1937) and EIIR Coronation Medal (1953).

He was a keen fisherman and excellent shot. He shared a small snipe and duck shoot and wrote a short booklet on the subject. Though there is a hyphen in his name, the family do not use it. His V.C. is held by the family at Knockgray. He died in Montreal on 25 October 1961, aged 82. On 5 November 1961 he would have had a 60-year association with Standard Life. He was buried privately at 11.00 a.m. on Saturday 28 October in the Pine Hill Section, Reford Family Plot, Lot 258, Mount Royal Cemetery, Montreal. This Cemetery opened in 1852, and is 165 acres with more than 162,000 graves.

He still owned Knockgray until he died, although the house, farm, shooting and fishing were all let. Kate died 11 August 1966.

Memorials include a tablet in the Museum of the Royal Highlanders of Canada, Bleury Street, Montreal which includes his name.

His name is also on the V.C. Roll of Honour at the Union Jack Club, Sandell Street, Waterloo, London SE1 8UJ.

William Hew Clark-Kennedy

Lieutenant Colonel of the 24th Battalion, Quebec Regiment (Victoria Rifles), Canadian Expeditionary Force

In the 1890s William Clark-Kennedy was a pupil at St Andrew's School, Southborough. During World War I, on the Fresnes-Rouvroy line, France, on 27 and 28 August 1918, Lieutenant Colonel Clark-Kennedy's battalion suffered heavy casualties.

Through his encouragement and collection and deployment of men the whole brigade was able to advance. Although he became severely wounded, Lieutenant Colonel Clark-Kennedy refused aid and dragged himself to a shell hole where he acted as observation officer.

He refused to be evacuated for over five hours, until he had gained a position from which the advance could be resumed. He died in Montreal in 1961 at the age of 82.

Other honours
Companion of the Order of St Michael and St George, Distinguished Service Order and Bar, Croix de Guerre

Image courtesy of the Victoria Cross Society

William's Write-up at the Victoria Cross Grove, Dunorlan Park, Tunbridge Wells

CHAPTER NINE

Brave to the End –
The Story of Captain Lionel Ernest Queripel 1920–1944

FOREWORD

Lionel was 19 when he joined the British Army and 24 when he was killed. Richard has done much work finding so many people who remember him in his short life.

We grew up knowing that our family belonged to the British Army. Sadly there are no more Queripels to carry on the tradition.

I think that this story will inspire the generation which is now growing up in a a very different world, sixty years later.

Rose Robinson (Lionel's late sister)

A MILITARY BACKGROUND

Lionel Ernest Queripel came from a good military background. If anyone can be described as a born soldier it was Lionel Queripel. His father, grandfather and great-grandfather all served the forces of the Crown for 100 years before him. His great-grandfather, Captain W. Watson (1809–1879), had served with the 89th Regiment of Foot in the Crimea, and his grandmother Mary Ann (born *c*.1815 at St. Peter Port, Guernsey), married Colonel Alfred Ernest Queripel (Lionel's grandfather) during the September quarter of 1872 at Clifton, Somerset. Alfred Queripel was born in 1848 at St. Peter Port, Guernsey and educated at Elizabeth College, Guernsey. He then trained as a veterinary surgeon joining the Army on 27 August 1870, and served in the Afghan War of 1879–80. He served with the Royal Artillery in India, where he became Chief Veterinary Officer under Lord Roberts. Mary Ann died in 1915 and when the war ended their daughter took him to California. His heart had been unsound for some time, but by that time he had two grand-children in England; he longed to see them and started for home. The Atlantic chill was too much, and he died at sea on 28 April 1921, two days out from New York. He was apparently a most loveable man.

Colonel Alfred Queripel's son, Leslie Herbert (Lionel's father) was born on 14 July 1881, and raised and educated in India. He attended The Royal Military Academy at Woolwich and was commissioned as a Second Lieutenant into the Royal Artillery on 22 November 1899. With his unit he fought with the International Force for the relief of Peking in 1900 during the Boxer Rebellion. He became Lieutenant on 16 February 1901, commanding 12 Battery 1902–3. He became Captain on 17 March 1908. Back in India, in 1911 he raised 33 Signal Company, a new venture, and became an expert in the new signals technology. He was promoted Major on 30 October 1914 and appointed Temporary Lieutenant Colonel from 1 April 1915. He served as Director of Signals on General Nixon's staff in Mesopotamia from 9 April 1915 during the First World War, reaching the rank of Colonel and being honoured as a Companion of the Distinguished Service Order (D.S.O.) in October 1915 and a Companion of the Order of St. Michael and St. George (C.M.G.) in 1918. In March 1915 he was appointed Assistant Director of Army Signals and Telegraphs, Force H.Q., to which was attached an Inspector General of Communications.

Mesopotamia 1915 – General Nixon's staff (Leslie Queripel middle row right end)

Lionel's father Leslie Queripel lived at 52 Warwick Park, Tunbridge Wells in Kent from 1926. The house was built in 1911 for Mr. Starmer, the then Dean of The Royal College of Music and organist of St. Mark's Church, Tunbridge Wells. His final command was of 28th Air Defence Brigade at Tonbridge. He retired in 1930. He was Vicar's Warden at the Church of King Charles the Martyr in Tunbridge Wells from 1940–1952. He married, first in 1914, Margaret Kidner who was born in Nynehead, Somerset in 1882. They married in the City of London (registered during the June quarter), but she sadly died in that year. He then married in 1918, Margaret's sister, Sybil Kidner, who was born in Nynehead (birth registered during the December quarter of 1891 at Wellington, Somerset).

Leslie Queripel

Sybil Queripel

Leslie and Sybil married at St. George's, Hanover Square, London (registered during the March quarter of 1918) and had two daughters, Meg (born 1918) and Rose (born 1924), and one son, Lionel. In later years Colonel Leslie Queripel used to sit outside the front door in a wheelchair. He died on December 31 1962, aged 81, and was cremated in Tunbridge Wells. His Military Papers are stored at the Liddell Hart Centre for Military Archives, King's College, London.

After Colonel Leslie Queripel's death, Sybil lived on the ground floor of the house, and converted the first floor into two bed sits/kitchen and bathrooms. These were occupied by Eileen Gall and Miss Davy, who paid a low rent in return for a small amount of help. In addition a room was let out to a tenant named Miss Ruth Pearson. Mrs Malloy came in to help in the house one morning a week, and Mr Ashdown on Saturday mornings to mow lawns and sweep leaves. Sybil continued to attend Parachute Regiment functions. She was a keen gardener and did her own shopping and cooking until she left Tunbridge Wells in 1978 to go to the Walhatch Country Residential Home in Forest Row, Sussex. She sold 52 Warwick Park in May 1978. Sybil died in 1983 and was cremated in Eastbourne. Lionel's elder sister Margaret (Meg) married Donald Mackay who retired as Deputy Manager, Windscale, Calder Hall. They had a son, Robert, and a daughter Jane Margaret who died in 1987. The younger sister Rose moved to Buxted to live on the edge of the New Forest having married Dick Robinson O.B.E., who retired from the Prudential after over 30 years. He was in the Territorial Army (HAC) and served to the rank of Major, Royal Artillery in the war. They had two sons, David and Philip. Sadly Dick passed away in 2009 and Rose in 2011.

Colonel Queripel's brother, Lieutenant Commander C. M. (Mervyn) Queripel (1883–1914) entered the Navy through Osborne and was killed in action in H.M.S. *Bulwark* in 1914. Lieutenant Commander Queripel's burial took place on 1 December at Woodlands Cemetery, Gillingham.

EARLY YEARS

Lionel was born on Tuesday 13 July 1920 at the Manor House, Winterbourne Monkton, Dorset. Queripel is a Guernsey name. Therefore the "Qu" is pronounced "K". His elder sister, Margaret (Meg) was also born here in 1918 at the home of their mother's uncle. Aunt and uncle used to help when a baby was born in the family. The house is still in the family. Meg and Lionel were both christened in the church there. Younger sister Rose was born in Kirkee, India in 1924 when her father Leslie was commanding the 16th Brigade Royal Artillery.

In 1926 Lionel's parents, Leslie and Sybil bought 52 Warwick Park, Tunbridge Wells and Lionel's first school was not far away – a short walk to St. Clair Ladies Private School, 25–29 Frant Road on the corner of Roedean Road. The Principal was Miss C. E. Desprez Vickery. He went to kindergarten there as did Meg and Rose. It was a girls' school but there were a few boys. Hector Munro, who was a friend of Lionel's at the school remembers that there were about 12 boys out of around 60–70 pupils. He went with his sisters, and they had a very good early education. Hector remembers having tea at Warwick Park, and if Lionel misbehaved then Colonel Queripel would tell him off, but if Hector misbehaved he would just laugh it off.

52 Warwick Park, Tunbridge Wells

Lionel then was sent to Durnford, Langton Matravers, Dorset from 1928–34. This was a Preparatory School for Boys established in 1893, and there would have been around 90 boys in 1928. The school was at the top end of the long village street and the village shop at the bottom. Many of the rooms and dormitories had views across to the Purbeck Hills.

Nicholas Elliott's excellent book *Never Judge a Man by His Umbrella* written in 1991 recalls his own schooldays there. He entered the school in September 1926, two years before Lionel. He recalls the Headmaster, Mr Pellatt, whom the boys referred to as "T.P.". He had owned the school since it started, and was an unorthodox Head.

St. Clair Ladies Private School Building in 2007

The fees (around £90 per term) were probably the highest of any private school in the country. The school had no telephone, and had virtually no plumbing, apart from an indoor unheated swimming pool. At 7 a.m. every boy had to jump in both in winter and summer, having run naked from their respective dormitories. There was no heating in the dormitories, and no running water. Breakfast was at 8.30am, following the plunge and early school. The meal awaited on tables when the boys all came in. The tea had usually been poured a long time earlier, so was usually cold. Eggs were usually congealed on the plates. Sausages were served once a week, but most boys disposed of them under the table as they tasted of sawdust. You were not allowed to leave anything on your plate at the end of the meal. At the end of the day, prayers took place in the dining room, which involved kneeling in the muck the boys had created earlier in the day, which had not been cleared up. Every Sunday the matron would give out a weekly ration of sweets brought back from the holidays. The older boys waited around the corner and took the sweets off the younger ones. There was a lot of bullying at the school. In the summer term it was customary for the school to have a half holiday once every new boy had swum the length of the school bathing pool at Dancing Ledge. Those who failed were not popular at all. In 1939, the school was sold. Durnford was requisitioned by the Army later that year and was acquired by the owners of the Old Malt House when the Army gave it up in 1948. The main buildings were either pulled down or sold. Interestingly the school's most famous pupil was Ian Fleming, the writer of the James Bond novels.Lionel moved on to Marlborough College in Wiltshire on Friday, 27 April 1934. His school number was 259. He spent four terms in a junior boarding house called 'A' House. David Clemmow was in 'A' House with him and recalls Lionel and him having to run up and down the cellar steps of 'A' House as junior boys. Lionel joined his senior boarding house (B3, Housemaster E. G. H. Kempson) in September 1935 where he spent the rest of his Marlborough career.

Frederick N. Hicks recalls:

> Lionel and I were in the same dormitory for our first term, normally bedtime starting at 9. 30 p.m. getting ready, and prayers with lights out at 10pm. Geoffrey Chilton, our easy to get on with Housemaster treated all 18 boys on Saturday nights by allowing us to have a

free-for-all pillow fight for 15 minutes before lights out to burn off our energy and settle ourselves. Also it allowed us to get to know each other better, as we had different desks in house, and were in different classes. The fight started with boys in beds either side, then ended up in a rough and tumble and wrestling to see who could get the upper hand.

It was great fun and over the Saturdays the stronger boys became apparent from the weaker boys, ending up with the two best wrestling each other – Lionel Queripel and Frederick Hicks! He was bigger and heavier than me. Sometimes he got the better of me and other times I got the better of him – it was later in medical training that I realised this was because I was fortunate in having a high muscle power body weight ratio which enabled me to be surprisingly capable for my smaller size. All my life these Saturdays have been happy memories! My vivid memories of Lionel came flooding back when one day the front page of the Daily Mirror or Express carried the news that Captain Queripel had been awarded the VICTORIA CROSS. Could it have been that our struggles together to outdo each other helped sew in him the will to win the battle to defeat the war enemy?

Incidentally, Michael Birley remembers Lionel as the one more likely to win a V.C. than most of his contemporaries at Marlborough. He also recalls him as a "fairly tough opponent on the rugger field".

Members of the Marlborough House Platoon – Lionel in the centre flanked by Howard Stephens (left) and Kenneth Terry (right), also killed in the R.A.F.

He was of reasonable academic ability but never reached the elite 6th Form, his final year being spent in Maths 5b in which he had a middling position. His sister Rose remembers he was not good at maths, but his great asset was common sense. His height was 5ft 10ins, broad shouldered. She remembers him as the older brother who was very kind to her. He spoke French fluently, and worked in a wine shop in France run by Mme. LeClerc during school holidays. He spent two or three Easter holidays in Wimereux, just north of Boulogne. Here he posed as a complete Frenchman and spoke French unless or until English day-trippers became unpleasant, then good English (from a schoolboy) was most effective. As his mother Sybil said "All would go well until they got out of hand, or showed any disrespect to Madame; the effect of a firm English, 'Good morning, Sir,' from a tough looking young English boy had a magical effect".

Lionel represented his boarding house at both boxing and rugby, where he played scrum half. He also excelled in the Officers Training Corps, being promoted to Cadet 2nd Lieutenant in his final term. He became a "House Captain" or House Prefect.

Michael Gregson, who was slightly older, remembers Lionel as being "short, stocky, quiet and very pleasant; also a very good rugger player".

B3 House Rugby Team Michaelmas 1936. Lionel seated extreme left of middle row, just in front of housemaster E. G. H. Kempson

Nigel Anderson recalls:

> a cheerful, friendly man, but not effusively so, with a sense of purpose without being dogmatic about it and not likely to be diverted from his goal, either in the start or finish of it. There was something about him which I cannot define other than to say that he had a firm personality.

David Swann told me that:

> we were a trio together – Queripel, Andrew Wilson and me. He was a dear friend of mine, and we were all in B3 together. We used to go to 'Treacle Bolly' – the other side of the Kennet River from the school. Here there were flatlands rising to a hill on the Marlborough Downs. In a U-shaped section of valley on wet days there was a lot of mud around. It was easy to make a slide and we would toboggan down. Lionel often fell off and we all laughed at him.
>
> … My girlfriend (later my wife) came down at weekends in the family Rover and used to say to me 'you will make sure Lionel is around won't you?'. She was very taken by Lionel. We also used to play golf at Ogbourne St. George. He was far from academic – charming – agreeable.
>
> … The V.C. was very much in character. He was ingrained with the glories of army service. It was the main characteristic through his school days with his inheritance (family background) and inclinations, together with his physical ability. He enjoyed the Corps. It was taken for granted that he would join the army.

Kenneth Dunlop, who called him "Queri", was in the same House:

> He was great fun – a born comedian. When he was about 16 if you asked him a question he didn't know the answer to he would reply 'I'm afraid I'll have to ask my wife on that!'

Once playing a house game of hockey, I think Queri was playing at right-back, the ball came over near to his goal-line, so he gave a swing and missed the ball completely. He then gave everyone watching a wave and ran back and as it approached the line gave a huge swing (sticks) and hit the ball over people's heads to the other end of the pitch.

He wasn't a great academic, but was a good sportsman at House level. He was a stocky strongly built man, with very long arms. He had a cheerful temperament. He was never cross with anyone, very even-tempered, and was popular with everyone. He was very laid-back, and did just enough work to keep out of trouble.

Jock Knight and Lionel were both members of the 1st XV Rugby pack in the autumn of 1938, and the only memory Jock has of him is as "a rather squat, energetic and silent wing-forward".

Greville Selby-Lowndes was a friend of Lionel's in both junior and senior Houses, but was slightly older:

For a term or so I shared a study with him and one other. He was never a dominant character – he never shouted the odds. He was quiet and modest, but he would never let you down or the house or the school (nor his regiment and its men at the end), always reliable, he was always a loyal friend, but quite undemanding. He was short, but well-liked, popular but never pushy. He was a good scrum-half in rugby. Owing to his tough physique and slightly bandy legs, he could always keep the opposition guessing, and probably himself too, as to which way he was going. I completely lost touch with him until, in hospital in Tilburg, Holland in February 1945, when I saw his name on a list of missing people that the army was trying to trace.

Close-up of Lionel in the B3 House Rugby Team

In a few holidays, Lionel helped with the local Sea Cadets under the guidance of Captain Cable. Lionel's sister Rose remembers:

we were all at boarding school with normal holidays in Tunbridge Wells. The family had an annual fortnight spent at Pevensey Bay in the last two weeks of August, between 1926 and 1939. We went swimming, made monumental sand buildings and played deck tennis. There were always old friends to meet each year – we had bicycles and explored, mostly in Sussex. A day at Pevensey Bay was a ride of 30 miles each way.

Rose remembers that Lionel was a good rugby scrum-half, but working hard to pass the Sandhurst entry exam (which he did well) was more important. She knew that away from home he had a good social life, but she never heard mention of any special girlfriend.

His mother, Sybil recalled that:

he was never a brilliant scholar and did not shine in class. This was because he always dug down on a subject until he understood it, the result was that in exams he always confounded his tutors. When his form master tried to dissuade him from taking School Certificate that year, he said, 'I haven't time not to' – he passed. When the Sandhurst exam was coming, once more the same thing happened, 'I haven't time not to' – he seemed always to have that sense of urgency. When the results came out his form master wrote, 'I am sure that no-one was more surprised than you, to see your name in the first half of the list'.

Lionel left Marlborough on Tuesday, 20 December 1938, and was admitted to The Royal Military College, Sandhurst on 27 January 1939. According to the entry in the Gentleman Cadet Registers of the College (most pre-war records were lost or destroyed during the Second World War) he was in 4 Company RMC. His "Ability to Train" and his "Ability to Lead" are both listed as: Below Average.

He left Sandhurst on 21 October, 1939 and was commissioned as a Second Lieutenant 108181 on 22 October into the Royal Sussex Regiment. He had been a member of the last term to pass out at the start of the Second World War. He joined the Royal Sussex Regiment as he had links with the county. First, the much-loved family holidays were spent in Sussex at Pevensey Bay. Secondly, until the county boundary was moved to the Borough boundary, sometime in the 1930s, the part of Tunbridge Wells which included the family house was in Sussex. So it seemed a natural progression.

THE ROYAL SUSSEX REGIMENT

In December 1939, the 2nd Battalion Royal Sussex Regiment moved from Belfast to Maiden Newton, Dorset where Lionel would have joined it. The Battalion had been stationed in Ireland at the outbreak of hostilities. The 133rd Brigade was to be strengthened by the addition of the 2nd Battalion. In April 1940, the 2nd Battalion moved to France as part of 133 (Royal Sussex) Brigade, 44th Home Counties Division. The other battalions in 133 Brigade were 4th and 5th Royal Sussex.

From 1940–42 Lionel was involved in the Defence of the South-East coast, which he knew well. The Brigade was manning the defences of South-East England against invasion. The family used to have holidays in Pevensey Bay. While he was on the coast, Lionel collected from Tunbridge Wells a wind-up gramophone, some ropey records and some books given by others for the cause. A small group of people in Tunbridge Wells collected these items. After the outbreak of the war, his sister Rose only saw him two or three times. Rose remembers that he enjoyed riding a motorcycle, but never owned one. In the early war days he had some sort of liaison job, and at least once he came home on one for a day visit.

He spoke fluent French and was taking troops into France in 1940 as interpreter for detachments of the regiment going to the front, and then coming back. The last time he did this was when he met survivors of Dunkirk boats in this country. Thousands of British and French troops were safely evacuated as the advancing German Army swept through northern France. The evacuation was completed on the night of 3 and 4 June, the final stages being conducted under fire from German machine-guns. In all some 335,000 British and French troops were safely landed, in what Sir Winston Churchill described as "a miracle of deliverance".

Bill (Badger) Balcombe who had joined up in 1939 did two months' training in Chichester and then went to Seaford for field training. The first officer he met at platoon training was Lionel Queripel. He described Lionel as a "smashing man". He remembers joining a train for Seaford at Uckfield, and Lionel opening the First Class carriage door, and inviting Bill and others to join him. This was to save them having to stand or "rough it" in Third Class! He told them on the train "you will all be Sergeants soon!"

Bill knew him for two to three years and recalled:

> He would always be the last one to leave, sending others to safety first. He trained us, but he was just starting out, and we had to call him Mr Q. Lionel was a young subaltern at the time. We were training at Seaford and went to Steyning Rifle Range to practise.

Lionel became a Lieutenant on 22 April 1941, being given the temporary rank of Captain on 28 July 1942. This meant that at the end of the war, had he lived, he would have reverted to the rank of

Steyning Rifle Range December 1939. Royal Sussex recruits from Seaford doing their six weeks fieldcraft training before posting to Units. Lionel is front row, fifth from left

Lieutenant. Incidentally from 16 September 1943 he was given the additional rank of Acting Major which allowed him to wear major's rank insignia. In summary his rank of Lieutenant was permanent and part of the peacetime establishment of his regiment. His rank of Captain was temporary, while his regiment was expanded to its wartime establishment. His rank of Major was an "acting" rank, while he was engaged in a particular task i.e., his attachment to the 10th Battalion, The Parachute Regiment. This explains why there are some photographs taken of Lionel wearing major's rank insignia. These had to be altered for official display after the posthumous award of the Victoria Cross.

When the threat of invasion receded the Division was marked for operations overseas. In May 1942 the 2nd Battalion sailed in a large convoy to the South Atlantic as part of 44th Division. At that time they sailed for "an unknown destination", but with news that Tobruk had fallen in June, they were rerouted for Suez. They disembarked at Suez on 24th July 1942. Members of the 2nd, 4th and 5th Battalions joined the 1st Battalion in the Western Desert. The Division joined Eighth Army at the time of Rommel's threat to the Delta. The three battles which took place in the desert at El Alamein in 1942 marked the climax of Hitler's plan to wrest Egypt from the British. The three battles were known as the First Alamein, Alam Halfa, and El Alamein – where Rommel was finally defeated in Montgomery's finest triumph.

General Montgomery arrived on August 12 and summoned all the staff for his famous "pep" talk. He realised that there was a vital point which was not defended. This was Alam Halfa, a ridge in the rear of El Alamein, which commanded a large area of desert. Because there was a shortage of available troops to defend it, the 44th Division was sent for. Montgomery had toughened and trained the Division on the Sussex and Kent beaches.

The Royal Sussex Brigade were to hold the Alam Halfa Ridge, and in order from west to east lined up – 4th Battalion, 2nd Battalion, Brigade Headquarters, and 5th Battalion. The 2nd Battalion was under the command of Lieutenant Colonel Kenneth Hooper. The Ridge was the key to the battle. If the Germans could pass it to the east, they would shift northwards and meet the British armour on favourable ground, behind the main part of 8th Army. There was a real shortage of defence around the ridge, so everyone was set to digging as fast as they could. Rommel could arrive at any time. The digging was difficult as the soil was very rocky and hard.

2nd Royal Sussex – The Eve of Alamein. L.to R: Lionel; Lieutenant M. Henry (killed, Arnhem); Lieutenant Matthew Lees; Captain George Langridge; Lieutenant P. Pafford; Lieutenant Montgomery

On 31 August, Rommel attacked shortly after midnight. A formidable assault was launched by the Germans – 15th and 21st Panzer Divisions, the 90th Light Division, and the 20th Italian Corps. Three simultaneous thrusts were made, with the heaviest from the south. At dawn, the whole desert south of the ridge was covered with German tanks and transport, and at about 7.30 a.m. the tanks dashed forward towards a minefield. No. 133 Brigade were on the west and 131 Brigade on the east. Their positions were well dug in, encircled with minefields, and supported by a field regiment and numerous anti-tank guns. Looking down from their position, the Royal Sussex could see the 22nd Armoured Brigade meeting the enemy, whose axis of advance was directed towards their ridge and then north to the Ruweisat Ridge. By night the 133rd Brigade sent out strong fighting patrols, up to four or five miles.

1 September saw the final repulse of the enemy after some costly attacks during the day. General Montgomery said, "this battle never received the interest or attention it deserves. It was a vital action, because, had we lost it, we might well have lost Egypt. In winning it, we paved the way for success at El Alamein and the subsequent advance to Tunisia". Losses at Alam Halfa were some 2,000 men in the Eighth Army. Alam Halfa provided the pivot for his defeat of Rommel's final thrust, and Montgomery then reformed the Eighth Army in preparation for his autumn offensive. The arrival of fresh divisions and new equipment enabled him to form 10th Corps.

The Royal Sussex Brigade now left the 44th Division and joined the 10th Armoured Division of the 10th Armoured Corps. To provide the new Armoured Division with its infantry, 133 Brigade had been detached from 44 Division, re-equipped as lorried infantry and on 29 September joined the new armoured division. A very important part of the armoured division was its infantry brigade. This included the "lorried infantry" brigade, who were ordinary infantry transported by lorries. The 10th Armoured Division under Major General A. H. Gatehouse consisted of 8th Armoured Brigade, 24th Armoured Brigade, and 133rd Lorried Infantry Brigade under Brigadier A. W. Lee. This comprised 2nd, 4th and 5th Royal Sussex Regiment and one company of the Royal Northumberland Fusiliers. The motor battalions had many more armoured carriers than the lorried battalions. The former's radios were all protected in carriers, whereas those of the lorried infantry were mounted in unarmoured 15cwt. trucks. The tasks of lorried infantry were:

(a) The attack and clearance of hastily organised enemy anti-tank front by day, or more probably by night.

(b) The attack, in co-operation with tanks and artillery on an enemy anti-tank front which has had time to dig in.

In the three weeks of available training time, the Brigade concentrated on task "a". The battle plan did not envisage the motor or lorried brigades mounting formal set-piece attacks as part of the breakthrough battle. There was intensive training during this period, including a number of divisional exercises, each lasting several days.

On 21 October the commander of 133 Lorried Brigade produced a message to his men referring to the numerical advantage of Eighth Army but went on to advise:

> But a superiority of weapons and tanks and equipment will avail us nothing, unless the men behind those weapons and in those tanks also possess a superiority of will-power to fight them harder, more ruthlessly, more daringly, and, most important, longer than the enemy. Thus the success or failure of this forthcoming battle depends, in the end, upon us, each and every one of us, from the Commander-in-Chief down to the individual private, individually and collectively. Let us see to it that the 133rd Royal Sussex Lorried Infantry Brigade provides an extra surprise to Master Rommel in the hardness of its hitting and its lasting power. Let us make him say 'Gott straffe these men of Sussex – do they never tire?'

The Battle of El Alamein opened on 23 October. The 10th Corps were to go in on the second night, to deepen the gap in the enemy minefield made by the assaulting divisions. This attack made no headway. The 133rd Lorried Infantry Brigade moved hardly any distance at all during the night. As dawn broke they received orders to disperse. On the 25th the two forward battalions of 133 Lorried Brigade, with many men not in slit trenches lost about 60 men and several trucks to enemy shelling before new orders reached them changing their role and permitting them to move further back. By 26 October, Montgomery resolved to pursue the battle of attrition with infantry until Rommel's resources were used up. He would launch the Australian Division northwards on 26 October and then deliver his knockout blow down the axis of the coast road. The Brigade was withdrawn on the third night, and, after a brief respite, was sent in to the attack again on 27 October. No. 133 (Royal Sussex) Infantry Brigade lay dispersed on a patch of desert about five miles south-east of El Alamein railway station. Montgomery had launched his attack four days earlier and the Brigade was now waiting impatiently to follow the armour of its parent division, 10 Armoured, through gaps in the defences created by the New Zealand and Highland Divisions. The Brigade, as lorried infantry, would be required to move fast. Although their immediate task had not been specified, their expected role in the battle was to deal with pockets of resistance in the wake of the armoured break-out.

At midday the three Royal Sussex battalion commanders were summoned forward to an "O" group with their commander, Brigadier Alec Lee. They were told to meet him some 15 miles forward, near a feature nicknamed "Kidney Ridge" in an area recently captured by 51 Highland Division. The battalions in the meantime prepared to move forward. As the afternoon progressed, battalion "O" Groups were called forward for orders and reconnaissance. The main body of troops joined them after dark to be launched almost at once into a frontal attack against fixed enemy defences which had already held up the armoured break-out for three days.

With the vulnerability of his armour weighing on his mind, the corps commander, Lieutenant General Herbert Lumsden, decided to seize a sector of the axis defensive belt with his only available infantry – 7 Motor Brigade of 1st Armoured Division and 133 Lorried Infantry Brigade. Two strong points were picked out and codenamed "Snipe" and "Woodcock". The motor brigade was to attack with two battalions on the night of 26 October, either side of a kidney-shaped ring contour. At the time it was thought to be the crest of Kidney Ridge, a feature that ran right across the front. As the battle progressed, after much confusion, it was found to be an indentation. Initially he only used the motor brigade. Although it was apparently his intention to relieve it with 133 Brigade, the latter was not warned to take part until too late to influence 7th Brigade's battle. This situation regarding the motor brigade was, however, unclear to senior commanders and during the morning of 27 October, 133 Brigade was warned to relieve them that night.

Moving forward ostensibly to 2 Rifle Battalion's relief, 133 Lorried Infantry Brigade had delayed its start and its artillery support, for an hour owing to a number of confusions, mainly a lack of information on the rifle battalions exact location and its survival. Finally, with an hour's artillery support laid on "Woodcock" but well west of "Snipe", in case of the riflemen's survival, the 3 Lorried Infantry Battalions set off. At 2230 hours, the Brigade advanced: 5 Royal Sussex left, objective "Snipe". 4 Royal Sussex on the right, objective "Woodcock" and 2 Royal Sussex in reserve. The 2nd Battalion was further cheered with a rum issue "with the compliments of the commander of the Highland Division".

The morning of the 28 October found the 5th Battalion on the left, dug in on a forward slope, secure but unable to move due to hostile artillery and sniper fire. The 2nd battalion was brought up on their right, thus extending the line. The attack was ill-conceived ending in disaster, with the 4th Battalion being practically wiped out. Their survivors were absorbed by the 2nd Battalion. Both commanding officers of these Battalions were killed – Lieutenant Colonel Murphy, commanding the 4th, and Lieutenant Colonel Kenneth Hooper, commanding the 2nd, who was shot by a sniper while visiting the forward companies on 28 October. On the extreme right, the survivors and rear details of the 4th Battalion were taken under command of the 2nd Battalion and formed a defensive flank. Thus 133 Brigade now occupied a salient some 1,500 yards deep to the south of the kidney feature. When dusk fell on the 28th the two surviving battalions of 133 Brigade, 2nd and 5th Royal Sussex were still in their isolated and exposed positions well west of the main defence line.

That night the 2nd Battalion mounted a series of patrols to destroy sniper positions and locate others for treatment by our guns and mortars. The following day the Battalion had the satisfaction of accepting the surrender of 41 members of 115 Panzer Grenadier Regiment, shelled out of their position. On 29 October the forward troops were ordered to withdraw some 500 yards to the reverse slope of Kidney Ridge which they did that night. The Royal Sussex Brigade, though sadly depleted, now joined the 51st Division for their attack on the night of 1–2 November, in conjunction with the 2nd New Zealand Division. It was named "Supercharge", for it broke the enemy line and let the armour through after the Brigade had captured the position known as "Woodcock", where there had been many losses.

Montgomery decided to make his effort just north of Kidney. So it fell to 133 Brigade to attack again and assist the final breakthrough. "Supercharge" was to strike the enemy with the Highland Division on the left and the New Zealand Division on the right. No. 133 Brigade under the command of 51st Division was to advance and form a hard shoulder protecting the left flank. The 2nd and 5th Battalions were, respectively, given the task of recapturing "Woodcock" and "Snipe" on the nights of 1 and 2 November. Both Battalions mutually supported each other, and the operation was supported by massive close artillery fire. Learning from recent experience in which lorried infantry had brought heavy losses in vehicles, the Sussex battalions had planned to advance on foot with picks and shovels carried by the men and only essential vehicles following. A special artillery barrage was prepared for 133 Brigade starting some 20 minutes after the supporting fire for the main operation, that is at 1.25 a.m. Though the Brigade had to await reliefs by troops of 153 Brigade, both of the Sussex battalions were on their start lines in good time. The 2nd Royal Sussex took "Woodcock" during the night with the 5th swinging south to take "Snipe" the following night.

In the words of Christopher Nix, commanding 2nd Battalion, "the attack was completely successful, although I had some very anxious moments. The Battalion was magnificent and fairly tore into the enemy and after an hour's hand-to-hand fighting on the enemy position, all opposition died away". Although they were reduced to a strength of two battalions, the Brigade played a vital part in this battle. The number of prisoners taken by the Brigade was estimated at over 500.

In another part of the line near Galal, a patrol of the 2nd battalion captured General Enrico Frattini, commander of the Italian Parachute Division, and his staff. The Carrier Platoon, forming part of the mobile column which engaged and rounded up these Italian officers, was commanded by Captain Lionel Queripel.

By this time the outcome of the Battle of El Alamein was decided. Armoured cars of the Royal Dragoons, which had moved up behind 133 Brigade, burst out to the south-west and were soon harassing the enemy's rear areas. Rommel realised it was time to withdraw, and despite Hitler's exhortation to stand fast ordered the withdrawal of what was left of his mobile troops. No. 133 Brigade reverted to 10th Armoured Division and took part in the pursuit as far as Mersa Matruh, rounding up about 3,000 prisoners.

The *Egyptian Gazette* of 8 November, 1942, gave the following account of their last battle on this front:

> The Sussex had captured two vital features, driving a wedge into the enemy line. It was certain that the Germans would try to win back the ground. At first light they attacked with tanks, and overran some of the forward troops. They shelled the Sussex line and raked it with machine-gun fire. Every weapon they could bring to bear opened up at the slightest hint of a movement. But the Sussex held on grimly. They remained out there in their lonely salient for a whole week. Then the crisis passed. The Sussex were relieved and went back to rest.

The Brigade went back to reorganise in the Canal Zone.

WITH THE PARAS

Born in the desert, flowered in Italy, withered at Arnhem, yet did not die …

One of the improvements that was brought forward after Alamein was the need for a fully trained and operational parachute regiment. It was felt that Rommel's armies would have been defeated much quicker, and more prisoners and booty taken. So in October 1941 three men were sent to start a parachute training school at Kabrit, a village in the Suez Canal Zone on the edge of the Great Bitter Lake. On 3 May 1942, No. 4 Parachute Training School became operational in order to train members of the SAS and agents who were going to be parachuted into enemy areas. No. 4 Para Brigade was to be created around this training facility. On 12 December the brigade commander, Brigadier Shan (later Sir John), Hackett and his Brigade Major P. H. M. May, completed their parachute course there. Brigadier Hackett took command of 4th Para Brigade on 1 January 1943.

The weather was good and it only took ten days to train each group of recruits. However it was very soon realised that the training facilities were inadequate for the needs of training a brigade as opposed to a simple parachute training school. The facilities were not ideal, the Drop Zone too hard for basic training, and sandstorms and great heat made it uncomfortable. Recruits jumped off backwards from the tailboard of a lorry moving fast across the desert, with the additional hazard of the occasional cactus. This practice was later halted! A great deal of valuable preparation was achieved at Kabrit in spite of the conditions.

In December 1942, the 2nd Battalion Royal Sussex Regiment had been chosen to select volunteers, of whom there were 200 officers and men, which has been quoted as "nearly all who were fit for that kind of activity", to become the 2nd of the Brigade's parachute battalions, and redesignated as 10th Battalion, The Parachute Regiment (10 Para). Originally when the Battalion was scheduled for conversion it was known as "S" (for Sussex) Battalion. Attempts were made to retain the "S" in 10 Para's title but the War Office ruled against it. However the War Office felt that a regular infantry battalion could not be asked to be removed from its regiment and incorporated into the Army Air Corps. So the 2nd Battalion Royal Sussex could retain its original identity, enabling the gaps that would be left to be filled by infantry reinforcements. It was bolstered by men of the 4th (T.A.) and 5th (Cinque Ports) Battalions.

Lieutenant Colonel F. B. I. Ken Smyth O.B.E. of the South Wales Borderers was placed in command of 10 Para, and its core foundation was around 100–200 all ranks of 2nd Battalion Royal Sussex. They were incorporated with the 4th Brigade. They joined up at Kabrit before moving to Ramat David. The volunteers included Lieutenant Lionel Queripel, who became "A" Company Captain, a position he held until his death. At that stage he was second-in-command. Sergeant Springford, Provost Sergeant at the time, had served with the Military Police. On one occasion he had apprehended a Lieutenant Queripel in Brighton, and was surprised to find that Captain Queripel was now his Company Commander. But a more just and charming man, a more able commander there could not be, as Sergeant Springford was the first to testify.

A new site was found in northern Palestine, and the move was made to a new camp around Ramat David on 13 March. Conditions were much improved, and more aircraft and equipment became available. Morale was good, although the necessary early morning start was not popular. Another airfield was used at Afula, 6 miles to the south of Nazareth. This is where the parachutes were packed and stored. During the first two months the men packed their own parachutes. Exercises were also carried out in Cyprus and around Lake Tiberias, which offered better conditions for airborne and para training.

The already trained 159 Para Battalion joined 4 Para Brigade at the outset and was redesignated 156 Battalion, The Parachute Regiment. The 4 Para Brigade, with only two battalions still lacked a third battalion to bring it up to strength. The low response from volunteers from 2nd Battalion Royal Sussex resulted in a recruiting campaign throughout Middle East Command. This resulted in the building up of 10 Para, and allowed the formation of 11 Para to begin. By late May 4 Para Brigade was considered ready to join its parent division 1st Airborne, itself just recently arrived in Tunisia. This gave heart to the men of 4th Brigade, and the advance party left by air for Kairouan on 20 May. Not long after the main body were able to move in secret, but had to remove their parachute "wings". Red berets were issued for the first time at Kairouan and in August the men received the Army Air Corps Badge – a silver eagle surrounded by a laurel wreath.

The 1st Airborne Division were amassing at Mascara and Msaken, near Sousse. The 4th Para Brigade (including the 10th Battalion) were the last on the scene. The long journey from Ramat David had been by rail to Port Said, then by sea to Tripoli, ending with the road journey to Msaken. The Division was complete by 10 June 1943, except for the 11th Battalion. A period of intense training ensued in preparation for Operation Husky – the invasion of Sicily on 9 and 10 July. No. 4 Brigade was held in reserve for this operation, which was not successful. During their stay General Sir Bernard Montgomery visited the 4th Brigade that month to give a pep-talk.

After the final defeat of all forces in Sicily several weeks later, the invasion of Italy became a certainty. No. 4 Para were selected to support British land forces and they were briefed for a landing on two drop zones around Reggio, just a few miles ahead of the landed troops. The overall plan was for troops to land at Salerno to join up with the 8th Army who were advancing, and then a joint push on Rome could be put into operation.

On 8 September an Armistice was signed between Italy and the Allies. However the Germans did not intend to surrender Italy. Meanwhile Major- General Hopkinson, commanding 1st Airborne Division, received orders to occupy Taranto, and hold it against the enemy. Taranto was a major port and naval base. So on the evening of 8 September the 2nd and 4th Para Brigades sailed from Bizerta in North Africa in a minelayer and five cruisers of the Royal Navy and in the American cruiser Boise, bound for Taranto. This was to take place at the same time as the landings at Salerno, and no opposition was met at Taranto. Under the terms of the recent Armistice, a large proportion of the Italian fleet was to sail to Malta to surrender. The Allied flotilla was able to observe the Italian fleet heading for Malta. The invasion did not go totally smoothly. Supplies were slow to arrive and there were shortages of both manpower and communications.

The task of 4th Brigade was to form a bridgehead against possible German attack while the rest of the Division were landing. While the 1st Para Brigade formed a perimeter fence around Taranto, the 2nd and 4th Brigades pursued the fleeing Germans. The northerly advance by 4th Para Brigade was made on parallel roads. The 10th Battalion were to go via Palagimo to Castellaneta, and 156 Battalion through Massafra and Mottola. By midnight on 10 September both battalions were near Castellaneta, and they attacked at dawn the next day. The battle raged all day and "A" Company, with 2nd in command Captain Queripel, spear-headed the frontal assault, while "D" Company carried out a flank attack from the north-west.

Sergeant K. D. Banwell, as No. 1 Platoon Commander in "A" Company, the point company, led the advance with Captain Queripel. While proceeding up the dusty main street of Castellaneta, Sergeant Banwell saw a water-trough on the right of the road. He decided to wash his face in the cold water for refreshment. But as he approached, a German machine-gun fired at him from the end of the road. He ran and dived straight into the trough. His own sten gun was still useable, and he was able to fire back. Private Martin ran over to join him but was shot as he did so, the only fatal casualty during the morning's advance.

By dawn on 12 September, the 10th and 156th Battalions occupied the town. The 10th had lost one man killed, one officer and two other ranks wounded. On 13 September, the 10th was relieved by the 4th Battalion and moved north of Mottola by the main road between Taranto and Gioia del Colle, where they were billeted in farms. The 4th Brigade's next target was the capture of Gioia del Colle, together with its airfield. This was needed as an airbase to cover the Salerno landings. The Brigade needed a fighting patrol from the 10th, from which "B" Company was selected. A five-hour battle followed, and by midday on 16th they had inflicted considerable damage on the enemy, while obtaining useful information on their positions, strength etc.

On 18 September the 1st Air-landing Brigade took over from 4 Para Brigade and pushed forward towards the plains of Foggia. The 10th and 156 Battalions withdrew to Taranto, although they did later come back to Gioia and Bari for a few days break. The camp was at Bari because there was less damage there than at Taranto, but the mosquitoes made sleep difficult.

Captain Queripel and Sergeant Bentley and other officers and senior N.C.O.s spent a 48-hour vacation on board H.M.S. *Greyhound* – which was at that time engaged on patrol against "gun-runners" off the coast of Albania.

Before they had left North Africa the Division had already been told that it was highly likely to be sent back to the U.K. This was to enable them to prepare and train for Operation Overlord, the invasion of Europe planned for 1944. So it was decided on 29 October, 1943 that the 1st Airborne Division would be returned to the U.K. save for the 2nd Independent Parachute Group. The 10th Battalion prepared to move during the third week of November and on the 24th embarked at Taranto on H.M.S. *Staffordshire* in bright sunshine. They arrived in Liverpool on 10 December, before arriving in Rutland at midnight as the snow was just falling. The men were billeted in the villages near Oakham. The 156 Battalion went to Melton Mowbray and the 11th Battalion to Leicester. "A" Company were billeted at Somerby, "B" Company in Thorpe Satchville, "D" Company in Burrough on the Hill, and Support Company at Ashby Folville. H.Q. Company moved to Somerby. Captain Carr and Sergeant Banwell were responsible for putting on entertainment in Somerby Village Hall. As training permitted, companies took turns to visit the various pubs in Somerby and to take in a live stage show. In Somerby there was also a Land Army hostel for girls from Nottingham and Leicester, and needless to say a number of betrothals ensued!

Gerry Dimmock, who was with the MT Section of the 10th was Captain Queripel's driver, and drove him to many functions around the area in his jeep. Local people would invite the officers for meals to their country houses. Gerry remembers him as "the most kind man one could ever wish for. He was very considerate, he always brought a drink out for me". Gerry knew him from Kabrit up to Arnhem, where he was shot down before the DZ (Drop Zone).

Sergeant Banwell remembers Captain Queripel as:

a very quiet and shy man, but nevertheless a popular officer. He was seldom seen without his curved pipe, which was a permanent feature. The Company used to do so many marches and always, coming back from Somerby we would come through the village of Thorpe Satchville. He would call a halt outside the 'Fox and Hounds', a public house, order two or three men to go in to get the beer. The remainder to lie down, with their feet up on the wall. I would fill his pipe, light it and enquire if anyone had trouble with their feet.

Sergeant Banwell, incidentally, died at the end of August 1999, having made his 1,000th jump at Arnhem in 1984 at the 40th Anniversary of the battle.

Lew Read was a Sergeant who served with Lionel Queripel from early days in 7 Platoon, "A" Company, Royal Sussex. He remembers how Captain Queripel, a wonderful officer, always made sure the men's feet were OK after a route march. He would inspect their feet. Lew Read remembers him as being very strict on certain things, but he thought the world of him.

The winter of 1943 and spring of 1944 consisted of intensive training, but leave was also taken, and there was time for keenly contested recreation – boxing, athletics and football. They developed high morale mixed with deep feelings of comradeship. In February 1944, the 10th were the first troops from 1st Airborne Division to partake in a parachute refresher course organised at Ringway, near Manchester – now Manchester Airport. The Central Landing School came into existence on 21 June 1940 as a reaction to the German invasion of Western Europe. In July extra facilities were set up at Tatton Park, located just 5 miles south of Ringway. By 1942 a great deal of progress had been made in improving tuition and techniques, although some quite serious injuries and occasional accidental deaths did occur.

Douglas Dakota transport aircraft were sent from the USA to Ringway from January 1944. Dakotas carried 20 fully equipped paras, compared with just 10 in the Whitley bombers, which greatly increased the numbers that could be trained. The two sites were fully utilised throughout the war years with 114,300 descents made during 1944 alone.

It was during February that Queripel attended a Company Commanders Course at the School of Infantry in Durham. Major Anson, "A" Company commanding officer went as Instructor at the Staff College and Captain Queripel became acting O.C. In due course he was promoted to Acting Major but, unfortunately he injured himself playing rugby and he went into hospital. After an absence of more than 21 days he had to revert to the rank of Captain. Soon after Major Anson returned and took over the Company again with Captain Queripel as second-in-command.

General Urquhart, the new Divisional Commander visited the Battalion on 25 January and was pleased to find that the 10th were up to full war establishment. In early March there were inspections by Field Marshall Montgomery and His Majesty King George VI. The King invited General Urquhart and two Brigade Commanders to dinner on his train. During dinner he said to Lieutenant General Sir John Hackett:

> I am sure that in this splendid lot of men there are any number who could win a Victoria Cross, and I shall be surprised if before very long some don't. The sad thing is that there are all too few winners of the Victoria Cross who survive. What I want to see in the Army is live V.C.s.

The 1st Airborne Division fulfilled his prediction, but of the five V.C.s from the Battle of Arnhem only one lived to receive it.

By the spring of 1944 larger scale exercises were taking place frequently. During May the Battalion was billeted in the cotton town of Holmfirth, Yorkshire so that field firing training could take place. By the end of that month the troops were more than ready for action. It was in the summer of 1944 that Lionel Queripel went into hospital to have a knee cartilage removed. He was passed fit for active service remarkably quickly.

By now they were ready to take part in what was to be the supreme Anglo-American effort of the Second World War. Four Airborne Divisions were available to take part in Europe's invasion. Two were British – the 1st and the 6th, and two American – the 82nd Airborne, and 101st Airborne. An important part of the final plan, codenamed OVERLORD, involved the landing of the Allied Airborne forces closely behind the invasion beaches to secure important communications. They were also to stop the movement of reserve troops in the area. The second part of the plan, codenamed Market Garden, became the first to actually come to fruition.

Once the landings in Normandy started, life became very tense, and the Division was placed on frequent standby before events overtook the need for operations. There were numerous aborted or unrealised operations planned between D-Day and Market Garden. Operation Comet was the first of two plans to capture the main bridges over the Rivers of the Maas, Waal and Lower Rhine and smaller rivers and canals. This was cancelled in the early hours of 10 September.

OBJECTIVE: ARNHEM

In September 1944, the plan known as Operation Market Garden had two elements: Operation Market covered the airborne plan, and Operation Garden the ground plan. For the latter, the British Second Army, which was led by XXX Corps and the Guards Armoured Division, were to move forward from Neerpelt, advance through Eindhoven and Nijmegen to Arnhem. For this to succeed it was vital for back-up from the air. The plan for Operation Market was for 101 Airborne Division, commanded by Major General Maxwell Taylor, to capture the bridges between Eindhoven and Veghel; Brigadier General James Gavin would lead 82nd Airborne Division to capture the bridges from Grave to Nijmegen; and Major General Roy Urquhart's 1st Airborne Division with 1st Independent Polish Brigade were to capture the bridges over the Lower Rhine at Arnhem. This was a total area of 100 square miles, stretching from the Dutch frontier to the Rhine. The waterways were the Wilhelmina and Zuid Willemstaart canals and the rivers Meuse, Waal and the Lower Rhine. The first four crossings were allocated to the two American divisions, and the most difficult task, capturing the bridge at Arnhem was given to the 1st Airborne Division, which included Captain Queripel. They were to hold it until relieved. The river here was 400 yards wide, and the bridge almost 2,000 feet long.

For the purposes of this story we shall concentrate mainly on the Airborne forces and in particular the actions around Oosterbeek. The plan for 1st Airborne Division was on D-Day to land the Air-landing Brigade, who would in turn secure the landing areas for the 2nd lift; then to drop the 1st Para. Brigade and Reconnaissance Squadron (jeeps in gliders) who were to take the Arnhem bridges. The gliders would land the artillery and anti-tank guns in support. On the second day the 4th Para Brigade would be dropped, with the rest of the divisional units. The 4th Brigade with the Air-landing Brigade would then establish a bridgehead defence around the environs of Arnhem. On the third day the Polish Para Brigade would drop south of Arnhem, and take over the eastern perimeter of the bridgehead. In order to complete the landing of the whole airborne force it was essential to have at least three days of clear weather.

Planning for the operation began on 10 September. The idea was, in Field Marshall Montgomery's words, "to lay an airborne carpet from south to north across the three great rivers traversing Holland, capturing the road bridges intact in the process". It was hoped it would end the war by Christmas. There had never been an attempt to send such a huge airborne force, together with vehicles, artillery and equipment, which would be capable of fighting on its own, deep behind enemy front lines. Besides transporting heavy equipment – jeeps, artillery etc. – the gliders were to ferry more than a third of the 35,000 troops required; the rest would parachute in.

Major Urquhart, 42, the commander of the 1st British Airborne Division was in command of an airborne division in battle for the first time. He refused to believe reports that the German Army was in a bad way and that only training units were left. He therefore sent a Spitfire to reconnoitre the Arnhem area. The photos that were obtained showed that he was right. They showed German armoured vehicles on the edges of the woods next to the drop zones intended for 1 Para Brigade in 2–3 days' time. However his superiors refused to take any action on this information. There was to be a total failure to pass down available intelligence to all units who needed it.

There were many other problems with the operation. First, there were just not enough aircraft to be able to transport the three divisions in one airlift. So four days flying were required. This meant only one parachute brigade was available for the first attack on the bridge at Arnhem. Another problem was that the Americans were only willing to operate in daylight. A daylight drop of such size had never before been attempted. Another problem was the necessity of selecting dropping zones and landing zones some seven miles from base. The dropping and landing zones for 1st Airborne Division were on open heathland well to the west of Arnhem.

At 17 American and seven British airfields, troops began to arrive on Friday 15 September. The 1st Airborne Division was near Stamford. Briefings for the operation were held for officers that day and soldiers the following day. In Holland, the situation on the ground was worsening as back in England the men of 10th, 156th and 11th Battalions and other Divisional troops gathered at airfields at Saltby, Spanhoe and Cottesmore. They were preparing to take part in the largest operation of its kind in the entire war. There was a gathering of low cloud and fog forming across the country. In Belgium on Sunday 17 September, XXX Corps under General Horrocks was ready to break out of the small bridgehead they held on the far side of the Meuse-Escaut Canal and move north-east to meet up with the U.S. 101st and 82nd Airborne Divisions. This was to take place at the river crossings at Eindhoven, Grave, and Nijmegen, and, within 48 hours, with 1st Airborne Division at Arnhem.

Two Brigades of 1st Airborne Division were to land on the first day, with 1 Para Brigade of three battalions aiming to take the Arnhem road and railway bridges and seize the pontoon bridge nearby. Three battalions of 1 Air-landing Brigade, arriving by glider, were to secure landing and dropping zones for further lifts and to make up the western sector of the Arnhem defensive perimeter. The tasks given to 4 Para were to drop during the second day on the most westerly landing zones and to move in to Arnhem. Here they were to set up a defensive perimeter on the high ground to the north, and relieve 1st Parachute Battalion. The operation began before dawn and continued all morning. More than 1,400 bombers had left British airfields, followed at 9.45 a.m. by 2,023 troop-carrying planes, gliders and their tugs. The sheer scale of the operation brought people out of their houses to stare in disbelief. The huge airborne force was heading for its targets. There was a constant drone of aircraft which could be heard for miles.

By 1400 hours on Sunday 17 September a total of 331 British aircraft, 319 gliders and 1,150 American planes towing 106 gliders had laid an airborne "carpet", concentrated over three zones between Eindhoven and Arnhem. Over a period of 1 hour and 20 minutes around 20,000 parachutists and glider-borne infantry had landed far behind German lines. Two brigades of infantry and divisional back-up arrived with the first lift of 1st British Airborne Division. Totalling some 8,000 men they were commanded by Brigadier Hicks. His task was to secure the drop zones around Wolfheze and surrounding areas for subsequent drops. General Lathbury's 1st Para Brigade had been ordered to capture the main road and pontoon bridges in Arnhem itself. Under Lieutenant Colonel John Frost, 2 Para made good progress moving south to the Lower Rhine. They met little opposition and set a fast pace. They soon began moving towards their targets, although as the Americans reached some of their objectives they found the bridges had already been blown up. Their objective was the Arnhem Bridge, which was eventually reached and secured.

The relief force of XXX Corps, was also encountering difficulties back at the operation's start line. With only three days to make 60 miles along a narrow, well defended road, the XXX Corps armoured column ran into trouble almost immediately when German artillery picked off the nine leading vehicles, effectively bringing it to a standstill for almost an hour. By the end of the first day, the column had travelled a mere seven miles. British and American troops were at or near their objectives by midnight on the first day. After long marches and some fierce encounters, they had gained most of their objectives. Fog prevented the planned take-off at 0700 hours on Monday 18 September.

The weather cleared by 11 o'clock to allow the 127 Dakotas of 314 and 316 Groups, 1X U.S.T.C.C. to take off – carrying the 4th Brigade, 4 Para Squadron R.E., 133 Para Field Ambulance, and detachments of the R.A.S.C. The second lift was rerouted along a more northerly route to Holland. 1,336 American C-47s, 340 British Stirling bombers, over 1,200 gliders, and over 250 Liberator bombers made up the convoy. They were protected by 867 fighter planes. The lift consisted of 6,674 airborne troops, 681 vehicles and trailers, 60 artillery pieces, and nearly 600 tons of supplies. The 10th Para flew in 33 C-47s from Spanhoe and 1 C-47 with Advance Party from Barkston Heath, vehicles in 7 Horsas from Keevil and a Hamilcar from Tarrant Rushton.

The Germans had a stroke of luck. On the first day the body of an American soldier shot down in a glider was discovered. On him was found a copy of the complete operational order marked "NOT to be taken in the air". General Urquhart wrote, "Thus the selfishness or wilful disobedience of one soldier gave the Germans an immediate compensation for the advantage we had of surprise". This meant that anti-aircraft fire was much heavier resulting in more casualties on the second day.

In the early afternoon the heavy drone of massed aircraft approached from the south-west, and it wasn't long before the leading 36 Dakotas came into view. They were flying at 700 feet with serials following at one minute intervals. They were escorted by RAF Spitfires and Tycoons. In less than ten minutes, 2300 men of 4 Para Brigade were dropped. Twenty miles from the Drop Zone, Flight Sergeant Carter's stick of "A" Company, 10 Para, having hooked up, were surprised when the alarm rang and there were cries of "abandon aircraft". The officers, C.S.M. and 16 men were then evacuated from the plane. Carter jumped last with the American crew, while the aircraft crashed in flames.

It was after 2 p.m. that the three battalions of the 4th Brigade began dropping while being fired at by mortar and "spandau". As the Dakotas came overhead the Germans opened up from the woods and trees lining the main road. As the aircraft came in, the commanding officer of the King's Own Scottish Borderers (K.O.S.B.), Lieutenant Colonel Robert Payton-Reid, led a bayonet charge with his H.Q. men and cleared the wood edge in time. On Drop Zone Y at Ginkel Heath, protected by the K.O.S.B., and a platoon of the Pathfinders, all three battalions of 4 Para Brigade dropped in tight formation, guided by green smoke. The gliders containing the remainder of 1st Air-landing Brigade and divisional troops also landed safely. Some of the parachutists were caught up in tall trees and were shot by the retreating enemy.

Despite the heavy fire along the last 20 minutes of the run-in, the American pilots had maintained their close formation and speed. Many were hit by flak and six were shot down before the drop; one went down in flames with the loss of all the crew and 18 paras of 156 Battalion. The other five managed to drop their sticks (or the majority of them) of 10th and 11th Battalions before having to make forced landings. A total of 4,000 men landed in the second lift, which gave the potential to make a huge difference to the fighting strength of the division. However it was unfortunate that they were late into battle, and did not have sufficient time to influence events before the light faded.

However, because radio communications had broken down, 4th Para Brigade had not been told in England that the plan had not been achieved, and that the 1st Battalion had not yet taken the high ground, but were desperately fighting their way to the bridge at Arnhem. The three Parachute Battalions of 4 Para Brigade were quick to organise themselves. The enemy soon began to retreat with many surrendering. Brigadier Shan Hackett arrived at the H.Q. Rendezvous with five prisoners of his own. There was sporadic shooting in the woods for a while. In spite of the difficult landing conditions all units rallied quickly at their R.V.s and sent out their own patrols. No. 156 Para went to the north-west corner of the Drop Zone, with 10 Para in the north-east and 11 Para in the south-east. No. 10 Para had to hold their position, while protecting 133 Para Field Ambulance who were close by. The medics were quick to set up and were already looking after casualties from both sides, who had suffered during the drop and fighting that followed. Everyone had been surprised at the amount of shells and mortars that greeted those who were being dropped. They had not been warned beforehand to expect any problems, and the men wondered whether they had been dropped in the wrong place. The Germans of course knew where the landings were to take place from the captured documents. No. 10 Para were heavily engaged and suffering casualties. However the Battalion was ready to move in order to take up positions along the Arnhem-Utrecht road within 90 minutes of the first landing.

The aircraft in which "A" Company Commander, Major Pat Anson had been travelling was shot down south of the Rhine. The plane had been hit by AA fire, but the troops managed to jump out. That evening Captain Queripel took over command in his absence. Not long after landing, Brigadier Hackett was briefed and told that 1st Para were in trouble. He was not pleased to learn that he was to relinquish 11th Battalion, who were to proceed to Arnhem immediately. He requested that the 7th King's Own Scottish Borderers be placed under his command instead, which was agreed.

The 4th Para Brigade received no new orders, and so proceeded with the original plan. This was to move towards Arnhem as soon as they were able. However the loss of 11th Para meant Brigadier Hackett had to review his original plans. Progress was slow because only 156th Para was able to move off to the position vacated by 11 Para. They were on the far west side of the Drop Zone. At 1700 the 156th Battalion headed east along the Arnhem-Utrecht railway line towards Oosterbeek Station until they came across heavy enemy fire. They left a platoon behind to guard any prisoners and help the wounded. The 10th Para were to follow with the other brigade troops once 133 Para Field Ambulance had dealt with existing casualties and were able to move forward. It was almost dark when the casualties were cleared and the 10th battalion was able to move down to the railway, where they halted for the night. By dusk 156 Para reached a wood north of Oosterbeek, some six miles from where they had landed. A night attack was out of the question and so the Battalion halted. The 7th K.O.S.B. arrived shortly afterwards, and they came up against strong opposition. They were to guard Johannahoeve Farm, which had been designated the landing zone for the transport and artillery of the Polish Brigade due to arrive on the third day.

The Brigade had already lost over 200 men, nearly 10 per cent of its strength from the aircraft which had been shot down, before the battle had begun. Brigadier Hackett was concerned that the Division lacked direction as isolated units were fighting their own battles without any definite objective. After meeting with Brigadier Hicks, who was in temporary command of the Division, he was reassured eventually:

> I arranged with Brigadier Pip Hicks, now in command of the Division, that the task of the Brigade for the next day would be to advance between the railway and the main Arnhem-Ede road, with the intention to secure the high ground at Koepel, keeping a firm left flank on the road.
>
> After returning to my HQ, I sent out the necessary orders to all units; 156 Bn to secure Koepel; 10th Bn. to occupy the base on the main road north of LZ "L"; 4th Parachute Squadron RE (in the infantry role) to act as backstop west of Wolfheze. Brigade axis – the railway. 7 KOSB, now under command, were around Johanna Hoeve Farm, but committed to their task of protecting the LZ for the gliders of the Polish Parachute Brigade.

At dawn, the 4th Para Brigade were to proceed hastily to secure an area of high ground known as Koepel, a wooded ridge to the north of Oosterbeek and the railway line. It was from here that the Brigade was to advance towards Arnhem on what was thought to be the left of the 1st Parachute Brigade. This would allow a double assault to be made. No. 156 Para was to move forward keeping the railway line on its right, and to the left 10 Para, under Lieutenant Colonel Ken Smyth would keep its left hand boundary as the Arnhem-Amsterdam road.

TUESDAY 19 SEPTEMBER

The plan was for Lieutenant Colonel Des Voeux's 156th Para to move first to take three areas of high ground – the first overlooking the Johannahoeve Farm, the second in the woods near Lichtenbeek House, and finally the area known as Koepel, three miles from Arnhem. To support them, 10th Para were to advance on their left flank. Once Koepel was secured, the Brigade was then to attack in the direction of Arnhem on what was believed to be the left flank of the 1st Parachute Brigade.

No. 4 Para found that the Germans had reinforced overnight. They had extended their troops along to the west hoping to trap the Brigade from the north. This would allow them to attack the forthcoming Polish landing zone, which was due to be operational that morning. No. 4 Para Brigade, after occupying ground north of Arnhem, had moved forward during the previous afternoon and night. As the troops advanced they ran into heavy fire. "A" Company immediately occupied positions in the wood to the north of the main Arnhem-Ede road. "D" Company, commanded by Captain Mike Horsfall, went forward on the north side and "B" Company moved into reserve. To the right 156 Battalion moved to man the front between the road and railway and 7th Battalion K.O.S.B. held the rear. Successive attacks against the Germans were proving costly with casualties mounting in both 10th and 156th Para. The Germans were using mortars, "spandaus", Dornier aircraft and artillery and this all increased during the morning. The attacks were west to east both north and south of the Dreijenseweg.

By midday the 10th Battalion and "A" Company, 7th Battalion K.O.S.B. were near the pumping station at La Cabine. "D" Company came under heavy fire from German outpost positions of the 9th SS Panzer. They exchanged fire with the German infantry until the Battalion's mortars could be brought into use. Shortly the mortars began to fall on the enemy line and the defenders were suitably subdued. However ammunition was now in short supply and soon exhausted. Lieutenant Colonel Smyth soon realised the problem and asked for further reinforcements. For some reason Brigadier Hackett's H.Q. limited him to one company.

With two rifle companies closed up on each other, he chose Captain Queripel's "A" Company at the rear and furthest from the enemy. Queripel was to make a base around the pumping station north of the main road, enabling the road to Arnhem to be kept open. "A" Company, under the command of Captain Queripel attempted to attack the enemy left flank, but they also encountered heavy resistance and were forced to withdraw with heavy casualties. Close fighting continued for several hours, often hand-to-hand in the woods. On the whole the 10th did not suffer as badly as the 156th, but the Battalion was ordered to withdraw and save its strength. The 10th were able to withdraw under cover of smoke. The rearguard platoon suffered losses, with several men being cut off and taken prisoner.

As they withdrew they came under heavy cross-fire from German troops dug into positions in the woods. Lieutenant Clarke recalled a vivid moment in the morning's battle – of Lionel Queripel sauntering across the fire-swept road, pipe in mouth, to give a laconic report on "A" Company to Colonel Smyth. At this very moment, the Signals Officer himself had been receiving a farewell message from Peter Ware, whose "B" Company positions were being overrun by the enemy armour. Food and ammunition were both in short supply. Although they were backed up by mortars and light artillery, they were attacking a line numerically greater and with stronger fire power. It soon became obvious that they would not be strong enough to continue towards Arnhem in this direction. The only side which was at present free was the main railway line to the south. There was little alternative but to withdraw the remains of the Brigade across the railway. Then they would have to move east to join the remainder of the Division at Oosterbeek. Brigadier Hackett received orders to withdraw 10th and 156 Battalions to the south of the railway and to try to advance along the Heelsum-Arnhem road.

So soon after 1500 hours they started withdrawing towards the Wolfheze level crossing and tunnel beneath, before retreating to the south across the Ede-Arnhem railway line. The idea was to move 10 Para back first, to capture the level crossing, through which the withdrawing units could pass. This was in spite of the threat that the Germans pressing from the west might arrive there ahead of them.

No. 10 Para had been given one of the hardest and least enviable tasks involving disengagement and withdrawal while in close contact with the enemy. The line of retreat was across the proposed landing zone of the Polish gliders, and was being defended by 7 K.O.S.B. The Germans meanwhile had moved west along the line of the Amsterdam road and were based to the north of 4th Brigades area of operation. They were by now covering the landing zone thus hampering 10 Para's efforts to reach Wolfheze. Their advances that afternoon were placing 4 Para's plans in jeopardy. Three battle groups, numbering 6–7 battalions were advancing in a three-pronged move. The centre group's objective was Wolfheze, which was vital to 4 Para because this was the only available place where they could get their motorised transport across the railway cutting.

Captain Queripel

A decision had been made in England to postpone the drop of the Polish Para Brigade south of Arnhem again due to the poor weather conditions. This was a huge blow to the British forces. But a further part of this Brigade was flown in. Twenty-eight out of 35 Horsa gliders reached the landing zone. A squadron of Messerschmidts hit many of the machines, and anti-aircraft fire caught others. Gliders, many on fire, crash-landed on the field or ploughed into trees. So at around 1600 hours while 10 Para tried to withdraw across open fields, gliders of the 1st Polish Brigade began to swoop down between the Ede-Arnhem road and railway. They landed in the middle of 10 Para's retreat and the advancing Germans. As they crossed the open ground German armoured vehicles and infantry had appeared out of the woodland behind them and opened fire. Understandably the Poles could not make out which were friends and which were enemy, so fired indiscriminately, causing casualties on both sides. There was general confusion, and many acts of bravery ensued. Under heavy fire, some men raced in to try and help the Poles unload jeeps and anti-tank guns from the gliders, others helped the wounded to safety. However only two of the anti-tank guns were recovered, one of which was taken by an officer of the 10th Battalion. A signal had been sent from Divisional H.Q. on Tuesday morning requesting that the Drop Zone for the gliders be altered but this signal never arrived.

It was then agonising to watch supplies being dropped behind the German lines. One hundred and sixty-five aircraft left England to resupply 1st Airborne Division. Thirteen planes were lost and five dropped their panniers. The remaining 147 planes flying at 900 feet and in loose formation dropped 390 tons of ammunition, food and medical supplies which were so desperately needed. Unfortunately most of it went to the Germans, who distributed it to the Dutch population of Arnhem. Only an estimated 31 tons were retrieved. Of the 150 planes which returned to England, 97 had been hit by flak. One hundred men were lost, of whom 52 were killed.

There was then quite a scramble to reach the safety of the woodland to the south, resulting in some of the glider loads having to be abandoned. As they retreated 10 Para, together with some of the Polish soldiers, returned fire along with some of the brigade defence units. They came under heavy fire before they reached Wolfheze and in the village itself many men were killed and wounded. The enemy was the 16th SS Grenadier Depot and Reserve Battalion. In fact the Germans who faced the 10th and 156th received the highest casualty rate of any unit during the whole nine-day battle.

What remained of "A" Company, under Captain Queripel, was dropped off in a small wood some 500 metres north-east of the crossing to hold off German attacks coming across the landing zone. The remainder of the Brigade found the village and level crossing clear of the enemy and set up for the night. No. 7 K.O.S.B. also withdrew south, leaving its "B" Company occupying a defensive position half a mile to the east of "A" Company, 10 Para. No. 156 Para also reached the railway line and joined up with 10th Para, which consisted by now of only 100 all ranks out of the 500 men that had arrived the previous day.

A BRAVE LAST STAND

Tuesday the 19th had not been a good day for the 1st Airborne Division. Virtually everything that could go wrong had gone wrong. The Polish troops had landed in a German attack, cargo supplies had gone astray, and battalions were unable to break through to the bridge at Arnhem. In addition there were numerous casualties, pushing the Division towards final destruction. It became a sleepless night for the remains of 4 Parachute Brigade, with constant enemy shell-fire and mortars. Food and ammunition were in short supply. They were still some 2,000 metres from Oosterbeek, where the rest of the Division were encamped. The two companies who were already under strength did not survive the night. Half a mile to the east of Wolfheze the Brigade found a small drainage tunnel running beneath the railway line. This was only just large enough for a jeep to negotiate. The slow process of moving all the Brigade's vehicles began.

The railway embankment had proved a barrier for vehicles, and as the Germans possessed the only crossing point the Brigade could be cut off. Hackett felt he had to withdraw south of the railway line. Thus the 10th began to withdraw. Their route led across fields in the direction of Johannahoeve Farm and to its west. This created an easy target for the enemy. This created havoc, and it was during the withdrawal that Captain Queripel won his V.C., giving his life to save others.

No. 10 Para held out until the early hours, and the few remaining survivors were despatched by Captain Queripel, who remained in position until the end to cover them. During the afternoon his Company had been advancing along a main road towards Arnhem when they came under heavy machine-gun fire. He had been ordered to take some men from "A" Company and two other battalions and defend a small area of woodland, north-east of Wolfheze, to hold off the Germans following the Brigade withdrawal. This area was vital to the defence and came under heavy attack from the Germans. They were forced to fight off repeated attacks throughout the day and into the night. Captain Queripel reorganised his troops, which meant crossing and recrossing the road while under intense fire. While carrying a wounded sergeant to the regimental aid post Queripel was himself hit. Although wounded in the face and arms, he led an attack on the machine-gun crew, killing them all and capturing two machine-guns and an anti-tank gun. This had been taken from the British. Later in the day he received further wounds in both his arms but continued to encourage his men in the face of fierce resistance.

He was cut off with a small group of men, and they took up position in a nearby ditch. Mortars and "Spandaus" kept firing at them, making the position untenable. The paratroopers faced horrendous firepower, especially from the Spandau Machine-Gun, otherwise known as the MG 34. Bursts of fire were constant mainly between knee and hip height. The enemy seemed to have vast supplies of ammunition, while the paratroopers were only armed with what they could carry. In spite of his bad wounds he continued to encourage the men to defend with hand grenades, pistols and the few remaining rifles. He realised that they would have to withdraw. Despite protests from his men, Queripel ordered them to leave, while he covered them with his automatic pistol, and a few remaining hand grenades. One of the men, J. L. Jevans later recalled Captain Queripel shouting "Colour Sergeant get these men out!" Sergeant Joe Sunley recalls the situation well:

> Late in the afternoon I was approaching Wolfheze with several men of the 10th under Captain Lionel Queripel. We came under heavy machine-gun fire from tanks. We took cover in a shell-hole near the railway embankment at the foot of a tree. We had only small arms and grenades. As the German armour came nearer, Captain Queripel said "Sgt. Sunley

get the men back"; and on my orders they left. I remained, but the Captain told me that the order included me as well. I said, "Sir, if you stay, I stay", but he was adamant saying "that's an order Sgt. Sunley" and I had to leave him, and that was the last I saw of him. He stayed there and held back the German advance so that our troops could get back over the railway. He died there fighting to the end. Capt. Queripel was magnificent. He knew that we would be overrun and told us to retreat. When he died, the world lost a valiant soldier, an officer and a gentleman.

Others who were with him included Sergeant Shand, B. Pick and N. Masters. This saved their lives, and it was the last time anyone saw him. It was only when other Germans moved in that Queripel was killed. He died from his wounds later that day. He was officially reported as wounded and missing. It was believed that he had been captured, and it was not until some time later that it was established that he had been killed at the Wolfheze crossing.

The Battalion Roll of the 10th Battalion, The Parachute Regiment – Arnhem 1944 – lists every man. The entry for Lionel Queripel states: "Wounded or died near Wolfheze during the retreat from the Leeren Doedel area 19.9.44 age 24".

Ton Schemkes, who was a 13-year-old at the time, has spent his life researching the Battle, especially the 4th Brigade's movements. He believes that Lionel fought his last action near the pumping station. This was on the north side of the Amsterdamseweg (Arnhem-Ede road). Lionel was in slit trenches south of this road. He tells me that at about 7 a.m. the first platoons, 4 and 5 of "A" Company reached the north side of the road, and 3 Platoon the south side. Opposite the Waterworks 3 Platoon crossed the road and "A" Company occupied the Waterworks area. The other companies of the 10th arrived in the woods at the south side of the main road. Many German attacks came in from three sides on the north side, with tanks, machine-guns, infantry etc. From about 1200 hours until 1400 hours, "A" Company was under extreme heavy attacks and Captain Queripel had his hands full inspiring his men. Many times he crossed the main road to inform Lieutenant Colonel Smyth and to receive new instructions.

He apparently also came into the civilians' underground shelter to relax and bring cigarettes and chocolate. He showed the civilians how to recognise the difference between the English and German gunfire. Years after the war these civilians recognised this friendly officer from a photo in a book as Captain Queripel.

A Private who was with them recalls:

> … One of the anti-tank guns was captured by the enemy. It had caused a great deal of trouble, as it was being protected by two Spandau Machine Guns. Captain Queripel gathered six of us and we went down the side of the road to knock it out. Capt. Queripel individually knocked the two enemy machine guns out by hand grenades and we recaptured the anti-tank gun. It was evident that our position was becoming impossible to hold. We were given orders to start to withdraw, but it was difficult to cross the road to get into the woods at the other side. So we had to throw smoke bombs onto the road. Although the enemy was shooting in the smoke, no-one was hit.
>
> After crossing the road we found we were fighting a rearguard action. Fighting our way through the woods we were being attacked on three sides. With Capt. Queripel we took up positions in two trenches. Here we were about 12 of us. We were under very heavy fire and we heard and saw the Germans walking between the trees in the wood. Capt. Queripel inspired us to keep fighting.
>
> With Capt. Queripel we were five of us in this trench. One German stick bomb landed in our trench and the Captain hurled it back at the enemy. It exploded and we heard a terrible cry. Capt. Queripel realised the terrible position we were in, and he decided that we should try and escape, leaving him to cover us as we left those slit trenches. He at first ordered us to

leave, but we refused to leave him, but then he gave us a direct order and we had to obey it. The last we saw of him by looking quickly back over our shoulder, he was throwing grenades at the enemy. Most of us did get through the woods in the end and carried on fighting to the end of the Battle.

Dr. Adrian Groeneweg of the Airborne Museum, Hartenstein is not sure where Lionel was killed. He always understood it was east of the pumping station on Amsterdamseweg. He says that there are no reliable eye-witness accounts available, apart from a list made up by the Red Cross Dutchmen who collected the bodies along Amsterdamseweg whom they buried at Renkum. The list does not mention the exact places where the bodies were found, but Captain Queripel is among them.

Harry Dicken, who was with Battalion H.Q. Intelligence Section favours the pumping station theory, and says it would be unlikely that Lionel, wounded as he was, could have made it to Wolfheze.

The wounded sergeant helped by Captain Queripel was Frank Fitzpatrick. When his machine-gun section had been attacked by a Panzer tank he was wounded in the neck and shoulder and left for dead. Unfortunately the three men who saved his life all ultimately lost theirs. Captain Queripel was first. Captain Drayson, Medical Officer was killed by a grenade while looking after the wounded. This grenade caused further wounds to Sergeant Fitzpatrick. The third, a medical sergeant died in 1963. Sergeant Fitzpatrick took morphine tablets during his capture and transfer to P.O.W. Camp at Fallingbostel. Sergeant Springford was wounded with Captain Queripel, but eventually reached the same P.O.W. Camp.

The situation was now very critical. Major General Urquhart decided on the night of 19/20 September to withdraw Hackett's Brigade and bring it into the Oosterbeek perimeter. Attempts to reach Lieutenant Colonel Frost at the bridge in Arnhem were abandoned. The Germans were still unaware that they were at last on the run and only just about able to maintain any cohesion. Hackett's 10th Battalion now only had 250 men, and 156th had 270. Urquhart planned to make a stand, pull in all the troops, and hold on until XXX Corps arrived.

The 156 Para set off at first light in order to make a right-flank attack on the Wolfheze-Oosterbeek road. However they were soon under heavy fire and suffered many casualties. "B" Company of 7th K.O.S.B. arrived safely at Wolfheze to find no British troops, so moved towards the river. However they were soon surrounded by the enemy. They were ordered to surrender, with some of 156 Battalion taking flight into the woods. The 4th Parachute Brigade had been virtually wiped out. At around 0600 on 20 September, Shan Hackett's much depleted battalions headed for the divisional perimeter. He ordered 10th Para to move to the east thus bypassing the enemy, leaving 156 Battalion engaged with the enemy.

The 10th Battalion now took the lead from the 156th Battalion and started to move south-east to towards the divisional perimeter. They sped through the woods, even though they were only 70 men in strength, facing machine-guns and snipers on route. They then marched down the road to Divisional Headquarters. They were ordered to take several houses, and many of the remaining officers and men died defending these, while others were taken prisoner. A further group was still with the 4th Brigade fighting at close quarters. In the afternoon Shan Hackett decided to break out. It was shortly before 7 p.m. that he and seven officers and 60 men reached Divisional Headquarters.

The other two Battalions also withdrew. "A" Company of 7 KOSB were surrounded and taken prisoner. No. 1 Platoon managed to escape through the woods, but were captured the following morning. The 10th Para Battalion fought their way through the woods on Wednesday and marched into the perimeter under their wounded C.O., Lieutenant Colonel Kenneth Smyth. There were just 70 men. After a rest at the Hartenstein Hotel they were ordered to move out and hold a road junction at an outer defensive point on the eastern perimeter. An assault led by Captain Peter Clegg cleared the Germans out, enabling 10th Battalion to take over four houses on the main road.

Throughout the next day there were constant attacks on the houses, and two of them were set on fire. The C.O. was wounded fatally and also Major Peter Warr. In the other two houses, the survivors continued fighting for another day. All the officers were killed or wounded. After dawn the houses were attacked again. The position was hopeless and the platoon had to pull back having lost half its numbers. During that day, Thursday 21 September, around 3,600 survivors of the 1st Airborne Division held out in the woods and buildings around Oosterbeek intending to hold a bridgehead across the Rhine, while waiting for XXX Corps to arrive. They were attacked throughout the day. Also on 21st the Polish 1st Independent Parachute Brigade landed in the afternoon, after two days delay due to the weather. Their Drop Zone was south of the Rhine, near the village of Driel.

On Friday 22 the Germans shelled and mortared the Airborne positions heavily. That evening, XXX Corps's tanks began to arrive on the south bank of the Rhine opposite the bridgehead still held by the 1st Airborne Division at Arnhem, but despite repeated attempts over the next three days, it proved impossible to reinforce their positions. By the end of the battle the Germans had deployed some 110 artillery pieces around Oosterbeek. The survivors of 1st Airborne were now outnumbered by a ratio of 4:1. The Germans were concerned that the Poles might attempt to capture the bridge at Arnhem, so withdrew 2400 troops from Oosterbeek. They moved south and made attacks during the day at Driel.

On the night of Sunday 24 an attempt was made to try and reinforce the 1st Airborne Division with the 4th Battalion the Dorsetshire Regiment. Unfortunately they landed among the Germans who were prepared. Two companies were able to cross the river, but of the 315 men who crossed, only 75 reached Oosterbeek. The remainder were captured, and so the decision was taken to withdraw the 1st Airborne Division. At dawn the Division received orders to withdraw across the Rhine that night. The Germans made it as difficult as possible, breaking through a thin front line. The attack met more resistance as it moved into the British lines. It was finally broken up under heavy bombardment from the 64th Medium Regiment.

On the night of Monday 25 September the survivors from the units in the Oosterbeek perimeter were brought back across the Rhine in bad weather. British and Canadian engineer units ferried them across, covered by the Polish 3rd Parachute Battalion. This happened under cover of darkness and 2000 were ferried to safety. By early next day 2,398 survivors had been withdrawn, leaving 300 men to surrender on the north bank because the Germans prevented their rescue. Of the approximately 10,600 men of 1st Airborne Division and other units that had fought north of the Rhine, 1,485 had been killed and 6,414 were taken prisoner, of whom around one third were wounded. Only 136 men of 4 Para Brigade returned. A total of 582 men of 10th Battalion went in, 92 died, 86 evacuated and 404 missing. In the nine days of Operation Market Garden airborne and ground forces losses amounted to more than 17,000, of which over 13,000 were British.

The main problems had included the mistake of having the landings of 1st Airborne Division spread over a number of days. There were too few aircraft to carry the whole Army. Bad weather and the decision to make only three daily "lifts" hindered the effective force that the Allies were able to bring to bear on the ground. Also the distance between drop zones and the bridges meant the element of surprise was lost and large numbers of troops were unable to reach their objectives, giving the Germans valuable time to reinforce their positions. Delays in capturing some of the key bridges along the relief route had serious consequences for the British and Polish paratroopers in Arnhem. The failure to make use of intelligence on the German forces was also a major factor. Intelligence reports were largely ignored, as it was assumed that the reports were inaccurate or that the various German units were no longer combat effective. There had also been problems with who should take charge of the division and its deployment. To make matters worse, the paratroopers at Arnhem found their radios would not work, and with communication with the forces outside the town almost impossible, all effective control over the engagement was lost.

THE VICTORIA CROSS

Major Brammall's book *"The Tenth" A Record of Service of the 10th Battalion the Parachute Regiment 1942–1945* has an extract written by Sir John Hackett, 21 years after the battle. It tells how he was taken by jeep to St. Elizabeth's Hospital after he was seriously wounded on 23 September. He had been wounded for the second time while walking back from one of his visits of inspection to his units. He had been hit by splinters from a mortar bomb in the left thigh and stomach. He had decided it was a good idea to pretend to be a private soldier in order to disguise his rank in the hospital.

> Then I heard that 'Kidney' Smyth was in a room nearby. He was badly hurt, they said, and had no chance of survival. He was paralysed from the waist down, and growing weaker daily, but was still clear in his mind and in good heart.
>
> I had to be with Kenneth for several important reasons. One was that he was one of my Battalion Commanders and a friend. Another was that someone had to put together citations for richly deserved awards, and as the Battalion had been virtually destroyed I should have to do it myself. Only Ken Smyth could now help me and I had to have his story before he died.
>
> I therefore confessed to the Germans that I had been fooling them all the time and was not, in fact, a private soldier, as I had pretended, but a Major. I explained that I had concealed my rank in fear, and now wished to be treated like an officer and put alongside Col. Smyth.
>
> For several days now, until this calm and quiet man died, I spent my time with him getting his story and writing up the citations. All this I put together and when it was complete wrote a little letter to the Divisional Commander to accompany it. Sometime later the package was got out of the country through the Dutch underground and fetched up in due course at Division.
>
> It is perhaps also worth recalling what happened to the citations. Months later, when I eventually got back to England, I enquired about them. They had been received but, with regret, it had been impossible to put them in as recommendations for awards because they were not entered upon the correct Army form. So I had to write them out again in the accepted manner.

N. Masters of "A" Company claims that he and Sergeant Shand gave the citation for Lionel Queripel's award, and they later learned that he had been awarded the V.C. He described Lionel as having led them during the battle with "great gallantry".

Ton Schemkes tells me that the men who recommended Lionel for the Victoria Cross were: Jimmy Jones, Busty Bentley, Gurka Moate, Dave Hill, Taffy Davis, and Paddy Brown.

Christian H. Thoma, whose main interest is the NW European theatre wonders how the V.C. recommendation was made:

> As far as I am aware, VCs are only awarded when there is a recommendation by a senior officer. As the senior officer, Major Anson was either killed or injured when the Captain's action took place, I am hard pressed to determine who would have made the recommendation. Surely it wasn't the Germans!
>
> Because the few remaining members of his battalion were ordered to withdraw, leaving him behind to provide cover, it is surely impossible to know what exactly happened soon after. For instance, after being severely wounded, he may have run out of ammunition and surrendered. In the event, we know that he wasn't taken prisoner and sent to hospital as his body was later found by the Dutch, Therefore either he died fighting or perhaps the Germans shot him after he surrendered.

Ton Schemkes says that after leaving him nobody knows what happened to this brave officer, except his grave was found at the General Cemetery at Renkum after the war. If he was killed in action his field grave must have been in or near the slit trench.

> In my opinion, in the last moment he was very heavily wounded, was taken prisoner and taken into a German Aid Post and/or Hospital near Renkum and died there. In Renkum there was a Health-Resort Hospital called 'Oranje Nassau Oord' occupied by the Germans and used as a hospital. Everyone who possibly knows about the deaths and burials, German or Dutch, have passed away.

The Archivist at the Airborne Forces Museum, Aldershot believes that Lionel was captured by the Germans, as his body was taken to Renkum, while others found in the area were taken the other way. He believes Lionel fought his last action at Wolfheze, but from the limited evidence available now, I believe that Lionel died defending his position, and was not captured, and that he died near the railway crossing at Wolfheze.

From the wording of the citation I would suggest that the Victoria Cross was awarded for the bravery leading up to the withdrawal, and the cover provided to enable his colleagues to escape. He would have known that his own position was hopeless, but was saving the lives of his men.

When Major R.E. Boone of 1st Airborne wrote to Colonel L. H. Queripel, D.S.O. about his son, he was writing on behalf of the whole Battalion:

> Lionel joined at Arnhem on Sept. 18th, and put up a truly remarkable performance. His bravery and devotion to duty were outstanding. His Company Commander was shot down some distance away, and Lionel had taken over the Company. He was last seen in a bomb crater at dusk on September 19 to the west of Arnhem. He had by then been wounded in the face and arms, and covered the retreat of some 8 men who were with him. He had also rescued a wounded sergeant under fire and had picked up and thrown back a live grenade that had been thrown into the crater. He has always been one of our most popular and likeable officers, and we are all very proud of him.

His Citation for the Victoria Cross was in the Supplement to the *London Gazette* and is dated Thursday 1 February 1945, Numb.36917, p.669:

> The King has been graciously pleased to approve the award of the VICTORIA CROSS to:-
> Captain Lionel Ernest Queripel (108181), The Royal Sussex Regiment (1st Airborne Division) (Dorchester).
> In Holland on the 19th September, 1944, Captain Queripel was acting as Company Commander of a composite Company composed of three Parachute Battalions.
> At 14.00 hours on that day, his Company was advancing along a main road which ran on an embankment towards Arnhem. The advance was conducted under continuous medium machine-gun fire which, at one period, became so heavy that the Company became split up on either side of the road and suffered considerable losses. Captain Queripel at once proceeded to reorganize his force, crossing and recrossing the road while doing so, under extremely heavy and accurate fire. During this period he carried a wounded Sergeant to the Regimental Aid Post under fire and was himself wounded in the face.
> Having reorganized his force, Captain Queripel personally led a party of men against the strong point holding up the advance. This strong point consisted of a captured British anti-tank gun and two machine guns. Despite the extremely heavy fire directed at him, Captain Queripel succeeded in killing the crews of the machine-guns and recapturing the anti-tank gun. As a result of this the advance was able to continue.

Later in the same day, Captain Queripel found himself cut off with a small party of men and took up a position in a ditch. By this time he had received further wounds in both arms. Regardless of his wounds and of the very heavy mortar and spandau fire, he continued to inspire his men to resist with hand grenades, pistols and the few remaining rifles.

As, however, the enemy pressure increased, Captain Queripel decided that it was impossible to hold the position any longer and ordered his men to withdraw. Despite their protests, he insisted on remaining behind to cover their withdrawal with his automatic pistol and a few remaining hand grenades. This is the last occasion on which he was seen.

During the whole period of nine hours of confused and bitter fighting Captain Queripel displayed the highest standard of gallantry under most difficult and trying circumstances. His courage, leadership and devotion to duty were magnificent, and an inspiration to all. This officer is officially reported to be wounded and missing.

This was the third V.C. won at Arnhem, the 126th of the war and the 46th awarded to the Army. An Army despatch rider came to Tunbridge Wells to tell Lionel Queripel's father that his son had won the V.C. At that time his mother described him as "just an ordinary boy". His father commented that "My son's battalion was very badly cut up. Only 80 men came back, and not a single officer. It seems to be a foregone conclusion that our family goes into the Army".

The Dutch Red Cross would have recovered all the bodies in October 1944, and Lionel would have been temporarily buried in Renkum Civil Cemetery. On 1 February 1945, the date of his citation, he was officially reported "wounded and missing". The Dutch Red Cross made a list of all the bodies collected. The list does not mention the exact places where the bodies were found, but Captain Queripel is among them. His death was not confirmed until 4 April 1945, when the Canadians finally liberated Arnhem. Canadian and British forces had crossed the Rhine east of Arnhem Bridge to liberate the northern part of Holland. The Graves Registration units of 2nd British Army started to locate the field graves of all the men who had been killed, died of wounds, or been reported as "missing believed killed". They were then to bring them all to a central location. The Report form was very detailed and gave such details as Army Number, Rank, Name, Cemetery or place of burial, plot, row and grave numbers. Also height, build, colour of hair, fingers and hands, nature of wound, identity disc, documents or other effects on the body, clothing, boots, equipment and general remarks. A map reference of where the body was found was often added, and the place of burial. The form was signed by the officer conducting the exhumation.

The Arnhem Oosterbeek exhumations did not start until a year after the original burial and in some cases over two years. Work began three days after the liberation of Arnhem, on 20 April 1945, by a Graves Registration Unit led by Captain J. T. Long. A field was given on perpetual loan by the Netherlands Government. It had been identified as a suitable site to accommodate up to 2,000 graves by Lieutenant Colonel Stott on 4–6 June, and the site was levelled by 25 June. This became the Arnhem Oosterbeek War Cemetery, administered by the Imperial (now Commonwealth) War Graves Commission. It is more commonly referred to as The Airborne Cemetery. It was consecrated on 25 September 1945 in the presence of British military representatives and Dutch personnel. Information about the many hundreds of missing men was very sketchy, owing to the fact that so few men survived the battle. It took some months before the names of prisoners taken by the Germans were known. It was not until April and May 1945 when survivors of the prison camps returned, that full information could be obtained and verified. By 20 July 1945 some 1,450 graves had been located and marked.

Those who returned to Oosterbeek in the summer of 1945 were overwhelmed by the situation they found. The devastation of their village was immense, but they had no time to dwell on it. They started to build some basic housing and clearing rubble. They were eternally grateful for their freedom. In September 1945 some 1,200 children of Oosterbeek attended the cemetery for the first time. At that time it was just small heaps of sand with white iron crosses. They all held a bunch

Oosterbeek Cemetery

of flowers, and listened to "Abide with me". They placed the flowers on the graves, and have done ever since at an annual remembrance.

In a letter from Major R. E. Boone to Lieutenant Baker dated 24 June 1945 Lionel was still listed as missing. Lionel was not officially reported dead until his obituary appeared in *The Times* of Friday 6 July 1945. Various articles suggest that he was captured by the Germans and died in captivity, but his sister Rose denies this, and there is no evidence to suggest that this was the case.

Lionel's Grave

So Lionel was buried in Arnhem Oosterbeek War Cemetery on 24 August 1945. His grave is one of 1763 Allied soldiers, sailors and airmen who lost their lives during the period Sept. 1944–April 1945 as a result of hostilities in the area. The cemetery is in the northern suburbs of Oosterbeek, four miles west of Arnhem on the road to Wageningen. The entrance to the cemetery is a short distance along this road opposite the town cemetery. Lionel is buried in Plot V, Row D, Grave 8.

The Victoria Cross was presented by King George V1 to Colonel and Mrs Queripel at Buckingham Palace on Tuesday 18 December 1945 in a ceremony at 11.00 a.m. Seven other awards of the Victoria Cross were also made to next of kin on that day, including Mr and Mrs Tom Brunt of Paddock Wood, who received the award for their son, Captain John Brunt who was killed in Italy.

Sergeant L. A. Read paid tribute to the memory of Lionel Queripel in a letter:

Capt. Queripel V.C., the only V.C. in the Battalion, was my platoon officer back in 1940 with the Royal Sussex. He was one of the finest men I was privileged to serve under – always the last officer to return to his mess. His first thought was for his men. He was not familiar but greatly respected. One hears of V.C.s being given for impulsive bravery, but not Captain Queripel. Anyone who knew him would have expected him to do just what he did. I believe he came from a military family – they should be proud of him.

Another officer described Lionel as "determined – rather dour, but with a quiet wit which soon endeared him to all of us. There was no stopping him once he had decided to do something".

B. Pick described Lionel as "a well-made man, strong and fit and very considerate, who never seemed to lose his temper. He was a soldier you could depend on. If anyone was getting behind on a route march he would help carry their guns or ammo".

Sergeant Tex Banwell remarked:

By all accounts no V.C. was better earned. I am certain that as long as there is an A Company 10th Battalion Parachute Regiment man alive, he will forever be in their thoughts. An Officer and a Gentleman".

On Wednesday, 29 June 1972, Lionel's mother, Mrs Sybil Queripel, accompanied by her two daughters, presented the family collection of medals including her son's V.C. in trust to The Parachute Regiment for the future. He was also entitled to the 1939–45 Star, Africa Star, Italy Star, France and Germany Star, Defence Medal and the 1939–45 War Medal. They were held by the Airborne Forces Museum in Aldershot, although of course the originals were not on display. The other medals on display in a case belong to Captain W. Watson, Colonel A. E. Queripel C.B., Lieutenant Commander C. M. Queripel, and Lionel's father Colonel L. H. Queripel, C.M.G., D.S.O. They have since been moved to the new Imperial War Museum, Duxford.

The reverse of Lionel's V.C. is engraved as follows:

CAPTAIN LIONEL ERNEST QUERIPEL
R.SUSSEX R. (1 AIRBORNE DIVISION)
19th
SEPTEMBER
1944

WE WILL REMEMBER HIM

There are a number of memorials etc. around the country in honour of Lionel, his schools and regiments. There is a Durnford School War Memorial window in St. George's Parish Church, Langton Matravers, Dorset. This was dedicated on 18 May 1974.

* * * * *

At Marlborough College, like all Old Boys who died in the Second World War, Lionel's name appears in two places in the Memorial Hall, which was opened in 1925 to honour the College's war dead. His name is carved – together with those of some 240 others on the main western entrance to the Hall, over which is inscribed the single, gilded word: "REMEMBER".

In addition there is a Book of Remembrance kept in a locked cupboard in the Hall in which there is a very short entry for each old boy killed in the Second World War. The entries are very terse, limited to little more than name, dates at the College, and date killed.

On Saturday 8 October 2005, a Memorial Plaque in honour of Old Marlburians who were awarded The Victoria Cross, The George Cross or The Albert Medal was unveiled. This was carried out by Lieutenant Colonel E. C. T. Wilson V.C. in the West Lobby of the Memorial Hall. The plaque is about 10ft high and 4ft wide. It includes 15 names in total, including 13 V.C. holders in chronological order.

* * * * *

The 10th Battalion, The Parachute Regiment are remembered at The Imperial War Museum at Duxford. The Museum holds Lionel's medals, as well as the Queripel family medals.

* * * * *

In Somerby each September there is an Arnhem Service and Parade and in All Saints Church there is an Arnhem Memorial Window. To the left of the Memorial Window is another plaque:

> In Proud Memory
> Of the Officers and Men
> Of The
> 10th Battalion Parachute
> Regiment
> Who were trained in this
> Area and gave their lives
> For their Country
> In September 1944 at
> ARNHEM
> Their Comrades place this tablet here

In addition, in the church is a kneeler to Lionel, with the wording "Captain L E Queripel V.C. 10th Battalion" on one end on a brass plaque on wood. The red kneeler simply has The Parachute Regiment crest in the middle.

The Queripel Kneeler, All Saints Church, Somerby

There is also a plaque in the Village Hall. The plaque was made by John Daniels, a Deputy Keeper at Leicester Museum and unveiled by the Lord Lieutenant, Colonel Sir Robert Martin.

IN THIS HALL IN SEPTEMBER 1944
THE 10th BATTALION THE PARACHUTE REGIMENT
WAS BRIEFED FOR THE ARNHEM LANDING
FROM WHICH SO MANY DID NOT RETURN.

REMEMBER FOR GOOD, O GOD,
ALL PAST AND PRESENT MEMBERS OF THIS REGIMENT.

A TRIBUTE FROM THE LEICESTER BRANCH
OF THE 1940 DUNKIRK VETERANS ASSOCIATION
AND THEIR FRIENDS. 1972.

AT THE GOING DOWN OF THE SUN
AND IN THE MORNING
WE WILL REMEMBER THEM.

Village Hall Plaque, Somerby

Also in the Village Hall is a stone tablet on the ground which says:

To Commemorate
The 50th Anniversary of
The formation of
The 10th Battalion
The Parachute Regiment
1942–1992

* * * * *

Early in November 1988 a function was held at the Royal British Legion, Main Street, Egremont in Cumbria to honour the fact that the Royal British Legion there had connections with two V.C.s including Lionel. (The other was Private Harry Christian who lived nearby and is buried in Egremont Cemetery). The local padre at Egremont was Rev. Ray Bowers, who attended with Mrs Bowers. The next man to follow Lionel out of the aircraft at Arnhem was Ray Bowers, who was Branch Chaplain of the Cumbria Branch of the Royal British Legion. The Cumbria Branch of The Parachute Regiment Association use the club for their meetings.

A photo of Lionel and an extract from his citation appear in a glass frame on the wall, and there is a replica Victoria Cross.

* * * * *

In June 1956, the wardens of the Dyers' Company suggested that the Worshipful Company associate itself with the 10th Battalion, The Parachute Regiment. The offer was officially accepted on 27 June 1957.

Since then the Dyers' Company has made an annual Christmas gift of £25 to battalion funds and has made a number of most generous donations for specific purposes. These included a portrait of Captain Lionel Queripel V.C. for the Officers Mess. This was presented on 4 May 1960 at a dinner in the Officers Mess. The replica of his V.C. and the citation were later presented to the unit by Mrs Queripel, and were hung in the mess, next to the picture of her son.

* * * * *

At a meeting of the Tunbridge Wells Council on Wednesday 7 February 1945, the Mayor Alderman C. E. Westbrook said that he was sure the Council would wish him to refer to the highest military award of the Victoria Cross to Captain Lionel Ernest Queripel. As they all knew, Captain Queripel was a member of a most esteemed local family and it was deeply regretted that the officer had been posted wounded and missing. The Mayor felt he was sure that it was the unanimous wish of the Council, that an expression of admiration and congratulations should be extended to Captain Queripel, in recognition of outstanding bravery in action and to Colonel and Mrs Queripel, whose son had so bravely upheld the military tradition of the family and brought great honour to the town in which they resided. The Mayor was also sure that they would wish to express to Colonel and Mrs Queripel the sincere hope that they might still receive good news of the safety of their son.

When the Courier printed the Council minutes about Captain Queripel they ended with the following tribute by Herbert Hope Campbell:

> We who are the burghers of your native town
> Hail you today, with your illustrious name
> Your knightly valour wins for you renown
> We glory in your courage and your fame
> May we be worthy of your daring deed
> Performed by you in England's hour of need.

Lionel's name was only added to the Tunbridge Wells War Memorial in 2005. An appeal for names to go on the Memorial went out on 31 May 1946. Although Lionel's death was confirmed on 4 April 1945, his sister Rose says "our parents never had any knowledge of an appeal for names. I had no idea there were names on the memorial until 2004, when I was told that Lionel's name was missing. I understand that there are many more missing likewise".

Lieutenant Colonel John Powell from Groombridge wrote a letter to the Kent and Sussex Courier, which appeared on 15 October 2004. Having visited Oosterbeek cemetery, he learned from the Book of Remembrance that Lionel came from Tunbridge Wells. This led him to investigate why his name was not on the War Memorial. "Inquiries with both the Commonwealth and War Graves Commission and The Royal Sussex Regiment Association confirm that his name is not recorded on any memorial in the U.K. save for the Royal Sussex Regiment Book of Remembrance in Chichester Cathedral". Further inquiries with Tunbridge Wells Town Hall confirmed that no application was made to have his name included.

Subsequently as a result of this, a commemorative plaque was added on Thursday, 24 February 2005. A special feature appeared in the Courier on 8 July 2005. John Powell had received numerous responses from readers, and this put him in touch with Rose, Lionel's sister. He then approached Tunbridge Wells Borough Council and the Royal British Legion who responded quickly.

Lionel's Name added to the Tunbridge Wells War Memorial

* * * * *

The Victor Comic No.83, September 22 1962 had a front and back cover comic strip entitled "The Courage of Captain Queripel" as part of their series on V.C.s in full colour.

* * * * *

On the 50th Anniversary of 10th Battalion, The Parachute Regiment, 138 sat down to dinner at The Leicester Moat House, Oadby, on Saturday 11 April 1992. Of the 138, 65 were members of the wartime "Tenth". Guests included Mr and Mrs Robinson – Lionel's sister and her husband.

* * * * *

St. George's Chapel, Chichester Cathedral has been the Memorial Chapel of the Royal Sussex Regiment since 1921. It was rededicated on 11 November 1921. The names of the 1,024 who fell in 1939–45 have been recorded in a Memorial Book beside the altar.

* * * * *

There is a Queripel House at 1 Duke of York's Square in London SW3. It is on the site of the old Duke of Yorks Headquarters, the H.Q. of the 10th Parachute Battalion, T.A. It was developed as an office block when the Duke of York's was sold off. It is now part of a retail and office development completed in 2003. There are now a collection of companies behind the old facade. The name "Queripel House" appears outside. Inside reception there is a plaque on the wall to Lionel, which originally listed his regiment as "The Sussex Regiment". This has now been rectified. In addition there is a full-length memorial window of six panels with Lionel's name and the V.C., pictured with parachutists descending.

256

Window at Queripel House, London

* * * * *

Rose and her husband, Dick attended the Service in Westminster Abbey on 19 May 2003 when H.M. The Queen dedicated a long overdue memorial to all V.C. and George Cross winners. They were among the honoured guests who were invited.

* * * * *

Lionel's sword was originally held by the 4th/5th Royal Sussex, a T.A. regiment, at Hastings, and taken on charge by the T.A. Trust. On 3 July 1966, a Council of Colonels decided to convert the Home Counties Brigade, of which the Royal Sussex Regiment was a part, into a single large regiment – The Queens Regiment – which formally came into being on 31 December 1966. On the formation of the Queens Regiment, the 4th/5th Battalion became a company of the Queens Regiment, T.A. The sword was therefore loaned to the Queens, whose officers carried it on ceremonial parades. In order that

Dick and Rose Robinson at Westminster Abbey

it should be properly identified and honoured the Royal Sussex T.A. Trust in 1988, arranged for it to be engraved with Lionel's name and date and place of his award of the V.C. At the same time a duplicate was also engraved, to be held by the Royal Sussex Regiment Museum in Eastbourne.

His original sword was held by "D" (Queens) Company, The London Regiment, T.A. in Edgware until 2007. It was carried by their officers on ceremonial occasions, but was still officially on loan from the Royal Sussex Regiment. In view of its significance (and value) arrangements were made in 2007 to return it to the Eastbourne Museum, who will pass the duplicate to the London company to carry on parade, as they were happy with this arrangement.

* * * * *

The Royal Sussex Regiment Museum at Eastbourne has a display concerning Lionel's deeds. Up until 2007 the display stated that Lionel died in captivity. After consultations with Rose, Lionel's sister, it was decided to amend the wording as follows:

> Captain Queripel was never again seen alive, but his body was recovered by the Netherlands Red Cross from the scene of the action after the battle and buried with other members of the 10th Parachute Battalion in Renkum Cemetery. His remains now rest in Oosterbeek Commonwealth War Graves Cemetery.

Mrs Rose Robinson and members of the family visited the Museum on 19 September, 2007 to see the new display, together with the author.

* * * * *

On Thursday 26 April 2007, the Mayor of Tunbridge Wells, Councillor Ron Weeden, hosted a road naming ceremony at Barratt Kent's new homes development at Connaught Park, Sandhurst Road, High Brooms, Tunbridge Wells. Barratt Kent approached the Tunbridge Wells Borough Council who suggested the five V.C. names who should be recognised with new road names – including Lionel. The "Queripel Close" sign was unveiled by the Mayor, and Richard Snow, the author who said a few words about Lionel's life.

* * * * *

Plans in Dorset were being put on hold in 2007 to commemorate local heroes. The former Mayor of Dorchester had called for a scroll of honour to honour the county's soldiers to be displayed in the Council Chamber. But in March 2007 members of the Council's Policy Committee put the matter on hold to determine what criteria war heroes needed to meet. Committee members received letters from local residents in support of this, which recognised three V.C. heroes, including Lionel. The matter is due to come back before the town council at a later date.

In June 2007, it was reported that H.R.H. Prince Charles wanted to pay tribute to local war heroes by naming streets after them in his Dorset suburb of Poundbury. The List included V.C. winners (with Lionel) and a trooper who survived the Charge of the Light Brigade.

The Prince, through his Duchy of Cornwall Estate, also hoped to commemorate battles in which the local regiment, affectionately known as the Dorsets, took part. But the tribute turned into a bitter row after the Duchy's suggestions were thrown out by local planners. The Duchy has reluctantly agreed to go back to the drawing board.

The decision has infuriated local veterans who say it is an insult to brave men and women who gave their lives for their country. Members of Dorchester Town Council's Planning Committee preferred instead to have the streets names after farms owned by the Duchy of Cornwall's estate.

* * * * *

Lionel's name is on the V.C. Roll of Honour at the Union Jack Club, Sandell Street, Waterloo, London, SE1 8UJ.

* * * * *

There is also a kneeler in All Saints Garrison Church, Farnborough Road, Aldershot, Hampshire. It is here because the church is the home church of The Parachute Regiment. Lionel's name is in the Book of Remembrance, and the kneeler is Parachute Regiment purple with the regiment's crest in the top middle. Above it on a white plaque attached to wood it states:

In Memory of
Captain Lionel Ernest Queripel V.C.
10th Battalion The Parachute Regiment
Arnhem 19th September 1944

Captain Lionel Queripel

CHAPTER TEN

All for Valour –
The Story of Captain John Henry Cound Brunt 1922–1944

FOREWORD

As a lad growing up, every day was filled with action, for John lived to find out and have fun. He was a sportsman at heart and failure was not to be reckoned with: but challenge and experimentation was the yardstick by which he lived his life. In the School Chapel he attended daily prayers, and Faith through prayer was the reason he attended the early prayer service that the Army Chaplain took every morning. It was on this inner strength that he drew in times of great danger when life and death decisions had to be made. John packed more into his twenty-one years of life than most of us do in a lifetime.

After his death the war poet W. H. Phillips wrote a poem for John with an Epitaph which is reproduced below p.328.

Dorothy Miller, John Brunt's late sister

Captain John Brunt

Dorothy Miller and Family at unveiling of plaque to John Brunt, Priest Weston 15 May 2004

A SOLDIER IS BORN

John Henry Cound Brunt was born on Wednesday 6 December 1922 at the New House, Priest Weston in the sub-district of Chirbury, Salop. The birth was registered on 28 December, and he was baptised on 23 January 1923.

New House, Priest Weston

His father Thomas Henry Brunt was a farmer who was also born in Priest Weston, a tiny village at the base of Corndon Hill, some three miles from Churchstoke. His mother was Nesta Mary Brunt, formerly Cound. His mother's maiden name Cound is French, and she was born in Churchstoke, Montgomeryshire in 1893. She was listed on the 1901 census as Resta Cound. She was the eldest daughter of John and Mary Ann Cound of Churchstoke Hall, Churchstoke. They were both born in 1859 in Montgomeryshire. John was a farmer, born at Mont Kerry and Mary was born at Mont Llanwynog.

Tom Brunt

Nesta Brunt

Nesta served as a Volunteer Auxiliary Nurse during the First World War nursing wounded soldiers on Salisbury Plain. His father Tom joined the Shropshire Light Infantry and spent most of the war based in Aldershot training men how to handle and ride horses. At the beginning of the war there were no tanks, and horses were used to draw wagons for everything. Soldiers on horseback were part of the communications network. Men coming out of the cities such as Manchester and Birmingham had no knowledge of horses. But on the farms, everyone had horses for various purposes and everyone could ride one – there were no buses, cars, or trains! Tom spent some time in Suffolk during the 1914–18 war. He had a Squadron of Yeomanry at Beccles.

It was after the First World War that Tom and Nesta Brunt married and farmed the New House Farm near Priest Weston. It was there that the children were born – Dorothy (13 May 1920), John, and Isobel (5 October 1923). They were all born in the same Cottage Hospital at Churchstoke about three miles away. Tom Brunt grazed hill ponies on Corndon, and when the children reached school age he started to teach them to ride. Dorothy was the first to go to Chirbury School and her father saw her out of the yard on her little grey pony, Polly, at the age of four. She found her way across the fields and then down through Marrington Dingle onto the road that led to the village. A year later John joined her; but his little brown pony was on a leading rein. That lasted for two days only, for young as he was, he was determined to ride on his own. Mother was always waiting for them to come into the yard at the end of the day. In the holidays mother would take the children for picnics on Corndon Hill. There they picked bilberries and climbed up to the stones on Stapley Hill.

Dorothy was eight years old when her father decided to move from Priest Weston to Berghill, a farm near Whittington, not far from Oswestry. It was here that John began to show a fearlessness and complete disregard for danger that was the mainspring of his character. It first started with the comic "Tiny Tots" which they had every week. In it were drawings and instructions on "How to teach yourself to swim". John studied these and one day asked Dorothy to go with him across the fields as far as the canal. It so happened that the Shropshire Canal went through the farmland. No sooner was he there than he took his clothes off and jumped into the canal. There was nothing Dorothy could do but stand and watch. Eventually he climbed out and they wandered back to the house. His mother wanted to know why John had no clothes on and when he told her he had been swimming in the canal she asked him what on earth he thought he was doing and he told her that he had, in fact, taught himself to swim. And the blame was put on "Tiny Tots".

The family lived for about two years at Walford Hall, Baschurch and it was then that John attended Baschurch Elementary School. He went on to Welsh Frankton School, and when he was older and stronger the daredevil antics became really serious: one day he was swinging himself along the guttering of the dutch barn which was about sixty feet above the level of the farmyard and no one dared shout to him in case he fell. Of course he was scolded, and of course he would not do it again. But that did not deter him climbing damson trees that once hung over the brook, or the great walnut tree that grew out of sight of the house.

H. Clayton Jones, a friend, remembers the morning when John, as a lad of about nine, was introduced to him by his father. He was to Mr Jones something of a problem child at that time, but he very soon revealed his daring nature. When the other children assembled in lines on the morning of John's entry into Welsh Frankton School he calmly watched the proceedings from the school roof, on which he sat astride. He came to school on a bicycle, but he scorned brakes, and often finished a wild journey down Brow Bank in the hedge. With equal abandon John would attempt to ride any animal he could manage to mount, and on one occasion got astride an old boar, which dumped him without ceremony into the pig trough, after wildly careering twice round the paddock. When a boy of about 16 or 17 years of age he fought three adult gypsies who had picked a row with him. For this last exploit John apologised to his father, which incident illustrates his quiet, and in many ways, sensitive nature, for in spite of his personal daring he was never an exhibitionist.

His mother recalled that:

> when he was ten he won a school swimming championship, though he never learned a stroke and the only bath he had been in was in our bathroom. He had a year to train, but didn't bother, just jumped in and somehow won through. John was like that.

The children – John, Dorothy and Isobel were taken to school by the postman on his return journey. It was a Dame School, run by Miss Tudman and her sister. Dorothy remembers:

> The lessons were composed mostly of copybook writing, adding, simple spelling, and we did learn to read simple books; but mostly we were read to. Then at lunchtime we ate our sandwiches and played in the garden. When it was time to go indoors her sister rang a little bell, and saw that we brushed our boots, and washed our hands before going back to the classroom which happened to be in the front room. In the corner was a big screen which had pictures pasted all over it. John, my brother, spent most of his time behind the screen because he was considered by Miss Tudman to be misbehaving. He managed to find a little stool from somewhere in the room and he used to stand on it. From this position he could see over the screen and he made faces at us all. Fortunately Miss Tudman had her back to the screen.

Tom bought a car, called an 'Overland', and he used to take the family to the coast. Rhyl in North Wales was always popular. The children used to paddle, but John, of course, went swimming and they had to keep an eye on him in case he took off for America!

Eventually he was old enough for Tom and Nesta to send him to Ellesmere College, a Woodard School, in rural North Shropshire. These schools have a firm conviction that education is best determined within a community whose life, thoughts and actions are shaped by Christian belief and practice. The College, founded in 1884 is now an independent co-educational boarding and day school of 490 pupils aged 8 to 18. The prospectus stated that:

> Success at Ellesmere is founded upon high quality classroom education coupled with a strong commitment to extra-curricular activities, be they artistic, sporting or outdoor pursuits. Ellesmere College is a member of the Woodard Corporation, the largest group of independent schools in the UK. Ellesmere offers day, weekly boarding and boarding facilities within a five day teaching cycle with sport and extra-curricular activities at the weekend. Although a Church of England foundation, the College welcomes pupils of all faiths and nationalities.

Prebendary E. E. F. Walters, College Chaplain from 1930–36 has written that one morning in 1933 he received a letter from Sir Offley Wakeman of Yeaton Peverey Hall (built by Aston Webb between 1890–1892 6 miles from Shrewsbury). He was at that time Custos of Ellesmere.

> It came at a time when, like many of the Public Schools, Ellesmere was struggling for existence. He wrote this note to me, saying that a man on his Estate was trying to start a canning factory and had very little money for the education of his son. However, Sir Offley was evidently very impressed with Mr. Brunt's enterprise and he suggested that I should go and see Mr. Brunt and his son. I remember clearly that when I saw the boy, despite the fact that he talked such 'broad Shropshire' that it was not easy to understand him, some instinct seemed to tell me that here is good material who could become a credit to the School.
>
> If I remember aright the School Fees for a Boarder were only £105 a year; they certainly were not more than £90 a year in 1930 – incredible as it may seem today.
>
> I asked the Father what was the maximum he could afford and, after a moment's consideration, he said, 'I am afraid the idea is impossible; I couldn't, at this stage, produce more than £15 a term. The Provost (Archdeacon Lambart) at the time had given Messrs Evans-Prosser, Howard, Sumsion (Bursar) and myself (these four were known as the 'Inner Circle'!) discretion to reduce fees when necessary to meet the urgent need of filling places in the School.
>
> However, half-fees or less was a problem. Anyhow, I told Mr. Brunt to hang on for a time. I approached two people and secured a promise of £25 a year and £20 a year from another for at least four years provided School reports were satisfactory.
>
> And so, John Brunt came to Ellesmere. I remember him well as a boy of real character right from the beginning. Of course, he got teased about his Shropshire accent and accepted this so good-naturedly that it soon ceased.

At the school his energy and enterprise was funnelled into sports of all kinds. He entered Meynell House in September 1934 when he was eleven, and within a few days there was hardly a person in the School who was unaware of the fact. For six years his irrepressible personality was to enliven, exasperate, charm and delight boys, Masters, Matrons – and indeed any person who was in the School for more than a few hours. He used to get on the nerves of several masters. Former Pupil Vic Rowles remembers that new boys had to stand on a locker in front of Meynell House boys and sing a song.

Old Ellesmerian Terry Thornton tells me the daily routine was as follows: Reveille at 0700 with the younger element getting up first. Breakfast at 0800; Chapel at 08.45; morning lessons up to 12.20 with a break at 10.20. (In 1938 or 1939 the whole school paraded for P.T. in this break). Lunch at 1300. Games (OTC on Tuesdays). Tea at 1615 followed by lessons until 1830; Chapel at 1900 followed by prep until 2120 for fifth and sixth forms, earlier for junior forms. Lights out for juniors at 2130 and seniors at 2200. Last post played at 2100.

The weekend routine was: Timings the same on Saturday morning. Games until supper time. Evensong followed by "reading prep": an hour with no talking spent in the day room. Sunday Chapel at 1030. Walks or golf in the afternoon followed by evensong and reading prep.

John was always in the thick of everything that was happening. He was like a volcano, occasionally dormant, never extinct, usually erupting violently. In a word he was the bane of every Prefect's life, until he became a House Prefect himself, and later a School Prefect. But nobody, boy, Prefect or Master, ever found him unkind or cruel – he had no vice in him. His spirits were lively enough to make him forget School rules, though not rules of conduct; and his exuberance found humour in the dullest lessons and the most tedious of duties.

Among Old Ellesmerians who were at school with John, John Taylor recalls:

> he was a sensible chap, but not immune from brushes with the authorities. He was a mischievous lad who did land in a scrape from time to time out of sheer zest for life. He and I were in trouble for some misdemeanour … it may have been as slight as running in the corridor … but a senior prefect had vowed to punish us to the maximum. So I spent the last day of one summer term evading the said prefect being led by John Brunt. But for his excellent field craft we would have paid a price. Were I ever to be in a tight spot, he was the one I would have chosen to be a colleague in crime. That was nearly 70 years ago, but he is still an athletic, fearless, clever 15 year old in my mind.

James Ogden recalls that John Brunt was

> the first chap I met on my first day at Ellesmere-summer term 1936. He was alone in the day room of Meynell House knocking balls about on a small billiard table. He was extrovert, forthright and humorous. My only other recollection, trivial but typical, was of a late afternoon class-room in the winter. The lights failed and total darkness ensued. There was an almost instant crack as a piece of chalk hit the blackboard behind the master's head. Not a second passed before, in pitch black darkness, the master's voice roared "BRUNT!" I do not remember what followed. I do not think it possible for anyone to dislike Brunt. My shadowy memory of him is one of resourceful, innocent mischief; lively as a firework, and for some unknown reason kind and sympathetic.

Kenneth John Clarke, known as K. J. Clarke 3 who was in Woodard House remembers John Brunt being "a very fair prefect, and the toughest guy in the school". A. A. Jilani's first impression was that John was "the tough guy of the House". He remembers him as a

> very colourful personality with a sort of dominating presence, jovial and vivacious, bubbling with energy and full of life. I realised I should always keep on his right side! He was a 'rough and ready' type of person, not so fussy about his dress and turn-out. The amount of energy he possessed was simply stunning! With his qualities he was naturally not only the outstanding figure in the House but he was also a sort of legend throughout the entire College.

Malcolm Love was a very junior boy who had been sent on punishment exercise – rolling the cricket pitch with a crowd of others, and he forgot to turn up. (In the summer it required about

14 boys to roll the cricket pitch). Brunt was the School Prefect in charge and let him know in no uncertain terms. Then he suddenly relented, grinned and said: "Ah well, you've given me a really nice smile, you're excused!" This was no unusual occurrence apparently. Malcolm also said that absolutely everyone referred to him as "Charlie Brunt". However not everyone knew this, more commonly he would just have been referred to as "Brunt".

Charlie Emberton recalls, as a junior, being

> caught running in the Crypt corridor. John Brunt was waiting just around the corner at the ante chapel end, which was strictly forbidden. He was waiting for me hands on hips and legs astride. I ran straight between his legs and he said: 'Little man don't you ever do that again!'

Peter Wright recalls his love of dirty stories and jokes, and can still hear John Brunt telling a house prefect that he had seen a pretty girl running. "Her United Dairies were going!" he told him. Alan Baddeley recalls him as "a bit of a clown", and remembers the annual school photo, taken one summer where John appears twice, both clear images. "The photo was taken by panning the semicircle of 350 boys and John, standing at the end on the right raced the camera to the left and appears on the left as well!" Apparently the headmaster insisted John's father bought two copies!

Geoffrey Sale's friend Harry Dutton was a "mad electrician".

> He had an induction coil, and we used to join hands in a circle and get an electric shock. You could alter the amount of shock you received by pulling out a knob in the centre. One day we thought 'Let's try this out on Brunt', so we got him in and stood in a circle. Harry pulled the knob out as far as possible to produce the maximum electric shock. Brunt then took it by himself and held it. He began to sweat a bit, but managed to hold on to it for about two minutes. None of us could have held it for more than two seconds. Harry then decided he'd had enough and switched it off. Brunt's hand was paralysed and we had to prise the coils he was holding from his hands! It was two or three minutes before he got the use of his fingers back.

During the last three years Alan Baddeley either slept in the bed next to or opposite him. Peter Northcote remembers being in the same dormitory, which had about 70 beds, 35 each side. There was no heating, only cold water to wash in, and only one bath a week was allowed.

Terry Thornton told me that:

> in 1935 the Reds senior and junior dormitories were side by side with only a low wall dividing them. A full partition was put up a year or two later. There were about 10 or 12 beds on each side of both dormitories. A third dormitory was added in a smaller room at the entrance to the other two in about 1938. There was a row of wash basins, cold water only, at the end of the dormitory. A certain amount of horseplay was tolerated but I do not remember any bullying. In 1938, as school numbers grew, the Gymnasium was pressed into service as a dormitory and very cold it was in the winter. We were even allowed to wear pullovers in bed. Then the new dormitory over the new science block came into use.

Peter Northcote continued, "Charlie Brunt", as he was affectionately known, was in the Juniors and with his strong personality was always getting into trouble.

> We used to stick him in the laundry basket and put him in the cold shower, not that it seemed to have much effect! He was small and a very active, wiry, athletic person. He had the sort of character that didn't sense danger, and probably the war came at the right time for him.

Geoffrey Rice recalls a group returning to school in January 1941.

> We were staggering up to the School in deep snow and on icy surfaces. The journey back
> was never a happy time. The conditions and fading light made it worse than usual. But I do
> remember it was Charlie Brunt who cheered us up and kept up our morale. He was in fact
> an inspiration to us.

Old Ellesmerian Spencer Harrison remembers John:

> He was older than I, but he was a friend of my brother. I think they were in the Corps band
> together and they were stalwarts of Form 5c. My brother obtained only a pass in art when he
> sat the School Certificate; and I do not suppose that John did any better; they were certainly
> no scholars!!

He continues:

> John was in the sanatorium at the same time that I was in. We both had mumps. The
> sanatorium was presided over by some battle-axe of a matron and every afternoon we all
> had to take a laxative. John, being an older boy had to swallow a pill but I, being a junior boy
> had to swallow a dose of cascara. Dose time was in the afternoon when the matron had a cup
> of tea with us. John must have secreted his pills under his tongue as he had collected three
> or four. The matron's attention was diverted while John popped his pills in her tea cup and
> stirred it. I still remember the pleasure at seeing the old dear drink it!

It was at school that he had measles, which resulted in him having to wear spectacles. Michael
Barton can remember being in the sanatorium with John, when they were both caught by a mumps
epidemic. The end of term came while they were there, and they were unable to go home for a
couple of days. Michael remembers John as his senior being a very decent man and nice to him,
sharing his food etc.

Meynell House Athletics Team 1940. John is in middle row, third from left

As a young boy, he will be particularly remembered for his wild enthusiasm for every kind of game. As soon as the bell sounded, he was away with a ball or stick. If he could not play, he was to be found in the pavilion getting ready to be "telegraph boy", or blowing up footballs or whitening hockey balls. On Sports Day he invariably had the rake or the megaphone when he wasn't running. As he grew older, he began to excel as a player of games. Before he left Ellesmere, in July, 1941, he had won the Open Steeplechase, and was Runner-up to the Victor Ludorum. That year Meynell retained the Senior Steeplechase Cup, when he ran step-by-step with Alan Baddeley, and extended his hand unselfishly so that they could both cross the finishing line together. This was much to the consternation of the staff as house points were at stake and they would have preferred a first and second! Alan remembers:

> we steeplechased together stride-for-stride usually and though it was competitive I clearly remember our last year, when we came to the finish line, though he could have sprinted ahead as we ran side by side he put out his hand to shake hands to make sure the judges knew what the result had to be!

Geoffrey Sale remembers being on the finish line and recalls that they were in a terrible state, having run their hearts out. Michael Barton also remembers John Brunt being "sick all over the place" as he came in to the finish, but this did not prevent him finishing. Pupils and staff lined the drive leading to Founders Gate to welcome the winner. John Brunt always pushed himself to the limit – he was a giant of a man.

Leading the Steeplechase 1940

William Shepherd remembers that John was a very determined individual who drove himself to the point of exhaustion. He gained colours in Hockey (a stolid, very courageous goalkeeper), Rugger (a safe, courageous full-back), Cricket (a patient courageous wicket keeper and flashing slogger at the loose ball). Alan Baddeley remembers John keeping wicket to his slow left arm bowling for house and school and he can still recall many happy summer days spent this way and also the way he stood up to the quick men. He swam well and played Water Polo with tremendous energy. Gordon

Whittaker was Captain of the opposing Woodard team against John Brunt's team at the end of July 1942 and remembers the water being so cold that players had to be pulled out of the water at the end of the match. Vic Rowles can remember playing water polo when the water temperature was about 60 degrees F. A brilliant all-round athlete, John Brunt helped to win something like 15 sports cups during his last year at school, and he enjoyed table-tennis.

Terry Thornton remembers he "was of slim build but wiry. He coached the Meynell tug-of-war team, he was too light to be in the eight". Vic Rowles recalls John being in the seniors when he was in the juniors. The seniors came in for a wrestling match, with the house masters watching. "It took Michael Mobberley and myself to tackle John as he was such a strong boy!"

Rowles, Brunt and Mobberley

Roy Lambert was at Ellesmere with John, although Roy was younger:

> I recall that we, as a house, were blessed at the time with very efficient sportsmen, John being one of them. He was lively in many ways and got on well with all of us although as a younger lad it was hero worship by me.
> … He always got into tight places on the sports field. I saw him take fast balls in cricket on the chest without a murmur, head a high shot hockey ball over the bar as he had no time to get hand or stick into play, and as full back tackle dynamically anyone attempting to pass him with the ball. John was also great on the athletic field and never gave up even if he didn't always win.

On the Rugby field John Carter was in the same side when they used to play army sides, who used to be far stronger than them. Brunt was ready for them at any time. He used to "take a big army man on his shoulders and toss him off!" John Carter remembers one big player knocking him and half a dozen others flying. Brunt was there waiting for him, and just leaned down and put him on his shoulder. He then walked to the edge of the pitch and threw him down.

Coaching the Tug-of-War Team

Alan Baddeley recalls, "If you were caught in your own 25 having John behind you was a great strength (I was a humble forward!)".

John Taylor recalls:

> I guess that he was 15. He was not very big for his age. I think he had a rapid growth rather later than most of his contemporaries. But his daring on the rugby field more than compensated for his size. He was quite the smallest on the field and probably the youngest by a long way. The picture of John Brunt in my memory is rather like that of a spitfire swooping in for a low-level attack. He was adept at a flying tackle over an unbelievable distance. And, while he appeared to be 4ft something, it was a normal Saturday afternoon's entertainment to see him executing his tackle on huge 6ft somethings. If he experienced fear, it was well controlled. It did not seem to exist in his life.

Robert Harding remembers John as a very popular guy, and he was the only one to have the tenacity to tackle the Headmaster, R. A. Evans-Prosser at rugby. The Headmaster was about 17 or 18 stone, and had asked John not to tackle him so hard. It is believed they collided once and knocked each other out. Michael Barton remembers the fearless Brunt tackling the fearsome Evans-Prosser in full-flight. This resulted in the Headmaster's cartilage problem in his knee, and he was unable to play rugby again. He did continue to play squash. Bill Thomas remembers this annual match between the staff and First XV. "Evans-Prosser playing at centre-threequarter burst through with only Brunt between him and the line. Brunt tackled with the result that not only was the try averted but Evans-Prosser damaged his knee". Robert Harding added, "He was very good at sport, but hopeless academically! When he joined the army he said he'd got the best job in the army – teaching P.T. to the A.T.S".

Intellectually, he developed strongly on the literary side, and took quiet pleasure in writing Essays and in mastering set books. Few things gave him more pleasure than his part in the outdoor performance of "A Midsummer Night's Dream" (he played "Snug the Joiner" in 1941), and when he wrote from the battlefield, his love of the beautiful filled his letters to the exclusion of the beastly. He was not a gifted scholar and books did not interest him unless they were adventure stories.

Because Ellesmere is a Woodard School the chapel was at the centre of things. "Chapel" according to Alan Baddeley "was compulsory, morning and evening every day and on Sundays a sung Eucharist and sung Evensong. Ascension Day and All Saints were half holidays". John's great love for the School Chapel was a measure of his

Acting the Part

childlike faith in the goodness of Man, and he took it for granted that people would naturally try to do the decent thing. This faith undoubtedly gave him confidence and insight into the minds of others. Alan Baddeley and John were frequently paired as Servers at the main Sunday services.

Prebendary E.E.F. Walters (College Chaplain) recorded that:

> John was only 14–15 when I left Ellesmere in 1936 but he kept up with one with occasional letters. Ellesmere had a great influence in moulding a character of great strength and the spiritual values which he learned there were a guiding factor in his life.

John was a country-bred boy and he loved the great outdoors, and he loved animals. Gordon Whittaker and John used to go off hunting rabbits outside Oswestry.

It was a great surprise to some people to see what a magnificent, natural instructor he was, both in the J.T.C. (Junior Training Corps or College Cadet Force) as a Sergeant and in physical training. Kenneth John Clarke remembers him looking very smart in his uniform.

John Blake was in his Platoon and recalls:

> Charlie was my Platoon Sergeant in the Corps. I was a raw recruit. On one Field Day I didn't have my own rifle and so borrowed a bandsman's rifle. Charlie found out and shouted out 'you're no bloody good to me without a rifle!' He then took it off me and hid it until after the action. There were only about 100 rifles available.
>
> I was very fond of him, though I didn't see a lot of him as he was in a different House. He was in Meynell, and I was in Talbot. He was an awfully nice fellow and a real tough guy. He was in all the first teams: wicket-keeper in cricket, full-back in rugby, goalkeeper in hockey etc. It was no surprise to me when he won the V.C.

Robert Harding remembers "Charlie" Brunt. Robert was one of his "fags" – he carried his books from one form room to another. John insisted on carrying every book from one lesson to another. "Imagine having to carry all those and your own!" Peter Scott told me that before he had a "fag", Brunt would walk around changing classrooms with a box-file piled high with books. Colin Smith recalls that "he always carried around between classes a box file on top of which were enough text books to satisfy the whole of 5C!" John Carter said he was well known for carrying all his books:

> His arms were fully stretched and he carried books up under his chin. One day he walked into a science class, where the master blew his top with him. He went over to his desk in the science lab. and scattered his books everywhere, shouting 'Brunt, what the hell do you need all those books for? Who are you trying to impress?'

His father found the school fees a constant drain on the meagre family income, but persevered with the help of the Headmaster, Rev. R. A. Evans-Prosser B.A. He was Headmaster at Ellesmere from 1935 until 1961:

> John left the College in July 1941. He came to Ellesmere as a very young boy. He grew bigger and in his last year he worked hard. When he left he was still the cheerful schoolboy, typical of the school story but rare in reality. It was for his tremendous enthusiasm in wanting 'to do something' that he was so noticeable. He was wildly enthusiastic about Meynell House and about Ellesmere.

John at Ellesmere

Roy Lambert remembers chatting with his friends as lads do, and when John left with others, to join the forces, they agreed that "he would either be killed or get the V.C". He was sorry both events took place quite soon afterwards. Although Colin Smith was four or five years younger, he remembers John as " a character larger than life and it came as no surprise to learn that he had been awarded the M.C. and the V.C. during World War Two". Terry Thornton also felt that "if anyone was going to win a V.C. it would have been John".

Alan Baddeley also felt that:

> If I had to pick among contemporaries one who would possibly win a V.C. John would be he. Someone who had the unselfishness, concern for others, courage and loyalty that he had and demonstrated all the time that I knew him, given that it was wartime, was likely to end up being recognised with an award like this.

A. A. Jilani said that:

> In later years when I heard that John Brunt was awarded the coveted Victoria Cross, I was not at all surprised because he possessed all those qualities. He was bold and selfless, the type of person who would gladly lay down his own life for his colleagues. Even at Ellesmere, John Brunt embodied all those qualities of a Victoria Cross holder. The most precious gems in the world are those with a rough exterior. That was John Brunt.

THE BRUNTS IN PADDOCK WOOD

The Brunt family moved to Paddock Wood, Kent in 1934, to rent "Woodlands", Maidstone Road. This was a double-fronted, bay window house. They lived there until 1950, when they bought The Old Vicarage, Church Road, at auction. They renamed it "Burnside" when the church built the new vicarage in Maidstone Road. "Woodlands" was taken down and the site became a Health Clinic, which was built in 1967. This was knocked down in May 2005, to make way for a new one to be built on the same site, which opened in May 2006.

Burnside

Tom Brunt had sold the farm in Shropshire because of the recession in the 1930s, which meant he could not make a living from the land and became manager of a canning factory at Walford, Baschurch in Shropshire, which lasted for a year or so. The family had moved into Walford Hall. He then attended a canning course at The Harper Adams College where he met Sam Smedley, who asked if he would go and work in a Smedley's Canning Factory, which he was having built in Paddock Wood: hence the move from Shropshire. Tom Brunt became manager on the site of what is now Waitrose Supermarket in Church Road. He rented a shop in Commercial Road to use as an office before Smedley's was completed, and had his name on the shop window. Tom Brunt was also Senior Area Marketing Officer for The Ministry of Food until he retired.

Paddock Wood market had closed down around 1934/35. Smedley's Canning Factory took over their site, and used the one storey, non-brick building with its corrugated roof as their workplace. They canned peas from local farms, as well as other fruit and veg. Smedley's closed and was replaced by Mack and Edwards Distribution (pre 1960), who occupied the land and demolished the older buildings.

In his school holidays, "young John", as he was affectionately known would come home. In his teens he was full of high spirits covering life and sport as it came his way. In giving him some batting practice at the wicket, Paddock Wood historian Jack Walker was obliged to tell him that he could not hit every ball for six, to which he replied – "but they count more".

He had a reputation as a reckless young man, continually in trouble either fighting with the local gypsies, or riding bare-back over the local farms to the annoyance of the farmers.

Paddock Wood resident Kathleen Gibson remembers John Brunt "riding on his bike with no hands – he never touched the handlebars! and we all admired him". Edna Whenmouth (née Gurney) remembers that he was a good-looking young lad, and all the girls fancied him. The late Eric Knight was one of the gang, and remembered that John "was one of the lads who made his presence felt". He remembers John riding his bike on the towpath by the Medway River in East Peckham. He passed them and went straight into the river. Ron Goldfinch used to mix with John and related that John was often slower than the others getting undressed. They used to tease him that it was because he was a public school boy. The last one in the water used to pay for the beer in the pub that night. On one occasion John turned up and said that he wasn't paying tonight. He made straight for the river with his clothes on.

Ron remembers earning about 5 shillings a week, and that beer was cheap in those days. The price was the equivalent of half a week's wages. They used to call in at The Bell for a drink. John was 4–5 years older than the rest of the gang. The gang realised that John was a cut above them – his father had a good job. When John joined up he had the chance to go as an officer, but he didn't take it up. Ron can remember going shooting pigeons in Dover one day, and recalls what a pleasant young man he was. "When we later heard he had been killed in the War we all said: 'that's typical of John!'"

Fred King remembers John coming home on leave before he was commissioned. He played football and rugby and they had a few beers in The Kent Arms. He used to sneak his father's car and go out for rides. He can remember playing around the St. Andrew's Rec. They used to play 20-a-side football. Fred says, "You couldn't wish for a better bloke". Bill Hardcastle occasionally used to take John on his motor bike for a glass or two of cider at The Queen in Queen Street, just outside Paddock Wood. Terence Priest can recall being taught at Sunday School in Maidstone Road by John Brunt. This was in a hall by the church on a Sunday afternoon.

John used to help train the Home Guard in Paddock Wood, assisted by his father who was commander of The Home Guard from about 1940–43. His father wrote to the Principal of Ellesmere College on 20 September 1944 explaining that his son had been driving the family car when a bomb exploded only 10 yards away on the other side of a hedge, ripping the sliding roof off. He went on to say that only the previous week two German planes came down in the village and John had mounted guard on one of them. He walked over to the second one as it exploded, killing one NCO and wounding seven or eight others.

John spent his last days in Paddock Wood before joining the army, helping with the Hop harvest. Percy Smith recalls hop-picking with John:

> When the pole-puller went by, John said something to him, and the pole-puller chased John across the field! He made a great many friends of all ages. He was welcomed in almost every home in the village, owing to his daredevil, fun-loving, thoughtful and considerate nature. Lads of his own age soon learned that it was senseless to dare him to do anything.

John's mother was Secretary of the Paddock Wood Red Cross and Comforts Committee in 1945. She worked with the Voluntary Aid Detachment during the war, and was on Queen Alexandra's Roll of Honorary Service. She was also in later years a Governor at Paddock Wood Primary School. The Brunts worked hard for the troops during the war.

Eric Silletto remembers going for an interview with Nesta Brunt at "Burnside" for the headship at the Primary School. Mr Brunt met him at the door and was very kind in making him feel relaxed. While waiting for interview their conversation included cock fighting, which Tom Brunt was interested in. He had a glass case display of cock-fighting items. Mr Silletto was offered the job, and enjoyed a glass of cider after the interview. Tom Brunt had collected antiques and sporting prints to decorate the house, one of the most interesting in the district.

Mabel Jenner can remember being taken to the Apple Growers Association by Tom Brunt. He was Manager there based in Marden. She turned up at "Woodlands" and went with him. She wrapped apples, and these were done up for export. It ended when the troops took it over to use as a bakery.

Mr and Mrs Brunt soon became very involved in village affairs, serving on various committees, and were especially active with the church. Tom Brunt was a warden for 12 years and a member of the Parochial Church Council.

The Brunts left Paddock Wood in 1964 and the church magazine commented:

> Mr and Mrs Brunt are due to leave Paddock Wood after living here at "Woodlands" and later at 'Burnside' for the last 30 years or more. In their time they have given real service and friendship to many people, not least the church of Christ as seen in St. Andrews. Mr. Brunt

was church warden for 12 years, then Hon. Treasurer, a member of the P.C.C. for many years. He ran a Boy's Bible Class for many years. Mrs. Brunt was an active member of the Mothers Union and was for 22 years the Treasurer here.

Until his retirement Mr Brunt was a plant health specialist for Kent and was awarded the M.B.E. in October 1961 for his services to agriculture. Tom and Nesta Brunt retired to Wombourne in Staffordshire, after Tom had suffered a stroke, and they were both in their late seventies. They decided that "Burnside" was too big for them to live in during their retirement. Tom Brunt said, "It was a very difficult decision to make. We both love Kent, and are reluctant to leave our friends in the village". Also their youngest daughter Isobel wanted them to be living nearer to her. She and her husband both taught at Dudley College of Further Education, about seven miles from Wombourne. Tom Brunt died in 1967 and Nesta in 1974, both in their eighties. They are buried in the churchyard there, along with Isobel who died in 1985.

EARLY DAYS IN THE ARMY

John volunteered for the Army on leaving school. He cheerfully told his father "It's no use hanging about". In 1941 he trained as a Private with the Queen's Own Royal West Kent Regiment. He was 18 years old when he enlisted. He took part in strenuous training at the Infantry training camp at Maidstone, and in the Battle-school in the Wrotham Hills, while at an O.C.T.U. (Officer Cadet Training Unit).

Prebendary E. E. F. Walters (College Chaplain) records that:

> War had broken out before he left school and he announced that he would like to go to an O.C.T.U. I remember one of the Senior Staff saying to me though John was no fool, it was doubtful whether he would qualify. John said, 'Well, I want to give it a go' and so he went for an interview. He came back triumphant at his acceptance!

The Regimental Depot of the Queen's Own Royal West Kent Regiment changed its title to 224 Infantry Training Centre as soon as war had been declared on 3 September 1939. This became the basic training centre for all six battalions of The Queen's Own. Its task was to put up to 2,500 Militiamen at a time through an 18-weeks' training course, at the end of which they would be ready to take their place in platoons in the field. A hutted camp had been constructed at Sandling Park, on the Maidstone to Chatham road. The camp later became known as "Invicta Lines".

By the autumn of 1941 fewer men were available for the Army intake, and it became impossible to send reinforcements to battalions of their own regiment just where and when they were wanted. A system of "linked" regiments was therefore evolved, by which The Queen's Own was linked with the Queen's Royal Regiment (West Surrey). The I.T.C.s of the two regiments were amalgamated, that of the Queen's Regiment moving from Guildford to Maidstone. The Combined I.T.C. then became 13th Infantry Training Centre at 'Invicta Lines'.

John excelled at all types of games, and he boxed (winning two or three Regimental Championships, until his eyes were injured, and he had to give up boxing.) He is believed to have won his first Championship within a week of joining up! He played rugger and cricket, and coached every game.

He was asked to play cricket for Kent. The wicket keeper had been called up and John was in his element. He quickly became a Corporal, and he became well known as a P.T. Instructor. He did well, remarkably so for one who had no marked academic abilities, and as an officer, especially as patrol and platoon leader, he soon proved his worth. He suddenly found himself a man, and then, his sense of responsibility required courage and faith and it was these that stood him in good stead. The next winter he found himself at Sandhurst on an Officers Training Course. When he graduated to Officer status, there was much excitement at home. His father took him to London to be fitted out for his uniform. Everyone was very proud of him, and there was much celebration in Paddock Wood.

John joined His Majesty's Forces with his bosom pal, Arthur Howell. John in the army, Arthur in the R.A.F. In September 1943 Arthur was killed when his Lancaster bomber crashed. While in the trenches John wrote a sad letter to Arthur's parents (his handwriting was very good). The letter recalled how they cycled to Maidstone together to join up. He also mentioned that he felt the war was turning.

John was granted his commission on 1 February 1943 with the Sherwood Foresters and was posted to North Africa. Although he was commissioned in the Sherwood Foresters (Notts and Derby Regt.) he never served with them. It is believed that he became very friendly with Captain Alan Money from near Sleaford, an officer of the Royal Lincolnshire Regiment on the boat and asked for (and received) permission of the C.O. of the Notts and Derbys to be posted to the Lincolns. The 6th Battalion, which he joined was a territorial Army Unit which drew most of its recruits from Grantham and the surrounding towns.

He was flown to Tunis to join the 6th Lincolnshire Regiment on 11 April and found himself on the dusty Goubellat Plain. He had been flown from Algiers (the Allied Forces H.Q.) to reinforce their officer strength for the final battle of Tunis. The 6th Lincolns were part of 46th Division which had sailed for North Africa on 8 January 1943, arriving in Algiers on the 17th. When John arrived they were positioned a few miles from the redoubtable Djebel Kournine that was holding up the tanks of two armoured divisions. The enemy was the Hermann Goering Division, whom they would meet later in Italy. The task of 46 Division was to gain the hills north-east of Bou Arada and this side of the lake called Sekret El Kourzia, in order to launch the armour of First and Sixth Armoured Divisions into the Goubellat Plain and on towards Tunis.

The 138 Brigade's move forward was delayed by a handover to the Guards, and this meant that their attacks, planned for darkness, had instead to be carried out in the hours of daylight. They achieved outstanding success. A new area was reached during the early hours of the morning of 21 April, and among the trees and boulders the Battalion settled down to rest until the following night. The first part of the advance was across a ravine and as it was crossed, a sub-tropical storm was experienced with torrential rain and incessant thunder and lightning. It was a misty morning, and the Lincolns, who led off from Horseshoe Farm, made good progress. Companies of K.O.Y.L.I. (Kings Own Yorkshire Light Infantry) and Lincolns crossed over open cornfields to take Argoub Hamra. The attack on 22 April preceded an attempt by armour to break through to Tunis, and would involve the Brigade carrying out a night advance and attack on high bare features dominated by Argoub Sellah. However the advance was actually accomplished in broad daylight in an area of cornfields sprinkled with poppies, which was in full view of the enemy. The Germans held the high ground with the Hermann Goering Division, who fought for every inch of the steep hillside, which was covered with anti-personnel mines, but "D" Company soon got on top. The advance through the cornfields was wide open to attack. The wounded lay in the corn which made it difficult for the stretcher bearers to locate them. By 23 April the battle of Bou Arada was over. It was expected to be won in five hours, but in fact it was 33 hours before the last enemy positions were finally taken. The C.O., Lieutenant Colonel J. Y. E. Myrtle, D.S.O., was killed by a mortar bomb. In addition the second in command, Major K. G. Barrell, had to be evacuated with a temperature only a few hours after he took over. So the command was placed under Major F. C. L. Bell, M.C. However the attack proved successful, allowing the armour to pass through as planned.

After a few days rest the Lincolns, together with the York and Lancasters fought an unpleasant small battle at Djebel Kournine on the morning of 27 April. This was a bare rocky hill with twin crests, known affectionately as the "Twin Tits". The hill overlooked flat ground that was the valley which marked the way through to Tunis. It was strongly held by the enemy, the Panzer Grenadiers, who were dug into the rock face, and had already resisted several attempts to flush them out. On the night of the 29th an officer and ten men from each company volunteered to carry out a silent attack, but they were unable to achieve their objective. Lieutenant Colonel Bell recalls "we had been told to take it. I sent some men up, with John Brunt down below to make diversionary noises". The Germans were fully alert. In their positions at the top of the hill, they only had to pull the cord of the stick-grenades and roll them down the slope. After an eventful night the Patrol was withdrawn and joined the rest of the Battalion for a well-earned rest. The following day the Battalion moved to the Medjez el Bab area where they debussed and a meal was prepared.

For the final battles of Tunisia more British divisions were deployed than had been assembled on one battlefield since 1940. On 6 May 1943, First Army launched Operation STRIKE, a thrust on Tunis from Medjez el Bab. This was begun by a huge air attack and artillery bombardment. Over 16,000 shells fell in two hours on the front of one assaulting British division alone. By mid-morning on 6 May, the armoured divisions were moving towards Tunis to find only scattered and occasional resistance. At 4 o'clock in the afternoon on 7 May the leading British Army troops entered Tunis. They surged round Tunis to Hammam Lif and across the neck of the Cape Bon Peninsula.

The 6th Lincolns had positioned themselves in a gully at the foot of Longstop Hill, and on the 12 May they were to be found in cornfields near Massicault, on the main Medjez-Tunis road. From then until the end of the campaign the Battalion did not catch up with the enemy. Although sporadic enemy resistance continued until 12 May, after three years of fighting the North African campaign was effectively over. On the night of the surrender, General Alexander sent a signal to the Prime Minister, Winston Churchill: "Sir, It is my duty to report that the Tunisian campaign is over. All enemy resistance has ceased. We are masters of the North African shore".

John Brunt took part in the final stages of that campaign and was present when the amazing victory was won. His frequent letters (no Old Ellesmerian kept in closer touch with his friends from Ellesmere) enthused on the beauties of North Africa. He was involved in the strife towards Cape Bon and took part in eleven engagements in sixteen days. He was slightly wounded in the Tunisian fighting, and indeed was wounded several times during a two-year period, but never seriously.

By 12 May the Battalion was on the move again. They kept marching through the day, though it was quite upsetting to be sweating along the road seeing load after load of prisoners of war going past in trucks. They eventually reached Oued Zarga. Here huge barbed wire cages had been constructed to contain Italian and German prisoners of war. The Battalion's orders were to guard the prisoners. This was hard under the conditions as the days were hot, with little shade to be had. However there was a river close by, which the troops were able to swim in. Soon it was time to leave and the Battalion boarded a train for a long journey westwards to a location about 20 miles west of Algiers.

On arrival training was undertaken. While the weather was good, the heat made daytime exercises much more exhausting. The troops in the 46th Division were trained in combined operations, which although an intricate means of warfare remained untested. In this part of Tunisia the final rehearsal of the Italian assault landing took place – a difficult task as it involved the making of a beachhead and the off-loading of vehicles, tanks, guns and supplies.

The North African campaign ended too quickly afterwards for John Brunt to taste any more action. He was inconspicuous among the rest of the subalterns during the reorganising and training phases near Algiers and Djidjelli, and again in Palestine training Junior Leaders and even as far afield as Baghdad. At the end of June/early July, 138 Brigade moved to Djidjelli, a small town on the coast to carry out training and general exercises including the use of landing craft. They pitched their tents just a few yards from the sea. As progress was made, the exercises were extended from landings on the beach to include advancing inland to take fixed objectives. During training a break was made for a sports day in the form of a swimming gala at the Quay in Djidjelli with competition from the Navy.

For some time it had been intended to use 46 Division in a proposed X Corps landing on the toe of Italy. But towards the end of August the task of the Division began to emerge. It was to be one of the assaulting divisions in the U.S. Fifth Army, in charge of which was Lieutenant General Mark W. Clark. In the second week in August the Division left for Bizerta, a port which had been laid low by bombing. Here Exercise "Jennifer Dryshod" was carried out as a final rehearsal for an assault landing, the making and extension of a beachhead, the off-loading of vehicles, tanks, guns, and supplies.

On 1 September, Divisional Headquarters were established on U.S.S. *Biscayne*. Throughout the whole period the Battalion was stationed at Bizerta there were active air recces. Several raids of moderate intensity took place. The areas selected for the troops were in the open and the ground was very dusty. However thanks to the R.A.F. and the U.S. Army Air Corps recce planes were unable to breach the defences, and nights remained undisturbed. The Lincolns embarked on 4 September, in infantry landing craft of the United States Navy. By 5 September embarkation was complete, and the next day the convoy began to form up in the Bizerta roadstead. Owing to the risks involved the Battalion had to be split up among nine ships. That night (6th/7th) a hundred enemy planes made a raid on Bizerta. In spite of an intense barrage from upwards of 150 guns on shore and nearly all the ships at sea, a few enemy aircraft got through and dropped bombs in the harbour, in and around the town, and on the convoy in the harbour. Amazingly no casualties were suffered by the convoy.

At dawn on 7 September the convoy set sail. Able and Baker Companies were each carried in L.C.T. (Landing Craft Tank), which, owing to the long period of time on board, sailed straight to a beach near Palermo. Here troops were able to disembark for six hours to stretch their legs and have a swim. It was uncomfortable for the soldiers and many still had desert sores that refused to heal. The landing craft made them all violently seasick at first. However regular meals and gallons of hot tea provided by the Navy made all the difference and were gratefully received. The crossing was largely uneventful until midday on the 8th when it was announced on the BBC that Italy had surrendered.

SALERNO AND BEYOND

An armistice had been signed between Italy and the Allies on 3 September 1943. Meanwhile American and English troops prepared to land at Salerno, just south of Naples. They arrived early on 9 September and were met by fierce resistance from the Germans under Field Marshall Kesselring. Operation AVALANCHE consisted of the Fifth Army landing force, which comprised the U.S. VI Corps, and the British X Corps – 46th and 56th Infantry Divisions, with the 7th Armoured Division in reserve. Both were near novices to war, having been blooded in North Africa in different but equally unpleasant and bitter battles. The 6th Lincolnshire Regiment, and John Brunt, were part of 46th (North Midlands) Infantry Division 138 Brigade. The British X Corps was under the command of General Richard McCreery. They were all part of the U.S. Fifth Army under General Clark. Their orders were to land on the 20 miles of beaches at Salerno, 50 miles south of Naples, and take that port.

John Brunt

General McCreery was worried that the beachhead would turn out to be too extensive. His X Corps represented the Northern Attack Force for the invasion, with the 6th Corps the Southern. His main assault troops, the 46th Division (Major General J. L. I. Hawkesworth) on the left and the 56th on a wider front to the right, would establish a beachhead. This would include Salerno as far south and inland as Battipaglia, the hills overlooking Highway 18 to Naples, and the airfield at Montecorvino. The plan was to land on two beaches, known as Red Beach and Green Beach. It was planned to land the Lincolns on Red Beach, the most northerly beach in the operation. Unfortunately the Assault Brigade, which landed at 3.30 a.m., suffered very severe casualties and by 7.30 a.m., as the Battalion began to land, the Germans had reoccupied Green Beach, the southern beach of the Division. It was also not an easy task on Green Beach, where companies of the K.O.Y.L.I. and the Lincolns were put ashore. Through the sun's glare the enemy were able to observe the beach from the hills. The disembarkation of Green Beach had to be suspended. The K.O.Y.L.I. and Lincolns hastily headed for the dunes, and were later able to move forward down tracks from the beach. "C" Company landed just to the south of Green Beach from a LST (Landing Ship Tank) known to its American crew as a Large Slow Target (top speed 9 knots). This indeed it proved to be, and the ship was badly damaged by enemy tanks at close range just as she landed. The Company, however, was very lucky suffering only a few casualties, although Support Company detachments and The Royal Artillery also on board, were not so lucky. The LSTs were crowded and uncomfortable. They were designed to carry armour for short distances so there was very little space for troops below the decks. The heat in the holds where the vehicles were stowed and the men were supposed to sleep was unbearable.

"C" Company turned north, waded the River Asa, crossed the enemy-occupied Green Beach just inland and met up with the rest of the Battalion which had landed safely on Red Beach. The main German assault was made against X Corps, who were seen as providing the bigger threat to Naples. In spite of a few problems, both 46th and 56th Divisions managed to hold their ground, with air and naval gunfire support. During the afternoon, the Battalion was ordered to attack the south-west in order to take Green Beach from the rear. Their task was to try and flush out the Germans who were in control of the exits from Green Beach, which meant the battalions had to approach them in the flank and rear. This proved an unpleasant and difficult task, making progress slow with a number of casualties being suffered. It took until the early evening before the enemy began to withdraw with their tanks.

The landing at Salerno found Lieutenant Brunt commanding No. 9 Platoon in "A" Company with considerable dash and exceptional skill. The Battalion, having assembled, was then ordered to move south-east, establish a base in the area of Casella, a farm near the Asa, and then clear up southwards to Green Beach. Able Company was to move back to the area of Granozzi and then with the aid of tanks clear up south-east and parallel to the sea up to the line of the River Asa. Able Company, with John Brunt, moved off at about 1500 hours to carry out their task. It wasn't until shortly after dark that a runner arrived with information that Able Company had moved forward to the Asa. Here they came across a few enemy on route, whom they engaged. They were now concentrated about a mile south-east of the Battalion. They rejoined the Battalion about midnight.

By 1200 hours on 10 September the Battalion was in readiness. The Brigade commander ordered the Battalion to proceed as swiftly as possible to Salerno to assist the Special Service Brigade in making the Vietri defile absolutely secure, and protect Salerno from attack from the north-west.

No. 2 Commando was positioned around Vietri, under Colonel Jack Churchill. Vietri-Sul-Mare is a little fishing village tucked between the hills and the sea on the Italian coast about four miles west of Salerno. Northwards runs the pass to the Plain of Naples, which is completely dominated at Vietri by Dragone Hill on the west and by San Liberatore to the east. It was essential to make the left flank safe before darkness that night otherwise nothing would prevent the Germans attacking during the night. In response to Colonel Jack Churchill's call, the commanding officer of the 6th Lincolns arrived at the Headquarters. He apologised pointing out that he would be unable to attack before dusk as he was unfamiliar with the terrain and the Regiment was not fully prepared. He promised to send a company to strengthen the 2 Commando position north of Vietri and relieve two troops on the western approaches to Salerno. So the 6th Lincolns and the K.O.Y.L.I. moved into the hills, and the commandos descended into Vietri for a rest. This would leave 3 Troop of

2 Commando to attack. Very shortly the positions held by 3 Troop were relieved by a company of Lincolns together with a section of tanks. The Commandos had carried out their objective in seizing Vietri and also the high ground to the Cava defile. However they did not have the necessary manpower and fire support to hold off the Germans.

When they arrived at Vietri, the Lincolns found an improved situation on Dragone Hill and for that night companies were engaged to the east of the Pass – on San Liberatore. One Company relieved a dangerous situation early the following morning on Dragone Hill, providing good shooting at various targets for the rest of the day. Dragone Hill is 1,500 feet high with precipitous slopes. They also captured Commando Hill west of the town, and progressed up the Vietri defile. On 11 September a patrol from Able Company, led by Lieutenant Brunt reached San Pietro without contact.

On the right of the Vietri defile the Lincolns carried out probing attacks throughout 12 September. On 14 September the Commandos were relieved by the York and Lancasters. Along with the Lincolns they held their positions for the next week under incessant shell and mortar fire. On the night of 14 September the Hermann Goering Panzer Division attacked from the north on high ground dominating 46th Division's area, an approach which was finally repulsed after intense fighting. This German Division had fared badly in Sicily and North Africa. They had an effective force of fewer than 15,000 men, 30 tanks, 21 assault guns as well as ample field artillery.

From Salerno and over the Volturno, John Brunt led Number 9 Platoon into many bitter encounters with the enemy and soon created a reputation for being a magnificent fighting soldier and a trustworthy leader. He was aware that his Platoon liked him, and he himself gained a lot of satisfaction from realising that his own Platoon casualties were the lowest in the entire Battalion.

Once the Germans realised that Salerno was the target for landings, they brought in more reinforcements, creating difficulties for the Fifth Army bridgehead. However the Fifth Army resisted strongly, and with the support of firepower from the battleships off the coast, by 15 September the Germans retreated back to the Volturno River. They had been pounded mercilessly from the air and had fought hard to break through the British ranks. The Schmaltz Battle Group from the Hermann Goering Panzers pounded away at the Lincolns and the York and Lancasters. Although they gained a little ground into the Cava defile, the infantry held firm. The Germans decided to pull out of the battle on 17 September.

The positions on Dragone Hill and San Liberatore became familiar to the Battalion, and the whole area was mountainous with some dense woods. The harbour in Salerno could be observed from these positions. The Battalion were always aware that there was nothing behind them apart from the sea. They could always see there were landing craft in the bay. It was a standing joke that they were there to take them off only if the Lincolns were able to reach them. However, any movement in the open was liable to mortar and artillery fire. Headquarters became established in a large house on the hill above Vietri. However the terrain was bad, the weather hot, and there was little drinking water. Against a formidable barrage, all they could do was hold on, keep up the patrols and look out for any sign of a German advance. From 10 to 20 September 1943 the Battalion made patrols from here to establish the whereabouts of the enemy both day and night.

The Battalion was responsible for covering the Vietri defile and Salerno up until the night of 19/20 September, when it was relieved by the 2/5 Leicesters. The Battalion then moved into Salerno, where accommodation for the whole Battalion was found in the Theatre Royal. The Battalion then enjoyed three days well-earned rest, which gave plenty of time for everyone to get washed and cleaned. All through their stay in the hills, water had been a serious problem, and there was none available for washing. Following their rest, "D" Company captured the Costa Pinano ridge overlooking Cava (to the north of Vietri) on the night of 22/23 September. "D" Company were ordered to capture Costa Pinano and "C" Company to occupy a pimple six hundred yards to the south. As movement was only possible on mule tracks, this made obtaining supplies more than usually difficult. The Battalion attacked during the early hours with two companies but they met opposition in an area which had been reported safe by another unit only a few hours previously. The night was clear and Spandau tracer was able to establish a well-organised defensive position. After some fierce fighting, "A" and "B" Companies were sent to reinforce the attack. There was no progress around the pimple until after dark, when 11 Germans gave themselves up and reported that the rest of them would like to do the same. They said they had felt like surrendering since the first attack but had faced such fire when they showed themselves that they decided to fight on until nightfall. The remaining 24 men surrendered during the night and "C" Company were able to occupy the pimple the next morning. After a battle in which there were many examples of personal heroism, the battalion reported that it had completed its task – the path was now clear for the advance of the 7th Armoured Division into the Plain of Naples. The Battalion had suffered heavy casualties, amounting to four officers killed and three wounded, 14 other ranks killed, 44 wounded and 28 missing.

The Battalion moved to Nocera in torrential rain, thunder and lightning on 27 September. Here they were to relieve a Battalion of Queens, but when they arrived it was found they did not need relieving, so the Lincolns settled down to join them. At first light the Queens left and it was realised that both battalions had been staying in an Italian Military Hospital, which was under the Red Cross jurisdiction. This situation was rectified by the Battalion taking up residence in a battered artillery barracks in the town. This provided a useful and timely chance to have clothes and kit cleaned and sorted out and for the troops to have a good rest. They stayed there until 6 October, spending most of their time training. They then moved north of Naples, concentrating in Ciaciano area with the rest of 46th Division. During their stay trips were taken to see Pompeii.

The Germans gradually withdrew from Salerno to the Volturno River, so that the Allied advance had to be delayed. This allowed the Germans time to build their defences north of the Volturno, running from the Garigliano River in the west to the Sangro in the east – this was known as the Winter Line. The Allies, following their successful landing at Salerno, had captured Naples and were now advancing towards their new objective, which was Rome. The German troops were able to hold Naples for several weeks and it wasn't until 5 October that the first British troops entered the city.

By the end of the battle for Salerno the Germans had certainly shown that they were a formidable and resourceful enemy. General Alexander pointed out that "The Germans may claim with some justification to have won, if not a victory at least an important success over us".

The advance continued slowly. It took another three weeks to cover the 30 miles from Salerno to the Volturno River, only 40 miles south of Monte Cassino, where Fifth Army arrived on 5 October. It then took a further nine days to cross the river. The crossing itself was made between 12 and 14 October.

The Germans were defending the banks of the Volturno with experienced men, 15 Panzer Grenadiers and the Hermann Goering Division. All along the river, the possible crossing places were being manned, with sufficient strength in reserve. Its banks were steep and heavily wooded, with the river itself broad and unfordable. It was now up to 46 Division to make one of the bridgeheads. The Division's task was to cross the Volturno on the western flank nearest the sea. By 12 October the autumn rains had set in and the Volturno was a thundering torrent. However that night the Division managed to cross on a wide front. Before the tanks were able to provide support for the infantry on the other side of the river, the enemy counter-attacked strongly but the 46th Division held out and the bridgehead was slowly enlarged. The Lincolns, with the rest of 138th Infantry Brigade, were in reserve when the 46th Division crossed the Volturno. The Battalion's task was to enlarge the bridgehead. This meant a slow, persistent and rather costly advance over flat ground across the river. This was dominated by high ground about two miles away, which was held by the enemy. It turned into a hard slogging match, and "D" Company's action was fairly typical. For this advance it was necessary to send forward fighting patrols to locate and engage with enemy opposition. If this proved unsuccessful, leading companies were to attack using the information gained. At night the enemy showed his presence by sniper and machine gun fire. By first light "D" Company had occupied their first objective which was a large farm, without any problems. The Germans held on as hard as they could to the second objective, covering all approaches with machine-guns until "D" Company was able to advance further.

The Battalion was then ordered to relieve the K.O.Y.L.I. This took place without further incident, and they were able to occupy approx. 1,500 yards of canal with Able, Baker and Charlie Companies forward, and Dog held in reserve. Patrols made contact with the enemy and action took place by sending them forward and then following them in greater numbers. On 23 October the York and Lancasters and the Lincolns, who had been engaged in patrolling in a forward position, carried out an attack to gain the road a mile ahead. This resulted in continuous and fierce opposition. The Lincolns were confronted with dug-in machine-guns, and it was not until the following morning that they were able to gain access to the lateral road. The Battalion's next task was to continue constant and penetrative patrolling. Recce patrols ventured out about two miles, bringing back some extremely valuable and detailed information about the enemy's position and the layout of the terrain ahead. It is certain that the Battalion learned a considerable amount about the art of patrolling during the few days it was in the area. It was not until 25 October that both X Corps and the 6th U.S. Corps had finally consolidated their bridgeheads. On 27 October the Battalion was relieved by the Queen's and moved east during the night in order to consolidate with the rest of the Brigade, just a few miles west of Capua. It wasn't until the final stages of the battle of the Volturno that the Battalion had been heavily involved, so their casualties were small, four being killed and six wounded.

November turned out to be a quiet month. At the beginning the Battalion was bivouacked near Capua, in or around a few burned-out farms and orchards. It was during a short break from operations that the Battalion was visited by the Divisional Dance Orchestra, which proved extremely popular and a welcome distraction. On the 6th they moved forward to the Garigliano River. The Fifth Army was temporarily halted opposite the lower reaches of the Garigliano and above the headwaters of the Volturno. General Clark's idea was to concentrate his main force in order to clear the approaches to the mouth of the Liri Valley, which was protected by a number of large hills (Montes). McCreery's task was to clear the Montes on the left flank using 56th Division on the right and the 46th on the left. During November and December, the Fifth Army made several attempts to break into the Winter Line, in order to occupy the mountains on both sides of the gap at Mignano. The road to Rome runs through here. The Lincoln's task was to reconnoitre the Garigliano for suitable places to cross over a three and a half mile stretch and attack any enemy found to the south of the river. They mounted intense patrol activity both during the day and at night. The terrain for several miles either side of the river was very flat and open. From there it rose gently, and was then thickly covered by olive groves and orchards. In addition to the patrols, the Battalion snipers had been busy and made regular excursions to the river. This proved very effective and demonstrated to the enemy that they were not going to have things all their own way. On 15 November, General Clark ordered everyone to rest, allowing time to reinforce and regroup the divisions, as well as to set up supply routes and build up reserves. On 17th the Durham Light Infantry took over from the Battalion, and the whole Brigade moved back giving time for training. The Battalion found themselves being billeted in the badly bombed and shelled village of Carinola, but everyone had a roof over their heads. The time spent in Carinola allowed everyone to get their clothes and kit dried and cleaned and to get some badly needed sleep.

On 1 December, the 46th and 56th Divisions carried out an attack in order to capture the whole of the Camino Massif. This consisted of a number of rocky mountain peaks between 2,000 and 3,000 feet. 138 Brigade started this operation in reserve and was not engaged in the first five days of the battle. On the night of 6 December the Lincolns moved north to occupy Colle la Croce before midnight, and then sealed off the road below, cutting off the remainder of the German forces to the south. The following day, after being bombarded all night by heavy machine gun fire from various positions in San Nicola, they went in to the village in the early light of morning. On 10 December they received orders that the Battalion would relieve the Scots and Grenadier Guards in the Rocca Valley during the night of 11/12 after being relieved by the K.O.Y.L.I. on San Nicola. This relief was completed rapidly and without any major problems.

The weather throughout these operations was certainly not favourable. Torrential rain fell constantly, which turned the low-lying terrain into a sea of mud. For several days everyone was soaked to the skin. It was with some relief that a change in the weather took place on 12 December, as the sun came out for most of the day which allowed both men and ground to dry out.

The Battalion remained in position covering the Rocca Valley until the 26 of December. As there was no enemy counter-attack, this became a period of constant and active patrolling. Their position was extremely exposed to enemy observation from the San Ambrogio ridge across the Garigliano 2,000 yards to the west. Therefore only essential movement was permitted, and the whole Battalion lay low. This was fully justified, for during the whole 14 days in and around Rocca, none of the company positions were shelled or mortared, in spite of an ever-increasing amount of artillery activity from the enemy in the area. Snipers were operating by day, but the enemy were not, and so only one German was seen and killed by the snipers.

AWARDED THE MILITARY CROSS

At Carinola, where the Battle Patrol was formed, Lieutenant Brunt was a natural choice as Patrol Commander, with Sergeant Reginald Tindall as his second in command. Inspired by his personality, the Patrol quickly gained its own individuality. They introduced their own particular brand of discipline, which somehow never ran to problems of dress. The Patrol was able to attract the natural born fighters in the Battalion, and was bonded together into a bold and trusted group of hard-hitting, resolute men who continuously tore enemy patrols to pieces. Later he had the then rare experience of being named in a long despatch by a War Correspondent for his prowess as a patrol leader at night. Reginald Tindall told me "We went out every night looking for trouble. We all carried tommy guns, grenades and phosphorous bombs. Our role was to bring back any information we could to Battalion HQ". Oliver Hardy, who served with John, remembers him as "a likeable man who always did his job, and was very keen and enthusiastic. People thought the world of him". Lieutenant Colonel Leonard Bell recalls him going out on patrol one night and coming back with a pig! The troops were very pleased as they could cook it.

During those wintery days of December and January 1944 the Patrol was in almost constant action, and nearly always on special assignments calling for huge amounts of all-round courage and fortitude. Lieutenant Brunt and the Battalion Battle Patrol received orders to attack and destroy an enemy post situated in some houses during the early hours of 15 December 1943. This took place at the main road junction 200 yards north of the River Peccia. In an effort to crack the enemy's line, Brunt's platoon crossed and re-crossed the River Peccia so many times, it became known as "Brunt's Brook". In what was described as "the darkest night", Brunt led a fierce onslaught which placed the enemy in a position of utter confusion. The Battalion lost many men in the matter of an hour or so. The Regimental History records the following about Brunt's M.C.:

> On the night of 14/15th December (1943) a Battle Patrol led by Lieutenant J.H.C. Brunt was ordered to destroy an exposed enemy post in some houses at the main road junction 200 yards north of the River Peccia. This patrol had been formed in November for special patrol tasks, and consisted of two sections each of sixteen men, all armed with Tommy guns or Brens. The action on 15/16 December was their first real encounter with the enemy. After an intense bombardment for five minutes, Lieutenant Brunt led a section in to the assault. This was carried out with the greatest dash and determination. The first two houses yielded two enemy, who were killed. The third house proved to be the main centre of resistance. Close fighting with grenades and Tommy guns followed. Eight enemy outside the house

were killed and those remaining inside the house received a liberal dose of grenades and Tommy gun fire. When all resistance had been silenced, the patrol withdrew, having had one man killed, and six wounded. Apart from ascertaining that the enemy belonged to 1st Battalion 2nd Herman Goering Panzer Grenadier Regiment at least twelve enemy were known to be killed and any others in the house killed or wounded. From subsequent reports of varying degrees of reliability, the enemy may have suffered no less than twenty-five killed in this action. For his outstanding part Lieutenant Brunt was later awarded the Military Cross, and his runner Private Hindmarch the Military Medal. Sergeant Potterton also played a conspicuous part, and though twice wounded, remained in action to the end.

The Citation for 4468508 Private Thomas Hindmarch tells us:

Private Hindmarch was acting as runner to the Commander of the Battalion Battle Patrol, which was ordered to destroy the enemy post at 907115 during the early hours of 15 December 1943. After an intensive thirty minutes fighting the Patrol was ordered to withdraw, while the Commander, Sergeant and Private Hindmarch stayed behind to bring in a wounded man. In going forward to the wounded man, the Sergeant was wounded. Private Hindmarch immediately dashed forward into the open firing his Tommy Gun in the direction from which fire had been opened.

There he resolutely remained while the Patrol Commander obtained and flung a smoke grenade to cover the removal of the wounded man. He had been carried about 60 yards when a German again opened fire and killed the wounded man. Private Hindmarch promptly killed this one remaining enemy. Throughout the action Private Hindmarch displayed courage and determination of the highest order.

A military observer gives the following description of a battle patrol commanded by the gallant Lieutenant, which appeared in the Kent and Sussex Courier on 29 January 1944:

The last pale vestiges of light pass reluctantly from the earth. Advancing night and the thickening fog hide the battalion perched high on the mountain. As the landscape changes from light to dark life on the hills begins to waken. Weapon pits and positions on the forward slopes are fully manned. Last touches are put to weapons now fully cleaned and oiled. Along the muddy tracks patrols creep out to look, to listen, and perhaps to fight. They all go the same way, towards the river and its tributaries curling at the feet of the waiting Army. Its flooding waters are streaked now and then with vivid flashes as shells burst about its banks. Among them is the Battle Patrol, whose task is to patrol the area of the River Peccia and destroy any enemy attempting to cross. At a convenient tactical point the Patrol Commander, Lieut Brunt ("Woodlands," Paddock Wood) sets up his base, and together with L/Cpl. R. Farrowby (Scunthorpe, Lincs.) and Pte. R. Pearson (Darlington), goes forward to the junction of the Rivers Peccia and Garigliano.

By this time the heavy mist had cleared very considerably, and after a short wait Lieut. Brunt saw five Germans on the opposite side of the river. He and his men immediately followed them, stalking their quarry along the banks of the Peccia. Unfortunately at this juncture, the moon appeared from behind a thick cloud and Brunt saw one of the Germans pointing at him across the river.

Further stalking was useless. Lieut. Brunt's Tommy Gun was blazing across the river before the Huns had time to collect their wits. He was followed almost immediately by Cpl. Farrowby and Pearson, who flung grenades across the stream. It had been impossible to take prisoners as had been hoped, but three Boches lay dead in the mud of the opposite bank and the remaining two ran for their lives as soon as the first grenade fell.

As a result, 258297 Lieutenant Brunt was awarded the Military Cross (M.C.), for "gallant and distinguished services in Italy", *vide* p.937 of London Gazette No. 36394, dated 24 February 1944. (Listed without Citation). This was recommended by Lieutenant Colonel David Peel Yates, D.S.O., O.B.E., commanding officer 6th Battalion, The Lincolnshire Regiment.

The following is the content of the recommendation for Brunt's M.C.:

> Lieutenant Brunt was in Command of the Battalion Battle Patrol which was ordered to attack and destroy an enemy post, situated in some houses at 907115, during the early hours of 15 December 1943. The enemy was found in occupation of three houses, in and around which they were systematically exterminated. After about 30 minutes close fighting with Tommy guns and hand grenades, at least eleven enemy had been killed. One man of the Patrol had meanwhile been seriously wounded and was lying in the road. Ordering the remainder of the Patrol to withdraw, Lieutenant Brunt went forward with one man to bring in the wounded man. He had gone about 60 yards with the wounded man on his back when one remaining enemy opened fire and killed the wounded man. This German having been killed himself, Lieutenant Brunt rejoined the remainder of the Patrol. Throughout this action, Lieutenant Brunt was continually in the forefront of the fight, killing enemy and cheering on his men. It was largely due to his courage, determination and outstanding leadership that the Patrol carried out their orders to the letter.

An article by Edna Bayne in *The Shropshire Magazine* 1984 states:

> Lieut. John Brunt and his patrol, eager for action, went out early on the morning of December 15, 1943, to destroy an enemy post. Night and the thickening fog hid the battalion perched high on the mountain. As darkness fell life on the hills began to waken.
>
> At convenient tactical points the patrol Commander set up his base, and together with his 20 men made the descent down the rocky, winding pathway and along the appointed route to the River Peccia …
>
> The Patrol divided into two groups for an attack on the first two of the three houses which appeared to constitute the enemy position. In the garden of the first house they found two Germans, one of whom was receiving attention for a slight shrapnel wound. John dealt with them and this raised the alarm. At once the air was alive with the crack of fire and counter fire.
>
> The second group came under concentrated light automatic fire as soon as they were within range of the second house. Ignoring the spattering bullets and the fragments of bursting grenades, they settled down to the task of stamping out all resistance from this house. They plunged into the defensive inferno, and with grenade and tommy-gun quickly reduced the position.
>
> During the action which followed one of John's men, Private Kenny was wounded. (This was 4468889 Private Bernard Kenny, 6th Bn., Lincolnshire Regiment, born c.1923.) Straightaway John went back to get him out without any thought for his personal safety.
>
> His example inspired his runner to follow, and joined by the Sergeant, all three found themselves in front of the house. In an attempt to cross the road, the Sergeant was wounded. John, now in full view of the house, sprang forward and threw a grenade.
>
> As he dashed across the road with a shout of 'I'm coming', it was left to the runner to cover him with fire. John reached the wounded man, placed him on his shoulders and carried him away. Unfortunately, a German came out of the vines and fired a burst into the man's back, knocking him off John's shoulder and killing him outright.
>
> Characteristically, John placed his comrade down, kissed him, saluted, and then turning to his runner, shouted to him to get out. Then, though slightly wounded himself, John

fired his sub-machine gun for all he was worth and killed the German who shot Private Kenny.[Kenny's body was never recovered and he is mentioned on Panel 5 of the Cassino Memorial, Italy.]

As no firing came from the other two houses in the vicinity John decided to withdraw, having carried out his orders to the letter. They had scarcely moved back a yard when a machine gun opened up from a flank, and as they entered a small village on the return route, a red Very light went up, and for three minutes the village was alive with bursting shells.

But not a single man was touched. The Patrol had succeeded. The enemy were identified, their position strewn with dead and wounded Germans. It is certain that at least eight were killed or seriously wounded. Our own losses were one killed, five gravely wounded- one slightly wounded.

On the following night the Patrol was sent back a few miles for a well-earned rest.

Although it was realised that the enemy would probably react to this set back there was no positive move until a week later. There had been a thick mist all day with sunlight above it giving a very eerie effect. The guns were quiet and the visibility gave the impression that it was night time. A strong enemy patrol approached a forward platoon of Able in the mist on the afternoon of the 21st. The Platoon was not aware of the enemy until they were among them and were rounding the enemy up before they had a chance to take up their weapons. The Platoon Commander was killed and 14 prisoners taken, though the enemy Patrol Commander was also killed.

By the 21st the weather had again broken and in order to continue patrolling great determination and fortitude needed to be shown. Nightly patrols went out in pitch darkness and heavy rain, wading through flooded fields, and swimming the River Peccia. The efforts of those concerned did not escape those in command, and a special message was received from the Divisional Commander on more than one occasion commending their efforts.

Christmas passed by almost unnoticed, and on the 26th/27th the Battalion was relieved by 2 Hampshires. The Battalion were then able to take two days well-earned rest at Galluccio before again going into action. They had spent a long time in the line and everyone was ready for a good sleep and the chance to sort out their gear. All the soldiers had been exposed to the dreadful conditions, patrolling had meant being wet through and probably swimming the River Peccia each way. The weather had been bitterly cold – snow and rain were constant, and no cover was available. At Galluccio covered accommodation was found for everyone with the added luxury of meal times at the normal time and hot food being available. On the 25th, the Commanding Officer Colonel David Peel Yates temporarily assumed command of 138 Brigade, and command of the Battalion devolved on Major F. C. L. Bell, M.C.

On 29 December the Battalion again went into the line, relieving the York and Lancasters for four days on the River Peccia. The weather was still bitterly cold, snow and rain were frequent, and there was no cover available to shelter from the elements. Preparations were made for an attack across the Peccia on the night 4/5 January. The Brigade were given the task of protecting the left flank of the 6th U.S. Armoured Infantry, who were to capture an isolated hill – Mount Porchia – covering the approaches to Cassino. The York and Lancasters were on the right, and the Lincolns on the left. The river although only 25 feet wide, was swollen by rain and snow coming off the mountains, and this presented a major obstacle. Two fords had however been found, and these were to be used by Baker Company and the Battle Patrol, who would capture a small bridgehead, enabling Able to pass through to the final objective.

Baker Company were successful in crossing the river by moonlight after which they captured a group of farms, which was their objective. Casualties were light and 22 prisoners were taken. Meanwhile the enemy was constantly firing shells and mortar bombs onto the river line and the area to the south. It turned out to be the heaviest bombardment of enemy artillery fire ever encountered by the Battalion, and casualties soon mounted up. The Battle Patrol, who were looking for a suitable crossing place, were caught in heavy fire from a Nebelwerffer (six-barrelled rocket mortar). The enemy had evidently prepared full contingency plans for any attempt at crossing the river and was now using these to full effect.

After they learned of Baker's success, Able were ordered to cross the river and pass through. However as they crossed they met heavy artillery fire, which resulted in fifty percent casualties. The moon had gone down and this meant that progress was slow. The remainder of the Company had to withdraw as they were too weak and disorganised for other duties. Evacuation of casualties was commenced in very strenuous circumstances, because the whole area was under continuous heavy fire.

A member of his Battalion wrote in the "*New Poacher*", the Organ of the 6th Battalion, The Lincolnshire Regiment that: "On the dark 5th of January, 1944, he (John Brunt) led his Patrol forward under heavy fire. He had pleaded with the doctors in a rear hospital to be allowed to leave a sick bed to take part in the attack. He was back again in the same hospital twenty-four hours later with concussion after a piece of shrapnel had almost split his helmet, but only because he was forcibly led from the scene of the fighting by an N.C.O., who realised he was a very sick man". Reginald Tindall remembers John being ordered to rest in hospital, but he discharged himself and came back in his pyjamas! "He was a man that liked to be at the front".

The *Kent and Sussex Couriers* of 21 and 29 January 1944 tell us that John Brunt had been wounded in action in the Mediterranean theatre of war. "His work with his unit has always been full of thrills and adventures, as he was in charge of the unit's battle platoon and worked mostly at night filching men from the enemy's lines for purposes of identification of units employed against our front. In a letter to his father he said he hoped to be back in the line again shortly".

The Battalion was then relieved by the D.L.I., and rested for a few days after returning to Le Vaglie. Reginald Tindall remembers John "firing a revolver for reveille out of the window". A belated Christmas was celebrated on 9 January.

On 11th January the Battalion returned to Rocca D'Evandro for a short spell to relieve the Hampshires until 15 January when the two Units exchanged positions again. The Battalion passed into Corps reserve at Gallucio and while they were trekking from Rocca there was too much talking for the liking of the commanding officer. To mark his displeasure the next day, the whole Battalion had to climb the adjacent mountain, carrying full equipment including mortars and machine-guns. While at Gallucio the Battalion had a visit by the Divisional Dance Band including a special guest – the Canadian female vocalist – Inga Andersen.

Following these preliminary skirmishes, the next phase of the plan was the main assault on the German Winter Line. X Corps was to cross the lower Garigliano River, and advance up the Ausente valley behind Castelforte, to threaten the rear of the Liri Valley defences; 2 (U.S.) Corps were then to mount a frontal attack towards Cassino. On 17 January X Corps attacked across the Garigliano with the 5th, 46th and 56th Divisions, opposed by the German 94th Division. Bridge-building was slow, as the proposed crossing place and its approaches were under enemy observation and so they were subject to accurate artillery fire.

"The *New Poacher*" continued:

> He (John) returned from hospital this time to be in an uncomfortable situation over the Garigliano. The crossing of the Rapido River was to be preceded by British attacks at two points on the Garigliano. The first of these attacks, on the coast where the Garigliano reaches the sea, was a diversion intended to draw the Germans away from their defences in the Liri Valley. The second British attack, at the south-west edge of the valley was intended to capture the heights overlooking the Rapido and to protect the American's flank when they made the main crossing. The first British attack on the night of 17 January caught the Germans by surprise. They quickly captured the town of Minturno, near the mouth of the Garigliano, and established a large, secure beachhead on the north side of the river. With

reinforcements, the Germans were able to prevent a second attack. The Patrol, still as game as ever, was caught in heavy shelling that caused many casualties in the ranks and left many shaken. The Patrol that moment was in pretty poor shape, but on receiving an order from the Commanding Officer, Lieut. Brunt turned to the men he had left and remarked, "We have still to go up that hill," and without another word turned and started to climb. He never looked back. But he knew that every man who could walk straight and some who could not were following him.

The 46th Division were due to cross the river on the night of 19/20 January. However the Germans then opened the sluices of a dam higher upstream on the Liri, causing the Garigliano to be higher and run faster than usual. So any crossings had to be abandoned. The eventual night crossing on the 20th was extremely cold and even the coldness of the water could be appreciated from within the boats. The Garigliano became swollen with water from the mountains and flowed very swiftly, so great care had to be taken in steering boats with which the soldiers were not familiar.

After a long night march which included a crossing by assault boat and ferry, the morning of 21 January found 138 Brigade established in the loop of the Garigliano, east of Castelforte, where they relieved two battalions of 169 Brigade. On the right were the K.O.Y.L.I., and on the left the Lincolns with the York and Lancasters in reserve. Once over the river, the companies took up their positions on the slopes of the mountain. While there the Battalion withstood determined counter-attacks by the 71st Panzer Grenadier Regiment. The intense cold was indescribable. Men resorted to wrapping themselves in their Gas Capes to try and keep warm, but this meant they were soon soaked in condensation.

The 46th Division had by now taken up position in a restricted bridgehead over the river, and they began to enlarge it, capturing a number of hills which overlooked the river where it turned north. The next few days were spent reorganising the Battalion on a three-company basis. "A" and "C" Companies were amalgamated under Major T. C. Charity, M.C. and the Battle Patrol went to enlarge "B" Company, which had started with very low numbers. On 26 January, the Brigade was ordered to enlarge the bridgehead over the Garigliano and secure Monte Tuga, the Battalion's objective being Monte Rotunda. Before that however, the enemy had to be cleared from a smaller peak, Castello, and this was brilliantly carried out by an attack which included all the Battalion's armoury. On the night of 26 January, the Lincolns, moving forward against Hill 334 south of Monte Rotunda captured an officer and his command of forty men. By darkness the Lincolns were firmly dug in on the hill. Following that successful infiltration the Battalion took Monte Turlito, the planned objective for the D.L.I. The Battalion then remained in reserve for a few more days before moving to Campo, north of Monte Camino, on 31 January 1944, for a few days well-earned rest. By now the Battalion was very weak. Four Officers and 150 men joined as reinforcements on 2 February.

The ground was bare, rocky unyielding terrain. All the mountain sides seemed to be steep and artillery had constant problems clearing the tops in order to reach targets. The Germans always seemed to have the best of it, however high the mountains captured, they were always able to withdraw back to even greater heights. When the Battalion moved forward it always took two days to reach the desired location. The limits of human endurance were being tested constantly, traversing the mountains was a major trial in itself, and it was always intensely cold.

General Hawkesworth commanded 138 Brigade, which now consisted of 5 Hampshires, the Lincolns, the K.O.Y.L.I. and later the York and Lancasters. For the new attack he directed them to capture first Cerasola and Faito, and then Monte Feuci half a mile to the west. After a short rest and some welcome reinforcements, on 7 February, The Lincolns endeavoured to capture Monte Faito, 2,600 foot high. This was very steep, rocky and with very little cover. The whole area was totally under constant observation by the enemy from San Ambrogio to the north-east or Castelforte to the west. By 8 February the Lincolns, who were concentrating on Faito, twice captured and were twice driven off the barren summit of Hill 803. At this time an enemy message was intercepted "Faito must be held at all costs", and consequently the weight of mortar fire and frequent counter-attacks followed. A company of Lincolns were pinned in the gully below Hill 803, and it was decided at midday to put off the attack on Faito for the moment, as the Battalion had lost 110 men. The mountains all around were so high and steep that it took twenty-four hours for the wounded to get to the Field Ambulance. Instead the K.O.Y.L.I. were ordered to attack north from Cerasola, and the Lincolns were then to attack Hill 803. But neither attack happened, for the K.O.Y.L.I. "O" Group was put out of action in heavy evening shelling of Cerasola. Almost at once the enemy, following up the Lincoln company withdrawal from below Hill 803, became a dangerous threat. At midnight 2 Coldstream Guards relieved both the Lincolns and the K.O.Y.L.I. and on 10 February the Battalion went back to their previous billets at Le Vaglie for two or three days' rest and reorganisation.

On 14 February, the Lincolns crossed the Garigliano again, to oversee a sector on the extreme right of the bridgehead and take over from the Leicesters. They were to cover the lower slopes of the mountain range, with Cerasola and Ornito towering over them. When the Battalion took up position, the enemy were closer than expected and on the first night they approached "C" Company's positions and covered the area with machine gun fire. The next night an operation called "Variety" was planned and executed. A fighting patrol under Lieutenant Todd attacked two farms which had been nicknamed "Flanagan" and "Allen". The Patrol killed all six occupants, broke up a counter-attack, then withdrew. By day, the Battalion's gunners and mortars were able to be on the lookout for enemy patrols. At night, a week of aggressive patrolling meant the Germans had to withdraw about 500–600 yards. It had been a very long spell in the line, lasting more than two weeks, but the days and nights were amazingly quiet except when the patrols encountered the enemy.

On 15 February 1944, the Abbey at Monte Cassino was bombed by the Allies on a clear sunny day, which was observed by the Battalion. Wave after wave of aircraft flew over and dropped their bombs on the Abbey.

It wasn't until 1 March 138 Brigade was relieved by 1 Guards Brigade and moved to Le Vaglie, where everything possible was laid on to entertain and look after the men. Everyone had a complete new issue of clothing, which was very welcome. Everyone thought that when the Battalion was relieved they would be going out of the line for a long time, and this included speculation that they may be returning to England. Then everyone was told they would shortly be going to another country for a period of recuperation, reorganisation, and training, but that their destination was definitely not England. On 6 March the Battalion moved for just one night to the temporary staging camp at Pignatoro, near Capua. Once again that night was bitterly cold, with snow and frost. They then took the train to Taranto on 7 March, with the R.A.S.C. Band coming to the station and playing "The Lincolnshire Poacher" as the train left. The journey took 48 hours arriving in Taranto on the 8th, and they went into a staging camp which was about 3 miles from the town. There were E.N.S.A. shows, theatres, cinemas, and a whole range of entertainment. On the 16th they left Taranto in M.S. *Batory*. After the baggage had been slung on board via nets, the men followed again in the same way.

So ended the first Italian campaign. It was the toughest of all, although it consisted of only four major battles – Salerno, the Volturno crossing, the Camino operation and the battles around Castelforte. In spite of the fact that the battles, after October, were interspersed with long periods of inactivity while on the defence, the strain was constant. Patrolling, especially in the atmosphere of the Garigliano valley, resulted in a constant nervous tension, which made the battles something of a welcome distraction. There were long periods of never ending routine, of morning and evening "stand-to", of constant sentry-duty, and of patrols, which seemed to continue for ever. Periods of rest and inactivity were usually short, and the nearby villages had little to recommend them in the way of entertainment. Casualties during the previous six months had been fairly heavy, being a total of 23 officers and 495 other ranks killed, wounded or missing in action.

John Brunt is reputed to have said to his friends something along the lines of "I've won the M.C., now for the V.C.!" He acted as Intelligence Officer for a period from March 1944, before being rested.

The Division was certainly in need of a break. Since the landing at Salerno, there had been little opportunity for rest. The previous three months, in the snow and rain of a hard Italian winter had pushed endurance to the limit. Even the periods of rest out of the line resulted in long marches, carrying heavy kit, to reach the shelter of some half-destroyed hill village, where only a few days later men were faced with the long trek back.

The voyage to Egypt was pleasant and uneventful with warm sunshine and a blue sky. The Battalion arrived at Alexandria. A waiting troop-train took them to a staging area at Quassasin. The sweeping sands at Quassasin Camp, after a crowded uncomfortable truck ride, offered a gritty welcome. When the wind blew the camp was covered in clouds of sand which left a fine deposit on food and clothes. The incessant midday sun made battledress uncomfortable, but in the cold evenings it was more bearable. From this camp everyone was sent to Cairo for four days leave.

There were numerous cafes, bars and nightclubs, which proved very welcome to everyone. There were trips round the city and the bazaars, trips to the Pyramids and Sphinx and camel rides. There were plenty of things to do and only a short time in which to enjoy them. It was wonderful for men who had not seen civilisation for over a year.

John enjoyed leave in Cairo, where he spent four happy days. Having come to the conclusion that the army were being somewhat unfair to unwary troops fresh from the fighting, he struck a blow for the oppressed Other Ranks by letting the wind out of all four tyres on the car of the Provost Marshall!

Jack Chapman remembers how well John got on with his batman, Len Trask, a Welshman. They thought the world of each other, and Jack remembers once when they fell out with each other John shouting "Shut up man, you're like a bloody baby!" It was in Egypt that John Brunt came into the Battalion clubhouse and said "my batman was the smartest man in the Officer's Mess last night – he'd got my clothes on!".

John also visited Jerusalem, and spent some time training Junior Leaders in Palestine. No. 139 Brigade had already gone ahead to Palestine, and shortly after the end of leave in Cairo, the remainder of the 46th Division moved by road and rail to the lines of hutted and tented camps around Nathanya. This was the aim of the five hundred mile journey across the Suez Canal and through the searing heat of the Sinai desert. Nathanya was pleasantly situated on the shores of the Mediterranean. On the long stretches of sand dunes the Infantry sweated and took part in intensive battle training and the quiet of early morning was spoilt by the clatter of Bren guns and the occasional sound of mortars. Tank training was also involved. Training was hard and relentless, but there was still ample opportunity for relaxation. Weekends were much enjoyed in Tel Aviv or Haifa, where cinemas, shows and cafes were in abundance and well supported.

John also spent some time in Damascus recuperating from his time in hospital as a result of being injured. The Division had moved up into

John in Damascus

Syria on 3 June. It was a fascinating journey, passing over the bridge into Jordan and then along the eastern shore to the Sea of Galilee. Here in the mountains the last stages of training took place at Dimas, a hutted camp high in the Syrian mountains between Damascus and Beirut, the two principle cities. Company training and combat with the support of tanks were fully practiced.

In the end, the stay was only 13 days, and of that time only two days were spent on training with tanks. The heat was unbearable and unrelenting. The Division were soon needed to continue the war and the long trek back to Egypt and Quassasin began on the 16th, with most of the travelling being done at night to avoid the day's constant heat. This was completed by road and rail over three days.

The heat seemed even more intense than the previous visit, and welfare amenities were non-existent. At the end of the month the Battalion embarked at Port Said in two ships, the Britannic and the Durban Castle. There were high hopes that the Division were destined for home and then France – anywhere but Italy – and so it almost happened. But when the Division sailed Taranto was its destination.

The news was good. Rome had fallen; there would be no more battles in the too well-known hills across the Garigliano. The invasion had established a firm footing on the Normandy coast.

John had found this rest period away from the fighting rather quiet and was delighted to be back with his regiment in Italy.

TOWARDS THE GOTHIC LINE

They arrived in Taranto on 3 July, followed by a two-day journey by cattle truck to Pignatore, near Capua, where training continued. The weather for once was good, and life far from unpleasant. Trips were organised to Capua to see films and shows, and occasional concerts were organised in the camp area. While at Pignatore the whole Battalion visited a Field Hospital for each soldier to give a pint of blood. No one needed persuading as they all knew the need for blood transfusions in looking after the wounded. Following a short stay there, the Division moved north through the remains of Cassino, through Rome and northwards to rolling country around Bavagna on 23rd. Some hard training on a platoon level took place here during the 31 days spent in this area. This period was enjoyed by everyone in spite of a lack of amenities other than the opportunity to take part in sport and a successful "fair". During this period King George visited Italy, landing at Perugia, not far away from the Battalion location. So they were used to line the route from the airport on a hot day.

Back in Italy for the second time, as temporary Captain and second in command of "D" Company, and Acting Adjutant, John Brunt was transferred from 5th to 8th Army, being one of the troops who were secretly switched from coast to coast to take part in General Alexander's surprise push.

Now that Rome had fallen (6 June 1944), Allied Forces felt they would be able to head north to the German Gothic Line, between Pesaro on the Adriatic and a point 12 miles south of La Spezia on the Ligurian Sea coast, south of the River Po. The Line was naturally strong and had been heavily fortified by the Germans. Field Marshall Alexander's plan,

John and friend in Naples

by a secret concentration of the 8th Army on the Adriatic Coast, was to attack the Gothic Line. The decision was taken that the main thrust of the Allied attack would be on the Adriatic side of the Gothic Line. This was intended to draw the Germans over, leaving the way clear for an attack on the other side. In order for this to be achieved, the Allied Forces were regrouped, bringing the bulk of the Eighth Army over to the Adriatic. A Conference at Division H.Q. for commanding officers made the intention quite clear, the Eighth Army's ultimate objective was to be Vienna. After further training, the Division was hidden away in rolling countryside around Sasso Farrato, after a journey north which was completed by 23 August.

The Allied attack on the Adriatic sector began on 25 August, and this took the Germans by complete surprise. The Battalion moved forward at dawn on the 31st to a position which enabled them to see across the River Foglia. At 2200 hours the C.O. held a meeting in two 3-tonners backed end to end, following which orders were given for the capture of a ridge some 1,000 yards from the Foglia. Just as dawn was breaking Baker Company were scrambling up this ridge and reached the first farm without opposition, establishing Battalion H.Q. here. The second farm was reported clear, but as Baker made its way down the forward slopes towards the ridge which had been named "Cow", fierce small arms fire and some mortar bombs slowed their progress. The advance had started in the early hours and soon after midday in the hot sun, with the support of artillery and a squadron of tanks, the companies took the enemy's fortified positions at incredible speed. It was a tremendous sight to see the demoralised Germans emerging from their concealed positions on the hillside with their hands raised as the companies approached. This action was a complete success and by 1430 hours, 22 prisoners had been taken and more than 10 killed. The defences had been very well constructed, very deep and with concrete emplacements in places. General Sir Charles Keightley, the Corps Commander, subsequently congratulated the C.O. upon what he described as a "model tank and infantry battle". By the early hours of 1 September, they had breached the main fortifications of the Gothic Line on the Adriatic.

No. 138 Brigade were among those whose role was to capture the bridge at Ponte Rossa over the Ventena, a small stream – on arrival on the night of 2/3 September it was found to be virtually dry. That whole area of the Adriatic was intersected by rivers, which generally were dry after the summer. At the start tanks could not be used owing to the limitations at the existing ford, and a second crossing for them had to be captured by the Lincolns. The advance could not begin before midday, and two tanks were lost at a very early stage. The undulating countryside and fierce resistance delayed what had been intended to be a swift advance. Both the Lincolns and the K.O.Y.L.I. were forced to send in infantry and tanks to attack before the Ventena was breached by the latter that night. The York and Lancasters were then ordered to pass through and capture Morciano and San Clemente. Two companies swept over the river bed, and up the slopes to capture the village of San Andrea. Over sixty prisoners and four anti-tank guns were captured, and a tank taken out. The two remaining companies came behind in tanks making for San Clemente.

On 9 September 138 Brigade were sent to relieve 169 Brigade of 56 Division at Gemmano – a large, prominent, bare and dominating ridge south of the River Conca. This was destined to become an important point in the defence of The Gothic Line. Four villages stood on its bare slopes – Villa at the eastern end, then Gemmano and Borgo, and finally to the west Zollara. Just west of Borgo a rounded hill with a farmhouse on its summit was known as Hill 414, and in between with a cemetery in it, the bare ridge with a large cross on it was Hill 449. To the south a spur jutted out to Farneto.

The relief of the Queen's Brigade, who had faced a difficult time there, was somewhat complicated. The plan had been for the K.O.Y.L.I. to relieve what was left of two battalions which were holding Gemmano and Villa, while the third battalion attacked north through Farneto. The Lincolns were then, after winning this skirmish, to pass through and capture Hill 449. But the Queen's attack was unsuccessful, and in the morning the K.O.Y.L.I. were on Hill 414 with two companies in Gemmano and one in Villa, while the Lincolns were waiting below. Failure by two battalions to capture this difficult feature had brought Fifth Army's advance to a halt. On 10 September the

Battalion continued the assault; this was done in broad daylight four hours after receiving orders. Their route would lead them over country with very little cover, and without the support of tanks. Meanwhile the plan was for the Lincolns to capture in succession Hill 449, Zollara and the southern spur. When the companies advanced through Villa towards Gemmano they faced intense artillery and mortar fire, and suffered many casualties before they even reached Hill 414 from which the attack was to start. Just after noon, under a blanket of smoke, one depleted company made a daring assault and managed to reach the lonely cross. But the bare hillside was exposed to enemy fire from the right flank, and four hours later attempts were still being made to dislodge the Lincolns from their hard-won positions.

That night the Durhams took over Gemmano. The K.O.Y.L.I., who had been relieved from defending the village, were to move on to Hill 449 and the Lincolns would then clear the spur southwards as far as Farneto. But enemy patrols and skirmishes that night caused a lot of confusion. Sections of the enemy managed to get back into Borgo and Hill 449. Fierce exchanges took place, and the enemy was never completely dislodged from Hill 449. Not until 1700 hours was the hill taken, with relief later that night provided by another Battalion of the Brigade.

During the clearance of the battlefield a soldier of the 6th Lincolns was found with clenched fingers gripping the cross on Hill 449, where he had fallen in the first attack. There were 150 casualties including 33 killed and "B" Company had to be disbanded. These were heavy losses, and the Battalion stayed beneath Gemmano village until September 14. The fighting had been very bitter and the artillery fire was the fiercest and most concentrated that the Battalion had yet come across. *The Times* later compared conditions with those of the Somme in the First War. It was true to say that the German resistance and defensive fire could not have been greater.

The Battalion violated the neutrality of San Marino, crossing its borders early on the morning of the 16 September. By 17 September the Lincolns had crossed the River Marano without any problems, and with the support of tanks they advanced towards Montelupo, where the road led to the town of Domagnano on the eastern approaches to San Marino City. It was here that they met some opposition. Three houses on the right of the track were taken in successive platoon attacks and fierce close fighting. Ahead, at Montelupo, a large yellow farmhouse called "Yellow House" with a round bare knoll behind it was the next in line, and it was successfully taken after the Carrier Platoon made a wide outflanking movement. This was a success capturing its objective and 45 prisoners, and a useful map with markings on it. Two tanks were knocked out by close range bazooka fire as they moved up the track. The Battalion was held by intermittent fire on a narrow ridge which resulted in every effort to deploy and advance being checked. Four hundred yards away on the left a white building was still holding out, and when the attack took place casualties were heavy. Eighteen of the 22 men who attacked were accounted for within the first 100 yards. Two more fell shortly, and only Lieutenant Stockdale and Corporal Lewis reached the buildings through a barrage of fire. Lieutenant Stockdale was killed, and Corporal Lewis, who was severely wounded, was taken prisoner. However when some of the enemy withdrew he managed to crawl back with some useful information, and just before darkness fell a troop of 46 Recce Regiment who had come a long way round, captured the place after constant fighting. Many prisoners and their belongings and equipment were captured but the Battalion lost 95 men. As the light was fading the York and Lancasters passed through the Lincolns and took the remainder of the town of Domagnano together with around 20 prisoners. One carrier crew will remember the battle well for, while evacuating wounded, the driver went the wrong way and drove into the enemy positions and was taken prisoner.

On 20 September, the Lincolns moved into Serraville to take up position protecting the right flank of the Division, but a feared counter-attack never took place and they were able to rest. For a week the remains of farmsteads on the outskirts of Serraville provided the Battalion with some shelter from the incessant rain, and tired men were able to rest after several weeks continuous fighting. By 25 September, 8th Army had breached the Gothic Line west of Pesaro. In the meantime the Germans had reinforced their ranks, and were now waiting for the rains to start.

John wrote:

> We are fighting again now – you may have heard over the BBC about our Division cracking the Gothic Line. I thought it was rather hot of the War Office to let such news go over the wireless, but I suppose we are so good that Jerry knows at once when we are in the line … We are having a grand time now, much better than a year ago – Salerno time! I was a lucky chap to come out of that lot alive.

The Battalion advanced, on 6 October, to an area south-west of San Angelo. The weather was still horrendous and order and counter-order followed. The Lincolns were ordered to hold the Monte Albano ridge. On the 9th when darkness fell, the Battalion squelched through the mud to the Fiumicino, crossed by a bailey bridge, and then were kept in reserve 1,500 yards east of Monte Gattona. On 11th October, the Battalion took the ridge where the village of Montiano stood. An enemy sentry was found asleep behind his machine gun! He and the other 21 were taken prisoner with the exception of five who resisted and had to be killed. On the night of 12 October the Lincolns crossed the Rigossa, and having taken an enemy platoon by surprise, on the hill overlooking Montiano from the south, marched into the village before midday. By the morning of the 15th the Lincolns had advanced to and taken the nearer end of Monte Romano at its western extremity, which was the last real problem on the road to Cesena. Here they were counter-attacked throughout the day, but in the evening 139 Brigade took over for the final time before the Division was relieved. On the night of 15 October the Leicesters relieved the Lincolns on the near slopes of Monte Romano. It was a difficult relief because the enemy were close, and a company of the Lincolns stayed behind. The Battalion moved to Serraville on the 17th and, a week later, to Urbino for rest and training.

In two months of non-stop fighting 46 Division had met and defeated five German divisions. Sixty miles had been covered as the crow flies. Ten rivers had been crossed, most of them in the face of fierce resistance. Almost two thousand prisoners had been taken. General Keightley, the commander of 5 Corps said:

> I would like to take this opportunity of congratulating you most sincerely on your brilliant success in the fighting of the last few months. Throughout this phase of the battle of Italy, which has resulted in forcing the enemy through the much publicised Gothic line, 46 Division has been engaged in all the toughest and most bitter actions. Throughout all your operations your commanders have shown skill in leadership and your troops the greatest gallantry.

Perhaps the finest tribute was paid by the Commander of the Canadian Corps, who said to General Hawkesworth, Divisional Commander "I think if ever a Division has earned the title of 'The Iron Division' 46 Division has".

No. 138 Brigade had now moved to the university city of Urbino, which had suffered badly by the collapse of roads and bridges caused by the heavy rain. The ten days spent there were very pleasant ones and provided a chance for some much-needed relaxation. There were plenty of film and stage shows and dances were held. This was, however, cut short by orders to concentrate in the area of Bertinoro on 3 November. Bertinoro, which lies on a ridge running parallel to the main Cesena-Forli road was nearly halfway between those two towns. From a view point here Forli and its airfield were clearly visible.

The 46th Division attacked Forli on the night of 7/8 November. Just after midday on 8 November orders were issued for the crossing of the Rabbi River. That night 138 Brigade made the crossing, wading through three feet of rapidly flowing water. Shortly Charlie Company discovered an atrocity carried out by the Germans. Nine Italian men were found down a well with their hands tied, and shot through the head. The recovery of their bodies made even Captain Brunt turn white. A quickly carried out advance, practically unopposed, brought them up to the Montone River in the afternoon. Storms prevented the crossing of the river until 12 November, when the Lincolns were the first to cross. They waded the river south of Terra del Sole and swinging right captured the village. The bridge, though damaged, was soon repaired in order to carry vehicles. Able Company with one section of Carriers advanced across country, clearing the little farmhouses which featured all over the countryside. 15 November enabled some reorganisation and patrolling to take place. Over the next week they were able to obtain much detailed information about enemy positions.

17 November saw the Division lined up on the Cosina Canal. From north to south there was 46 Recce Regiment, 5 Foresters, 6 Lincolns (in a holding role) and 2/5 Leicesters. Together with 4th Division, the 46th continued to force the enemy back until they reached the River Lamone at Faenza on the 24th. The Battalion had retired to Forli on the 22nd, where they were billeted. A canteen and a cinema were available, as well as a mobile bath unit. However, things were not completely quiet as the town was still under shellfire from long range guns at all times of the day or night. On 24 November, the Battalion were given less than six hours' notice to move. However, this lasted until 5 December, so they had a really good rest.

During November 1944, the incessant rains turned the battlefield into a ghastly morass. Allied losses were high, with the Eighth Army losing 14,000 killed or wounded alone. General Vietinghoff, the replacement for Kesselring, was able to observe that the Fifth Army had been weakened. So he launched a counter-offensive to recapture some of the lost ground which the Germans had surrendered in September. By December conditions for combat could not have been much worse.

FOR VALOUR

By early December, the 6th Battalion, the Lincolnshire Regiment, were operating near Ravenna fighting against the Germans who were withdrawing northwards up Italy. On the night of 3/4 December 5th Corps, led by 46th Division, began its attack on Faenza. The Division had established a bridgehead over the Lamone four miles short of the town. Because there was only one bridge which could be used to supply the Division, the Regiment suffered through lack of carriers, tanks and anti-tank guns. On the evening of 6 December the Lincolns took the village of Ragazzina near Faenza, where some of the enemy were still in bed but others staged a fight. After heavy fighting over the period 6–8 December, the 6th had established defensive positions at Faenza. At dawn on 8 December, 46th Division reported that there was extra shelling on its front and more German infantry and armour, which showed no sign of dispersing. Towards midday, radio interception identified 90th Panzer Grenadier Division around Celle. All British Brigades were put onto the defensive expecting to be on the end of a major counter-attack. Although objectives had been gained plans for any further advance were cancelled by Brigade on the afternoon of the 8th. The average strength of the Rifle Companies was down to 65 but "A" Company had suffered so severely from constant shelling and German counter-attacks that it was relieved of its forward position by the Carrier Platoon under Captain Brunt on the evening of 8 December.

Early the following day there was a huge concentration of artillery fire against the Battalion's positions. The German 90th Light Division had delivered an all-out assault which was aimed at destroying the bridgehead. Although the forward platoons of one company were outfought, the attack was held with the help of a troop of the Queen's Bays and the support of the gunners, the 71st Field Regiment, who provided much-needed defensive fire. It was the Carrier Platoon who took the initial onslaught. It had been shortly after 7 o'clock in the morning that the enemy had started firing. An hour later it was obvious that the main weight of the attack was being launched against the Lincolns, southwards from Celle. The three Companies of the Lincolns were all below strength because of recent losses and were endeavouring to hold a front of about 1000 yards. Then tanks began to move forward. Despite the bombardment of shells and the aerial attacks of fighter-bombers, the tanks continued to advance. They overran the Carrier Platoon, whose withdrawal was covered by the heroic action of Captain Brunt, who was firing any and every weapon he could lay his hands on, and who single-handed held up the enemy infantry. Two tanks and an anti-tank gun were taken out in attempting to hold the onslaught. The Platoon at Fondi di Sotto, reduced to an officer and seven men, held on grimly and determinedly to its position, and the main attack was held at Ragazzina. By 11 o'clock the enemy's first effort petered out.

During the lull the Lincolns were able to make some adjustment to their positions. The Platoon at Fondi di Sotto was withdrawn, and the Carrier Platoon were positioned on the left to plug the gap between the Lincolns and the K.O.Y.L.I. Here a further attack in the afternoon was driven off, with Captain Brunt directing fire from the top of a tank.

Bill Goddard was a Corporal in "D" Company at the time, and remembers that:

> We got into a fight, and I got wounded by an 88 shell fired from a Tiger tank. From the same shell, my namesake and friend 20 year old Pte. Goddard was killed (on his grave it mistakenly says that he was a Lance Corporal.). The Section was wiped out, and I crawled back to the starting point, an old farmhouse, where the medical people took me in, dressed me and then left us. I ended up with shrapnel in my leg and left elbow. Sergeant Whittle stayed behind with us to look after the wounded. He gave us a running commentary of what was going on outside – John Brunt's brave deeds – and because of this deed we were able to be stretchered out of the farmhouse that night. If John Brunt hadn't carried out that action, I wouldn't have got out. We all admired his courage, he gave us confidence.

The Regimental History of the 6th Battalion tells us:

> Soon after dawn shelling increased and minor counter-attacks were repulsed. Able (Platoon) had suffered severely, so it was decided to relieve them with the Carrier Platoon under Captain Brunt, M.C. This relief was completed during the early evening (on the 8th).
>
> In the meantime, preparations for a further attack by Dog (Platoon) were put in hand, but at 3 p.m. this was called off by Brigade and orders issued to hold firm in present positions, so D.F.'s for mortars and artillery were developed, and two Priests placed in support for anti-tank protection, and one two-pounder anti-tank gun guided to the Carriers' forward positions.
>
> Just before dawn the C.O. went to visit companies and had reached Able, who were in the area of Tac (Tactical) H.Q., when an unprecedented concentration of artillery fire struck the ridge. Hurrying back to Tac H.Q. to deal with the obvious counter-attack he found that both the Carriers and Charlie Company were hotly engaged. For the next three hours a furious battle raged, both sides using artillery to the maximum. The Carriers took the initial onslaught, and their positions became untenable after the two tanks in the area had "brewed-up," the two-pounder gun destroyed by a direct hit, and their communications destroyed. It was a relief to hear Captain Brunt's excited voice on the air telling of his situation, and he was ordered to hold firm some 300 yards east of his original positions and on Charlie Company's right. Charlie and the other Carrier section came in for trouble next, but withstood the assault magnificently.
>
> Major Murray, the Battery Commander at Battalion H.Q., responded magnificently, and it must be mainly attributed to the shooting of his guns that the enemy never pierced our defence, although, as it was later known, the full force of the 90th Light Division was launched against us.
>
> Sgt. Green's Carrier section beat off one fanatical assault led by an officer who tried the ruse of advancing with his hands up. The Carrier Platoon were too old soldiers to fail to notice the grenades in his hands, and plugged him with .45 and sent his men reeling down

the hill. This effort yielded a marked map showing the complete enemy plan, a little late, but nevertheless interesting as Battalion H.Q. proved to be the final objective of the 90th Light.

The Battalion on this day, the 9 of December, acquitted itself magnificently, and many deeds of valour which will remain unsung were performed. Suffice it to say that the counter-attack was brought completely to a standstill with the loss of 200 yards of ground on the right, but at the cost of considerable casualties.

The 90th Panzer Grenadier Division had in fact failed in its primary aim of eliminating the British bridgehead south of Faenza.

Edna Bayne in her article for *The Shropshire Magazine* in 1984 recalls:

Back in Italy for the second time, John Brunt became Captain, and second in command of "D" Company, and we know that later his Commission was made permanent. Although he managed to lend his own particular dash to the job of getting the morning and evening meals up to his Company, he chafed at administrative routine. It was no fun for him and he longed for a chance to get back with the Company. He wanted to be up and doing. He had not long to wait.

At Forli, the C.O. appointed him O.C. Carrier Platoon, much to John's delight. Before the Battalion moved out towards Faenza he was ready for a last grand fling before the withdrawal for rest and reorganisation.

John had celebrated his 22nd birthday on December 6th, 1944, in the thick of fighting. It was now December 9th with very little, if any, respite. At 'stand-down' things were generally quiet, apart from some slight shelling from the enemy. When this became a barrage, it was obvious that some sort of move was to be attempted by the enemy. John ordered a sharp look-out to be kept from all windows for any sign of a counter attack.

John fought a magnificent action, his coolness, bravery and devotion to duty, and complete disregard of his own personal safety under the most intense and concentrated fire was beyond praise.

Wherever the fighting was heaviest, there you would find John, moving from one post to another, encouraging the men and firing any weapon he could find at any target he could see.

Exhausted after having taken such a strenuous part in this action, he was granted a few hours' rest. Night fell. Over the wireless the C.O. called for Captain Brunt, and John had to be disturbed, dog-tired as he was.

The conversation began. Characteristically he volunteered to repeat a difficult job. However, the C.O. dissuaded him, and congratulating him on his work said, 'You're very young – very young; be careful. I'm watching you. I am just behind you'.

The next morning, with the battle won and the glory of it his, John was as eager as ever, watching here, there and everywhere in the event of further trouble, while breakfast was being prepared – their first meal for about 48 hours. He was standing in the doorway of his Platoon Headquarters, drinking a mug of tea with his men, when he was greeted by a stray mortar-bomb, which fell at his feet. John was killed outright. He died with his Platoon around him. It was the only enemy fire for that whole day.

It was announced in the *London Gazette* on 8 February 1945 (Number 36928, p. 791) and the Press on the following day 9 February that three new Victoria Crosses were to be awarded. The awards were to Lieutenant (Temporary Captain) John Henry Cound Brunt M.C. (posthumously); Jemadar R.A.M. Sarup Singh, 1st Punjab Regiment, Indian Army (posthumously); and Sepoy Bhandari Ram, 10th Baluch Regiment, Indian Army.

The Citation reads as follows:

War Office, 8th February, 1945

The KING has been graciously pleased to approve the posthumous award of the VICTORIA CROSS to:-

Lieutenant (temporary Captain) John Henry Cound Brunt, M.C. (258297), The Sherwood Foresters (Nottinghamshire and Derbyshire Regiment) (Paddock Wood, Kent).

In Italy, on the 9th December 1944, the Platoon commanded by Captain Brunt was holding a vital sector of the line.

At dawn the German 90 Panzer Grenadier Division counter-attacked the Battalion's forward positions in great strength with three Mark IV tanks and infantry. The house, around which the Platoon was dug in, was destroyed and the whole area was subjected to intense mortar fire. The situation then became critical, as the anti-tank defences had been destroyed and two Sherman tanks knocked out. Captain Brunt, however, rallied his remaining men, and, moving to an alternative position, continued to hold the enemy infantry, although outnumbered by at least three to one. Personally firing a Bren gun, Captain Brunt killed about fourteen of the enemy. His wireless set was destroyed by shell-fire, but on receiving a message by runner to withdraw to a Company locality some 200 yards to his left and rear, he remained behind to give covering fire. When his Bren ammunition was exhausted, he fired a Piat [Projectile Infantry Anti-Tank missile launcher, the British equivalent of the bazooka. This fired a hollow-charge warhead from the shoulder] and 2in. Mortar, left by casualties, before he himself dashed over the open ground to the new position. This aggressive defence caused the enemy to pause, so Captain Brunt took a party back to his previous position, and although fiercely engaged by small arms fire, carried away the wounded who had been left there.

Later in the day, a further counter-attack was put in by the enemy on two axes. Captain Brunt immediately seized a spare Bren gun and, going round his forward positions, rallied his men. Then, leaping on a Sherman tank supporting the Company, he ordered the tank commander to drive from one fire position to another, while he sat, or stood, on the turret, directing Besa fire at the advancing enemy, regardless of the hail of small arms fire. Then, seeing small parties of the enemy, armed with bazookas, trying to approach round the left flank, he jumped off the tank and, taking a Bren gun, stalked these parties well in front of the Company positions, killing more and causing the enemy finally to withdraw in great haste leaving their dead behind them.

Wherever the fighting was heaviest, Captain Brunt was always to be found, moving from one post to another, encouraging the men and firing any weapon he found at any target he could see. The magnificent action fought by this Officer, his coolness, bravery, devotion to duty and complete disregard of his own personal safety under the most intense and concentrated fire was beyond praise. His personal example and individual action were responsible to a very great extent for the successful repulse of these fierce enemy counter-attacks.

The next day Captain Brunt was killed by mortar fire.

Also on that day, 9 December 1944, where action ended with the battle over the River Lamone, West of Faenza at C. Magnana (Map Ref: 271234 Italy 1:25,000 Sheet 99-1 NW) Private Robert Seymour Boagey 4809828 won the Military Medal. His Citation reads as follows:

At C. Magnana this soldier was with a Carrier Platoon Section consolidating the position. At dawn on 9th December 1944, he was on Observation Post duty and, spotting a Mark 1V Tank and Infantry advancing, ran to inform his Platoon Commander. Together they manned a Bren Gun, Private Boagey observing. An intense Artillery concentration fell on the area and the Tanks opened fire causing a number of casualties.

Regardless of this Private Boagey kept the gun firing at the advancing Infantry of whom fourteen were seen to drop. As the wireless set had been destroyed, Private Boagey was sent to a Company Headquarters just in the rear to call for Artillery fire on to the Tanks, now four in number. This he did, passing over ground swept by the MGs of the enemy armour. A little while later the Carrier Platoon withdrew slightly to a new position, and by this time the enemy were in great strength and in very close contact. Several squads of enemy armed with Bazookas attempted to infiltrate to deal with our own Tanks.

In spite of incessant Mortar and MG fire, Private Boagey and his Platoon Commander went forward alone successfully shooting up these parties and forcing them to withdraw. On one occasion to get a burst at a bunch of enemy Private Boagey stood up and resting the Bren on his shoulder his Officer was able to bring effective fire to bear. The aggressive action taken by Private Boagey in assisting his Platoon Commander in the face of intense Small Arms and Shellfire to a large extent was responsible for the failure of the enemy attack in this Sector.

The courage and devotion to duty displayed by this soldier were of the highest order.

The Regimental History of the 6th Battalion tells us that:

> By noon things had settled down and casualty evacuation was interrupted only by spasmodic, if heavy, shellfire. Carrier drivers did magnificent work in this direction.
>
> In anticipation of further assault that night every effort was made to strengthen our positions, but the night was a quiet one. The following day Company Commanders from a New Zealand Battalion came up to recce for our relief that night. It was while they were there that the news of Captain Brunt's death from a stray mortar bomb was received.
>
> Our casualties for the few days fighting had been heavy, amounting to 12 killed, 85 wounded, and five missing, so it was not, therefore, surprising that the New Zealand Battalion decided to take over our forward positions with one company of 140 odd strong.
>
> The relief on 10 December 1944 was quickly completed and the Battalion started off on the long trek back to Forli. Transport met us just off the main Forli- Faenza road, and by 8 o'clock on the 11th of December companies were in the billets they had previously occupied.
>
> The Battalion were in no real fighting shape after three months fighting, and our move to Porto San Giorgio, south of Ancona, was most welcome, heralding rest and opportunity for most necessary training. The move was uneventful, and on arrival preparations went ahead with a swing interrupted only by alarms of a move to foreign parts. However Christmas and New Year were well spent before the alarms were realised.

Forli had fallen on November 9, Ravenna on December 4, and Faenza on 16 December. This action was in fact the last serious action in which the 6th Lincolns were engaged. Shortly afterwards they were sent to Greece to maintain civil order. In April 1945 they returned to Italy and moved into Austria at the end of the war. After service in Austria, the Battalion was disbanded in February 1946.

So ended 46 Division's second campaign in Italy. What had been achieved? The Division had advanced more than 80 miles, fighting all the way. Eighteen rivers had been crossed. Nine German divisions had been severely beaten and bruised. Nearly 3,000 prisoners had been taken. The Division had suffered over 4,000 casualties. Sixty-eight Officers and 624 had been killed.

The Citation did not have Brunt's regimental affiliations quite correct. Although they stated that he was from the Sherwood Foresters (the Nottinghamshire and Derbyshire Regiment), he was attached to the 6th Battalion the Lincolnshire Regiment at the time. His application for a regular commission in the Lincolnshire Regiment had not, unfortunately, come through before he was killed and his name is not therefore to be found in the Regimental Roll of Honour.

John Brunt was killed four days after his 22nd birthday and was buried with full military honours, before he could add another notch to his Tommy gun. Although there are those who feel the story has been exaggerated he was reported to have had 87 notches on the gun he carried with him, and supposedly would have been able to add another 30 from that day. Each notch represented a German he had killed in battle. His father had hoped he would bring the butt of the gun home when he had finished out in Italy.

Tom Brunt told the press:

> All his life he wanted to be a soldier. While he was at Ellesmere College his eyes suddenly failed him and he had to wear glasses. He could not see without them, but he was a crack shot when we used to go out shooting.
>
> You know, I never knew him as a man, only as a boy, and a youth. He was only 18, straight from college, when he joined up. He had been abroad nearly two years. It was only a few days after his birthday that he died.

Mrs Brunt told the Press he was a born soldier and that this war was a crusade as far as he was concerned. She said "the first news I had that John might get a V.C. was from his batman, Private Len Trask. He sent me such a wonderful letter. "Myself I miss him," he had written. "He would never ask me to go anywhere where he wouldn't go himself. He was a grand fellow. We had a teamwork spirit together by killing as many Boches as we could…"

Mrs Brunt added that there was one last letter from him. It stated "I'm doing O.K. So don't worry, I'll always be O.K".

"John was very proud of his school," Mrs Brunt told the *Courier Newspaper*. "He would have been pleased about the award – for us and for the school". Mrs Brunt remembered a younger John, in 1936 and referred to an item of swimming news in the school magazine. Two of the learners, it stated, were well launched by the end of a fortnight, and one of them had the temerity to capture second place in a junior event of the sports. "We always pulled John's leg about that," she said. "He was such a loveable, homely boy," she went on. "There was hardly a house in the village he had not been in and helped with the washing-up, or something of that sort. He chose his career and he did his job. He did it well".

The Rev. R.A. Evans-Prosser, Headmaster of Ellesmere College, in a personal tribute said:

> I knew Lieut. (temporary Captain) John Brunt better than any of the recent Old Boys. Perhaps it was because he wrote so regularly from whatever part of Europe he was; or it may have been because there was a very close bond between us ever since, in 1940, he brought me down in a crashing tackle at Rugger. That tackle sent me to hospital with a broken knee! John Brunt loved his life and enjoyed every moment of it. His letters were full of joie de vivre. There was never a complaint. He threw his whole heart and soul into his rugger and his boxing and his fighting. In one of his last letters he was thrilled because in his battalion he had trained 10 of the 11 winners in the bouts, and at the same time he sent his best wishes to his friends in the lowest school certificate set, who were just about to face the ordeal of that examination. Whether he wrote from Tunisia, where on one occasion he said it was so hot that the ink on his pen dried up "twixt pot and paper", or from arctic Italy, he never gave any other impression than that he was engaged in a great and thrilling adventure. Truly he gave his life in accordance with the Ellesmere motto: Dimicans pro patria. [The School Song is Pro Patria Dimicans – Fighting for his Country].

Prebendary E. E. F. Walters (College Chaplain 1930–36) recorded that:

> In a letter to his mother, in later years, John told her that he regularly attended the Holy Communion Services, even on the battlefield. He wrote a letter to me, on one occasion, saying, 'the Padre' came up into the front line and held a Communion Service; 'it was

wonderful to experience the peace of God amidst the field of battle' – a memorable phrase.

A Mr L. Bedford who was CQMS of Headquarters Company remembers "Johnny Brunt" saying that he would die happy if he won the V.C.

At the Sunday morning service in Paddock Wood in February 1945, after the announcement of the V.C. to John Brunt, the Rev. E. Thompson read the Citation to the congregation. He called for a minute's silence and offered prayers for victory. Following this the "Last Post" was sounded by Sergeant S. Clark and Private S. Smith of the Home Guard, after which the National Anthem was sung. The Vicar preached on "Bravery".

Reference to the Victoria Cross so gallantly earned by Captain J. H. C. Brunt was made by the Chairman, Colonel E. R. P. Bolleau at the outset of the Tonbridge Rural Council meeting on Friday 16 February 1945. Very proud that the officer was in the rural district, they offered congratulations to his parents, coupled with deep sympathy that their gallant son was not permitted to live, and wear his coveted decoration. Captain Brunt's father was well known to them and his energetic work in the Ministry of Food and as an officer of the Home Guard had commanded the respect and admiration of all concerned.

John Brunt's V.C. and M.C. were presented to his parents by H.M. King George VI at Buckingham Palace on Tuesday 18 December 1945. Also decorated the same day with the V.C., were I. A. Bazalgette; A. F. E. V. S. Lassen; D. S. A. Lord; R. A. M. Palmer; W. B. Weston; J. H. Grayburn; and L. E. Queripel. (see Chapter 9).

John's father met Viscount General Alexander at the ceremony, and when he said to him "I expect that you know many men who should have been awarded this medal". The General replied, "No, because there is always only one who will do the unexpected and that day it was your son".

The V.C. and M.C. are on display at The Royal Lincolnshire Regiment Museum, Museum of Lincolnshire Life, Burton Rd., Lincoln, Lincolnshire LN1 3LY. These were left to John Brunt Miller, Dorothy's son. They were given on loan to the Museum by the family in April 2000 rather than keeping them in a bank vault, although both regiments had been keen to house them. The Royal Lincolnshire Regiment tied in the presentation with the opening, by H.R.H. Prince Andrew, of an extension to the museum. He turned to Dorothy and said, "Your brother was a very brave man", and she replied, "We would rather have John back than those medals".

Tom and Nesta on their way to the Palace

His other medals are also in the Museum:
1939–45 Star
Africa Star
Italy Star
The War Medal.

The following notice appeared in *The Times,* 6 December 1946:

> BRUNT.- In proud and ever-loving memory of our
> Dearly beloved only son, CAPT. JOHN HENRY COUND
> BRUNT, V.C., M.C., Sherwood Foresters, attd. 6th
> Lincs., on this his 24th birthday, killed Dec. 10, 1944.
> 'O Valiant Heart'

THE BEST CIVILIAN, OFFICER, AND GENTLEMAN IN THE BATTALION

Mr and Mrs T. H. Brunt received a letter from Lieutenant Colonel F. C. L. Bell, 6th Battalion Lincolnshire Regiment dated 12 December 1944, and the dreaded War Office telegram arrived on 15 December 1944, at their home in Paddock Wood.

The letter read as follows:

John and his Medals at the Museum in Lincoln

Dear Mr. Brunt,

This letter to tell you of the death of your son John, grieves me so much that if it appears disjointed you will forgive me, as I feel so very much at his loss.

John was killed outright by a mortar-bomb which fell close to him on the morning of 10 December and we buried him in our Divisional Cemetery. I cannot give you exactly where at present.

John was one of the most popular officers in this Battalion, his light energetic personality was a delight to all who met him. Not only shall I feel his loss there, but also in the field where he was one of the most forceful and courageous leaders I have ever had the honour to have under my command. The day before he was killed during a very strong enemy counter-attack, he carried out feats of daring that will long live in our memory, he was a terror to the hun and a constant source of inspiration to us all and it was to a great extent to his efforts that the enemy were so successfully checked. Here again I cannot give you details at present but will do so later on if you would like me to tell you. I will see that poor John's effects and kit are safely despatched to you.

I hope you will take comfort in the knowledge that your son's memory is a glorious one in the eyes of everyone of his battalion and on their behalf I want you to accept our sincerest sympathy. As for myself I feel the loss of my friend John most deeply and send you my sincerest regrets.

Please do not hesitate to write to me if there is anything I can do for you or about which you would like to know.

Yours sincerely

F.C. Leonard Bell, Lieut. Col.

Reports conflict as to how John died. His death certificate simply records "Killed in Action". (Incidentally it also states that he was born in Wales. The confusion undoubtedly stems from the fact that Priest Weston was included in the Forden catchment area, and Forden is in Wales, but Priest Weston is in Shropshire.) We do know that it was the day after his heroic deeds, and that he was hit by a stray mortar while off duty. It was only a short distance away and it is believed that it was the blast from the bomb that collapsed his lung … and he was gone. It is believed to have been one of only two mortars fired that day, and that the Regiment withdrew shortly afterwards to Greece. It was only four days after his 22nd birthday. His commanding officer Lieutenant Colonel Leonard Bell told the present author that they were on a ridge with the odd tree, and the attack was from the west. John was sitting outside his slip-trench. He said that they were "in the open, and that everyone was on duty at the time, you slept when you could. I was on a hilltop behind the Battalion".

Other reports mention that he was in the doorway of a farmhouse or barn, and that a stray shell dropped almost at his feet. Other sources quote that he was dozing in the sun waiting for his batman to bring him breakfast or a cup of tea. He was carried in to the house and died with his Platoon around him. Oliver Hardy, who served with him tells me that he was killed in the open, while Jack Chapman mentioned that John had been talking to "Lumpy Lawson, a jeep driver from the north of England. They seemed to be good friends, as they were always talking to each other".

Another report stated that Captain Brunt had been severely wounded when a lull came and his radio operator, Private Chapman, judged it safe to make breakfast. Private Chapman wrote to John's parents:

> Captain Brunt was fearless. He had done a remarkable piece of work, and like all of us he was dead beat. I was on duty on the set which was the only and main means of communication. For once there was a lull. A call came for the Captain and before he spoke over the air he said: 'Chappie, my back is in agony. Half the house fell on my shoulders'. After a few hours sleep a peaceful sunny morning greeted us. What irony of nature! As I was cooking our first meal in about 48 hours, a shell greeted us and killed Captain Brunt. It was the only enemy fire for the whole day, and it had to kill the best officer and gentleman in the battalion. I brought him in and saw it was hopeless, the last straw after those nightmare days and nights. I smoked a cigarette to hide a tear. He was loved by all.

John Brunt is buried in Plot 3, Row A, Grave No. 8 at Faenza War Cemetery, Italy. His headstone bears a Foresters badge and a V.C. Under the badge is the wording :

CAPTAIN
J. H. C. BRUNT. VC.,MC.
THE SHERWOOD FORESTERS
ATTD. THE LINCOLNSHIRE REGT.
10th DECEMBER 1944. AGE 22

Under the Victoria Cross:

HOW BRIGHT
THESE GLORIOUS SPIRITS SHINE

To find the cemetery take the Bologna-Ancona altostrati A14 and exit at Faenza. The War Cemetery lies 1.5 kilometres south-east of Faenza and is approached by a secondary road which branches off the main road Bologna-Forli (Route No. 9.) just east of the town. The cemetery is permanently open and may be visited at any time. The war cemetery was formed in the winter of 1944 for the burial of those who were killed in the static fighting before the advance was renewed in April 1945. There are now over 1,000, 1939–45 war casualties commemorated in this site, which includes 11 from the Lincolnshire Regiment. Of these a small number are unidentified.

John Brunt's Grave

Among the tributes to John Brunt was a poem by William Henry Phillips, which is reproduced at the end of this chapter. This was published in *War-Time Rhymes and Peace-Time Rhythms* by the Devonshire Press in 1946.

A few days before his death, the O.E. Chronicle received his Christmas card, and in his last letter, he asked them to keep him a place in the O.E. Cricket XI, and to book his table at the May O.E. dinner. The O.E. Chronicle of February 1945 reported "we shall remember his honesty of purpose, his cheerful friendship, his loyalty, his zest in life, and his great war service. To his friends his loss is heavy to bear. We offer our sympathy to his parents and his sisters in their deep sorrow".

A Memorial Service was held at 7 p.m. in St. Andrews Church, Paddock Wood on Wednesday 27 December, the Eve of Holy Innocents Day, 1944. There was insufficient room in the temporary church, and there were as many standing round the open door and under the windows as there were inside.

The Vicar, Rev. E. Thompson's Address paid tribute to "Young John" as he was known in the village and included the following:

> Speaking paradoxically we are here tonight to pay a meed of honour to one whom we never knew. And, to speak paradoxically again, we are met in a spirit of deep reverential pride, which extinguishes boasting on the one side and overcomes sorrow on the other. A "pride" that rises high above either boasting or sorrow.
>
> You will bear me out that we knew John as a public school boy who used to come home for the holidays from a fine public school in the north-west of England, a high-spirited and somewhat boisterous lad filled with life and activity, only desirous to lend a hand, and do a good turn to any where need should call, yet withal, able to hold his own against the rougher element of the village, withal tender hearted and loved by us as a son and brother. This was the John we knew and remember. It is of another John we speak tonight, whom none of us saw.
>
> His school period drew to a termination, and without hesitation or reservation, rather the strong reverse, he decided to throw in his lot with the overwhelming cause of his Country. We had glimpses of him occasionally as he ran home for a Sunday from his Infantry training camp at Maidstone, fairly strenuous training; to get out of bed in the grey-dawn of a frost-held morning, and clad in a single cotton garment, to run three miles with a cold rifle barrel against one's skin. Then in the Battle-school on the Wrotham hills. Under the influence of such Spartan training John could hardly be expected to have a superlatively high regard for the Home Guard, but there is on record an occasion when, under a temporary command, there was a Bren gun to be carried to the top of a hill. The men looked at it, a little hesitant. 'No good waiting, men,' he said, 'this is the way to do it'. And seizing the gun, he threw it upon his shoulder and charged up the hill, nor laying it down till he had deposited it where it was ordered to be mounted.

Then John passed from our notice, and it is to a new John, a full-grown man that we are honouring tonight. He finds himself in Tunisia, in that Herculean strife towards Cape Bon, where he takes part in eleven engagements in sixteen days, and received the first of his three wounds. Then we read of him in the Holy Land, and Syria and towards Baghdad. Then back to the Central Mediterranean at the Salerno landing, where, you will remember, the operation once hung by a thread. Here is a glimpse of his part in that superhuman contest. It is dated 27 September.

Now just having lived through the worst thirteen days that I shall probably ever experience in the whole of my life, I can sit back and write a letter in a considerable amount of comfort. We have been drawn out of the line after forcing the Salerno Bridgehead and making the necessary gap for the armour to pass through. Gee! It was tough at times. Once I really thought it was all up for us, but no, not likely, every man held his own inch of ground, and each man's reward is now granted.

Later he found himself in that indomitable army whose task it was to crack the Gothic Line. He was stationed near a brook, which he crossed and re-crossed so many times, that it became popularly known as "Brunt's Brook". In the climax he led his platoon one night across the brook and successfully stormed a German strong-point, which gained for him the coveted Military Cross, and he became a Captain.

So he moved, forwards and backwards, now to refit, now to re-fight, always advancing, up that long weary Italian peninsula, 'til we hear he is on the Adriatic Front, in or about the city of Faenza, whence comes the news that he has fought his last earthly combat. The details of that tragic operation are not yet to hand.

John's C.O's letter about John's death was then quoted.

What a magnificent testimony! To quote a stanza from William Shakespeare, 'He gave his body to that pleasant country's earth, and his pure soul unto his captain, Christ, under whose colours he had fought so long'.

The Vicar continued:

I turn now to another aspect of his life, which, were he alive today, one would not venture to intrude into. Captain John Brunt was not only a brave man, he was a good churchman. Unlike many a present day public school boy, who goes to Chapel daily in term time because it is a rule of the school, and in the holidays goes nowhere on Sundays, John loved to attend his Parish Church. He was always at his early communion, and on more than one occasion helped me here at the Celebration of the Holy Sacrament, as a Server at the Altar; and I appreciated his help at the Office, because I was convinced of the pure sincerity of his personal life.

Even in the field of War, he would write home and mention how he had partaken of Holy Communion at such times as the Military Chaplain had come round to hold the Service. Here is a private testimony of a quite confidential nature.

He quoted John:

I said my prayers more than once that day, and I knew I had more than a rifle by my side. I prayed to God that I should be guided the right way, and I am convinced that is the reason I am alive today; believe me, I was finished more than once, but hung on. So did each one of my men, I am proud to say.

The vicar continued:

> Captain John Brunt was not only a brave man, he was a good man. Can we not see him going forward into battle, his right hand clasping his Master's, and his Master's other hand around his shoulder, and so they went in together?

After speaking about "death", he concluded his address:

> Thus we conclude our all too unworthy eulogy upon the memory of a brave and Christian man, and we humbly thank God that he has done wisely, as He ever does.

> *Life is all the sweeter that he lived,*
> *And all he loved more sacred for his sake;*
> *And death is all the brighter that he died,*
> *And Heaven is all the happier that he's there.*
> *May the souls of the faithful departed, through the mercy of God, REST IN PEACE.*

On 21 September 1946 the Mayor, Aldermen, Councillors and Burgesses of the Borough of Grantham, in Open Council, granted to the 6th Battalion, The Lincolnshire Regiment, the regimental privileges of marching through the Town with Colours flying, bayonets fixed and drums beating. The day also included a Thanksgiving Service. Amongst those present were John's father, mother and one of his sisters.

"Flying Colours", A Civic Tribute to the 6th Battalion The Lincolnshire Regiment, produced after this occasion, records about 9 December 1944:

> Then occurred an act of incredible and unsurpassed bravery, even in a Battalion where feats of personal valour were every day occurrences. The action of Captain J.H.C. Brunt, M.C., which won for him the V.C., showed not only incredible bravery and a complete indifference to personal danger, but revealed a perfect knowledge of the soldier's craft, a readiness to sacrifice himself for those he led, and a practical solitude for the wounded at the imminent risk of his life. The miracle of his bravery is equalled only by the wonder that he survived in the face of such tremendous odds. This gallant officer, who would pale at the sight of a recent atrocity committed upon some hapless Italians by the Germans, might have stood to Chaucer for the portrait of his Knight. His bravery was no flash in the pan, nor was it an exhibition of bravery for bravery's sake. His courage was necessary if the lives under his command were to be saved and the day to be won. It was necessary to be superhuman and he was. By one of the cruel ironies of war, Captain Brunt was killed by a random German mortar shell the next day. 'He was a verray parfit gentil knight'.

Lieutenant Colonel Leonard Bell called him "mad as a hatter! When he joined the regiment he asked 'What can I do sir'. He always wanted to do something. I was quite impressed, he seemed a bit keen, and he was a good chap. He was a jolly good Officer".

Eric Aspland, who was John's sergeant said that John was,

> A good man who led his men from the front. He was always in charge and never asked anybody to do something that he wouldn't do himself. He was very good with the men and was totally honest and a very brave man.

Jack Walker, the Paddock Wood historian wrote in "Contact" 1982 that a Mr E. Andrews of Talbot Road, Northampton had written to say that he was so proud to have served with John Brunt.

Mr Andrews also wrote to the "Old Codger" in the *Daily Mirror* of 16 March 1981.

> Captain John Brunt was the very best officer he had ever met in his army service of 14 years;
> to the people of Paddock Wood I would like to say, if we were all like John Brunt the world
> would be a better place to live in.

Another letter came to Paddock Wood from Mr W. Goddard of Louth. He stated that on 8 December he was wounded, and because of Captain Brunt's action he was brought out to safety. By coincidence his namesake, Lance Corporal F. C. Goddard, 20 years old, was killed by the same shell. Bill Goddard, who was in the Battle Patrol with John in the early days before being wounded, remembers that he wore thick lenses in his glasses, and felt he never looked the courageous type. He was "a good officer who was well-liked and who spent time talking to the ordinary soldier". He remembers John telling them that he must win the V.C.

Jack Chapman, who served with John Brunt remembers being with him in Italy. On one occasion they were with a jeep driver and took some food up to the Company that night. When they came back they heard some ducks and chickens in a hut. John Brunt said "you two go and get the chickens, and I'll make sure the owner doesn't come out". Jack remembers that "we cleared them out and there were enough to feed the whole Company!" Jack continued, "John Brunt would often say that he always felt he would die on the last day of the war, and as it turned out the day he died was the last day's action the Company saw".

To the older residents of Paddock Wood, John Brunt was more of a local hero than a national one, and knowing him as they did, no one was surprised when reading of his exploits, which led to his decorations. When the news of his death came through, the village went into mourning and as someone said "it was like losing one of your own grandchildren".

It is worth also recording that the front and back pages of the *Victor* Comic for 17 July 1965 record "Brunt VC" and his story in colour comic strip.

His nephew John Brunt Miller, who was born in Tonbridge, Kent in 1946, refers to him as "The December Man", which is very appropriate as he was born in December (6th). His M.C. was won in December (14th/15th) and his V.C. was won in December (9th). He was also killed in December (10th). Incidentally his memorial service in Paddock Wood was also in December (27th) and his parents received his M.C. and V.C. in December (18th). Interestingly his nephew John Brunt Miller was christened on December 9th (1945) – the anniversary of John Brunt's V.C. action.

WE WILL REMEMBER HIM: MEMORIALS

A Public Meeting was held on Thursday 22 February 1945 in the Church House, Paddock Wood to discuss the most appropriate way of commemorating the award of the Victoria Cross to Lieutenant (acting Captain) J. H. C. Brunt. At the meeting the National Anthem was sung and the official Citation of the award was read by the Chairman, Sir A. Marten.

After striking tributes to the memory of the gallant officer resolutions were passed:

> That this meeting records its deep appreciation of the gallant deeds of Captain Brunt V.C.,
> M.C., and of the distinction he has brought to this village by winning the V.C. It also offers
> its respectful sympathy to the parents of Capt. Brunt.

It was also resolved to have a memorial in his honour, and to open a special fund. The committee was as follows: Sir A. Marten (chairman), Mr Horace Simmons (secretary), Mr W. R. H. Faulder (treasurer) and Mrs F. C. Waghorn, Mrs A. B. Faulder, the Rev. E. Thompson and Messrs. H. E. Hall and G. L. Baker. Contributions could be made by and through committee members or at the National Provincial Bank, Paddock Wood. The nature of the memorial was to be decided at a further public meeting, but in the meanwhile suggestions were invited. It was emphasised that the fund was in no way to prejudice or interfere with any general war memorial at the end of the war.

In March 1945 it was reported that subject to the final decision of the subscribers, the committee of the Lieutenant J. H. C. Brunt V.C., M.C. Memorial Fund announced that the object of the fund was to provide a cricket pavilion for the Paddock Wood Cricket Club. The fund, which was still open, already exceeded £300. However it was eventually decided that the Pavilion should honour all who fought in the war from Paddock Wood.

The old St. Andrew's Church, Church Road, Paddock Wood was bombed in 1940. Drawings for the rebuilding of the new church were drawn up at the offices of Cecil Burns and Guthrie in 1945. On 9 April 1945 Mr T. Brunt, then Church Treasurer, stressed the points for a new site for the church. By December 1945 it had been decided that funds should be put to a memorial window in the church, and £500 had already been subscribed by local people for this purpose. The foundation stone for the new Parish Church in Maidstone Road was laid in July 1953 and the church consecrated on Friday 17 June 1955. One of the most important parts of the new building was the beautiful Victoria Cross window, in memory of John Brunt.

Jack Walker's *History of St. Andrew's Church, Paddock Wood,* tells us that:

> At or near the west wall is the beautiful rose window in memory of Captain John Henry Cound Brunt V.C., M.C. who lived in Paddock Wood. For a better view of this gem of stained glass and its representation it would be better to go well back in the nave. The window was by Miss Joan Howson of Putney who has much coloured glass work in many parts of the world as well as in this country. You will see the four arms of the Victoria Cross with its ribbons standing out prominently. In the centre is the British Lion above the Crown. To mention the whole citation by the War Office would stir the heart.

The small windows under the gallery contain extracts:

The memorial window to John Brunt

The rose window above is in honoured memory of John Henry Cound Brunt V.C., M.C. born December 1922. Killed in Action in Italy December 1944. Only son of Mr. and Mrs. T. H. Brunt of Burnside Hse., Paddock Wood. – & The Trumpets shall sound on the other side.

The right hand window quotes part of the Award Citation: "The Magnificent action fought by this Officer his coolness, bravery & devotion to duty & complete disregard for his own safety was beyond praise." "He was one of the most forceful & courageous of Leaders."

The church organ was moved from the north transept in 1973 into the gallery, when the interior of the church was refurbished, and this sadly obstructs the view of the rose window. In 1986 John's sister Dorothy, a teacher, became aware of this and said:

I am quite certain that my mother and father would not have wished to have John's window covered over with organ pipes. The people of the village contributed to have the window designed and made as a memorial to John.

Local historian Jack Walker also felt it was an insult to the medal. The Rev. Dennis Winter, Vicar of Paddock Wood said that there had been lengthy consultation with the church authorities at the time the organ was proposed, but there were no local complaints. He defended the position and design of the organ, saying it had not obscured any significant detail of the window except a regimental badge.

Also in the back of the church is the bronze wall plaque to 20 local men killed in action. This records the name of John H. C. Brunt V.C., M.C.

Also in Paddock Wood, John Brunt's name is remembered on the War Memorial for the 1939–45 War. Mr and Mrs Brunt were on the Paddock Wood War Memorial Committee. A Memorial Service was held on Remembrance Sunday, 12 November 1950, when the names of the fallen were unveiled. The service was conducted by Rev. G. W. Nightingale, Vicar assisted by the Rev. J. W. C. Jenkins, B.A., B.D., Methodist supported by Mr R. P. Edwin and Mr T. H. Brunt.

Names on the Paddock Wood War Memorial

Paddock Wood War Memorial

Two Union Jacks which were brought back by an ex-serviceman of Paddock Wood after seeing service with the British Army through France and Germany from D Day were used to unveil the new names on the War Memorial and on seats.

A parade which included the mens' and womens' Sections of the British Legion, the Red Cross, St. John's Ambulance Brigade, Boy Scouts, Girl Guides, Cubs, Brownies and detachments of the Civil Defence Corps and police formed up in Station Road, and headed by the Paddock Wood Silver Band, marched to the War Memorial to join in the service, which was attended by well over 250 people. Units of the army, the Royal Air Force and the Royal Navy were represented. Mr R. P. Evans was the parade marshall.

Addresses were given by Mr T. H. Brunt and Mr J. C. Walker, who said it was the duty of every citizen to remember the men who came to Britain's rescue in the dark days of 1940–41. Wreaths were laid at the foot of the memorial by various organisations and relatives.

The *New Poacher*, the organ of the 6th Battalion of the Lincolnshire Regiment, on 24 December, 1945 included a letter to the Editor from Tom Brunt, John's father:

> Would you ask his Battle Patrol and Platoon pals if any of them would like a really nice photograph of him, and if so kindly let me have their names and addresses and I will get our family photographer to take me some copies of his photograph just prior to leaving to join the Unit.
>
> In several Army circles at home it is reckoned that this V.C. was the finest in the war, being unexampled for constant and sustained bravery.
>
> His sister, Dorothy Miller, has just given birth to a baby boy, who is to carry on the name of John Brunt, and judging from the way he exercises his lungs about feeding time he looks like being a decent sort of successor. It is too early to say more just yet. John's other sister (Isobel) is at St. Felix School, Southwold, as a teacher in physical culture and social science. She too seems to have acquired some of her brother's toughness and is a great athlete.
>
> Give my regards to Trask, his late batman, and also "Chappy" who wrote me so wonderfully immediately after we heard the sad news.

In addition five houses in Paddock Wood, next to the "John Brunt V.C", pub were named "John Brunt V.C. Court". This is on the site of the old two-storey building that contained a hall above, and stables below, which was owned by the pub. Planning permission had been sought over a long period of time to build between three and eight dwellings. This had started in 1987, but it was not until November 1994 that outline planning permission was obtained to demolish the existing derelict buildings and the erection of a residential development of five dwellings. Full Planning permission followed on 13 March 1998, granted to Inn Business Group Plc., via Lambert and

John Brunt V.C. Court

Foster, Estate Agents. The houses were built by Canham and Son, Builders and the first occupants moved in during March 2000.

* * * * *

In 1945 Ellesmere College launched a memorial fund. *The Ellesmerian Magazine* for February 1945 in its editorial states:

> The death of Captain John Henry Cound Brunt was announced just before Christmas. The award of the Victoria Cross, for a series of brilliant actions on the day before he was killed, was announced in the New Year. He had been awarded the M.C. earlier in the Italian Campaign. His military career was short; but he had impressed his cheerful personality on all whom he met, and great tributes have been paid him by the officers and men of his Battalion. He is well known to many of the younger O.Es, and a wish has been expressed that his life should be marked in an especial way. A small committee has been formed, and this committee has decided to ask for subscriptions to a JOHN BRUNT MEMORIAL FUND. The money paid into this fund will be used to build a new Pavilion in his memory. It was in the old wooden Pavilion that he spent some of his happiest days, and those who knew him best, believe that this permanent memorial of his life would have appealed to him as the perfect memorial. An anonymous subscriber has started the fund with the gift of £1,000. We feel sure that many friends of this gallant young soldier would like to subscribe and, on behalf of The Ellesmerian we offer our co-operation, and hope that a worthy memorial will be raised to his memory.

The Appeal letter sent out from J. W. Nankivell, Editor of *The Ellesmerian*, R. A. Evans-Prosser, Head Master, and W. L. Sumsion, Secretary, states:

> We have written of John's life, always so cheerful, honest and full of service, because we believe his countless friends would be unwilling to allow his death to go unnoticed. His School life was a happy one, happy and fruitful to him and the School. He has died, knowing life as a schoolboy and as a brave soldier of exceptional promise and brilliant achievement. We feel sure that it would be your wish that his memory should be perpetuated in the School which he himself loved so devotedly.

The letter was sent to the parents of boys who entered the school in or after 1922, because they may not have known the addresses of many of the Old Ellesmerians of this period who were on active service. It was also sent to Old Ellesmerians who entered the school prior to 1922.

Old Ellesmerian Peter Bevin was the first winner of the "John Brunt bat" for scoring the most runs in a season, in 1950. The bat was bought by Mrs Nesta Brunt, John's mother who presented it to him.

John's parents paid a visit to Ellesmere College taking with them a portrait of John, painted by Harry Dixon, which they presented to the College, as a memorial to their son's memory, to hang in the new cricket pavilion. I believe this portrait now hangs just inside the Founders Gate at the College.

The John Brunt Memorial Cricket Pavilion was duly opened by John Brunt's mother on Saturday 23 May 1970. The ceremony had been postponed from 17 May the previous year, because of bad weather at that time. Also present were the Captain of the Cricket Team, Mr S. V. Taylor, and the Headmaster, Mr D. J. Skipper.

J. W. Nankivell, in his speech before the gathering said:

Portrait of John Brunt by Harry Dixon

This pavilion is a memorial to a young man; he lived for 22 vivid years. His friends here, in the years that followed his death, 26 years ago, contributed to the pavilion fund, to be built in his memory. Many circumstances prevented our building until last year when, happily, it was possible to combine with the changes made to the swimming pool behind it. John Henry Cound Brunt, Captain in the Sherwood Foresters, spent nearly all his boyhood in Shropshire. He was at Ellesmere, in Meynell, from 1934–41; he joined the army in 1941. His seven years here were to him a joy. He tolerated the classroom, though he never made any sort of claim to scholarship. It was his friendships in the House and the School that came first. He was keener on the active life; on all games and P.T.; keener on the corps than on the academic; and it was up here, on this pavilion, that for years his life was centred. He gained colours for Cricket, Hockey, Rugger; he was a good athlete and a leader in the Corps. He succeeded in the Army first as a soldier, then as a boxing champion and a cricket and rugger player.

After speaking about John's military exploits he continued:

I knew him well, perhaps better than most. He was not one to speak his thoughts fluently; one learnt of his inner life more from his letters, and he wrote to me regularly during his period of training, and he often told me, especially when in Africa and Italy, of his thoughts of schooldays, of the memories these playing fields held for him. He had a great capacity for friendship, and all those who knew him will remember him with affection and gratitude.

In reply Mrs Brunt spoke of the pleasure it gave her to have been invited to perform the ceremony, concluding,

John would have been delighted to know that this fine pavilion, standing on the playing fields he loved so well, was to be used by boys to gain the same delight that he found when he was here. He would have been doubly proud that you have felt it appropriate to give the pavilion his name and I am honoured to declare it open.

The Captain of School Cricket, S. V. Taylor, then presented Mrs Brunt with the key to perform the ceremony, after which the guests were entertained to tea in the pavilion.

* * * * *

On the evening of Friday 26 October 1976, an oil portrait of John Brunt was presented to his Regiment, The Worcestershire and Sherwood Foresters at a special ceremony. The portrait was accepted by Brigadier P. G. M. Litton, Chairman of the Regimental Association, who knew John Brunt personally. The painting was then handed over to the 1st Battalion of the Regiment, which was serving at Colchester. The ceremony took place at the John Brunt V.C. Inn. Brigadier Litton described John Brunt as a "charming man, a fine soldier, and a man of high moral standards".

The idea for a new portrait of Captain Brunt came during a discussion between Mr David Sheppard, landlord of the inn, since January 1976, and Mr Dennis Kent, a local antique dealer who was an amateur artist. Before starting the painting Mr Kent researched at the Imperial War Museum and consulted local people who had known John Brunt before he joined the army.

Whitbread Fremlins, the Kent Brewers, contacted the Sherwood Foresters Association and arranged the presentation. It was a nice occasion for a number of Paddock Wood people, and local historian Mr Jack Walker represented the family. The painting is now held by the Regimental Headquarters.

A further painting of John in his "Lincolns" uniform was painted after the war by L. Wells from a photograph. This was left by Nesta Brunt to John's nephew, Andrew Cameron, and subsequently to the Regiment.

* * * * *

In March 1999, the Paddock Wood Town Council approved a grant of £200 for the John Brunt V.C. Youth Award. This award was initially open to anyone attending Mascalls School aged between 11–16 inclusive, to be awarded to one young man and one young woman, irrespective of background, who could demonstrate a measurable achievement in five categories – physical, academic, artistic, spiritual and achievement. There were 19 entries in the first year, and the two winners were Gareth Owen and Emma Toulson. The prizes were presented by the Mayor of Tunbridge Wells, Councillor Alfred Baker on Bank Holiday Monday, May 3 1999 at the Civic Opening of Foalhurst Wood, which included a May Fair. In spite of being extended in 2001 to all children in Paddock Wood, the Award sadly fizzled out owing to lack of entries.

* * * * *

On 15 May 2004, a plaque was unveiled to the memory of John Brunt in Priest Weston, Shropshire, where he was born. The event was organised by the Shropshire War Memorials Association, who tracked down his sister and nephew. The plaque was unveiled by Mrs Dorothy Miller, sister of John Brunt, who was accompanied by her son, John Brunt Miller and her daughter Sarah Jane Miller.

Mr Clive Blakeway, of the Shropshire War Memorials Association, welcomed members of the family and friends, representatives of the Royal British Legion, Old Ellesmerians, and members of the local community and then asked Judge Peter Northcote (who was in Meynell House at Ellesmere College in 1935) to give a personal reminiscence of the man he knew when they were boys together at Ellesmere. Alan Baddeley (Meynell 1937) proudly read the official Citation. Mrs Miller reminisced about family life and childhood in Shropshire just prior to the Second World War before reading a poem dedicated to her brother after which she unveiled the plaque. The poem is to be found elsewhere in this story and is from the booklet *War-Time Rhymes and Peace-Time Rhythms* by William Henry Phillips (Devonshire Press).

The "Last Post" and "Reveille" followed the "Exhortation" by Mike Stanage, President, Chirbury Branch of the Royal British Legion.

The Plaque at Priest Weston

Dorothy recalls:

> We drove to Priest Weston, where already waiting for us were the British Legion representatives from Montgomery, Churchstoke and Chirbury. Then we saw it – the Plaque, in fine bronze; placed on the old brick wall that surrounds the Methodist Chapel. A grass bank led up to it from the road, and it was on this bank; under the Plaque that John placed our wreath, that had been made back in Belfast.
>
> We were suddenly surrounded by people and the Vicar of Chirbury came to greet me, and it was he who was going to conduct the Service.
>
> It was a strange feeling to be back in this tiny village after the best part of eighty years. The shop where we used to go and buy our sweets was no longer; but new houses were being built on the edge of the village, and the houses that I remembered were looking well with fresh paint and pretty curtains on the windows.

* * * * *

Other memorials to John Brunt include his name engraved on the War Memorial in the ante chapel at Ellesmere College.

* * * * *

In Lincoln Cathedral his name is on the base of a wooden altar rail in the Soldiers' Chapel of St. George. The altar rail, to the right of the altar, is "In Mem. Captain John Brunt V.C. + M.C", and another to Major C. F. Hoey, V.C. These were apparently erected by officers and men of the 6th Battalion, The Lincolnshire Regiment. They were paid for by the Regiment and were in place by 11 November 1951.

The altar rail at Lincoln Cathedral

* * * * *

John Brunt's name also appears on the V.C. Roll of Honour at the Union Jack Club, Sandell Street, Waterloo, London SE1.

* * * * *

A PUB RENAMED

On 3 September 1947 The Kent Arms in Church Road, Paddock Wood known locally as the "Rats Castle" was formally renamed "John Brunt V.C", in honour of John. It marked his connection with the town in which his family had settled in the early 1930s having moved there from Shropshire. The renaming followed a lot of discussion culminating with Tom Brunt giving his permission. He had not wished to upset the church in his decision.

It was also fitting that the naming ceremony should be performed by his father during the annual Hop Festival. This unique tribute to the memory of a courageous officer was paid by the management of Whitbread who wanted to make a more personal gesture of appreciation than public memorials could afford.

John Henry Cound Brunt

Temporary Captain in The Sherwood Foresters (The Nottinghamshire and Derbyshire Regiment), attached to the 6th Battalion The Lincolnshire Regiment)

John Brunt lived with his parents in Paddock Wood during his teenage years. On 9 December 1944, Captain Brunt's platoon was dug-in around a house near Faenza, Italy, as the German 90th Panzer Division counter-attacked the British forward position.

The house was destroyed by mortar fire. Switching to another position, Captain Brunt held back the enemy although he and his men were heavily outnumbered.

Inspired by his leadership and his use successively of a Bren gun, a PIAT anti-tank weapon, and a two inch mortar, his men regained their position and forced an enemy withdrawal.

Captain Brunt survived the battle but was killed by a stray shell on the following day. Subsequently, Whitbread Brewery renamed their Kent Arms pub at Paddock Wood *The John Brunt VC.*

Other honours
Military Cross

Image courtesy of The Worcestershire and Sherwood Foresters Regimental Museum (Sherwood Foresters Collection)

John's write-up in the V.C. Grove, Dunorlan Park, Tunbridge Wells

Tom Brunt presents a photo of John to Colonel Whitbread

The *Kent and Sussex Courier* for 5 September reports:

> In an impressive ceremony of dedication on Wednesday at Paddock Wood the new sign
> – bearing a portrait of the dead officer with the simple inscription 'John Brunt V.C', – was
> unveiled by Captain Brunt's father, Mr Thomas Henry Brunt, before many friends, villagers,
> and Whitbread officials.

Those present at the ceremony included Mrs Brunt, Captain Brunt's mother, Colonel W. H. Whitbread, Sir Sydney and Lady Nevile, Mr and Mrs Marchant and a large company representing the Services and other associations. (However none of John's colleagues was invited to the ceremony.)

Introducing Mr T. H. Brunt, Mr John Marchant, Managing Director of Frederick Leney and Sons Ltd., said:

> Those of us who knew John Brunt, first as a boy and then as a man, are naturally proud to
> be allowed, with his relatives, to take some small share in the fame which is so rightly his.
> Many of us have felt that we should like to pay tribute in a way which would be part of our
> everyday life and would also typify that friendliness which was his in so great a degree.
> Eventually it was suggested an inn should be named after him and a suitable sign raised in
> his honour. Happily for the project, Captain Brunt's parents were good enough to approve.
> It was around this spot that John Brunt spent his most impressionable years. From there he
> went out to win a fame which we shall not allow to be forgotten.

Mr T. H. Brunt said that he was grateful to those who had put forward the suggestion. He was quite sure nothing could be more fitting than this sign in his son's own village, and he unveiled the sign with these words: "Proudly and respectfully to the glorious memory of my son, John, who was killed in action in Italy, 10th December 1944, I name this inn John Brunt V.C".

Tom Brunt unveiling the pub sign   *Exterior Pub Sign*

Lieutenant Colonel F. C. L. Bell, D.S.O., M.C., Captain Brunt's commanding officer, who recommended him for the V.C., spoke feelingly of his many outstanding characteristics, and declared that his memory in the hearts of all members of the Sixth Lincolnshire Regiment would live for ever. He remarked that shortly after he had seen Captain Brunt in high spirits he was informed of his death on arriving at H.Q. "Everyone in the battalion was shocked and horrified that such a fine young man had met his death", he concluded.

A miniature replica of the sign painted in oils was then presented to Mr Brunt by Sir Sydney Nevile, Managing Director, Whitbread and Co.Ltd.

Those present were deeply moved by the simple ceremony. This is how Mr Sean Fielding of the *Tatler* had described it:

> No trumpet blew at that ceremony. They did not even stop the traffic. The village policeman was there, of course – a tall, lean youngster who had fought with the Welsh Guards in Anderson's First Army – but he did no more than raise a gently reproving hand at a boy whose farm tractor was spitting and bawling over-much and making it difficult to hear what young John Brunt's father was saying as he stood below the new sign. High above the strong sun was shining. The air was soft. The hops were ripe again and through their ordered ranks moved the pickers, women and children – and men.
>
> It was good to be there; good to meet John Brunt, Senr., and to see the wise crinkle of smile-lines at his eyes matched by those of his wife and daughter. This, you knew, was England, the real England, the true England, the England of hope and glory, her integrity unmatched, her solid uncompromising worth unsullied. These three people, father, mother, daughter, were clothed in a dignity and pride which acutely and instantly communicated itself to all others. The shoulders of the men became subtly squarer; the hands of the women were crossed before them in classic repose. It was good to be there.

The pub boasted two original exterior signs. The one on the front in Church Road stuck out from the wall, and there was one on the swinging pub sign across the road. This was a head-and-shoulders portrait of John Brunt in uniform. The sign was designed by Kathleen M. Claxton, and was built at Whitbread's Wateringbury Brewery. The other featured John Brunt and a large V.C. and ribbon. This sign hung on the wall above the entrance in Old Kent Road.

In 1951 Whitbread issued the first series of 50 metal plaques 2 inches by 3 inches, featuring Kent Inn Signs. Five series of 50 each were produced. These were available in the featured pubs and No. 43 was "The John Brunt V.C", bearing the head-and-shoulders portrait of the bespectacled young officer. Also available later were matchboxes with a picture of John Brunt and the wording "A Whitbread Fremlin House. 'John Brunt V.C', Paddock Wood, Kent. Bob and Eileen welcome you. Paddock Wood 3765".

John Brunt V.C. Matchbox

It was the only public house in Britain to be named after the holder of a Victoria Cross, yet in 1997 its name was changed to "The Hopping Hooden Horse – JBVC". (The initials were for John Brunt, V.C.) In recent years, the fortunes of the 19th century pub had apparently declined and a growing reputation for rowdiness seems to have been the catalyst for the name change.

The *Courier Newspaper* of 14 February 1997 reported that drugs, trouble and after-hours drinking were a thing of the past. It stated that for a while, the reputation of the pub left much to be desired. A new manager, John Whaley, 50, originally from Newcastle-upon-Tyne, was determined to give the pub a new image. He was granted a new licence on 7 February and announced that he had plans to turn it into a "real community pub".

Food, darts teams, quiz nights and live music were all on the cards, and he said that his ideas had already helped to boost trade. He also said that his employers, Inn Business had promised to revitalise the building by giving it a complete facelift. "I think the problem in the past was that the pub never really had a proper manager, so it was left to run on its own without anybody in charge. But now I'm here for good and I shall get it back on the right lines", he promised. Mr Whaley, who was divorced, said he decided to accept the job because he wanted to make a fresh start. He said local residents were very friendly.

The pub suddenly closed on Sunday 1 June 1997 after a final night disco. After concerns about the pub's reputation, the owners, Whitbread, sold it to the Hooden Horse Inns pub chain. There were already ten Hooden Horse pubs in Kent. Richard Fulcher, an area manager for Buckingham-based Inn Business, the new owners told the *Courier Newspaper* that "it is going to be a sophisticated pub with restaurant-quality food". Following rumours that it was going to be turned into a Mexican restaurant he added "There may well be a couple of Mexican dishes on the menu, but it certainly isn't going to be a Mexican restaurant". He confirmed that the building, some of which is listed, was to undergo a complete renovation, with "in excess of £100,000" being spent to give it a "traditional rustic look". Mr Fulcher said: "It is to be called the Hopping Hooden Horse, because of the hop cultivation in the area … And will have the initials JBVC after the name to retain the tradition and history of the town". So it was given a facelift, and offered a new Mexican menu, and boasted a lounge bar festooned with hop-bines.

The Manager of the John Brunt VC, John Whaley, was posted to the job of manager of an Inn Business pub in Milton Keynes. He said,

> It came as a big surprise when they told me what they were going to do, and it's a pity because I'd more than doubled the trade in here since I started. But I hope that when it re-opens, it will set new standards for Paddock Wood, because at the moment all the pubs are the same and I think the town needs something different.

Four bar workers lost their jobs, and he added. "Obviously the new company has a completely different staffing policy … it's been a shock for us all". His father, Bill, described receiving the news as a "bombshell". Within a week the pub was already being pulled apart. This led to a storm of protest and regulars complained that the new name and image insulted the memory of a local hero. Within just two days of the article about the pub's future appearing in the *Courier Newspaper*, a campaign to retrieve the original sign had been launched, and a petition started in support of the name being retained. Norman Packer, a Paddock Wood resident for more than 30 years said,

> It should never be allowed to happen. This place is part of our history – named after a guy who fought for our country. To put just four letters at the end of the new name is an insult! I've sat back and let things happen all too often before, but this I feel really strongly about, and I think you'll find there are a lot of people who agree with me. It's absolutely disgusting that they're even considering getting rid of the name.

The petition signed by hundreds of names was eventually intended for Ashford-based Hooden Horse Ltd, a wholly owned subsidiary of Inn Business.

Opposition to the plans was also voiced at the 2 June meeting of the town council, where members called for the sign to be found and either re-hung at the renovated pub, or put up elsewhere. It was felt that the Council were in favour of the plans, and Bob Akehurst challenged them by asking what right they had allowing the name change.

Alex Bensley, the owner of Hooden Horse Inns, who was showered with letters of complaint from locals, was reported in the *Courier* as saying:

> All our pubs contain the corporate Hooden Horse name, and there was simply no way we could have made the place work under the name John Brunt V.C. The pub had a bad reputation and it needed to be turned around. We are doing that by spending up to £50,000 on the bar and the kitchens.

He said he sympathised with local residents, but explained that the main swinging picture sign had been kept by Whitbread, who sold the pub to Inn Business. He also claimed that many

INDEX